PORT-ROYAL

The Drama of the Jansenists

Port-Royal of the Fields.

PORT-ROYAL

The Drama of the Jansenists

by Marc Escholier

Hawthorn Books, Inc., Publishers, New York

PORT-ROYAL

First American Edition: 1968

Design: Gene Gordon

2394

Contents

PORT-ROYAL

The Drama of the Jansenists

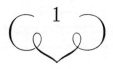

THE GOLDEN AGE

On September 2, 1599, a great company assembled at the royal abbey of Saint-Antoine-des-Champs, in one of the suburbs of Paris, on the site where the Hospital of Saint-Antoine rises today. Edme de la Croix, Abbot of Cîteaux, solemnly blessed Jacqueline Arnauld—not yet eight years of age— and invested her with the habit of a novice.

The child's grandfather, Advocate-General Marion, had obtained from Henri IV the promise that she would be made abbess of the Monastery of Port-Royal, a Cistercian convent founded in 1204 in the valley of the Chevreuse by the wife of a crusader. The Abbey of Saint-Cyr would be reserved for Jacqueline's younger sister, Jeanne.

Thus relieved of the task of establishing two of his daughters in the world, Monsieur Arnauld, a lawyer at the Paris Parlement * and son-in-law of Monsieur Marion, was able to marry off his eldest girl, Catherine, to a rich man. In noble families—or those of the upper middle class such as the Arnaulds— it was customary to offer the younger children to God in order to assure the older ones a position worthy of their rank.

When Jacqueline became Mother Angélique she recalled her receiving the novice's habit; she said with great simplicity that she "was delighted, as would have been any child of that age, to see that all the festivity was for her."

At the conclusion of the ceremony the little novice climbed back into the carriage with her family, and a great dinner was held for the whole company at the home of Monsieur Arnauld. After a brief sojourn at the Abbey of Saint-

---

* The chief judiciary body of France under the ancien régime.—Trans.

Antoine-des-Champs, Jacqueline was conducted to the Monastery of Saint-Cyr. Her sister Jeanne, who was to become abbess of this monastery, was then only six years old. She received her older sister ceremoniously and haughtily; Jacqueline must not forget that she was here in Jeanne's domain and that Jeanne could very well drive her out of it if she pleased. The two future abbesses lived and played together until June 24, 1600, the day when Jeanne in turn received the novice's habit with the same solemnity and rejoicing that had so delighted Jacqueline.

The following day Jacqueline Arnauld was taken to the Abbey of Maubuisson, near Pontoise, where she was to finish her novitiate. It was Advocate-General Marion who had chosen this convent for her, thus paying court to the king. Had not Henri IV been responsible for the election of its abbess, Angélique d'Estrées, the sister of his mistress, the beautiful Gabrielle? Henri, the *vert-galant,* often came to the monastery of Maubuisson, a discreet hideaway near Paris, to carry on his love affairs under the abbess' complaisant eyes.

When Jacqueline Arnauld entered this house Gabrielle d'Estrées had just died; even so, Monsieur Marion thought his granddaughter would better hold the king's attention if she were entrusted to the sister of the mistress he had loved above all others.

Jacqueline had the good fortune to find other children at Maubuisson— those of the abbess. This nun, whose profligacy had scandalized even Gabrielle d'Estrées, had twelve children by different fathers and reared them in her abbey, obtaining for each an education and rank corresponding to the father's status. One of the bastards was to become her coadjutrix; another was the companion of Jacqueline.

One day Madame d'Estrées took the small novice to another monastery over which she also presided as abbess—that of Bertancourt, near Amiens— and there she had the child receive the sacrament of confirmation. On this occasion Jacqueline found her first name changed to Angélique at the request of her parents, who thought to render discreet homage to Madame Angélique d'Estrées in this way.

On October 29, 1600, at the age of nine, the little novice made her profession and pronounced the vows that were to bind her forever. Having obtained letters patent from the king, Monsieur Arnauld asked Rome for the bulls that would permit his daughter to become coadjutrix to the abbess of Port-Royal, Madame de Boulehart.

In this petition "the professed sister Angélique Arnauld" was described as being seventeen years old, although in reality she was only ten; the substitution of her new first name for the one appearing on the baptismal register made it possible to conceal the child's age and to obtain these bulls in spite of canonical regulations. Later on, immediately upon hearing of the death of Madame de Boulehart, Monsieur Arnauld hastened with his daughter to Port-Royal. On July 5, 1602, the vicar-general of the Cistercian order had the nuns summoned to their chapter hall. A police lieutenant was present to forestall any resistance to the king's will, but the precaution was unnecessary. The nuns were very poor; having been told that the Arnauld family would come to their aid, they had been won over to Angélique in advance.

During the afternoon of that same day, the little girl of eleven, now abbess, knocked on the convent door and it was opened wide to her. Preceded by the cross and lighted torches, she entered the choir as the stone arches rang with the glorious sound of the *Te Deum.* The young abbess solemnly took possession of the abbatial chair and the keys.

The following September 29th, the Abbot of Cîteaux solemnly blessed her and installed her as abbess in the church of Port-Royal. More than three hundred persons were present, among them three abbesses—those of Maubuisson, Saint-Cyr, and Gif. Following the ceremony, the guests made merry in the convent, now established as the fief of the Arnauld family.

That same day Angélique made her first communion. No one had prepared her to receive this sacrament; the cobbler of the abbey, out of pity for the confused child, thought to lend her his manual of prayer. Mother Angélique later wrote of this event, "There was a great gathering and feast in the monastery cloister, such as would have been held in a secular house."

Some time later, the king came to the abbey in the course of a hunt. Preceded by the cross and surrounded by her nuns, the little Abbess of Port-Royal, lifted on high pattens to make her appear taller, welcomed the Béarnais. The king apologized for troubling the holy nuns; he had come only to see Monsieur Arnauld. The next day, passing on horseback by the walls where the community had gathered to look down on him, Henri IV cried out gallantly, "The king kisses the hand of Madame the Abbess."

In reality the abbey was governed by the prioress, Madame du Pont, under the supervision of Angélique's mother. Madame Arnauld put affairs in order, examined the accounts, dismissed the servants who were robbing the monastery, had repairs made on walls about to fall into ruin, and came to the help of those nuns who were without resources; she had one of them expelled— the youngest—because her conduct was provoking scandal.

On the other hand, no one took an interest in the spiritual life of the convent. Of the confessor himself Angélique was to say, "He scarcely knew the Lord's Prayer or a word of the catechism; his principal exercise was hunting." The monks conversed with the nuns only in regard to what they called "the good customs of the order." Racine, in his *Abridged History of Port-Royal,* summed up the matter in a few words: good cheer, idleness, indolence, libertinage. The season of the Purification was devoted to the Carnival; masquerades were arranged with the assistance of the confessor and the valets. Following the style of the day, the more coquettish of the nuns wore gloves and masks to protect their complexions; most of them had never received confirmation and did not even know what that sacrament was.

Madame Arnauld worried little about all this. "My mother," Angélique said later, "feared God. But at that time she had more love for the honor of the world." Over that honor, at least, Madame Arnauld did not cease her watch.

The little abbess had an ancient carriage brought out from the coachhouse for her own use. She went to see her sister Jeanne at the monastery of Saint-Cyr and visited her neighbors; she received her father's friends and took walks with them over her lands. "I had," she was to write, "a horrible aversion for the convent. I was alert and frolicsome." Angélique thought only of games, of chattering, and of amusing herself. The years went by; she became a young girl: Then she discovered profane books—an illustrated edition of Plutarch's Lives, and some novels. After following these heroes in their loves and victories, the young abbess found the long hours in the cloister monotonous; the religious life appeared to her to be an insupportable yoke from which she sought to be relieved.

Her paternal grandfather had been a Calvinist; saved by Marie de' Medici on Saint Bartholomew's Day, he became a Catholic through constraint and remained one through prudence. But several of Angélique's aunts were still Huguenots, and they advised her to leave the convent. Learning that her vows were invalid because of her extreme youth at the time she pronounced them, the young abbess thought of taking refuge in the Protestant citadel of La Rochelle; there she could marry, have a husband, children. . . .

Her daughter said nothing of this, but Madame Arnauld sensed danger; although exhausted by her pregnancies—she had in all twenty children— the abbess' mother sometimes arrived unannounced in order to assure herself that her daughter was leading a life befitting her situation as a religious. One day, fearing that someone had "discoursed to her about love," Madame Arnauld searched the abbess' furniture and coffers during her absence, but she found no suspicious writings. Monsieur Arnauld smiled. He knew Angélique and recognized in her his own blood; his daughter, he said, was too proud ever to consent "to live without honor."

It was important to the father for Angélique to remain in the cloister. Thus, immediately after she reached the required canonical age for an abbess, he made her ratify her vows, exacting her signature to an illegibly written document which he did not even give her time to read. The young girl dared not rebel, but "was bursting with vexation." She was never to forget her father's "trickery," and wanted less than ever to live the religious life.

Madame Arnauld installed a nun of Saint-Cyr in the convent, Madame de Jumeauville, to watch over Angélique. Informed by this supervisor that the young abbess put her amusements before everything else, her mother remonstrated with her sternly; even if she remained irreproachable, a nun should not leave herself open to suspicion. When Angélique appeared little convinced, her mother dissolved into tears. At this the abbess was moved "and humbly begged her mother's pardon, promising to live with all the prudence and circumspection she desired."

Thus there opened before the young girl a long, dreary existence that provoked what is called "cloister sickness." She languished and weakened. "I had great pity for myself," she said later. Port-Royal was in a marshy valley, where stagnant water bred fevers; stricken with malaria, Angélique was forced to return to her parents, who took her home with them to Paris.

In her father's house she rediscovered a forgotten world: great ladies clothed in silks, satins, and velvets brought in the latest court gossip. The young abbess grieved at having to live in retirement and being always clothed in serge. Worried at seeing her weak and feverish, her father took her to the family domain of Andilly, near Montmorency. There, beneath the fine shade trees, Angélique Arnauld was to rediscover the joys of family life. At the sight of her happy mother surrounded by her children, her nature suddenly revolted against the future imposed on her—a rebellion all the more painful because it was silent. She had, nevertheless, to return to Port-Royal; despite all the care lavished on her, her cure was taking far too long. Moreover, Angélique's mother guessed the conflict being waged in her daughter's soul. The sight of the world's pleasures was dangerous for a virgin vowed to God; Madame Arnauld did not like, she said, "to see nuns away from their cloisters."

Though still ill, the young girl was sent back to her convent. But to assuage the sorrow she felt at parting from her family, her parents sent along one of her sisters, little Marie, not yet eight, who was to go as a boarding pupil to Port-Royal and act as a companion to Angélique.[1]

Shortly after her return to the abbey, Angélique had a happy surprise: her younger sister Jeanne, now Sister Agnès, obtained Monsieur Arnauld's permission to leave her Saint-Cyr convent and spent some time at Port-Royal.

This novice knew no regrets or anxieties. She had adapted herself without effort to the existence that she would have to lead all her life; at the age of

---

[1] See Documents: *The Arnauld Family,* p. 318.

nine she knew the psalter by heart. "Self-sufficient and with a good opinion
of herself," she had her small affectations and loved her little pleated surplice.
Her future dignity as an abbess delighted her childhood years, and she always wore a little golden crozier attached to her rosary.

Jeanne "was prudent and exact," Angélique was to say, "but vain and
conceited beyond belief, even to the point of asking God why he had not
caused her to be born Queen of France." The novice had a pronounced taste
for pious devotions; she fasted, mortified herself, and sometimes had to be
led out of the choir in "fits of weeping." But proud and mystical as she was,
Jeanne now brought her sister a support that was to continue as long as they
lived.

An important event was about to take place. During Lent of 1608, a Capuchin named Basile came to the convent to ask shelter for the night, dinner,
and alms, in exchange for preaching a sermon to the nuns. Angélique accepted his offer, happy to hear a monk speak to her of God, for up to that
time she had heard only students sent by the Bernardines—and they had
stuttered so dreadfully that the nuns had been moved to laughter.

The abbess had the church bell rung and took her place in the midst of
her community. The preacher's voice rose as he spoke of Christ. This mendicant friar spoke to them of the birth of the Child in the stable; then of the
existence of God, who of his own free will cast aside his glory to become the
humblest of men.

Now at last Angélique Arnauld's rebellious heart opened wide. It was,
wrote her niece later, "God's first glance at her and her first glance at God."
For this Sovereign who had renounced his crown, the nun wished to suffer
and even to die. She was permeated by a hitherto unsuspected Presence, and
in the days that followed the young girl was aware of the first approaches of
grace.

Angélique spent that evening in meditation. The One who had accepted
first the litter of beasts and then the cross for her sake had truly become her
Spouse. "From that moment on," she said, "my joy at being a religious was
far greater than any of the unhappiness I had felt before."

Her niece, Angélique de Saint-Jean, later described the beauty of this new
life. "This hour was like the dawn of a new day which brightened within
her until it reached the fullness of noontide."

Carried away by her ardent Arnauld temperament, after "hating religion"
Angélique burned to give herself to Christ.

For a moment she thought of confiding in the monk whose sermon she
had just heard. But an instinctive prudence put her on her guard; she told
herself that she was only sixteen years old and that Father Basile was very

young; she let the Capuchin go away. Shortly afterward she learned that he had been unfrocked, was an apostate, "a stone of scandal."

Left to herself, the young abbess thought only of mortifications. How could she ever come close to the Crucified One, except through suffering? Angélique rose at night to pray in secret, slept on bare boards, and went so far as to burn her arms with hot wax. "What would you have had me do?" she later said. "I tried every means of suffering!" Then came scruples, the torments of an exacting conscience. Would the bride ever be worthy of the Divine Spouse? Angélique Arnauld was an abbess because her parents had deceived the sovereign pontiff by claiming that she had reached the age required by the laws of the Church. "I was cursed," she cried, "when I was made an abbess by men and not by God!"

She wanted to be relieved of the charge of the monastery, to become the lowest of lay sisters in the humblest of orders. This idea exalted her; if only she could live in silence for the God who dwelled in her!

At Pentecost in the year 1608 another Capuchin, Father Bernard, came to preach at Port-Royal; he was old, and his severe mien calmed the fears inspired by Father Basile. Angélique made her confession to him, avowed her unworthiness, and declared her intention of abandoning her charge. Imperiously, the monk dissuaded her from carrying out any such plan; in a century when Protestantism was every day gaining fresh victories, when so many priests were unworthy, the Abbess of Port-Royal must open the way to reform. Full of his subject, the monk ascended to the pulpit and adjured the nuns to renounce their easy existence; he demanded that they submit thenceforth to the strictest rules of their order.

The poor women, almost all of whom were condemned to the cloister by family necessity, were amazed and overwhelmed; having discovered the passion that burned within Angélique, they trembled for their peace and humble comforts.

Catherine du Pont, the prioress who governed the monastery in the abbess' name, was the first to protest; it was not proper to cast tradition aside to please the whims of a young girl. "She pointed out to me," Angélique later said, "that I was in the grip of a devotional fervor that might desert me within a few months. All this would lead only to disorder."

Angélique held her tongue; but every day the young abbess read and reread the rules for which the Cistercian order is indebted to Saint Benedict. The vow of poverty required that the nuns have no personal possessions. Nearly all of them had kept clothing, some ornaments, and small objects; they would have to give up these things which diverted their attention from God. On the contrary, the prioress thought that "these poor belongings" should be left with the nuns. It was in the interest of the community, she said, because each took care of what belonged to her. Angélique hesitated in the face of Catherine du Pont's authority. But Father Bernard himself went farther; he drew up a plan of reform which would bring back the spirit of Saint Benedict and Saint Bernard.

Naively, the Capuchin submitted his text to the vicar-general of Cîteaux, Dom de Morimond. The latter insisted, as did the other monks, on defending "good custom." He immediately warned Monsieur Arnauld that his daughter was being carried away by the sermons of the Capuchins and was on the point of upsetting the life of the Port-Royal community. Would it not be wise to remonstrate with her?

Worried, Monsieur Arnauld rushed to the monastery and took Angélique as well as her sisters Jeanne and Marie back to his estate at Andilly. There he spoke severely to the young abbess. She must learn to beware of mendicant monks; the Capuchins, he said, "want to get into our house to beg alms to take the place of what they could earn by running a good farm." When Angélique appeared unconvinced, her father grew angry. He described the Capuchins as "sneaks, hypocrites, and bigots."

Monsieur Arnauld had an even graver concern; Madame de Jumeauville had told him that his daughter was practicing austerities that could "ruin her health and shorten her life." Respectful but silent, Angélique resisted her father; exhausted by his anger, Monsieur Arnauld had to take to his bed. Should he die, he said, his daughter would be the cause of his demise. Frightened at this, the abbess promised to close her convent door to Father Bernard. But immediately afterward, in despair at the idea of renouncing an aim on which she had built all her future hopes, she in turn fell ill with a relapse of marsh fever. At this moment Dom de Morimond intervened; speaking in the name of the Abbot of Cîteaux, he demanded that Angélique send away any Capuchin who dared to present himself to her.

Exhausted, criticized by everyone, the nun felt deep bitterness toward her parents and superiors. "When I was incapable of making a choice," she said, "I was bound to a profession for which I had no vocation. Now everyone opposes my happiness and prevents me from living in accordance with the duties of that profession."

When Angélique returned to her convent she might well have considered herself vanquished. But a surprise awaited her: Father de Quersaillou, a Bernardine preacher sent by Dom de Morimond, chose as the text of his sermon the eighth beatitude: "Blessed are they who suffer persecution for the sake of justice." Without even daring to hope, the young girl asked herself if Christ had not once again spoken to her through the voice of a man. Much moved, she asked the monk to hear her confession, and not without fear she disclosed her plans to him. Far from reproving her as Dom de Morimond had ordered, the monk told Angélique that she was on the right road and that despite all obstacles she should carry her work to its conclusion.

The Bernardine was even able to have Madame de Jumeauville sent back to her monastery at Saint-Cyr; in this way Monsieur and Madame Arnauld lost their staunchest ally. Angélique's hopes rose: won over by her fervor, four or five nuns—the youngest—promised to follow her. But how could she impose on the prioress and the whole community the hard life of Cistercian nuns of former times?

Again the Abbess of Port-Royal's health failed; her attacks of fever became more frequent. The nuns who loved her for her youthful generosity saw her grow thinner and more sickly day by day. The time came when the abbess obtained through affection what she could not require through obedience. One day the most rebellious, the prioress, came to her. "Madame," she said, "tell us what it is you want us to do. We promise to do anything that will make you happy."

The wall had crumbled; the road lay open before her.

March 21, 1609, the feast of Saint Benedict, was a great occasion at Port-Royal. The poor nuns came to the chapter hall bringing their coffers and all their little belongings, offering everything that attached them to the world to the young girl whose sorrow had touched them so deeply. One of them, however, still refused to part with the key to the little garden that belonged to her, but in the end, won over by Angélique, she handed it over.

"It was the key to her heart," wrote Sainte-Beuve.

Angélique Arnauld had made the Abbey of Port-Royal into a true religious community. Father de Quersaillou easily persuaded her that she should reestablish the enclosure prescribed by Saint Benedict's Rule; encouraged by her first victory, the abbess instituted this reform. On April 19th, the occasion of the clothing of one of the novices, the latter's relatives and friends were not received inside the monastery; after the ceremony they had to arrange for the traditional banquet to be held outside the walls.

There was grumbling: "Our Abbess of Port-Royal is pleased to treat her daughters in this way. But she won't hesitate to open wide the door when Monsieur Arnauld puts in his appearance."

From that moment onward, Angélique's resolution was firm: her own relatives would no longer be permitted to enter the interior of the abbey. Not daring to confront them, she wrote her elder sister Catherine, now Madame Le Maître, asking her to tell her family that the enclosure was henceforth to be imposed on everyone. In her surprise Catherine did not dare to say anything to Monsieur Arnauld, but revealed Angélique's project only to her mother. Madame Arnauld shrugged her shoulders; her daughter, she replied, "would not have the impudence to treat her father in such a way."

As the days passed Angélique grew more and more aware of the trial that awaited her: a young woman not yet eighteen years old was daring to forbid access to the monastery to the head of the family who had made her its abbess. But if she abdicated, what would remain of the task she had undertaken? She begged heaven for courage in this most difficult struggle, one that would separate her from her own family. Only those of her religious who helped her carry out her first reform were taken into the secret; kneeling beneath the arches of the monastery church, they prayed at her side as during the vigil before a battle.

Since Parlement was in recess, the famous lawyer was on his way to Port-Royal to forget his troubles in the company of his daughter, the abbess. Announced by a courier, Monsieur and Madame Arnauld arrived at the monastery on September 25, 1609. In their company was Robert, the eldest of the children, as well as two of Angélique's sisters: Madame Le Maître and Anne.

The young abbess had her strategy planned. All doors were closed and the keys taken away from the extern nuns to whom they were usually entrusted—none of them would have dared to prevent the head of the powerful Arnauld family from entering the monastery. The rumble of the wheels of a heavy carriage on the flagstones of the courtyard was followed by a moment of silence. Alighting, Monsieur Arnauld was surprised to see that the great portal remained closed. Then the grid window, which permitted those within to see their visitors, was slid open; stupefied, the lawyer saw the pale face of his daughter behind the bars of the grating. In a very unsteady voice, Angélique asked him to go into a little parlor near the door where, from behind another grill, she would explain to him why the door had not been opened.

"What is the meaning of this nonsense? Is this the respect with which a child receives her father?"

Strong in his authority, the lawyer "insisted, urged, commanded, raged, and knocked harder and harder for the door to be opened." His outburst of wrath merely strengthened Angélique's resolution; the Arnaulds never surrendered to violence. Then the abbess' mother rushed up to the grating to heap reproaches on her daughter. Robert Arnauld, twenty years of age and already self-important, became angry in his turn. Son and grandson of lawyers, reared in the shadow of the palace, the fiery young man gave way both to indignation and oratory. He proclaimed that his sister was "a monster of ingratitude, a parricide who would be responsible for her father's death." As Angélique remained impervious to these anathemas, Robert addressed himself to the nuns whose hidden presence he suspected. Monsieur Arnauld was their benefactor; how could they allow "a person to whom they were so greatly indebted to suffer such an insult in their house?"

The daughters of Port-Royal trembled. The less fearful divided themselves into two camps. Those who supported their abbess "looked at one another and prayed in their hearts to God to give them strength." Others "condemned the ingratitude of Madame the Abbess of Port-Royal."

"How shameful," one of them said, "not to open to Monsieur Arnauld!"

The Angélique turned and faced them. "My parents," she declared, "made me a religious without asking my will. I do not ask theirs to live as a religious."

Monsieur Arnauld then demanded that his other two daughters—Jeanne and little Marie—be returned to him, for no one could refuse 'him this right. The lawyer had decided that as soon as the door was opened to allow the two to pass he would enter, using force if necessary. But his plan was foiled; led out through a hidden door, Jeanne and Marie suddenly found themselves standing beside their outraged parent.

Robert called on Jeanne as a witness to her sister's ingratitude; the novice replied with pious gravity that Angélique was acting in accord with the directives of the Council of Trent.

"Oh, so at last we are getting somewhere!" the young man cried. "And here's someone who presumes to tell us about canons and councils!"

From the start of this scene the abbess' other two sisters were the only ones to remain silent; overwhelmed and powerless, they witnessed the break between those they held most dear.

The grief-stricken look in their eyes no doubt calmed Monsieur Arnauld's anger. He returned to the grating and announced that he would agree to go to the parlor; Angélique immediately went into the room and sat behind the grill. There she suffered the harshest blow of all, the only one for which she was unprepared: for the first time her father appeared to her as a tired old man. He spoke in a faint, almost gentle voice. Since he was being driven out, he would leave, but if he was never to see his daughter again, he had one last request: for love of him, she must not ruin her health by her austerities.

At this display of affection, Angélique began to choke with anguish. Her emotion was too strong, and, overcome by her love for her family, the abbess lost consciousness and fell to the floor.

Monsieur Arnauld had only one thought: his daughter was ill, perhaps dead! Unable to reach her side, he shouted, shook the grill which separated them, and called for help. Terrified, his wife and children rushed in and shouted in turn.

The nuns assembled in the convent courtyard did not know what had happened; the cries they heard made them think that the violence of the conflict was increasing and that the Arnaulds were attempting to force open the door. Finally some of them distinguished the powerful voice of Robert, the eldest, begging them "to take care of their abbess, who was at death's door." The nuns flew in and saw Angélique lying on the floor, and managed to revive her. When she opened her eyes she saw her father, his hands clenched on the grill, his face ravaged by grief. Summoning all her strength, she begged him "not to go away that day." Monsieur Arnauld was ready to grant his daughter anything she might ask.

Some moments later, still separated from her family by the grill, the young abbess lay on a couch which had been prepared for her in the parlor, and tried to talk with them. The conflict had abated; each no longer felt anything but remorse and affection. Angélique's parents agreed never to enter the interior of the abbey.

However, they were not to be entirely excluded and in the days that followed they were able to work out compromises. Even though he could not cross the threshold of the cloister, Monsieur Arnauld obtained from the Abbot of Cîteaux the right to supervise the buildings and gardens and took them under his charge. As for Madame Arnauld and her daughters, they were soon to receive permission to have free access to the monastery. Even so, Angélique's mother did not return to Port-Royal for many a day. In her indignation she had sworn that she would never go there again, and, bound by this vow, she allowed weeks and months to pass without seeing her daughter. Finally, on August 4, 1610, at the convent of the Jacobins, she heard a preacher declare that one is not bound in conscience to keep vows made in a moment of anger. Filled with joy, Madame Arnauld immediately ordered the horses harnessed and rushed to Port-Royal; reconciled, the mother and daughter experienced so much happiness that always afterward Angélique commemorated in her heart that evening of August 4.

The young girl had been so shaken that she never regained her equilibrium of earlier days. But had she not won this painful victory over those she loved, the abbess would have lost her power and her undertaking would have been short-lived.

For this reason those who were one day to be called Jansenists gave September 25, 1609, the name "Day of the Grating."

Monsieur Arnauld realized that Angélique would not long consent to bear an abbess' title that had been obtained by fraudulent means. He therefore resigned himself to sending a petition to the sovereign pontiff to confess his deception and to request new bulls.

The Roman court evinced great displeasure, especially in regard to temporal matters at Port-Royal, and demanded that the Arnaulds return the monastery revenues that had been paid to them after the death of the last legitimate abbess, Madame de Boulehart. However, the official of the Paris archdiocese who was charged with the investigation learned that the modest resources of the abbey had not sufficed to cover the expense of the upkeep of the nuns or of repair of the buildings; only Monsieur Arnauld's generosity had enabled the monastery to continue in existence, and the provident father who had wanted to endow his younger daughters with ecclesiastical benefices was now seeing his own income swallowed up by the convent in which they lived. The official's report calmed the suspicions of Rome in regard to Monsieur Arnauld's probity; and simultaneously Pope Paul V learned how a seventeen-year-old abbess had reformed her convent at a time when many communities lived in a way far removed from the spirit of the Gospels.

On November 23, 1609, new bulls granted Angélique Arnauld the right to occupy her abbatial chair without further qualms of conscience. It was an immense relief to her; up until that time she had, as she was to avow, "great trouble in holding chapter and speaking before it, because I was not legitimately in charge."

A strange coincidence: two weeks before the bulls giving authority to Angélique were delivered, the Inquisition censored a legal complaint brought by Monsieur Arnauld against the Jesuits. In the name of his client, the University of Paris, the lawyer accused certain persons in league with the Jesuits of having armed one of the Society's former students, who attempted to assassinate Henri IV. He demanded that Parlement expel the Jesuits as "corrupters of youth, regicides." These words were never forgotten by the Society. They were, it was said, "the original sin of the Arnaulds."

For the present, however, the young abbess had succeeded in reconciling her family with Rome.

Since her first profession had been declared null, the Abbess of Port-Royal knelt for the second time before the Abbot of Cîteaux on May 7, 1610. Again she pronounced the three vows of poverty, chastity, obedience. Several days later Ravillac's dagger struck its mortal blow at Henri IV, the sovereign who had made Angélique an abbess. At the time of his assassination Henri IV was preparing to invade the Low Countries in search of the Princesse de Condé, with whom he was hopelessly in love and whom he wanted to abduct from a jealous husband. He had stated baldly to his confessor, Father Cotton, "that he would make war to get the princess back."

Despite all he owed to the king, Monsieur Arnauld had never shown the same indulgence toward him as had other members of the court. Learning of the assassination, her father said to Angélique: "The late king mocked the sanctity of marriage by an infinite number of adulteries. God sometimes takes vengeance on public crimes by tragic ends like his."

Jeanne continued to live at Port-Royal with her older sister; for some time still she was to preserve the pride that she inherited from the Arnaulds. "Her great natural spirits made her presumptuous," Angélique said later. At first the novice did not want to give up her long-cherished dream of becoming Abbess of Saint-Cyr, but one day her elder sister realized that grace had worked a great transformation in Jeanne. "She truly became," she said, "another creature in submission, humility, and love of poverty."

The time came when the novice felt a "complete aversion" for her dignity as abbess, and no longer wanted to be anything more than the least of the nuns at Port-Royal. In 1612 she made her profession; now Sister Agnès, she abandoned forever the abbey her parents had obtained for her. Thereafter her desire to mortify herself grew constantly. Since she ate almost nothing, she fell sick; Angélique tended her night and day, often kneeling to beg her younger sister to take nourishment.

Sister Agnès' piety led her to pray interminably; sometimes she was found unconscious on the floor of her oratory. Angélique herself was no less intent on fulfilling her vows. Not wishing to ask her father's help after the Day of the Grating, the abbess sold her silver dishes to fill the needs of the monastery and to aid the indigent; she took care of the humblest of the lay sisters when they were ill, sitting by their bedsides, watching over them, carrying out the most repulsive tasks.

The Abbess of Port-Royal gave over her own apartment to the sick; she refused to ask postulants for the customary dowry, having always had, she said, "a great aversion to bargaining over girls." Postulants brought with them only what it suited their parents to give, and thus the abbey became poorer and poorer.

Yet Angélique made one requirement which seemed most surprising at that period: she accepted only those novices who showed a real vocation. Thus she accepted extremely poor girls after refusing the daughters of great houses with rich dowries who "believed that it was their right to enter religion."

After setting up the enclosure, the abbess brought about, not by pressure but by example, a third reform prescribed by the Benedictine rule: abstinence from meat of any kind. She simplified the nuns' habits: the pleated robe was replaced by a straight, sack-like dress without gathers or folds; the linen chemise was replaced by one of serge.

Other Cistercian communities were disturbed to see "ancient customs destroyed" in this way. The abbess and her sisters were considered "mad, infatuated, innovators, schismatics"; there was even mention of excommunication. But Angélique, supported by the Arnauld clan, felt strong.

Soon she saw another of her sisters enter the novitiate—little Marie, up to that time merely a pupil at Port-Royal. On September 14, 1616, this young girl joined the community for the rest of her life, having made her profession under the name of Marie de Sainte-Claire. Thereafter known as Marie-Claire, she later told her father that on that day she knew such joy that "after receiving this grace, she no longer wanted anything except to die."

Having already given three of his daughters to the convent, Monsieur Arnauld intended at least to keep with him a fourth child, Anne: she who had stood by silently with her older sister, Madame Le Maître, on the Day of the Grating. This great moment, however, had made a deep impression on the mind of the child, and in her turn Anne was drawn to Port-Royal. Earlier, when she was very young, she had admired the austerity of her Huguenot aunts who "showed just as many outward virtues as many Catholics"; at one time, she had hesitated between her own religion and Protestantism.

Later on she had taken a great fancy to such love stories as *Astrée*. But one day, after reading Saint Jerome's letters on virginity, the young girl spent some time in meditation. She suddenly became aware of an immaterial Presence, and she fell to her knees before it. Then the Divine Spouse drew near and placed on her finger the invisible ring that was to bind her forever. Although Anne lived in the world after this, she did not belong to it.

Witty, graceful, and pretty, she refused the offers of marriage that came her way. One day, finding herself with her mother at the residence of the Duc de Guise, she told one of his close friends, the Capuchin Father Archange, of her desire to enter the convent. The monk was visibly dubious of her vocation and believed that she had been disappointed in love. "Father," the young girl said with all the solemnity of the Arnaulds, "I swear to you that should your Monsieur de Guise wish to marry me, even though I am a young person of no importance, I would not wish to have him; I must be married to a Lord who is greater still."

When Anne charged her sister, Madame Le Maître, to tell Monsieur Arnauld of her intention, he refused to grant permission; so long as he lived he would never consent to this daughter's becoming a nun.

Anne was too clever to argue with her father; she knew that with patience she would win when the moment came. She even pretended to give up the convent willingly, and for a whole year Monsieur Arnauld saw her taking part in entertainments of every sort. But already she felt only "indifference and disgust for the world." Who could oppose so strong a will? Monsieur Arnauld ended by giving in; one day when he was in a good humor, Anne begged him to allow her to retire permanently to Port-Royal in such endearing terms that her father became resigned.

On October 9, 1616, after a last night spent with her parents in the house reserved for the guests of the abbey, the young girl went with them to the last Mass she would attend with her family. During the reading of the Gospel she heard Jesus' words: "My yoke is easy and my burden light," and at this the novice turned to her parents with a smile of happiness.

The moment of separation came. Monsieur Arnauld left alone, almost furtively, in order not to reveal his suffering. After Anne had embraced her mother with all her strength, she lost courage and burst into sobs. Madame Arnauld was thoroughly upset, and on rejoining her husband she told him that their child had been unable to hide her tears. At this the poor man suddenly rebelled and, deciding to take his daughter back, returned to Port-Royal. But he found Anne's decision strengthened despite her grief. Nevertheless, she later said that on that day she had been "so tempted, so agitated, that she feared she could never persevere."

There followed for her what Saint John of the Cross called the "dark night," and Anne experienced a complete emptiness of soul. Her sister Agnès consoled her by saying "that having left the things of this world and not as yet having been consoled by God, she was, as it were, suspended between heaven and earth."

Finally, little by little, the young novice discovered those daily joys which drew her back from the abyss: the great silence of Port-Royal, the "childlike simplicity" of the nuns; everything spoke of God's pervading presence. Brought up on the Bible, Anne expressed her own thoughts when she quoted the words of the prophet Hosea: "I will lead her into the wilderness and I will speak to her heart."

One night she was "completely enthralled merely at the sight of the stars, and, another time, at hearing the sound of three bells ringing together in gentle harmony."

Each day, after a frugal repast in the refectory, the nuns repaired in procession to the choir where they sang *Benedicite* and thanksgiving. Listening to these hymns, Anne found again the image of the lost world of her childhood. "It was for me," she said, "the memory of Paradise." And so greatly did she rejoice at feeling herself the bride of Christ that when she was alone she danced like David before the Ark.

After this the fatigue and trials of the novitiate became as nothing to her. Under the direction of the mistress of novices, who was her sister Agnès, Anne threw her whole heart into all her tasks. In the kitchen she placed herself under the orders of the lay sisters; she cleaned the stoves and weeded the garden. Every night she rose at two o'clock to sing matins, and did not go to bed afterward. In the darkness the church was damp and cold; the nuns wore no more clothing in winter than in summer. Agnès Arnauld increased the humiliations; her younger sister must lose "that self-sufficient air" she formerly wore. Anne obeyed orders and joyfully submitted to all these mortifications. Agnès was not surprised to see her grow in this way; she had never really doubted the sincerity of Anne's vocation.

Angélique also rejoiced, but she was not to know perfect happiness until all the Arnaulds had approached "the royal portal of grace." One night she was told in a dream that her mother, as well as her eldest brother, Robert, would leave the world in their turn. She saw them in torment, both mounted on the same horse, their faces sad and downcast, coming to her at Port-Royal as though seeking a place of refuge.

So, without willing it, Monsieur Arnauld was to become the patriarch of a tribe dedicated to God as was the tribe of Levi among the Hebrews.

Step by step, Angélique drew closer to God. Saint Benedict's Rule regulated each moment of the day and night; but Angélique found that the religious discipline was never sufficient to reach the heights of the cross. The confessor was of little help, limiting himself to hearing his penitents and having them recite certain prayers. What was needed now was a patient and sure spiritual director, who would discover the workings of grace in each elected soul. Such a guide would console the nuns who felt themselves weaken or lose hope, and would lead those among them who had achieved love of God.

Angélique Arnauld, the reformer, remained a woman; she had need of the help of a priest who knew how to bring reason and lucidity to bear on hearts which grew too easily enthusiastic or downcast. But how few men among those consecrated for such a task were pure or far-seeing enough to carry it out? "Scarcely one in ten thousand," was the answer of Francis de Sales. Sadly, the abbess was to discover the truth of these words; the confessors who succeeded one another at Port-Royal did not contribute what she had expected from them. Angélique was forced to expel a doctor in theology, Dom Bomeceau, who had come to her highly recommended; he proved himself more gallant than pious, and held conversations with certain nuns in particular in order to say "silly things."

A Jesuit, Father Binet, maintained his dignity; but the turns and detours of his subtle piety made Angélique uneasy. "He was," she said later, "too wily with one like myself who likes sincerity and frankness, especially toward conscientious persons."

One day the abbess met the monk to whom her sister Anne had first revealed her vocation. Father Archange, the son of the Earl of Pembroke, had been expelled from his native England during the persecution of Catholics in that country, and had joined the Capuchins in France. "He was," Angélique wrote, "a man of excellent mind, of venerable and majestic mien, one worthy of the high rank of his birth."

Father Archange was to discover in the young woman the perseverance necessary for the accomplishment of great tasks. "God," he said, "expects something great of you."

He agreed to come to the help of the two confessors who for better or worse were following the progress of Port-Royal. "While one plants and the other waters," the Capuchin said, "I trust God will grant a happy increase."

In his flowery language Father Archange held before the monastery a gentle image of God. Agnès Arnauld, charged with the direction of novices, had exerted herself, as her niece later said, "to uproot self-love and human complacency from souls whom she watched jealously, with a jealousy all of God—wishing to bring them pure to Jesus." Father Archange moderated the excessive ardor of the novice mistress, saying to her "that she had in her charge tender children and little lambs. Were she to push them too hard, the whole fold could die within a day."

The monk revived Angélique's hope when it sank before the obstacles that were always cropping up. "Courage, courage, my good little abbess! Jesus Christ guards you as his beautiful dove in his breast opened by the lance."

Monsieur Arnauld still wielded his authority by fits and starts, and sometimes ran counter to Angélique's projects; moreover, the superior of Cîteaux showed little favor toward her reforms. It did not matter; the day would come, Father Archange declared, when "the tempest would change into a gentle calm, and indignation would be replaced by blessing."

Respect was due Monsieur Arnauld, the Capuchin said. But he did not have the right "to take from you the life of the soul; he was only the instrument used by God in giving you that life."

Finally, despite her desire to be humble, how could the abbess fail to appreciate the exquisite courtesy of the monk who remained always a nobleman beneath his rough habit? "You are misnamed Madame de Port-Royal," he said. "Your real name is *Madame de Cœur-Royal.*"

If the reforms introduced by Mother Angélique aroused the criticism of certain communities, many others asked the abbess to teach them her method of directing her religious.

With the authorization of the Abbot of Cîteaux, Angélique was successively to reform the abbeys of Lys near Melun, of Poissy, and of Saint-Aubin. For the same purpose, her sister Agnès lived for a while at the monastery of Gomerfontaine, and later at the Cistercian Abbey of Tard, not far from Dijon. The younger Marie-Claire was sent to a convent on the island of Auxerre. But the Abbot of Cîteaux reserved a still more difficult task for Angélique.

In the monastery of Maubuisson, where the Abbess of Port-Royal had passed her novitiate, shameless disorder continued. Although she was growing old, Angélique d'Estrées was still a living scandal, and was odious to the pious Louis XIII because she had sheltered the *amours* of the late king, his father. Despite his conciliatory nature, the Abbot of Cîteaux—now Dom Boucherat—was obliged to put Maubuisson in order. The project had already proved difficult, for one of the monks sent by the abbot had been locked up in a dungeon upon orders of Madame d'Estrées, who had him whipped every morning. The unfortunate man would have lost his life had he not succeeded in making his escape.

Finally, convinced that the decisive hour had come, Dom Boucherat made the canonical visit to Maubuisson which he had postponed for twenty-five years. Madame d'Estrées haughtily refused to receive her superior. A few days later, the Abbot of Cîteaux returned to Maubuisson armed with an order of Parlement, accompanied by the provost of archers. Angélique d'Estrées defied the assailants, who had to break down the doors and scale the walls. The armed men finally discovered the abbess and tried in vain to drag her from the mattress to which she clung. Finally, they had to carry her away, almost naked, in a carriage which took her to the Daughters of Penance in Paris, rue Saint-Denis, where she was locked up.

The nuns at Maubuisson had been quite satisfied with Madame d'Estrées; all of them feared what they called the "dreadful and savage reform" at Port-Royal. And now the abbess of that convent was being sent to them by the Abbot of Cîteaux. Angélique's spirits were extremely low on that day of February, in 1618, as she prepared to leave her own abbey for several years. Her nuns were in tears and already felt themselves orphans. Watching Angélique leave, her sister Agnès quoted the words of the Apostle: "Behold, we have left all things," and repeated several times the word "all" to express her sorrow.

Angélique took with her two professed nuns and her sister Marie-Claire, then aged eighteen. The abbess knew too well the difficulties of reform not to foresee the trials that awaited all four of them at Maubuisson; loyally she warned the professed nuns that they "must be prepared to risk their own lives with good heart." To Marie-Claire she showed the bed in the infirmary which would be reserved for her on her return—the Arnaulds did not gloss over the truth!

Angélique's somber predictions were to be realized; the two professed nuns would die from exhaustion and Marie-Claire was to suffer with fever for the rest of her life.

The reform of the abbey over which Madame d'Estrées had reigned was indeed a rude undertaking. Almost all the nuns at Maubuisson had been sent to the convent against their wills, either because they were younger daughters or because they came from poor families, and they had accommodated themselves as agreeably as they could to an existence they had not chosen. Several of them had gardens with arbors where they offered refreshments to their visitors; they gave plays to entertain their guests. In good weather the prioress would hurry through vespers and compline and lead the whole community along the ponds which bordered the Paris road. The monks of Saint Martin of Pontoise then came to join the nuns in dancing. Consequently, the abbess and nuns of Port-Royal seemed to them "like creatures from another world."

It was not, however, without emotion that Angélique returned at the age of twenty-seven to the scene of her childhood and the memories that still lived for her in this monastery. Going directly to the older nuns whom she had entertained in former days with her candid gaiety, she opened out her arms to them; for a moment a gentle happiness prevailed and there was a hope of peace. But the abbess knew that she could not reform the monastery unless she could infuse new vitality into it. As she had to act quickly, she opened the doors to girls without dowries, asking them only if they willed to lead the evangelical life.

The Abbess of Port-Royal obtained from the Abbot of Cîteaux authorization to receive a rather large number of novices at Maubuisson. Learning that their daughters would be received without dowries, many families sent younger girls who would "find an honorable situation in a well-established monastery."

Angélique tested the newcomers, of whom she kept only thirty-two—those whose faith was sincere and solid. Supported by the three nuns who came with her from Port-Royal, and by these novices, the abbess instituted the first of the dreaded reforms. The enclosure was established and grills and parlors prevented strangers from entering the cloister.

Angélique also preached silently, by her own example: the older nuns at Maubuisson saw her abandon her own apartment to the sick, as she had done at Port-Royal. Poorly clad, eating only herbs, she lived in one dark room. The gallant company of earlier days was replaced by the sick, often with repulsive diseases; through the grill, the abbess tended them with her own hands. "Madame de Port-Royal" soon became well known among the sick and suffering in the area. Angélique's companions and the novices received strict orders: they must carry out the most onerous duties and wait on the older nuns of the convent with devotion and respect. In this way, the abbess said, they would be won over more easily to the new spirit than by being hurt by "words they cannot bear to hear."

Angélique instituted a second reform. The older nuns had formed the habit of replacing the chanting of the hymns of the offices by discordant shouts, and this had become a form of amusement for them; now here, as at Port-Royal, the young abbess wanted the use of the slow harmony of the plain-chant, and pointed out its beauty to the novices. The older nuns at Maubuisson persisted in keeping up their racket, and thus in the church two sets of Christians faced one another, each choir chanting until it was exhausted in an effort to rise above the other.

The youthful fervor of the newcomers was already beginning to prevail when an event took place which compromised the whole effort: Madame d'Estrées escaped from the convent of the Daughters of Penance. One day in September, 1619, just as Angélique was entering the choir followed by the nuns, she saw her former superior appear before her. With a revulsion she could not suppress, the Abbess of Port-Royal faced this aging and debauched woman. She bore her Christian name and had received strange confidences concerning her past life; over these confidences Angélique had thrown a cloak as had the children of Noah when they covered their father's nakedness.

Haughty and determined to prevail, Madame d'Estrées addressed her former novice with ceremonious politeness: "Madame," she said, "I have come to thank you for the care you have taken of my abbey during my absence, and to request you to return to your own."

No less courteously, Angélique replied: "Madame, I would do so willingly if I could. But you know that it was the Abbot of Cîteaux, our superior, who ordered me to take over the direction of this convent: since I came through obedience, I cannot leave save by the same obedience."

Hearing this exchange one could have believe oneself in the palace of the Guises in the company of the amiable Father Archange. But now the voices rose; Madame d'Estrées proclaimed that she was the abbess and was going to occupy her chair in the choir.

"Madame," Angélique answered, "you are no longer the abbess; you have been deposed."

"I have given notice of appeal!"

This language was familiar to the Abbess of Port-Royal, daughter and granddaughter of jurists. "Your appeal has not been heard," she replied. "The judgment against you still stands." Then, seating herself in the abbatial chair, Angélique added: "So do not find it amiss if I sit in the abbess' place."

Madame d'Estrées said nothing but Angélique knew the struggle had only begun. She asked the young nuns to receive communion with her "to implore the help of the Holy Spirit in the tempest about to arise."

The service continued without incident; a great silence descended on the abbey. In the semi-darkness of the sanctuary the Abbess of Port-Royal saw the monastery confessor appear; he advised her to retire, for otherwise she would have to give in to force. Scarcely had she replied by a refusal when the church doors opened wide and Madame d'Estrées' brother-in-law, the comte de Sanzai, and four noblemen advanced, drawn swords in hand. The count announced to Angélique that she must leave immediately, while one of his companions fired off his pistol. The rule of feudalism had returned.

The Abbess of Port-Royal was not frightened; the violence of these men was nothing compared to that of her father's love which she had faced earlier. What did swords avail against God?

The daughter of the Arnaulds replied very calmly to the comte de Sanzai that, having been established in this house by the Abbot of Cîteaux and the authority of the king, she "could not be made to leave except by armed force."

As with one motion, each of the young nuns placed her hand in their abbess' belt "pressing me so hard," she told later, "that I thought I would suffocate."

Madame d'Estrées, sister of a marshal of France and cousin of a cardinal, had not foreseen the resistance of a young woman of no rank; without restraint she threw herself against her former novice and snatched at her veil in an effort to tear it off. Then those nuns who were faithful to Angélique, "who had been as lambs," she later reported, "became as lions." One of them, a girl of noble birth, defied Madame d'Estrées.

"Miserable woman," she said. "You dare try to remove the veil of the Abbess of Port-Royal. Oh, I know you; I know who you are!"

As she said this, the young nun, with no thought of the swords being brandished around her, tore off the usurper's veil and made her "draw back six paces."

This was too much. Madame d'Estrées ordered Angélique driven out immediately. The noblemen seized her and forced her into a closed carriage that stood waiting before the church. Immediately the daughters of the Abbess of Port-Royal rushed out, clung to the wheels and mounted the coachman's seat. The driver refused to obey Madame d'Estrées, who wanted the horses to start off with the carriage, even if the nuns might be hurt or killed. The planned abduction was a failure.

Freed by her companions, who now marched behind her in two rows, Angélique left on foot for Pontoise. The good people of that city had been angry at seeing the old abbess return with her friends. They had only dislike for the profligate sister of the royal favorite, Gabrielle d'Estrées, whom they had called "the filthy duchess." It is one of Henri IV's contemporaries who tells of the people's disgust at the "long royal debauchery."

All the inhabitants of Pontoise took their stand in favor of Angélique Arnauld, whose kindness had been attested to by the poor among them.

"Here come the daughters of the good Abbess of Port-Royal," they said. "They have left the devil in the monastery."

Arriving at Pontoise with her nuns, Angélique retired to a house given over to them by the vicar-general. One of the abbess' brothers, Henri Arnauld, now a lawyer, obtained from the Chamber of Abeyance of Parlement a decree for the arrest of Madame d'Estrées. Shortly thereafter the constable of the watch, surrounded by numerous archers, arrived to seize the former abbess, and she had to flee in great haste from Maubuisson with the comte de Sanzai and his friends.

The archers then came on horseback to Pontoise to seek Angélique and her daughters. Again on foot, the nuns left for the abbey. As night had fallen, each of the armed men carried a torch, and in this light the populace accompanied the nuns back to their reconquered domain.

It now become necessary to appoint an abbess to replace Madame d'Estrées at Maubuisson. Angélique agreed to the choice of a religious of high rank, the natural daughter of Charles of Bourbon, comte de Soissons, for it became evident that this august natural daughter of royal blood was the only one who could maintain her position at Maubuisson.

After Madame d'Estrées' flight insolent nobles from the country around, her friends and relatives, came to threaten the safety of the monastery, and it was necessary to keep a garrison there on constant watch. Arrested, imprisoned, and again with the Daughters of Penance in Paris, the deposed abbess engaged in endless lawsuits to regain her post. Madame de Soissons had only disdain for this chicanery, and under her guidance the Abbey of Maubuisson was again to know peace.

Angélique had to remain there for several months before the new abbess would be able to assume her functions. During that period the Abbess of Port-Royal learned how remote a great lady, even one who had entered a religious order, could be from a simple and fervent brand of Christianity.

Imbued with a sense of her rank, Madame de Soissons required the nuns to kneel as soon as they entered her room, to drag themselves in this position "to her side, and to address her with unparalleled ceremony and respect." Between a person of such high birth and Angélique Arnauld there was a gulf which neither of the two nuns was able to bridge during those long months.

When Madame de Soissons arrived, the Abbess of Port-Royal was dressed in her usual worn, patched habit. Her companions had to insist that in honor of Madame de Soissons she change to clothing more in keeping with her own dignity; but since dressed in this way she could not perform her humble daily tasks, her discomfort was so evident that Madame de Soissons had to advise her—not without secret contempt—to return to her old attire. What was more serious in the eyes of the noble abbess was the presence of young religious who were rich in faith but had come unprovided with a dowry. "She made it clear to me," Angélique was to say, "that I had taken in only beggars."

Beggars! The word wounded the young abbess who had great affection for the daughters she had chosen. She then made them an unwise promise: seeing that they were unhappy at the prospect of spending their entire lives under the direction of an overbearing superior, the Abbess of Port-Royal consoled them by saying that "if things did not work out well" she would receive them in her own abbey. But how could she impose on a monastery already so poor the presence of thirty-two religious almost entirely without resources? Anxiously Angélique wrote her sisters in the valley, asking if they would consent to this new sacrifice; she received a reply signed by every one of her nuns begging her to bring her companions with her, "because God will provide for them all." Angélique breathed again, for in those few lines she knew she had found Port-Royal again.

Madame Arnauld, to whom Angélique had also written, had the same thought. She replied: "I will help you in every way within my power." Shortly afterward, Angélique's mother went to Maubuisson with six carriages to take the novices away, and distributed among them monies she had managed to collect for the expenses of the journey.

Fearing that the arrival of thirty-two new members of the community would cause only trouble and discord at Port-Royal, Angélique ordered them to keep silence until the day she herself could join them. As they came within sight of the monastery tower they were to pronounce only the verse of the Psalm: "Set a watch, O Lord, before my mouth."

In his *Abridged History of Port-Royal,* Racine wrote: "These poor young women approached with trembling a house to which they had come, so to speak, only to starve." To their great surprise, they were received as though they were royalty. The nuns of Port-Royal approached their sisters chanting the *Te Deum* and thanking God for opening to them "the inexhaustible treasury of poverty."

When Angélique finally succeeded in leaving Maubuisson and regaining her haven, she loosened the tongues of the thirty-two mutes who had strictly obeyed her. Her niece, Angélique de Saint-Jean, later wrote: "The large number of daughters suddenly added to the community of Port-Royal only inspired a greater fervor; when someone throws a quantity of wood on a fire, it burns only the brighter."

In the course of these hard years spent at Maubuisson Angélique had known a great sorrow and a great joy.

In December, 1619, her irascible but loving father had been stricken by a cruel sickness which was to be his last. The abbess' thoughts never left him and often she awakened at night in anguish.

"Lord, save thy servant," she would murmur.

One of the religious who had come with her from Port-Royal, a young girl of nineteen, Isabelle de Châteauneuf, shared a room with the abbess, and would reply: "My God, thy servant hopes in thee."

For the rest of her life Angélique showed her undying gratitude to this companion, remembering the friendly voice that had risen to her out of the darkness.

The great happiness the Abbess of Port-Royal experienced at Maubuisson came to her from one who would one day be called Saint Francis de Sales.

She had greatly desired to meet the author of the *Introduction to the Devout Life*, who was already considered a saint. On November 6, 1618, Francis de Sales, then fifty-one years of age, arrived in Paris. Because of his position as Bishop of Geneva, he accompanied the Cardinal of Savoy, who was entrusted with negotiations for the marriage of Christine of France, younger sister of Louis XIII, to the Prince of Piedmont. One day the Bishop of Geneva went to the Abbey of Maubuisson to confer the sacrament of confirmation on one of the novices. From his first conversation with Angélique Arnauld he distinguished in her, as he expressed it, "a powerful soul."

The abbess found in Francis de Sales' ideas the image of that world to which she hoped to attain. Had she been given the guide she had been constantly seeking? "I found in him such great sincerity, together with so many graces and illuminations regarding my needs, that I placed my heart in his hands without any reservation," she wrote later.

Like Father Archange, but with greater talents, the Bishop of Geneva belonged to the spiritual family of Francis of Assisi, and his heart was delicately attuned to the "little poor man." He had the same affection for animals, for flowers, for all the beauties of nature which declared the glory of the Creator.

It is true that Francis de Sales did not reach the radiant degree of poverty attained by the luminous saint of Assisi or the extreme simplicity that reveals the supernatural qualities of a man. The Middle Ages, after all, had carried away with its own passing the secret of the primitives and of the builders of cathedrals.

In a pompous, ornate age, Francis de Sales often succumbed to the temptation of preciosity, but he was never guilty of bad taste. He was gentle, but not insipid. His flowery eloquence, his allegories laden with lilies, doves, and emeralds were always redeemed by the same great sincerity that conquered Angélique at the time of their first meeting.

Before her the Bishop of Geneva affirmed his faith in human nature. "Each of us possesses," he said, "a first and natural inclination to love God. He uses it as an instrument to hold us more gently in his grasp and to keep us with him."

Our weaknesses are only miseries. The Redemption "makes them more useful than original innocence ever was." To penitents appalled by their own evil inclinations, the Bishop of Geneva replied: "God has seen many more such things."

Above all, he wished to dispel the "foolish idea of virtue as something sad, quarrelsome, spiteful; a phantom that frightens people away."

Angélique told the bishop of her sadness at not having found, up to that time, priests or nuns who could inspire her with the confidence that leads to true submission. She desired only to obey, to abandon herself to a dominant will, but who, except a saint, possessed the qualities that she expected?

The Bishop of Geneva smiled and replied gently: "There is no need to look for universal minds. There is no harm, it seems to me, in collecting from several flowers the honey that we fail to find in one alone."

Francis de Sales feared that, in her desire to raise up saints, the reformer would turn away less strong-hearted souls who might be saved.

"My daughter," he said to the abbess, "wouldn't it be better not to try to catch such big fish, and take in more of them?"

What made the saint particularly apprehensive was Angélique's "promptitude," which made her hasten to tear down and rebuild everything around her. For Francis de Sales, God was not found "in wind, agitation, fire, but in the calm and gentle radius of an almost imperceptible breeze."

Wishing to guide Angélique, and not to hurt her, he expressed his thought in one of his familiar parables.

"Cherry trees bear fruit early: cherries which do not last long; but palm trees, princes among trees, do not bear dates until a hundred years after they have been planted." Therefore, the young abbess must moderate her impatience.

"Advance step by step," he said. "Do everything that you have to do gently and very softly."

Admonished with such delicate courtesy, Angélique confessed to him her self-satisfaction, and the extreme hastiness which often led her to treat people around her as stupid or foolish.

"Let your courage be humble," the bishop replied, "and your humility courageous. Beware of the words 'foolish' and 'stupid'; little by little train your vivacious mind to patience, gentleness, and amiability."

The abbess then accused herself of vanity, which she felt at certain times. Francis de Sales reassured her by evoking a biblical figure: these thoughts, he said, were like the birds which pecked about at the time of Abraham's sacrifice. What did he do? He drove them away with a reed.

Finally, Angélique dared to reveal what was at once her strength and her weakness: her pride. Francis de Sales consoled her: this sin is an insult to God's greatness only insofar as we yield to it, not in what we feel despite ourselves, as a natural impulse.

"Your heart," he said, "can be overwhelmed by awareness of your passions, but I think that you rarely sin by consent."

Did the abbess really want to break her pride? To overcome it there was only one instrument to use: love. "Never cease to love the love of God, for this is the king's highway," he said.

Angélique should set out in docile humility along this highway, led by a carefully chosen spiritual director. She should not look where she was going, "but with whom she was going"; finally, she must give up excessive mortifications. "Do not weigh down your weak body with austerities other than those imposed by your rule; conserve your bodily strength in order to serve God."

Thus calmed and reassured, Angélique summoned courage to speak about the Church: since the concordat permitting the King of France to appoint bishops and abbots, great ecclesiastical charges had become merely benefices. Many clerics desired only the most advantageous positions; sovereigns distributed them as rewards to their courtiers, to the relatives of their mistresses, sometimes even to heretics.

Francis de Sales was less disturbed by this than was Angélique; happily there was still a Christian Church, similar, he said, "to a garden with an infinite number and variety of flowers; each has its worth, its grace, its luster." Around these flowers gather the bees which "all contribute in supplying the hive with honey."

At the same time, the Bishop of Geneva revealed his hidden thoughts: there existed, unfortunately, bad nuns and priests who lived in what they believed to be the Church. "They are a multitude of wasps swarming around a dead body," the saint declared. It was indeed scandalous that the king appointed abbots who were "ruinous to pious devotion"; yet the evil came from sources higher still. Francis de Sales knew of the disorders of the Roman court, which contained "sick people who cherish their disease and do not want to be cured." He regretted the absence of a Council "which would reform the head and members." However, he added, Catholics should be silent so as not to cause unnecessary scandal; the only remedy was "to pray in secret that God would take a hand where men do not dare."

The following advice was addressed particularly to Angélique: if by ill chance the monastery of Port-Royal were one day to rise against Rome, it would know peace no longer and would court heresy. Had not Luther already been led astray by the mirage of a Church that had returned to the purity of the first centuries of Christianity?

Francis de Sales had often spoken to Angélique of Jeanne de Chantal, the future saint who had founded at Annecy, under the direction of the Bishop of Geneva, the Visitation order for the formation of "prayerful souls." In his *Treatise on the Love of God,* Francis magnificently described the mystical heights for which this order was destined.

Francis de Sales advised the Abbess of Port-Royal to write to Jeanne de Chantal; Jeanne's reply revealed joys, hopes, and fears which resembled her own. A correspondence then began between the two women, who found themselves, as Angélique said, "united as closely as one could possibly be to a person one has never seen."

The foundress of the Visitation was nineteen years older than the abbess; Angélique therefore addressed herself to Madame de Chantal "for guidance and enlightenment."

The Bishop of Geneva was only a luminous apparition in Angélique's life; the fact that he lived so far away and was so busy did not make him easily accessible. Jeanne de Chantal had more time at her disposal to follow her young friend closely, and went to see her each time she visited Paris. In the company of the older woman, Angélique abandoned herself to her old dream of resigning her charge as abbess in order to live in silence and contemplation of Christ; she wanted to leave Port-Royal and become, under Madame de Chantal's guidance, the last but most beloved of the Visitandines. Francis de Sales, who knew what Angélique's strength and faith could mean to endangered Catholicism, showed little favor for this plan. "God," he wrote her, "will use you for important things and in an extraordinary manner."

Thereafter, the Abbess of Port-Royal obediently sought only spiritual support from Jeanne de Chantal. The day came when she had the courage to reveal to this friend, even more plainly than she could to a confessor, the inner threat which terrorized her. Angélique had gone from reform to reform, from victory to victory, but now she trembled with fear of failing in that enterprise which was still her supreme purpose: namely, her own salvation. She felt living within her that most fearful of sins, the one that had damned the Dark Archangel—the pride from which the Bishop of Geneva believed he had absolved her.

Although not yet thirty years of age, the abbess had dominated her parents, convinced her superiors, triumphed over all rival communities. Through will power alone she had created a new Jerusalem in the valley wilderness of Port-Royal. Little by little, everyone had acclaimed her success; religious, priests, bishops vied with one another in praises that exasperated Angélique at times and that she bluntly called "nonsense." But how could anyone remain insensitive to so much adulation? "Monseigneur Camus of Belley confuses my ideas," the abbess wrote, "by his very vain and extravagant praises, for my wretched mind takes pleasure in them and I can scarcely bring myself to tear up his letters."

Thus a secret delight in vainglory filled Angélique's soul a little more each day. Her God wished to know only shame and suffering; how could grace penetrate a heart filled only with self?

If Angélique had lived under the direction of a confessor able to instill her with humility, if she could have renounced her dignity as abbess, she could perhaps have dominated the Arnauld pride; but she was surrounded only by blind admirers who became her courtiers. Accustomed to having every word obeyed from the start, the Abbess of Port-Royal could not bear to be contradicted. Everything had to be done the way she wanted. Before her mute and reverent daughters she could retain the appearance of sanctity even when each of her actions stemmed from demoniacal self-satisfaction. Over this viper's nest Francis de Sales had strewn lilies, quoting Scripture and calling on the mercy of the eternal God. Listening to Francis' parables the young abbess' hope had revived, but after his voice receded into the distance the flowers faded, the gems became tarnished. And God's terrible silence again reigned each time Angélique dared to turn her gaze on him.

One day succeeded another; death would come. Then judgment would be pronounced: was Angélique to be separated forever from the Divine Spouse without whom she could bear neither life nor death?

With a trust she had never felt before, the young abbess confided in Jeanne de Chantal: "I believe that my whole life is made up only of lies and hypocrisies," she wrote. "I have a fear of God that is servile and horrible, and such horror of death and hell that I feel no love at all; it seems to me that all my prayers and actions are merely products of the human spirit, and not of grace. I have extreme need of being humiliated and confounded."

On certain days, Angélique's natural youth and vivacity gave her an illusion of happiness. "Then," she wrote, "I am at peace and become too gay; often the thoughts in my mind are wiped out by frivolity." Wasn't this vain joy more dangerous to salvation than her terror?

Jeanne de Chantal had neither the knowledge nor the deep insights of a spiritual director. She could only reply with words whose meaning she well knew: "Look at God." Still, she realized how terrible this mute confrontation could be. Because of her incessant activities, she herself was often forgetful of the gentle and terrible Presence; she had to go from one community to another, building up in one place, righting things in another. Nevertheless, each time she paused, she, too, was filled with great fear of the Creator's unbearable majesty. The day came when Jeanne de Chantal could offer Angélique only her anguish. And this reply was to become the best remedy for the young abbess who was Jeanne de Chantal's "little novice." Forgetting her own fears, Angélique thought only of calming those of her friend. A sure instinct inspired her words: "Merely by the way in which you speak to me, I can see the depths of your heart and the Divine Spirit who abides there." Jesus, the nun continued, was holding Jeanne de Chantal "nailed to the cross with him"; already she bore the certain sign of predestination. Angélique praised "the divine wisdom which inspires and mortifies, which wounds and heals, which leads a soul down to hell and brings it back again."

Having succeeded in restoring peace to the foundress of the Visitation order, the abbess had the joy one day of seeing Jeanne de Chantal overcome the shadows that tormented her, renounce her own judgment, and at last abandon herself to the movements of grace. "I must no longer look," Jeanne wrote, "but must walk with eyes closed, neither willing nor knowing the way he is leading me . . . remaining simply lost and resting in him."

The saint was saved, and when Angélique returned to her wilderness she repeated to herself the words that had cured her friend. But the danger was ever present, and the one who would combat it had yet to appear.

During her long stay at Maubuisson Angélique had entrusted the direction of Port-Royal to her sister Agnès. The abbess saw in this move the possibility of eventually resigning her own position, and some time before her father's death she had beseeched him to agree to her withdrawal. Monsieur Arnauld had refused, but had decided that since Agnès was temporarily in charge of the abbey, she should be made Angélique's coadjutrix; in this way the younger daughter would be raised to a dignity that would in some small way compensate for her loss of the Abbey of Saint-Cyr. The lawyer sent his request to the court of Rome, expressing the desirability of granting Sister Agnès a title that would give her the authority necessary to direct the community during Mother Angélique's absence. The pope had hesitated for a while; it was not customary to lighten the work of an abbess who was only twenty-eight years old. However, Monsieur Arnauld's petition and his daughter's ever-growing fame convinced the Holy See to send the requested bulls in 1620. Agnès was cruelly disappointed; she very much wanted to avoid being made coadjutrix. Contemplative by nature, the young nun suffered because the duties of her position prevented her from lending herself "to that silence of heart and mind that is content only to adore and praise."

When, on September 6, 1621, Agnès was raised to her new dignity in the church of Port-Royal, the coadjutrix was unable to hide her sadness. Angélique, on the contrary, was completely happy to see her younger sister receive a charge which she would perhaps one day assume permanently. Coming from Maubuisson to attend this ceremony, the Abbess of Port-Royal sang the *Te Deum* so lustily that she became hoarse. At that point Agnès looked up at her with a mischievous smile, and with her finger pointed in her missal to these words from Scripture: "Before the Lord, here are two olive trees."

"I will not be alone here; we will be two," she murmured.

As the days and the years went by, the two olive trees were not to be separated.

In 1623, Angélique Arnauld left Maubuisson and returned to Port-Royal. There, the following year, she had the joy of seeing her youngest sister, Madeleine, clothed in the Bernardine habit. Thus, in succession, five of Monsieur Arnauld's daughters were won.

However, a new difficulty had arisen. After the arrival of the thirty-two novices from Maubuisson, the conventual buildings were too small to house all the nuns, now eighty in number. Moreover the abbey, built in a hollow of the valley, was inundated by rainstorms which caused the ponds to overflow; the water ran over the flagstones of the church and trickled down the infirmary walls. Finally, marsh fever spread among the nuns. Fifteen of them were to die within two years.

No one at Port-Royal would have been concerned about this danger if Madame Arnauld had not intervened. Now a widow, she was in charge of the whole family; consequently she decided to protect the health of her daughters and their companions by removing the community to Paris. With Angélique's consent, Madame Arnauld visited more than a hundred houses, and finally found one that could be transformed into a monastery—the Hôtel de Clagny, situated at the end of the faubourg Saint-Jacques, close to open country. In order to acquire this vast dwelling and convert it into a cloister Angélique had to borrow, and this debt long remained a source of great anxiety to her.

Louis XIII authorized the transfer of the convent to Paris, and at the same time praised the young abbess' zeal; Marie de' Medici proclaimed herself the foundress and benefactress of the new monastery. But neither the king nor his mother ever thought of coming to the help of the community, and the daughter of the Arnaulds was too proud to ask her sovereigns for money.

By 1626 all of the nuns had left their old abbey, thenceforth called Port-Royal des Champs (Port-Royal of the Fields), and only a chaplain remained. The nuns were all installed at Port-Royal of Paris.

It was not without regret that Angélique and Agnès abandoned the valley which had been the scene of the joys and sorrows of their childhood. Yet a great joy awaited the abbess: on February 24, 1626, she bestowed the Bernardine habit on her mother, Madame Arnauld, who, as Sister Catherine de Sainte-Félicité, left the world to live with her daughters and with God. From this time on, this fifty-three-year-old woman obeyed the abbess like a child, and dutifully followed the directions of the young novice mistress.

Some time prior to this Monseigneur Sebastian Zamet, the Bishop of Langres, to whom Madame de Chantal had often spoken of Angélique, had come to visit the abbess. The father of this prelate, a rich Italian banker, had arrived in France with the Medicis; the financier had made huge loans to Henri IV who, with amiable jocularity, called him "my money cousin." In his magnificent mansion the banker had often arranged splèndid banquets for the king and the beautiful Gabrielle d'Estrées; consequently his two sons had received many royal favors. The elder son took up the career of arms and the younger, Sebastian, devoted himself to the Church. He had become Bishop of Langres, a peer of France, and chaplain to Marie de' Medici.

At first Sebastian Zamet had led the easy life of court clerics, but one day an illness that threatened his life led him to religion. He then gave himself to God as he had given himself to the world—with ostentation. Even at the foot of the altar his piety revealed the *parvenu*. Monseigneur de Langres wanted to be surrounded by the most sublime minds of the Church in the same way as he had been surrounded at court by great nobles. When he presented himself to Mother Angélique, she thought she saw in him the representative of heaven whom she had long awaited.

Francis de Sales had died in 1622, and since then the abbess had been at odds with the Cistercian order to which she belonged. The new abbot, Dom Nivelle, had tried to put aside all the reforms at Port-Royal, pleasantly referring to them as "peculiarities." Angélique then asked the pope to release her from submission to the Cistercian order, and to make her subject to the Ordinary—that is, to place her under the secular clergy headed by the Archbishop of Paris. In 1627, Urban VIII granted the abbess' request. After this she was no longer even under the jurisdiction of the king, for at her request the queen mother, Marie de' Medici, persuaded Louis XIII to renounce his right to appoint the Abbess of Port-Royal, who in future was to be elected by her nuns for a term of three years. In this way Angélique had tried by every means to be relieved of the dignity which she owed to the favor of Henri IV. She intended to satisfy her dearest wish, one that had always been opposed by her father during his lifetime—to become a simple nun.

When Monseigneur Zamet appeared on the scene, the abbess had lost at one fell blow the saint who had directed her, her superiors at Cîteaux, and

the support of the monarch. Beguiled by the prelate's piety and desire to surpass everyone in serving God, Angélique believed that she could entrust herself blindly to this new spiritual director.

The bishop first required that she resign her position, and she prepared to
do this, although perhaps with no great precipitation. Her sister Agnès had
to abandon her functions as coadjutrix, and was sent by Monseigneur Zamet
with her younger sister, Marie-Claire, to the Abbey of Tard at Dijon.

In 1630, Monseigneur Zamet brought about the election of Genevieve Le
Tardif, a former novice at Maubuisson, as Abbess of Port-Royal. But this new
abbess had only the appearance of power: the monastery was in reality governed by the prioress, Madame de Pourlans, whom the prelate had brought to
Port-Royal for the purpose of directing the community according to his own
ideas.

Angélique regarded these great transformations with astonishment. Monseigneur Zamet showed only contempt for many of the religious of Port-Royal
who, in their simplicity and poverty, appeared "quite stupid," he said. Many
of them did not know how to write, and he had them labor, pen in hand, to
become "capable of everything" as the bishop required. Pupils were no longer
accepted unless they were daughters of either a marquis or a count. "In the
church, the use of perfumes, pleated linen, bouquets of flowers is required."

Preachers arrived from all quarters at the call of Monseigneur Zamet,
and succeeded one another with rapidity. The austerities which were practiced were spectacular: fasting on bread and water, submission to "terrible
disciplines and the most humiliating penances in the world."

Angélique was dazzled to see so many austerities joyfully accepted, until
the day she heard one of the nuns laughing at faults over which she had
shed many tears that very same morning.

The day came when the former abbess was saddened by the expulsion of
three poor nuns whom she had received through charity; these daughters, she
was told, "were a burden on the house." The precious letters written by Francis de Sales to the Abbess of Port-Royal were used to cover pots of unguents.

"I secretly asked myself," Angélique said later, "what was the use of all
this? Then I told myself, 'To destroy confidence in my own judgment.'"

Yet, despite her desire for humiliation—thereafter to be fully satisfied—the
former abbess could not conceal her mute suffering when she saw the ruin
of everything she had built up. Monseigneur Zamet surmised her feelings
and was irritated.

"You are hurting me deeply," he declared to Angélique on one occasion.

"But I have said nothing," she murmured.

"Your very shadow harms me," replied the prelate.

"Well, send me wherever you will; I will go," said the nun.

The authority at his disposal did not satisfy Bishop Zamet; the domain over which he wielded it had become too narrow for him. A monastery as modest as Port-Royal, buried at the extreme end of the faubourg Saint-Jacques, did not befit the Bishop of Langres. He decided to create a house in the heart of Paris that would be "favored by the great."

Supported by Louise de Bourbon, first wife of the Duc de Longueville, the bishop obtained authorization from Rome to found the Institute of the Blessed Sacrament, to be devoted day and night to the adoration of the eucharist. The ministers of Louis XIII were little attracted to this new devotion, but the king, having fallen gravely ill at Lyon, had been cured after receiving communion. After this, how could Marillac, the Guardian of the Seals, oppose the establishment of a house consecrated to the eucharist? In 1633, this convent was solemnly installed in the rue Coquillière, near the Louvre. The new community was the living reflection of Monseigneur Zamet, and displayed the ceremoniousness which the prelate owed to his Italian origin. The church itself was magnificent; those received as novices each had to have a dowry of ten thousand livres. They were required to be "of good mentality, capable of conversing with princesses." Their white and red habit was made of fine material and, as the bishop wished, was "augustly sovereign in appearance." Everything had to be agreeable so as not to frighten away the ladies of the court.

Monseigneur de Langres had decided to entrust the direction of the Institute to the most loyal of his religious, Madame de Pourlans. But this time his will was opposed by a prince of the church more important than himself. He had obtained control of the Institute only on condition that his authority be shared with the archbishops of Sens and of Paris. The latter, Monseigneur de Gondi, uncle of the future Cardinal de Retz, highly irritated at seeing his diocese invaded by the Bishop of Langres, removed Madame de Pourlans and demanded that Angélique Arnauld be appointed superior of the house of the Blessed Sacrament. Monseigneur Zamet was nevertheless successful in joining to her another nun, Anne de Jésus de Foissy de Chamesson, who constantly opposed her superior's plans and impeded her activities.

What could the former abbess do in this establishment ruled by Bishop Zamet? She had to attend the services, which were spectacles reserved only for the court. Endowed with a humane and very simple faith, the daughter of Monsieur Arnauld had always greatly distrusted flashy manifestations of piety. Thus she was extremely ill at ease in the presence of ecstasies, transports, and raptures, which increased in number around Monseigneur Zamet in a décor where the personages were swathed in long cloaks and scarlet fabrics.

Agnès, of a gentler nature and more of a mystic than her elder sister, had several years earlier transcribed at the order of her confessor, Father de Condren, the text of a meditation which she dedicated to the sixteen centuries that had elapsed since the institution of the Blessed Sacrament. In it each century was symbolized by one of Jesus' virtues: Holiness, Truth, Sovereignty, Possession, Infinitude. . . . This writing, with its rather precious piety, filled the Bishop of Langres with enthusiasm. He declared it "miraculous," and affirmed that it "did not express the thoughts of a nun but those of Jesus Christ within her." It was called the *Secret Chaplet* because it was to be circulated in handwritten form and never printed.

Now Archbishop Bellegarde of Sens, charged together with the Archbishop of Paris with supervision of the Institute of the Blessed Sacrament, had also been greatly irritated by Monseigneur Zamet's self-conceit. When he read the *Secret Chaplet,* so highly praised by the Bishop of Langres, Monseigneur Bellegarde believed that he discerned heresies in it. Whereupon this archbishop submitted the text to eight doctors of the Sorbonne, one of whom, Nicolas Cornet, later became famous. These theologians censured the *Chaplet,* finding in it, they said, "various extravagances, errors, and impieties." Placed in a bad position, Monseigneur Zamet found other theologians favorable to the *Chaplet,* and addressed himself particularly to Jean Duvergier de Hauranne, Abbot of Saint-Cyran.

This priest was still almost unknown to Agnès and Angélique. He had written to Angélique congratulating her on the "holy hardihood" that had led her to open the doors of the abbeys of Maubuisson and Port-Royal to girls without a dowry. At the request of the Bishop of Langres, the Abbot of Saint-Cyran closely examined the *Secret Chaplet,* and his knowledgeability made it possible for him to show that the text was orthodox on all points. To his own authority in the matter he shortly afterward added that of several theologians of the University of Louvain, among them Jansenius; all approved "the rapture and freedom of these loving praises."

Immediately the Jesuits entered into the picture. They had learned that Monseigneur Zamet's defender, the Abbot of Saint-Cyran, was responsible for two books severely critical of some members of their Society; the Fathers countered by attacking Agnès' *Chaplet.* There was gossip at court, where the nuns of the Blessed Sacrament were beginning to be considered visionaries.

Poor Agnès, unwitting cause of all this trouble, was appalled to see the rise of what was already called "the tempest of the *Secret Chaplet.*" "I cannot understand," she wrote, "how anything so unimportant could have such grave consequences."

Thus there entered on the scene almost all the actors in the tragedy of Port-Royal: the Abbot of Saint-Cyran, Jansenius, Nicolas Cornet, and the Jesuits.

Encouraged by his first success, and having decided to triumph over Bishop Zamet, the Archbishop of Sens submitted Agnès' meditation to Rome. Seeing that theologians had contradicted each other over a writing so innocent and almost unintelligible, the Holy Office wisely refused either to condemn or approve it, merely deciding that the *Chaplet* should not be disseminated "because such matters are not generally understood."

The Bishop of Langres could breathe again, and he owed his rescue to the Abbot of Saint-Cyran, whom he thereafter considered as the best of all theologians and most perfect of religious. Consequently, he introduced him as a preacher into the Institute of the Blessed Sacrament, telling the nuns that "God was giving them Monsieur de Saint-Cyran to guide them on the road to perfection."

The abbot objected in vain that he had a reputation for severity.

"You are not severe, Monsieur," the bishop replied, "but you are a lover of the truth."

Thus Monseigneur Zamet, after threatening the future existence of Port-Royal, led to Angélique the man who could give the complete fullness of a religious revival to the reform the abbess had begun.

Jean Duvergier de Hauranne had made his first studies in theology at the Sorbonne; considering them insufficient, he went to Louvain in 1600 to continue at the college of the Jesuits. Returning to Paris, Duvergier became the friend of the Fleming Jansen who, in accordance with the taste of the period for the Latin tongue, was to change his name to Jansenius. This scholar also came from Louvain, where he had devoted himself to studies in theology.

In 1611 the two young men decided to retire to a country house situated on a hill overlooking Bayonne, the home of Jean Duvergier's parents. There they spent some years together, studying the Bible and the Fathers of the Church.

Both had been struck by the weaknesses of most of the Catholic theologians of their time. While Protestants were discovering God in the psalms and prophets, many doctors of the famous Faculty of Theology at the Sorbonne were unable to extricate themselves from the scholasticism of the Middle Ages, losing themselves in subtle reasoning in an effort to reconcile the wisdom of philosophers with the teachings of Christ. Almost all of these humanists felt themselves closer to Aristotle than to Jesus.

Duvergier and Jansenius were convinced that Christians were needed, not "the babbling of the schools," to combat the Lutherans and Calvinists who claimed to go back to the sources of religion. Heretics should be answered in Christ's words, and with the writings of the Church Fathers. One must "find again the doctrine that was lost and once more acquire true knowledge."

For five years Duvergier's mother saw the two friends studying·the sacred texts from the first daylight hours to the middle of the night. Anxiously pointing to Jansenius, she told her son that "he would kill the poor Fleming by making him study so hard."

It was indeed a harsh test, but when Jansenius left his companion to return to Louvain each of the young men possessed a knowledge of sacred literature that would astonish their contemporaries. They continued to exchange ideas through correspondence; Jansenius was to discover "the heights and depths" of Saint Augustine and one day would set down the outline of a work devoted to this doctor in order to teach Christians about their final destiny. The correspondence between the two friends was taken up with this enterprise, and in order to forestall the curiosity of certain censors always quick to launch accusations of heresy, Duvergier and Jansenius agreed upon a certain language: the matter of the true reestablishment of religion constituted what they mysteriously called "the Pilmot affair."

All the prelates who approached Duvergier were fascinated by the extent of his knowledge, but he remained quite devoid of evangelical humility. The young theologian discovered in the Bible and writings of the Fathers only passages that would be pleasing to his hearers, and he intended to pay court to the great. One day the malicious and skeptical Henri IV asked his friends whether, if they ever found themselves alone with him on a desert island, they should not kill themselves—despite God's command—so that the king could sustain himself with their flesh and thus preserve his person for the welfare of his subjects. Duvergier hastened to draw up a reply which he gravely called "the Royal Question"; he discovered thirty-four cases in which a Christian has the right to put an end to his own life in order to prolong that of his prince! Henri IV's confessor, the Jesuit Father Cotton, was enthusiastic about this study and even affirmed that its author merited a bishop's miter and crozier.

In 1615, Duvergier published an *Apology* for Monseigneur Rochepozay, Bishop of Poitiers. This prelate had taken part in the fighting to defend his city against the Protestants, and after Henri IV's ascent to power this had brought down severe criticism on his head. Duvergier demonstrated in his *Apology* that ecclesiastics always have the right to fight and bear arms in case of necessity.

Favor was not long in coming to reward so accommodating a theologian: in 1620 the Bishop of Poitiers gave Duvergier the Abbey of Saint-Cyran in

Brenne. He thus became a dignitary of the Church only two years after the day he was made a priest, and was known thereafter as Monsieur de Saint-Cyran.

Was the abbot to pursue the career that had begun with so much promise? Everything would have borne him along in this direction had there not occurred an incident that was to change his whole existence.

At Poitiers, Saint-Cyran made the acquaintance of Father Condren, a priest of the Oratory, and the latter put him in touch with the founder of his order, Pierre de Bérulle.

The meeting was decisive; Bérulle became Saint-Cyran's friend and taught him how, through the incarnation and redemption, Christ had taken upon himself the fate of the world. As an image of the Messiah, he said, every priest should make himself "the living prayer of humanity."

In the light of his new discovery, Saint-Cyran's ambitions seemed contemptible to him; had he not already passed infinitely beyond any dignity he might covet? The day he had received the priesthood he had become "a king and more than a king." From the height to which he had been elevated, Jansenius' friend now took a close look at the condition of the Catholic Church which he had considered with indifference when he was only a student.

Who could help him along the road he now decided to follow? How very rare were the bishops, priests, and religious who were conscious of their mission.

In the presence of Vincent de Paul, Saint-Cyran was unable to hide his sadness.

"The Church of other days was a great river; today it is only mud. There is no longer a Church," he said.

It had been agreed with Monseigneur Zamet that Saint-Cyran would direct the Institute of the Blessed Sacrament solely by means of sermons; but so great was the abbot's influence that the nuns asked the preacher to become their confessor. At first Saint-Cyran refused; he would not take charge of consciences until the requests were made more pressing. The priest did not think he should assume this very heavy responsibility toward God until grace acted upon a soul and moved it irresistibly; then he would commit himself to it and always walk before it.

In this way Saint-Cyran was to receive the nuns' confessions one after another. Their superior, Angélique Arnauld, was the last to entrust herself to him. Accustomed to the gentleness of Father Archange, the suavity of Francis de Sales, and the deferential admiration of her confessors, she feared this stern man whose powerful forehead and penetrating eyes are shown against a dark background in the portrait by Philippe de Champagne.

Certainly Saint-Cyran did not have the scorn for these penitents which was shown by Jansenius, who said it was a waste of time to busy one's self with "that breed." Saint-Cyran was too much a Frenchman not to know the riches that can be concealed in a woman's heart; Angélique was the only one to recognize that when he would begin to lead her toward the narrow gate he would leave her no place of refuge.

From the time of their first meeting, Saint-Cyran did not hide from the superior of the Blessed Sacrament "that he had seen many abbesses reform their monasteries, but few had been able to reform themselves." This was a far cry from the laudatory letters that Angélique had regretfully torn up! She was one day to confess that "she had dreaded the great rectitude of this servant of God." His conduct toward the other nuns made Angélique feel that she was in the presence of the director she had so long sought. Yet an instinctive fear still militated against what "she loved and desired." She knew Saint-Cyran well enough to understand that she must consent "to the death of her will, of her discernment"; she must renounce reason and prudence, all the humble virtues inherited from her bourgeois ancestors, those that had guided her on a road that had seemed endless but also without pitfalls. Led by someone she did not know, the daughter of the Arnaulds had to cast herself into the terrible adventure of salvation.

At one time Angélique had wanted to avoid this fascinating danger, to act as though she were indifferent; but the idea of deceiving a priest by hiding from him the first movements of grace would have been the worst of betrayals. Moreover, had she not "wished so much for years to find a man whose strength of mind would dominate her own"?

It was useless to struggle against God; little by little her last resistances broke down. The day came when Angélique asked Monsieur de Saint-Cyran to hear her confession. This was an abdication; still it was not enough to want to surrender—it was necessary to be able to do it. There is nothing so easy as to appear before judges who have been won over in advance; but how could she disclose to an inflexible mind those petty faults and hypocrisies that were more difficult to avow than grievous sins?

"His great wisdom," Angélique said later, "made me dread revealing such stupidities to him."

One day she was forced to admit to Saint-Cyran that, despite her willingness to reveal everything, she feared she would never be able to do so if God did not grant her the necessary grace; would he pray for her to overcome the false shame that sealed her lips in his presence?

Saint-Cyran did not depart from the rule he imposed on everyone: Angélique must follow alone the road which still separated her from God. If she did not succeed in doing this, it was because she had not yet been touched by "the light of the heart," namely, grace; it was useless to attempt anything against the divine will. With gentleness—because he always avoided hurting anyone needlessly—Saint-Cyran only replied to Angélique that she should not "do violence to her mind." Hadn't she already made general confessions? Therefore it was useless for her to make one again. This discreet aloofness merely reinforced the nun's suddenly overpowering desire to confide in Saint-Cyran. Now it was she who in her turn prayed and pleaded until the man who had drawn her so powerfully finally consented to hear her —and so we find her on her knees before one who had become God's representative to her. The abbess' whole life, so holy in the eyes of the world, so poor when she judged it herself, rose up before her. Could she express all this? No. "The words failed to come." For two hours at the feet of the listening priest, kindly but inaccessible, the penitent sought for words, stammered, tried to confess her failings. It was all in vain; she could not express her desire to submit, her need of help.

That day Saint-Cyran went away without Angélique's having been able to make her confession. He had witnessed her struggle and he prayed for her; then, after several days during which the nun did not dare to ask him to come to see her, he spontaneously returned.

Again Angélique attempted to make her confession. She was completely astonished; almost without effort she disclosed every moment of her life, every turn of her most obscure thoughts. The priest heard her in silence with the ever fresh emotion he felt when he had a presentiment of God's first approaches to a soul.

Certainly as yet Angélique stood only on the threshold; as he had done in the case of each of the other nuns, Saint-Cyran was now to undertake on her behalf the most difficult task of all.

The Abbess of Port-Royal had expected to find a severe director who would impose heavy penances on her. She was much surprised: Saint-Cyran discouraged her austerities; he did not want the flesh treated as an enemy. "The body," he said, "is the first of the poor to whom we owe charity."

The priest always had, moreover, a certain distrust for ostentatious mortifications. In her blunt way Angélique said one day: "Monsieur de Saint-Cyran knew that voluntary penances are undertaken more for purposes of adornment than in order to cleanse oneself."

The priest preferred lengthy silent meditations to austerities; he wanted to instill "a spiritual silence that suppresses all motion, because God speaks to each soul alone."

Another surprise: this spiritual director had "great respect for the independence of each mind." One should not, he said, "bring pressure to bear on a person, but should expect to gain everything by leaving him free."

Saint-Cyran limited himself to helping persons in his charge to know themselves, to discover "the corruptions that hold them beaten to the ground," and
to liberate themselves from them. He also taught them how to speak to God:
prayer "should come from within, in the same way as true eloquence."

The priest used an expression which was to be immortalized by Descartes
at the same period: in order for the spirit to reign, a clean sweep (*tabula
rasa*) must be made of everything within; then would begin the slow work
of grace, a supernatural operation. The priest could only help the resurrected
soul to advance; he taught that divine love should be approached in "fear
and trembling," for we have never amounted to anything but nothingness on
earth, but also with "firm and constant hope," because we have been redeemed by the divine blood. We must "abandon ourselves to the winds of
God."

The penitent must first humiliate himself; "The soul rises only in descending." He must then take a long look at One who is still unknown; Saint-
Cyran called this "the hymn of silence." He must discover in the Gospel the
great force of "solid truths." He must confess his faults, repent, receive the
eucharist; the sacraments are the ways to the world beyond.

Here again Angélique expected more rigidity. Far from representing communion as a height no one could reach without painful efforts, Saint-Cyran
advised her to receive it frequently. To go to communion one had only to hate
the evil within one and to love God.

Angélique had always considered such hate and such love as insufficient;
she believed she had not done enough. "One always wanted more than he
wanted," she was to say of Saint-Cyran.

Finally the moment came when Angélique "surrendered her own discernment" and found again that inner fervor that had lighted her way in the
earlier days of Port-Royal. "It seemed to me I was another creature," she later
wrote.

Saint-Cyran witnessed the miracle to which he led people. After that it
was God alone who acted. The priest could only reveal to Angélique what
she carried within, then help her day by day to maintain her lofty and fragile
happiness.

The power of grace felt by the nun was described to her by Saint-Cyran in
words which took their full meaning on that day: "It is a movement of love
toward God; this love increases little by little as daylight does." When Jesus
became man, grace came down on earth; each time a human being raises
himself to God, the same miracle is accomplished again. However, these
riches are in greater danger than any earthly treasure; until the day he dies
each of the elect must obey the words of Saint Paul: "Cleave to the Lord, be
of one mind with him."

Saint-Cyran sometimes spoke with a sort of terror of the task of the priest. "A soul is a world," he said. Every one of us has his heights and his depths; each needs a different kind of help. "It is easier," he said again, "to undertake the political government of a kingdom than the spiritual rule of a single soul."

Angélique reveals what he accomplished. "Never before in my whole life had I known such perceptible consolations," she said.

The Bishop of Langres was greatly surprised when next he visited the Institute of the Blessed Sacrament which he had founded; no longer was he received as one inspired, whose orders came from God. The solemn austerities, the "sovereignly august" habit, the pompous services filled most of the nuns only with indifference and disdain. A deep silence had fallen over a house formerly so animated; the people of the court no longer were at ease, and withdrew with the feeling that they were intruding. A very close unity existed among the nuns themselves. Their eyes were lighted by the same joy; they held a hope in common, and this was expressed in their glances each time they came together.

At the Monastery of Port-Royal of Paris, also directed by Monseigneur Zamet, Saint-Cyran had met with a certain resistance, but within several days he had won over almost all who had rebelled. Agnès, who had been prejudiced against him, exclaimed, "No man has ever spoken as this man"; she asked him to become her spiritual director and, since he evaded this, she in her turn pleaded with him. She was never to forget that Saint-Cyran taught her "to listen to God who prays within us, to lose ourselves in his depths."

Soon at Port-Royal, as at the Institute of the Blessed Sacrament, there was an atmosphere of peace; it was almost as though the first ages of Christianity had returned.

Monseigneur Zamet soon recognized the origin of this silent revolution: Madame de Pourlans at Port-Royal and Anne de Foissy at the house of the Blessed Sacrament apprised the bishop of the influence exercised by the new spiritual director. The Bishop of Langres bitterly said that he was no longer anything but "the chaplain of Monsieur de Saint-Cyran."

Saint-Cyran did not take pride in victories which he in no way attributed to himself. Learning that the prelate was irritated because his authority was diminishing, the priest returned to his far-away abbey situated on the border between Berry and Poitou.

Monseigneur Zamet took advantage of Saint-Cyran's absence to try to recover his influence, but merely succeeded in dividing the nuns into two camps. The very few who remained loyal to him grouped themselves around Madame de Pourlans at Port-Royal and Anne de Foissy at the Institute of the Blessed Sacrament, but they were powerless before the new spirit that animated their companions.

The Archbishop of Paris, Monseigneur de Gondi, then intervened, sending Madame de Pourlans back to her Abbey of Tard. The same prelate authorized Angèlique to leave the Institute of the Blessed Sacrament, where she had always felt herself a stranger, and to return to Port-Royal. The new superior of the House of the Blessed Sacrament, Mother Le Tardif, had definitely withdrawn from Bishop Zamet and had become one of Saint-Cyran's penitents. The height of misfortune for the Bishop of Langres was that his protegée, young Anne de Foissy, realizing that she had no vocation for living in a formerly worldly Institute which had been changed into a real cloister, now returned to the world. Shortly afterward, the nuns who had come from Port-Royal also left the House of the Blessed Sacrament, and rejoined their own monastery.

After this Port-Royal subsisted on its own. Monseigneur Zamet made one more attempt to maintain the division, but Agnès Arnauld, who had been elected abbess there, wrote the prelate "humbly to beseech him not to come any more."

The Bishop of Langres was never again to appear at Port-Royal.

When, in earlier days, Monsieur Arnauld had wanted to ensure the future of his two younger daughters, Angélique and Agnès, he believed he had already established his eldest, Catherine, extremely well. Had he not given her as husband a royal counselor, Monsieur Le Maître, who had a hundred thousand crowns! Unfortunately the latter had proved to be a bad husband, fickle and dissipated, totally indifferent to poor Catherine. When finally he abandoned her, Monsieur Arnauld had only one alternative: to institute proceedings against his son-in-law for a separation. After obtaining from Parlement seven decrees in ten days, the lawyer found himself the legal guardian of his daughter and of the children born of her marriage.

After this, Madame Catherine Le Maître lived in her parents' home. There she met Francis de Sales, who heard her general confession and received her vow of perpetual chastity. Later the young woman was to retire with her mother and sisters to the monastery of Port-Royal and in her turn to become a religious.

Antoine, the eldest son of Catherine Le Maître, became a lawyer like his grandfather, Monsieur Arnauld. His renown outstripped even that of his forebear; the whole palace marveled at Antoine Le Maître's speeches to the court, garnished with Latin quotations and ornamented with mythological allegories. Chancellor Séguier did not want the king deprived of so valuable a man: Le Maître was made a councilor of state at the age of twenty-eight.

One day he wrote his aunt, Agnès Arnauld, announcing that he had just discovered the finest, most beautiful girl in Paris, and he intended to marry her. The nun was offended because her nephew dared tell her "tales of his love affairs; she had no ears for such dissertations." Above all, Mother Agnès was disappointed. "Dear as you were to me," she wrote Le Maître, "you have become indifferent. As you are placing yourself in a quite ordinary situation, I will also hold you in quite ordinary affection. You want to become a slave and at the same time remain a king in my heart; this is impossible."

Then, pretending not to have understood her nephew's letter, Agnès maliciously asked if the girl who had bewitched him was not that chastity which Antoine Le Maître had seriously wished to embrace in earlier days. At this point in her letter, the nun covered her nephew with praises that made him very uncomfortable. "You say that she is the most beautiful and the finest in Paris; you should have said in Paradise, since she is sister to the angels!"

Then in a tone of gentle raillery Agnès tried to persuade Le Maître that he was not made for playing the ladies' man. "The Gospel rightly says that there will be wolves in sheep's clothing, but not that sheep will wear the clothing of wolves. That is what you are doing; when one looks beneath your wolf's skin, one finds the wool of a sheep and a gentle spirit that breathes only peace."

The young man was annoyed, not knowing how to reply to such affectionate irony. But already grace was near; two months later, in August, 1637, Le Maître found himself at the bedside of his aunt, Madame d'Andilly, who lay at death's door. He listened as Saint-Cyran prepared her to leave the world; suddenly, as the supreme combat was ending, the priest's voice rose: "Go forth, O Christian soul, go forth from this world in the name of God Almighty, who created you . . ."

At that moment the veil that hid the future was torn aside for Antoine Le Maître; one day such as this the final words would be pronounced over his own dead body; after they had been said, no one could do anything further for him. Filled with anguish, the young man went down into the garden and for the first time meditated on eternity. A short time later he threw himself at the feet of Saint-Cyran, asking him to act as his guide on the road of the Gospel. With a strange premonition of future events, the priest spoke of danger: "I foresee," he said, "where God is leading me in entrusting me with your guidance. It does not matter; I must follow, even to prison and death."

At the request of his confessor, Le Maître continued for several months to practice law, but in the halls of justice he had eyes only for the crucifix, of which he had taken no notice before.

Madame Le Maître learned with joy of her son's decision, and she found him a retreat where "he could try to move his God by doing penance." It was a small lodging adjoining the monastery of Port-Royal of Paris. Madame Le Maître was to shelter there another of her sons, Monsieur de Séricourt, who was not long in deciding "to die to the world."

Lancelot, a young tonsured cleric of twenty-two, the son of a Parisian barrel-maker, was also soon "to bury himself alive" under the guidance of Saint-Cyran. Although he had lived in the community of priests of Saint Nicolas de Chardonnet, Claude Lancelot had never dared aspire to the priesthood himself, and was to remain a subdeacon all his life. When he first met Saint-Cyran he was, he writes, "like a man cast up by the sea on the shore of some island, awaiting the passing of a vessel that would bear him away."

In this manner there gathered around the Monastery of Port-Royal a group of men who were to call themselves *solitaries;* their number grew. All lived humbly and in poverty; each brought with him whatever possessions he had. Assembled in the abbey church before the grill that separated them from the nuns, they followed the offices; then they returned to their narrow rooms and from daybreak to nightfall prayed to God and meditated on the Scriptures. "Sing and make melody in your hearts," Saint Paul said to the Ephesians. "Each obeyed the apostle in his room," Lancelot wrote, "so that one heard the soft singing of the canticles; this brought to mind the image of the first Church of Jerusalem where, as Saint Jerome said of his own day, one heard from all sides, from fields and houses, the sound of psalms and alleluias."

At this time Saint-Cyran discovered the priest, selected from all the others, whom he was to take as his assistant. Of modest origin, this man had been appointed by Saint Vincent de Paul as confessor to the Hôpital de la Pitié. As soon as he came to know the spiritual director of Port-Royal, this priest, Antoine Singlin, was conquered, and he came to join the solitaries. Saint-Cyran chose Singlin because he found in him the grace that enabled him to lead others to salvation. He did not conceal from Singlin that such was to be his mission; above all else, a priest should impart the word of God "because it is through this word that we engender and revive souls, not limiting ourselves to nourishing them with the eucharist." He would be placed between the immensity of the divine, vast as "the monstrous grandeur of the oceanic seas," and the falsehoods of penitents "who are more cunning than foxes at hiding themselves."

Faced with a task whose extent he had not yet measured, Singlin was overwhelmed, and tried by every means to avoid the charge. Saint-Cyran had earlier entrusted some children to him; Singlin had trained and educated them and had spent happy days living among them, days that he wanted to prolong. Besides, the poor man had to admit weaknesses of his own, which, in his estimation, disqualified him for the proper exercise of the priesthood.

"You are not sufficiently tolerant of your own faults," Saint-Cyran replied. "We must lift ourselves up humbly and gently from our falls."

All Singlin's evasions were in vain; he had henceforth to share with the leader of Port-Royal the work of preaching and directing the nuns and solitaries.

Saint-Cyran saw very quickly that he had made no mistake in the young man. When he preached to Christians, Singlin did not seek oratorical effects; his simplicity was evangelical, his faith so strong that it moved everyone. More and more converts were won.

At that time Port-Royal was in the last days of its golden age.[1] Saint-Cyran upheld the faith of the nuns and followed the progress of the solitaries. He still corresponded with Jansenius, now Bishop of Ypres, who was writing a vast tome on Saint Augustine. Happiness reigned in the abbey and around it. "It is a sign that the Holy Spirit is with us," Saint-Cyran said.

But the hour of darkness was approaching. Port-Royal was to suffer persecution, and this struggle was to give to hitherto peaceful lives—which might otherwise be remembered only as a series of charming pictures—all the grandeur of martyrdom welcomed and accepted with love.

---

[1] This spiritual movement was only one aspect of the renaissance of Catholicism which is called the Counter Reformation—in opposition to the Protestant Reform.

2

THE COMBAT

The opening blow was struck at Saint-Cyran; the intransigence of his faith had made many enemies.

In 1625, a Jesuit, Father Garasse, had published a *Somme théologique des vérités capitales de la religion chrétienne.* This imposing title concealed the desire to accommodate the Gospel to the tastes of people in polite society; Father Garasse addressed himself to them with both ease and whimsey. His book made Saint-Cyran indignant. "He dishonors," he said, "the majesty of God."

Saint-Cyran had replied by publishing a compendium of the errors and falsehoods contained in Father Garasse's *Somme.* The Society of Jesus tried in vain to prevent the publication of this work, but was reduced to silence when the Faculty of Theology censured Father Garasse's book as "farcical, scandalous, heretical."

Several years later the Jesuits came in conflict in England with a papal legate who was an archbishop. A book inspired by Saint-Cyran vigorously defended the rights of the episcopate against the encroachments of the Society of Jesus. Thenceforth that Society was the declared enemy of a man who had dared attack it on two occasions.

Later on Richelieu's lieutenant, Father Joseph, attracted by Saint-Cyran's prestige, charged him with the guidance of the nuns of the Order of Calvary, whom the illustrious Capuchin himself had directed up to that time.

Racine, in his *Abridged History of Port-Royal,* had these ironical words for his Gray Eminence: "Although deeply immersed in the affairs of the world, he prided himself on being a great master of the spiritual life." Father

Joseph was, in fact, well known for his book on the method of prayer, which closely followed the *Spiritual Exercises* of Loyola. His "method" was intended to lead the nuns to God by means of intellectual disciplines similar to those conceived earlier by the founder of the Society of Jesus.

On one of his visits the Capuchin had seen the nuns who had been transformed by Saint-Cyran. Disdaining all exterior manifestations of piety, they no longer sought, Father Joseph said bitterly, "anything but supereminent perfection."

Like Monseigneur Zamet, Father Joseph felt a keen bitterness toward Saint-Cyran. But, since he was a man of broader views, he openly discussed the dangers that Saint-Cyran represented in his eyes: the priest was a threat to that honest mediocrity of minds necessary for the maintenance of order in the Church and in the state. Therefore his Gray Eminence began to pursue his rival with watchful hatred; when Saint-Cyran was later imprisoned, the conditions of his detention were alleviated only after the death of Father Joseph.

Even so, it was only when Saint-Cyran dared to attack Richelieu personally that his fate was sealed. The future cardinal had known Saint-Cyran at the residence of the Bishop of Poitiers when he himself occupied the bishopric of Luçon, "the most corrupt diocese in France." At that time Richelieu had been impressed by Saint-Cyran's theological knowledge.

"Gentlemen," he said one day to his entourage, pointing to Saint-Cyran, "you are looking at the most scholarly man in Europe."

The minister had quickly discerned the intellectual force of the priest and the prodigious influence he exercised over all who approached him, in addition to his knowledge; he should make such a man one of his creatures.

However, Saint-Cyran was not attracted to Richelieu, the politician, but to Bérulle, the mystic. Nothing could so have displeased the great cardinal.

As the spiritual director of Marie de' Medici, who placed all her confidence in him, Bérulle had contributed to Richelieu's rise to power. But the ideas of the two churchmen were soon found to be in opposition. Father Bérulle had conceived a plan for European union, according to which the Most Christian King of France should ally himself with the Catholic sovereigns of Spain and Austria. Had Bérulle's views prevailed the face of the world would have been changed, and the wars fought against the house of Austria and against Spain would have been avoided. France's power would have assured her of the first place in a European federation. Spoiled by gold from America, Spain had ceased to make any effort; the Emperor of Germany had only apparent power over his divided country, which was threatened at one and the same time by heretics and by the Turks.

But the idea of a European confederation, united by a common religion, brought only a disdainful smile to Richelieu's lips; wasn't it more to the point to impose the hegemony of the Bourbons on the Hapsburgs?

When it was a question of circumventing a king as timorous as Louis XIII, the man of God was powerless against the man of prey. Made a cardinal in 1627, Bérulle died in disgrace two years later.

Faithful to the memory of her spiritual director, Marie de' Medici made an attempt to realize Bérulle's projects with the help of what was then called "the party of devotees." For just one day, the 10th of November, 1630, the queen mother believed she had triumphed. In Bérulle's memory she wanted to bestow the bishopric of Bayonne on his faithful friend, Saint-Cyran; in that diocese the latter would find again the familiar countryside of his youth. But the very next day the most mercurial of kings assured the victory of Richelieu, and Saint-Cyran became one of the victims of the "Day of the Dupes."

Nevertheless, the cardinal was too wily a politician to show his rancor against the protegé of his adversaries; on the contrary, he felt that the moment had come to win the priest over to his own side. Richelieu had dreams of becoming the patriarch of the Church of France, which had great need of able men; hence he offered Saint-Cyran the diocese of Bayonne, which the queen mother had been unable to obtain for him.

Saint-Cyran knew the prime minister well enough not to be taken in; he knew that the very day he was elevated to the episcopate he would be bound in servitude. Richelieu never abandoned his creatures, but he used them as he saw fit.

Without hesitation, Saint-Cyran refused the miter. At this Richelieu was both surprised and irritated, for he now learned that the consciences of certain men could not be bought. Bérulle's disciple was condemned from that moment; the cardinal did not permit the resistance of a man on whom he "had no hold." Later, in 1642, Cinq-Mars, refusing to act as Richelieu's spy and even defying him, would pay for his audacity with his life.

Saint-Cyran was quick to understand that he would suffer for what he had done. One day he said to Angélique Arnauld: "The straight way obliges me to choose a prison rather than a bishopric. I would be right in thinking that to refuse the first would necessarily lead to the second under a government that wants only slaves."

From that moment on, Saint-Cyran never ceased to oppose the rights of a Christian to the demands of a tyrant.

When, for political reasons, Richelieu wished to have the Church annul the marriage of Gaston of Orléans to the Princess Marguerite of Lorraine, claiming that the dauphin had been victim of the "abduction of a minor," a single voice was raised among the clergy in defense of the indissoluble character of the sacrament of marriage—that of Saint-Cyran.

The cardinal had been displeased by the escape of the Institute of the Blessed Sacrament and the Monastery of Port-Royal from the hands of the vain but reassuringly pious Bishop Zamet; it showed that Saint-Cyran was capable of shielding subjects from legitimate authority. Now Richelieu, the statesman, mounted guard in his role as a man of the Church—could not great spiritual movements such as Port-Royal lead from one moment to the other to schism and perhaps even to heresy? Had not Luther broken off half of Europe from Catholicism on the pretext that he was restoring the purity of the primitive Church?

Saint-Cyran's words to Vincent de Paul, "There is no longer a Church!" had been heard all over Paris, and unfortunately recalled the Protestant revolt against the popes and hierarchy. Were not "the hymn of silence" and the lengthy silent meditations recommended by Saint-Cyran reminiscent of the "free examination" of the Huguenots?

Moreover the abrupt retirement of Antoine Le Maître, his withdrawal from the king's service while in full possession of his talents, was considered by Chancellor Séguier and by Richelieu as a loss to the state. Saint-Cyran was held responsible.

Finally, the latter's constant relations with Jansenius appeared treasonable to the prime minister. In 1635, the Flemish theologian had published a pamphlet entitled *Mars Gallicus*, in which he sharply criticized the alliance concluded by the great cardinal in the name of his Most Christian Majesty with the Protestants of Sweden, Holland, and Germany against the Catholic sovereign of Spain. Since Louis XIII had once more given a free hand to his minister, he was compared to Herod, who turned Saint John the Baptist over to his executioners; it was because of this libel that Jansenius had obtained the bishopric of Ypres as a token of the gratitude of the Spanish king. How could anyone remain the friend of such a man without at the same time becoming Richelieu's enemy?

Thus for years clouds had been gathering over Saint-Cyran's head.

Satisfying both his own bitterness and his desire to flatter the cardinal, Monseigneur Zamet turned over to the latter a very hostile memorandum concerning his old rival. In these pages the Bishop of Langres showed himself too superficial and filled with hatred for the document to be of any use, but soon thereafter an event took place which decided the prime minister to act.

Richelieu, who claimed to be a theologian as well as a statesman, had published a catechism when he was Bishop of Luçon. This work taught that, thanks to the sacrament of penance, in the absence of perfect contrition inspired by love of God pardon for sins could be obtained by "attrition," which consisted essentially of remorse based on a fear of hell. Since the cardinal had come to power his catechism had been accepted as gospel throughout France. However, on March 15, 1638, an Oratorian, Father Séguenot, had translated Saint Augustine's treatise *On Holy Virginity*, accompanying it with remarks completely at variance with the principles set forth in the Luçon catechism. Father Séguenot affirmed that attrition was not sufficient for valid absolution; God always pardoned those who loved him but never those who approached him out of servile and self-interested fear.

The pious Louis XIII, devoured by the terror of hell and incapable of love, was much affected by the Oratorian's opinion; already anxious about his salvation because he found himself allied to all the heretics of Europe against a Catholic king, the sovereign had spent a number of sleepless nights. Confronted with this danger, Richelieu came to some quick decisions: Father Séguenot was arrested and thrown into the Bastille, while his book was condemned by theologians acting under orders. Father de Condren, general of the Oratorians, was summoned to appear before the prime minister and explain under what conditions a member of his order had written so unfortunate a book.

Desiring to ward off danger to those closest to him, Condren at that time let it be understood that Saint-Cyran had inspired the book; the priest had, in fact, loudly proclaimed the insufficiency of attrition which he said he considered "as a human invention and the last watering-down of the sacrament of penance." No doubts remained in the cardinal's mind: it was due to Monsieur de Saint-Cyran that the king of France suffered insomnia! Richelieu raged with that violence later described by Retz in his *Memoirs:* "The formidable cardinal crushed rather than governed human beings."

On May 14, 1638, the constable of the watch, surrounded by men-at-arms, came to arrest Saint-Cyran. The latter had foreseen his fate, and shortly before had made himself read these words of the prophet Jeremiah: "I am in thy hands; do with me what thou wilt." Not for an instant did he harbor any thought of denying his ideas; it would have been, he said, "to break myself before God."

Therefore he calmly replied to the constable of the watch: "Let us go where the king commands me; I have no greater joy than an occasion to obey him."

Incarcerated in one of the unhealthful cells of the dungeon of Vincennes, which he would leave only to die, the captive was to know days and nights of anguish; deprived of all activity, separated from his penitents, he found himself isolated in a deep silence. Then he meditated—and was astonished and frightened. When he appeared before God he would have to give an account not only of his own actions, but of all the souls over whom he had taken charge; were they to be saved or lost? Was he not like the blind man of the Gospel who led the blind and fell into the pit along with them? In vain he prayed, in vain questioned the unseen Savior; he felt weighed down by an unbearable absence.

A mind less solid would have succumbed, but Saint-Cyran mastered himself. Prostrate, he tirelessly repeated the words of the Scriptures. Finally one day a ray of hope appeared. The prisoner had begged God to reveal the truth to him, even were he to be damned; he opened the Bible at random and his eyes fell on this verse of Psalm IX: "O thou that lifteth me up from the gates of death. . . ." King David's words restored peace to the captive, and never again did his hope falter.

Richelieu, however, wanted to complete what he had begun, and intended to prove Saint-Cyran guilty of heresy. The rebel was then to be judged and condemned as Urbain Grandier of Loudun had been three years earlier.

On the order of the cardinal, the guardian of the seals had a search made of Saint-Cyran's lodgings. Almost all of his writings were seized—they contained enough material for thirty volumes. However, the investigators did not discover the writings on the Blessed Sacrament which lay at the bottom of a coffer, and which contained material for an important book which the captive had begun to write. Unfortunately his nephew, Monsieur de Barcos, fearing to see his uncle accused of heresy, threw them into the fire. When he heard of "this burning," Saint-Cyran was crushed; those papers were dearer to him, he said, "than pearls and diamonds." But quickly he recognized that God's finger had pointed to their destruction because they represented something that he himself coveted, and that had been inspired by his desire to advance always further in knowledge. That day Christ's words were revealed to him in their full meaning: "I praise thee, Father, for those things thou hast hidden from the wise and hast revealed to little children."

Saint-Cyran was stripped of his arrogance; he must be henceforth only an echo of the Scriptures. True knowledge, which comes from God, is seated in a higher place than reason—in the heart. Accepting "his own voluntary ruin," Saint-Cyran no longer wished to listen to anything except the voice of God.

Thus the spiritual enterprise begun by Pierre de Bérulle drew to its close in the dungeon of Vincennes.

Saint-Cyran's arrest was not enough to appease Richelieu. In the cardinal's eyes a danger was presented by the solitaries who had withdrawn from the world and lived in a suspicious silence, linked together in no one knew what kind of conspiracy.

Shortly after the day Saint-Cyran was taken to the prison of Vincennes, these solitaries, already called the "Messieurs of Port-Royal," were advised by the Archbishop of Paris that, in obedience to a royal order, they must leave their lodgings on the faubourg Saint-Jacques, close by the monastery; it was feared at court that they had an unfortunate influence over the nuns.

After Saint-Cyran's imprisonment, his work had been carried on by Singlin. He replied to the archbishop that the solitaries did no more than attend the offices, during which a grill separated them from the nuns; hence they held no communication whatever with the latter.

The prelate had to execute the order he had received, but, knowing the fervor and correctness of the Messieurs, he authorized them to take up their residence at the Monastery of Port-Royal of the Fields, deserted since the departure of the nuns for Paris. Whereupon the solitaries repaired to that place, accompanied by the children formerly under Singlin's charge. Saint-Cyran did not want them returned to their parents, for he had always loved them and remembered Christ's words: "Unless you become as little children, you shall not enter the kingdom of heaven." Hence the prisoner had requested one of the solitaries, Lancelot, to devote himself "to their service." Such was the origin of the Little Schools of Port-Royal.

Madame Le Maître's third son, Monsieur de Saci, went to the Monastery of the Fields to join his two brothers, Le Maître and Séricourt. Saci himself had no need to give up the world; since the age of twenty-two he had been under the direction of Saint-Cyran, and later Singlin had persuaded him to become a priest. At Port-Royal of the Fields Saci became the spiritual guide of his two brothers and of the other solitaries.

The Messieurs and their disciples brought new life to the abandoned abbey, inhabited for the past twelve years by a single chaplain. This retreat in the Chevreuse Valley, called "a frightful desert" by people of the court, was in reality a verdant valley where forests, ponds, and gardens conveyed an air of peace. There the solitaries prayed and meditated, translated the writings of the Fathers of the Church, taught their pupils grammar, Latin, Greek, and rhetoric, labored with their hands in fields and gardens, and repaired buildings falling into ruin.

One day Monsieur de Laubardemont, a councillor of state sent by Richelieu, came to question the solitaries and even the children. Le Maître, who had been the first to leave the world—not without creating a certain stir— was particularly interrogated by the cardinal's emissary, but the former lawyer, who had also been a state councillor, was well able to look after himself. Insidiously, Laubardemont asked him if his great piety had not led to his being favored with visions.

"Yes, indeed," replied Le Maître, opening one of the windows of his room. "From this side I see the village of Vaumurier." Then, opening the second window: "And on the other side, the village of Saint-Lambert."

At Port-Royal, then in Paris and at court, this rejoinder created much merriment at de Laubardemont's expense.

He withdrew after seizing certain papers of no importance. But the solitaries realized they could stay no longer at Port-Royal of the Fields, and, on July 14, 1638, they left the valley. Their departure, which was called "the first dispersion," reminded them of the exile to which the people of Israel had been condemned in days of old.

Lancelot asked the father of one of his pupils, Monsieur Vitart, who lived at La Ferté-Milon, to give him shelter, and Le Maître and Sericourt came to rejoin Lancelot there. The dignity of the life of the solitaries and their goodness was so great that the peasants would rise silently and uncover their heads when the Messieurs passed their doors in the evening.

The nuns left the Institute of the Blessed Sacrament to return to their monastery on the faubourg Saint-Jacques two days after Saint-Cyran's arrest. Angélique Arnauld was made welcome by her sister Agnès, who had been elected abbess. Happy at being relieved of the charge of the convent, Angélique wholeheartedly assumed the duties of novice mistress.

Nothing remained of the dissension caused in former days by Monseigneur Zamet. Port-Royal would have returned to its golden age had not the nuns, deprived of their guide and knowing him to be imprisoned behind the walls of Vincennes, been torn by the feeling of their isolation.

No word came to them from the dungeon, for the Abbot of Saint-Cyran was in solitary confinement. Richelieu had him interrogated by de Laubardemont, delegated as his commissioner. But although the councillor of state had had no trouble obtaining the strangest accusations of sorcery from the nuns of Loudun at the time of Urbain Grandier's trial, he proved himself incapable of questioning Saint-Cyran. The official report he drew up was proof of his ignorance of theological matters, and the cardinal had to abandon his plan of having this layman handle the trial for heresy that he wished to begin. After a year had passed, the prisoner saw the ecclesiastic who had been appointed Laubardemont's successor enter his cell. He was Richelieu's confessor, Jacques Lescot, doctor of theology and professor at the Sorbonne.

The prime minister wished to prove that Saint-Cyran was a Calvinist; but he never succeeded, even though all the prisoner's enemies testified against him. When they were asked to bring accusations against the captive, Vincent de Paul and Father de Condren refused. In the numerous pamphlets written by Saint-Cyran, Doctor Lescot could not discover a single sentence suspect of heresy; the Jesuits themselves, to whom these documents were submitted, honestly acknowledged that they found them "worthy only of admiration."

Many of the friends of Port-Royal now intervened in the prisoner's behalf. The day following the death of Father Joseph they were able to arrange for

Saint-Cyran to be moved from the dungeon to a less unhealthful cell. It was high time: the captive had almost died there, and survived only because of this improvement in the conditions of his detention. It was thanks to his friends that he was no longer kept in solitary confinement, and could thereafter correspond with persons whose consciences he directed. Like the Apostle to the Gentiles in other days, from the depths of his prison Saint-Cyran preserved the faith of an increasing number of his penitents.

The man who had dared stand up to Richelieu "was never so formidable as after his detention," Le Maître was to say. "From his prison he directed incomparably more souls than he had done before in his whole life."

The foundress of the Visitation order, Jeanne de Chantal, deprived of the guidance of Francis de Sales by his death, besought the prisoner for a remedy against the doubts and anguish that again assailed her. Saint-Cyran sent her "the alms of the poor to help the poor."

In his letters, the prisoner revealed to Jeanne the existence of two "chains of action": one divine, for the salvation of souls; the other human, and reaching toward God. Grace, he explained, is the meeting of these two kinds of love. The captive asked Jeanne to bless suffering, which he called the "admirable figure presented by Jesus Christ on the day of his passion, when everything was destroyed." Madame de Chantal should lift her eyes "to the highest part of the cross, above our Lord's head."

Saint-Cyran's greatest conquest, however, was Angélique Arnauld's brother, Antoine Arnaud.

At Port-Royal Singlin and Saci had assumed the role of spiritual directors, but who was to defend the doctrine of grace before the Church and before the world? This combatant was to be the youngest member of a family which had already given most of its members to the same cause.

Antoine Arnauld was twenty-six years old when he met Saint-Cyran. He had pursued solid courses in theology at the Sorbonne, and represented what Bossuet could call "the flower of the school and of youth."

From the time of his first conversation with Saint-Cyran through the bars of the latter's cell, this young man fell under the extraordinary influence from which no one had yet escaped; an inner voice told him that the captive was a man who could light the way for him. "God called out to my heart," he wrote later. And he added that he was beside himself when he heard the prisoner answer all those questions he had asked himself without ever having been able to find their solution.

On Christmas Eve in that year of 1638, Antoine Arnauld wrote to Saint-Cyran. "Father—allow me to call you by this name, for God has made me want to be your son."

The prisoner discovered that the young theologian, soon to become a doctor of divinity and a priest, was as courageous as he was learned. Authorized to receive his visits and to correspond with him, Saint-Cyran prepared the youngest of the Arnaulds for the struggle that lay ahead.

"One must go where God leads and do nothing cowardly," he told him.

Antoine then learned something not taught by the faculty of theology: to meditate on each word of Scripture "as though weighing a piece of gold, and passing into the heart all the knowledge one has in one's head."

On February 28, 1641, the young man lost his mother. When Singlin carried the last sacraments to the dying woman, he would not allow Antoine to be present.

"It would have meant giving too great a place to nature," the priest explained later.

The time had come when strong souls were needed; the struggle had begun in the last citadel. Even so, Madame Arnauld charged her confessor with a message: "I beg you to tell my son that since God has bound him to the defense of truth, I adjure him to uphold it without fear, even should it lead to the loss of a thousand lives."

In the cell where he had been imprisoned for almost three years, Saint-Cyran received, at the beginning of 1641, an important book: *Augustinus*, written by his friend Jansenius. The latter, who had been professor of Holy Scripture at Louvain and then become the Bishop of Ypres, had finally finished his work on Saint Augustine. As did "the doctor of grace" in days gone by, Jansenius fought the heresy of the disciples of the monk Pelagius. Four hundred years after Christ's death, this monk had maintained that every man had it in his power to reach the supernatural world without the help of grace. In the sixteenth century this flattering doctrine had seduced the theologians of the Society of Jesus. Molina, the most illustrious of them, asserted in 1588 that there is present in each of us a celestial gift which Pascal would one day call that "sufficient grace which does not suffice." Molina affirmed, on the contrary, that God makes this grace efficacious for those who, by their merits, have won the right to enter heaven. The Holy Spirit restricts itself to giving to ordinary souls such grace as they need. Predestination is only a wise distribution of heavenly goods among Catholics. Saint Augustine had condemned the insolence of Pelagius "who counterfeits God's greatness." *Augustinus* attacked—without naming him—the spiritual heir of the heretical monk: Molina.

To satisfy and build up vanity—as this Jesuit had done—was, the Bishop of Ypres declared, "to extinguish grace, to do away with original sin, to depart from the cross, to reject Christ himself, and, finally, to raise to its full height the diabolical throne of human pride."

With Saint Augustine, Jansenius proclaimed the misery of every man "changed into a savage beast by his passions and capable only of giving himself over to earthly delights." He denounced the most dangerous of temptations, one that had led to Satan's fall: "Let those who desire to come to the holy city of grace cast themselves into the unfathomable depths of Providence; God's bridge will form beneath their feet. But do not let them believe they can begin to make this bridge themselves, for all human pride will march over it."

The Bishop of Ypres declared that the grace which alone can save us is reserved for the predestined, to those who know "the victorious delectation of the spirit.'

In Saint-Cyran's eyes *Augustinus* appeared at first as a living reminder of his studious and ardent youth. Here at last was the achievement of the work that Jansenius and he had dreamed of under the skies of Bayonne: the return to the Gospels and to the teaching of Saint Augustine. This rebirth of Christianity was the fruit of the plot to which two theology students had long ago given that mysterious name, "the Pilmot affair."

Gathering all his remaining strength, the prisoner deciphered the interminable Latin text; alas, he did not find in it the song of love that illuminated Saint Augustine's *Confessions* nor the luminous vision of Bérulle. Jansenius' book was only a theological treatise, scholarly and abstract. Having scant knowledge of human beings, the Bishop of Ypres—whose ascetic face and sharp features are shown in an engraving of the time—knew little of the tender love that animated Saint-Cyran and illuminated the Scriptures for him. Jansenius' pessimism, his obsession with Adam's fall and original sin, saddened his friend, who would have liked, he said, "more unction." The prisoner nevertheless admired Jansenius' erudition and especially the force of his language; thanks to his eloquence, Saint Augustine was now making a victorious reply to Molina and the Society of Jesus.

To those who obtained permission to visit him, Saint-Cyran declared: "Here is a book which will last as long as the Church!"

Only then did his friends have the courage to tell him of the death of his companion in the struggle. On May 6, 1638, eight days before Saint-Cyran's arrest, Jansenius had died of the plague—killed, it was said, by the dust that rose from the tomes among which he had spent his life. He had left *Augustinus* to posterity, but submitted the book in advance to the judgment of the pope.

Saint-Cyran had to face the future bereft of his friend. His strength declined; he felt mortally afflicted. Yet he knew that Antoine Arnauld would carry on his task. In a letter dated February 1, 1643, the prisoner entrusted this mission to the young theologian: "The time to speak has come."

Saint-Cyran knew what it would cost to unveil the truth; but since the salvation of mankind was involved, he would not be silent. "When I had to go into the great dungeon where I almost died," he wrote his disciple, "I thought it was a crime for me to remain silent."

Antoine Arnauld heard his appeal. He prepared to write an *Apologie pour Jansenius*.

As the youngest of the Arnaulds readied himself to enter the battle, the eldest, Robert, was living peacefully in the shade of the fine trees on his domain of Andilly, on the outskirts of Montmorency. He had added the name of this estate to that of his family, and so was known as Robert Arnauld of Andilly, then as Monsieur d'Andilly.

Thirty years earlier, on the Day of the Grating, he had accused his sister Angélique of being a "parricide." But he had long since been won over to the cause of Port-Royal. Andilly had been the first to discover Saint-Cyran at Poitiers, and had introduced the priest to Mother Angélique even before Monseigneur Zamet had entrusted Saint-Cyran with the spiritual guidance of her monastery.

After devoting a part of his day to religious devotions, Andilly frequented the court, fascinated by its splendor. There he was welcomed and loved; Anne of Austria had wanted him appointed tutor to the dauphin.

"What better could I do," she said, "than place the king in the hands of a man to whom God has given the heart of a king?"

Had the education of Louis XIV been turned over to Robert Arnauld d'Andilly, the religious history of France's *grand siècle* would have been different. But Mazarin feared the influence that such a preceptor could have over the queen. Anne of Austria had to abandon her plan and entrust the dauphin to the future Archbishop of Paris, Péréfixe.

After his friend Saint-Cyran was imprisoned, Andilly visited him and courageously delivered his messages. Then he would go back to the queen regent and pay his court to her; each year he brought her large fruits of various kinds, "monsters" gathered on his estate, which Mazarin smilingly called "blessed fruit."

Andilly had decided to do what he could to make God's voice heard by the noble feminine sinners of the Louvre and Saint-Germain. He led them, however reluctantly, to the Abbey of Port-Royal.

The most illustrious of these penitents was Anne de Rohan, princesse de Guémené. This descendant of the dukes of Britanny "was one of the most beautiful persons in the world," Madame de Motteville was to say, and she added: "She was a close second to Madame de Montbazon in the number of lovers she had." Arnauld d'Andilly wanted to open the gates of heaven to the princesse de Guémené. Of this, Madame de Sévigné wrote, "He was more anxious to save a soul housed in a beautiful body than others."

Madame de Guéméné had gone through many tribulations. In 1632, Richelieu had beheaded the most illustrious of her lovers, the duc de Montmorency, who had led the revolt of Languedoc against Louis XIII; later the eldest of her sons had gone mad. The younger one, the chevalier de Rohan, had been raised at the side of Louis XIV, but he had tried to turn over Normandy to the Dutch, and had paid for his crime on the scaffold.

At the time Arnauld d'Andilly undertook the princess' conversion, she was carrying on a scandalous affair with the Abbot of Gondi, the future Cardinal de Retz, who did not hide his intention "to do evil by design," as he himself put it. Nevertheless, the eldest of the Arnaulds gained ground day by day. Madame de Guéméné ceased to use powder and to curl her hair; she even went to Port-Royal of Paris where, her lover said, "she has escapades in place of retreats."

On one of his visits to the Vincennes prison, Andilly begged Saint-Cyran to guide the new penitent by correspondence. The captive considered the enterprise as onerous, "because it is more difficult," he said, "to give people of the world a taste for God than to teach Hebrew to a child." He nevertheless consented to exchange several letters with the princess. Saint-Cyran recognized her good intentions, but he scarcely believed that she could be saved. "Her present disposition," he wrote, "is in her soul like a spark of fire lighted on an icy pavement where wind blows on it from every side."

Nonetheless the Abbot of Gondi—the most formidable of these winds— was dismissed by Madame de Guéméné; she left her mansion on the Place Royale and installed herself on the faubourg Saint-Jacques, where she had a spacious dwelling built for herself. The future Cardinal de Retz was greatly vexed at losing his mistress.

"Monsieur d'Andilly has taken her away from me," he said.

With a neophyte's fervor, the princess in turn led to Port-Royal her best friend, Marie de Gonzague, daughter of the Duke of Mantua.

Marie, too, was very beautiful, and also had led a stormy life. She had seduced the brother of Louis XIII, Gaston of Orléans; wishing to break up a union that displeased her, Marie de' Medici had the princess imprisoned at Vincennes, where Saint-Cyran languished. Forced to give up the Duke of Orléans, Marie de Gonzague became enamoured of the handsomest of the nobles, the Grand Equerry Cinq-Mars, eight years younger than she. This time it was Richelieu who opposed the connection, as he did not consider Cinq-Mars of sufficient importance to be the companion of a princess. This contempt was one of Cinq-Mars' motives for becoming the cardinal's mortal enemy.

When Madame de Guéméné separated her friend from the Grand Equerry to lead her to Port-Royal, the fate of Cinq-Mars was being sealed. Refusing to accept Richelieu's policies, Cinq-Mars sided with Bérulle in favor of uniting France with the Hapsburgs of Spain—and peace. The conspiracy was discovered and he was executed.

Just before his death the condemned man handed the priest who attended him a lock of hair to which he joined a portrait of Marie de Gonzague, asking that both be burned in a brazier. Cinq-Mars' friend, De Thou, who was beheaded at the same time, had been one of Madame de Guéméné's lovers. Thus the two princesses saw the tragic deaths of two men they had known before they loved God.

Saint-Cyran was not mistaken: despite her good will, Madame de Guéméné's zeal soon waned. She returned to the world, to her lovers, to her mansion on the Place Royale; nevertheless, she retained an aura of devotion, a sort of romantic piety.

"Praying to God gives her great pleasure," the great Condé said of her.

As for Marie de Gonzague, she was always to retain close ties with Port-Royal. She later married the King of Poland, and from this remote country the queen corresponded constantly with Angélique Arnauld, telling her "that should she become a widow she would still have enough to be received at Port-Royal."

Its doors would indeed have been open to her, but Angélique never really wanted to see the arrival of this queen, who would have been, she said, "an excuse for relaxing the Rule."

The daughter of the Arnaulds had severe words for royalty: "Kings," she said, "are nothing before God; the vanity of their position draws his aversion rather than his love."

The Princesse de Guéméné led to Port-Royal another penitent, the marquise de Sablé. She was one of the blue-stockings of the Hôtel de Rambouillet, "getting the last ounce out of everything"; her wit, one of her admirers remarked, "caused a strange commotion in the world."

The marquise de Sablé's salon attracted the most illustrious women of the court: the Grande Mademoiselle, the duchesse de Longueville, Madame de la Fayette, and Julie d'Angennes, Duchess of Montausier. At the home of the marquise, these personages gathered with men of letters: Voiture, one of Madame de Sablé's lovers; Guez de Balzac; Saint-Evremond. The hostess' table was considered one of the finest in the land; a Jesuit entertained there said of her, "The civility of her mind extends even to the food she has served."

Disappointed in her marriage, Madame de Sablé also had a liaison with the duc de Montmorency, an affair which was later recalled by Madame de Scudéry in her novel Le Grand Cyrus; but the marquise decided to break off her relations with this handsome lover when she learned that he was courting Anne of Austria. It was high time; only shortly afterward Montmorency rebelled and was executed.

Subsequently the marquis de Sablé died of apoplexy, and his widow accommodated herself so well to her new situation that "it was a pity," Chapelain wrote, "it hadn't happened to her sooner." When Madame de Guémené took her to Port-Royal Madame de Sablé was fifty-seven years old, the age at which, according to Saint-Evremond, "religious devotion becomes the last of our loves." Angélique Arnauld welcomed this penitent with kindness; she was, the nun said, "well aware of the passions, the aversions, the temptations and deceits of the world."

The marquise asked what charitable works she should perform in order to redeem her past.

"All that is necessary," Angélique replied, "is to look at God."

But such a look of love was more difficult to achieve than any good work, for Madame de Sablé had never felt affection for anything but her own person. Until the end she kept up the good table, where, her friends said, the devil entrenched himself. Her physician wrote that she would not give up "a seraphic water that fortifies the flesh."

The marquise worried constantly about her health. On this subject, Tallemant de Réaux said: "She is a big lump who has nothing the matter with her except the things she imagines."

After her conversion she had a mansion built close by the Paris monastery of Port-Royal, and here she expected to devote her whole future to saving her soul. La Rochefoucauld came to see her there, and wrote some of his maxims while the marquise composed her own. More friends arrived to distract the penitent.

"Grace is needed for one to leave the world," she said, "but two graces are needed to make us hate it."

In the contract for her house Madame de Sablé provided for a window to open directly on the chapel choir so that she might hear the offices without leaving her room. "This was done," Agnès Arnauld wrote, "in order to take away her fear of contracting a disease in the church."

One day the marquise thought she had lost her sense of smell, and was terrified "at this sort of death in one part of her body." Mother Agnès had to calm her by saying that she herself had suffered the same infirmity for a long time without it ever having given her any trouble.

When Madame de Guémené, Marie de Gonzague, and Madame de Sablé found themselves together at Port-Royal, they engaged in endless chatter; the three women discussed only court intrigues, scandals in the lives of the great, and the latest plays—in a word everything that Angélique Arnauld called "deviltry." She would hurry to the side of the penitents, saying: "I am going to separate our ladies; they are ruining one another."

After being greatly tormented, as she confided to Mother Agnès, "by the fear of extinction," Madame de Sablé died at the age of seventy-nine, "at the very moment," one of her friends wrote, "when she was about to discover the secret of not dying." The marquise had asked, before her demise, to be given a place among the poor.

"That is something she never would have asked when she was alive," one of her intimates remarked.

Any contact with the poverty stricken had always filled her with fear of contagion.

On various occasions Saint-Cyran's friends tried to intervene with Richelieu in order to have the priest set free, but it was in vain.

"If Luther and Calvin had been shut up when they began to proclaim their dogmas, much trouble would have been avoided," the prime minister had declared when he had Saint-Cyran arrested. When the great Condé pleaded the cause of the prisoner, Richelieu replied: "That man is more dangerous than six armies."

In vain an appeal was made to the cardinal's Christian feeling.

"When it is a matter of crime against the state," he said, "one must close one's heart to pity."

But death came to Richelieu on December 4, 1642. In a letter written that day we read: "Fear of the Eternal prolongs life, but the days of the wicked are numbered." All of the prisoner's friends saw the hand of God in the event that had just taken place.

Louis XIII survived his minister by only five months. Although he regretted the great man's death, he breathed more freely. Nevertheless, out of respect for a formidable spectre, the king kept Saint-Cyran at Vincennes two months longer. Finally, at the entreaty of Mathieu Molé, President of Parlement, the captive was freed on February 6, 1643. Arnauld d'Andilly went immediately in a carriage to fetch his friend. So great was the captive's renown that the château guards lined up as he passed by, fired their muskets in his honor, and played fifes and drums.

On learning the great news, Mother Agnès entered the refectory at Port-Royal as a meal was being eaten. In order not to break the rule of silence, she untied the cord around her waist. All the nuns understood the meaning of her gesture, and although the silence was not broken, every heart was filled with joy. When Saint-Cyran returned to Port-Royal a free man, he aroused an enthusiasm which he considered excessive, for he thought of himself only as a sinner. At the request of the nuns he consented, however, to the celebration of a mass of thanksgiving. Exhausted by his captivity, the priest could not himself officiate and had to be content with receiving communion.

A supreme trial awaited Saint-Cyran. The bull *In eminenti,* in which *Augustinus* was condemned by Pope Urban VIII, was published on June 19, 1643. Everyone said the Jesuits had forced the decision on the pontiff when he was greatly enfeebled by sickness. It was then that Saint-Cyran rose up against his enemies, ready to resume the struggle.

"They have gone too far!" he said. And with a mystic's simplicity he added: "They have to be shown their duty!"

Saint-Cyran's strength was failing, but his spiritual heir, Antoine Arnauld, did not wait long to point out "their duty" to Loyola's sons.

The marquise de Sablé's spiritual director, Father Sesmaisons, had written a little treatise for the use of his penitents which allowed them to go to communion on the same day they attended a ball. "The more one is lacking in grace," the priest affirmed, "the more necessary it becomes boldly to approach Jesus Christ in the eucharist."

Thus what another Jesuit called "easy devotion" was provided for the benefit of the ladies of the court. On reading this text, which revealed the craftiness of Molina's successors, Antoine Arnauld felt the same indignation as did Pascal. In order to remind Christians of the spirit of the Gospels, he wrote a treatise on *La Fréquente Communion.* Because it was unexpected, it was widely read, and since it concerned souls, it caused a rude awakening.

Many Christians sensed the gulf that existed between the Scriptures and the doctrine of the Molinists; Louis XIII had lived in this way, tormented by doubts and fears. Now a doctor of theology had proclaimed what many believed: namely, that to commune with the Crucified we must know and love him, putting aside everything that separates us from him.

Arnauld's work was not presented as an abstract thesis; it contained the words of the Church Fathers, of Charles Borromeo, of Francis de Sales, of Bérulle. No one could escape the voice that said: "Love and rise up! Otherwise you are lost."

In the country, in Paris, and at court, those speaking of *La Fréquente Communion* referred to it simply as *La Fréquente.*

The Jesuits took up the cudgels against the young theologian who showed himself so dangerous from the start. They were soon to announce that the number of communions had considerably diminished after the publication of Arnauld's book.

This was true, but the only ones who drew back from Christ were "sinners hardened by their crimes," as Racine said later.

The discomfiture of the Jesuits led certain of them to resort to insults.

From the pulpit one of their number, Father Noiret, denounced his adversary as a "scorpion" and a "serpent with three-pointed tongue," and reproached him for "cutting off the nourishment of the faithful." This strange sermon drew attention to Madame de Sablé's confessor whom Arnauld had been considerate enough not to name. Honest people then read Father de Sesmaisons' treatise and were scandalized in their turn; others, not knowing the background of the matter, merely smiled, as did the maréchal de Vitry who, having come to hear Father Noiret's fulminations, said as he left the church: "There is something back of all this. The good fathers do not ordinarily get so worked up about serving God."

Dissatisfied with the clumsiness of their preacher, the Jesuits charged one of the most illustrious theologians of their Society, Father Pétau, with the task of replying to Arnauld. Alas, this theologian was too scholarly; a retired Latin teacher, he had forgotten his mother tongue. His interminable sentences and archaic style disappointed all thoughtful readers.

Having lost its case in France, the Society of Jesus intended at least to win in Rome, and Arnauld's book was submitted to the Holy Office. Several of his friends advised him to go to Italy to defend himself; Mazarin and Anne of Austria were insistent in urging him to do so. But Arnauld wanted to avoid giving the debates the publicity his presence would create, and which later would be harmful to the task he had set for himself. Thus he decided to disappear for a while and to seek a haven among friends, "placing himself," he said, "under the shadow of God's wings."

In Rome, however, the judges of the Inquisition found La Fréquente Communion to be an expression of Christian thinking that was perfectly orthodox. They had to absolve the book, censoring merely one passage which said that "Saint Peter and Saint Paul are two heads of the Church who are but one." This was because these words—which did not come from Arnauld's pen—might lead to an attack on the authority of the pope, Saint Peter's successor.

Saint-Cyran's last happiness was reading La Fréquente Communion. He himself was saving what strength he had to dictate the thoughts that came to his mind on the threshold of death, thus remaining faithful to his maxim: "A priest is a king, and a king must die standing up."

The ex-prisoner died on October 11, 1643, at the age of sixty-two, eight months after his liberation.

On hearing of the loss of one who had opened up the spiritual world to her, Mother Angélique refused to give way to grief; in his wisdom God had appointed the day of this death. The nun was heard to murmur only these words: "The Lord is in his heavens."

The persecution abated after Richelieu's death. Le Maître and his brother

Séricourt returned to the Monastery of Port-Royal of the Fields. Monsieur and Madame Vitart, who had welcomed the solitaries at Ferté-Milon, could not make up their minds to be parted from them; abandoning their home, they came to join their friends at the abbey, where they found a little lodging set aside for them.

The old buildings were again inhabited. The influence of Saint-Cyran's ideas and Antoine Arnauld's publication of *La Fréquente Communion* drew new solitaries to the abbey. Some of them came from the aristocracy, others from humble backgrounds, but most of them were descendants of old bourgeois families like the Arnaulds. The ambitions and cabals of the court, and the dissolute conduct covered over by an outward show of piety, had turned these magistrates, soldiers, and physicians away from the world. These grave and solid men lived at Port-Royal in an atmosphere that Lancelot called "the good, living odor of virtue."

Out of respect for persons, the solitaries always addressed each other as "Monsieur"; this title was the same for all, from the humblest of commoners to dukes. Such a sentiment of equality joined to a rather severe dignity that did not permit familiarity was an attribute of the French bourgeoisie of the seventeenth century.

Andilly, the eldest of the Arnaulds, still lingered for a while at court; then, at the age of fifty-seven, he left the worldly life to become one of the most affable of the solitaries. His fortune made it possible for him to have one of the marshes drained, to cultivate the valley and make it more healthful. A good gardener, he himself pruned the vines heavy with fine fruit in which he took such pride.

Anne of Austria, who became regent of the French kingdom after the death of Louis XIII, always had a great liking for "the good man of Andilly." Because they retained such excellent memories of the pious courtier, noblemen and ministers came to visit him "in the wilderness."

Andilly was very erudite and translated the works of Saint Augustine and Flavius Josephus; later he refused to become a member of the French Academy because he did not want to leave his place of retirement except at rare intervals.

Children came to add their games and laughter to this rather austere company. They were Saint-Cyran's young pupils whom he had put in the care of the solitaries during his imprisonment. At the time of the first dispersion they had been returned to their families or placed with others willing to take them in. Now they had all come back and were lodged in the Abbey of the Fields. Later when the nuns returned, these pupils went first to Paris, then back again to the Fields, where they lived at Les Granges, a building close to the monastery. Since there was no space for the youngest among them, they were installed in country houses at Versailles and Chevreuse belonging to two magistrates who were faithful friends of Port-Royal—Maignart de Bernières and Dugué de Bagnols.

Thus were founded the Little Schools of Port-Royal. So modest a title should have reassured the Society of Jesus, which would not have suffered the creation of colleges similar to those in which they received the élite of the kingdom. Renowned as educators of youth, the Jesuits did not want, Racine said, "for Port-Royal to dry up their credit at its source."

Moreover, the pupils accepted by the Little Schools were always few in number. Their principal instructors were Lancelot, who taught them Greek and mathematics, and Nicole, who devoted himself to philosophy and the humanities.

The Little Schools soon acquired a high reputation. Montaigne said that in former days colleges had been "a real jail for youthful captives where one heard nothing but the cries of tortured children and of their enraged instructors." In such colleges, he added, an adolescent was crushed by the burden of knowledge, "like a donkey laden down with relics."

The Jesuits were the first to bring a living culture to their students and to instruct them with benevolence. But Saint-Cyran wanted to go further: when the teacher addressed children, he said, he should "honor the Holy Spirit dwelling within them." Thus, in principle, all punishment should be avoided, and one should refrain from creating among pupils that spirit of competition which springs from egotism.

Each of the solitaries charged with teaching had only five or six pupils and was their constant companion, sharing their room and conversing with them familiarly. Lessons were taught in French; up to that time, teachers had used Latin, making a child's first schooling very difficult. Latin and Greek were taught as living languages and commented on orally; translations by the greatest writers were used in this connection. Written themes were reserved for students more advanced in Latin and Greek studies, since the teachers of the Little Schools discovered that "it is contrary to nature to begin by writing a language one is unable to speak." Spanish and Italian were taught mainly by means of conversation with persons who knew these languages perfectly, and their daily use was preferred to exercises in grammar.

Textbooks at that period were so tedious that the Messieurs had to write some themselves for the use of their pupils. Lancelot published several books on methods of learning languages, and in collaboration with Saci wrote a work on Greek roots which he arranged in French verse. Antoine Arnauld briefly put aside theology to write down the bases of textbooks of logic, general grammar, and geometry. Le Maître taught the art of speaking, the beauties of the French language, and the forceful harmony of Latin sentence structure.

The spirit of logic and clarity which characterized the teaching of the Little Schools contributed greatly to the purity of the classical age in France and to the molding, in the near future, of so great a writer as Jean Racine.

After leaving the Institute of the Blessed Sacrament the nuns obtained from the pope the restoration to their abbey property they had received while at the mission for perpetual adoration of the eucharist. Thereafter their monastery bore the name *Notre Dame de Port-Royal du Saint-Sacrement*. The nuns solemnly received the white scapular which symbolized their espousal to Christ, over which they wore the scarlet cross that signified the blood of the Messiah.

The donations received by the Institute enabled them to erect a church within the walls of the Abbey of Port-Royal of Paris, which up to that time had had only a chapel. This small edifice was the work of the architect Le Pautre, and enchanted Mother Angélique by its sobriety, discreet harmony, and exact sense of proportion. She was again the abbess, but this time it was by the will of her religious; re-elected three times, she was to carry this responsibility for twelve more years.

The community was now too large for the house on the faubourg Saint-Jacques. The abbess therefore obtained permission from the Archbishop of Paris to take back Port-Royal of the Fields and to divide the nuns between the two monasteries.

On May 13, 1648, after twenty-two years of absence, Angélique Arnauld, accompanied by seven professed religious and two lay sisters, had the joy of finding once more in the familiar valley the old walls she so often had reproached herself for leaving.

A new life began on that day. The monastery bells rang out. Behind a priest bearing the cross, the solitaries filed out to welcome those who, in the words of Le Maître, the eldest of their number, "were their ladies and their queens." The poor people formerly aided by Angélique, most of them now elderly, fell to their knees before her. As the nuns entered the choir in procession, a hymn rose from the depths of the church; the solitaries were chanting the *Te Deum* while the bells filled the air with a joyous clamor.

The Messieurs of Port-Royal had most willingly abandoned the abbey to those who were to occupy it thenceforth, and went to take up their lodgings in the old farm of Les Granges, built on a hill above the monastery. After a stay in Paris, their pupils came to join them there.

Mother Agnès had to remain in the abbey on the faubourg Saint-Jacques, of which she was the prioress, but her thoughts were with her elder sister Angélique at Port-Royal of the Fields.

"That place is closer to my heart than any other," she said. "Had our sisters in Paris known it, I think they would ask for the wings of a dove to fly to it and rest there."

The pupils being reared by the nuns were taken to the Fields; while boys were taught at Les Granges under the direction of the solitaires, little girls were educated in the cloister.

Nevertheless, the peace of Port-Royal was always in jeopardy. Only six months after Mother Angélique's return to the Fields, France was torn by the uprising known as The Fronde.

Isolated at the extreme end of the faubourg Saint-Jacques, on the edge of the city, the Paris convent could not be protected against the rioters. Consequently the prioress, Mother Agnès, decided to accept the hospitality offered her community by Maignart de Bernières, Steward of Petitions of Parlement, in his mansion on the rue Saint-André-des-Arts.

The nuns' nearest neighbors, who had counted on their presence, opposed their departure. Bernières and another friend of Port-Royal—also a lawyer, Le Nain—had to don their official robes, keep back the crowds, and escort the nuns to rue Saint-André-des-Arts. No one dared to defy these members of Parlement who had won the hearts of all Parisians by their revolt against Mazarin.

At Port-Royal of the Fields the abbess, Mother Angélique, also had to face the civil war. Soldiers who no longer knew under what flag they were fighting wandered over the countryside and pillaged it.

In one of her letters the abbess said that the horses and asses of the abbey had died of starvation; their places were taken by the livestock and harvested crops which the peasants, who rushed in from all sides, came to shelter in the monastery in the same way as in the darkest centuries of the Middle Ages. Port-Royal thus became a "Noah's Ark," the courtyard filled with chickens, ducks, and geese. There were horses beneath the nuns' dormitory and even in the chapter hall; one cellar alone held forty cows. "It was a miracle," wrote Angélique, "that beasts and people did not die from having been locked up together so long." The abbey church was filled with wheat, oats, peas, and beans; to reach the choir one had to step over cauldrons and all kinds of ragged clothing.

Girls whose honor was threatened came to seek refuge in the convent; sheds served as shelter for the frightened people, many among them sick and crippled. "Had it not been for the great cold," the abbess went on, "I fear we would all have caught the plague."

The cold presented a danger as well. Winter came and it was impossible to have heat, for the waggoners lived in the forest where no one dared to venture in quest of wood. The harvests were lost; everything was ravaged. The most necessary foodstuffs rose to unheard-of prices. "One is filled with a terrible pity," wrote Angélique, "to see this poor place." The abbess was here, there, and everywhere to welcome, lodge, and feed the army of unfortunates to whom she distributed the resources of the convent.

The solitaries, coming down from Les Granges sword at side, arrived with trowels in their hands to assist Mother Angélique. While some fortified the walls, others—former soldiers—mounted guard night and day over the most exposed parts of the abbey; some of them escorted the convoys of food which the nuns of the Fields sent their sisters in Paris to save them from starvation.

Among the abbey's defenders was the duc de Luynes, *seigneur* of the Chevreuse Valley. His pious wife had led him to the Monastery of the Fields and persuaded him to build in the near-by village of Vaumurier a small château where the couple intended to retire from the world. Since then the duchess, constrained for some time yet to live at court, had dreamed only of Vaumurier. But she died before she could reach her promised land. She was only twenty-seven years old when she passed away murmuring Saint Augustine's words: "O to love eternally! O to live eternally!"

The widowed duc de Luynes then became one of the solitaries.

The day came when the nuns had to leave the Monastery of the Fields because of the threat of roving bands. Mother Angélique and the religious came to seek haven in their Paris house on the faubourg Saint-Jacques, where a royal garrison had recently been stationed to ensure their safety.

Monsieur Luynes then assembled the solitaries and the peasants in his château at Vaumurier, and had the abbey protected by solid ramparts flanked with eleven towers, each thirty feet in height. Protected by a garrison of peasants commanded by ex-officers, the monastery was capable of withstanding any siege.

The duke also took advantage of the nuns' absence to raise the paving of the church, which so often had been flooded by rainstorms. At his order two large dormitories and seventy-two cells were constructed in the monastery. The day was to come when the nuns, driven out of their house on the faubourg Saint-Jacques, would have only this house of the Fields for shelter, and, by a strange coincidence, the number of choir religious at that time would be exactly seventy-two.

The peasants earned their livelihood from the work created by Monsieur de Luynes; without "the good duke" their suffering would have been terrible. The château of Vaumurier now sheltered more than a hundred persons who took their meals in the great hall at the table of the master of the house.

The Messieurs also helped the victims of The Fronde. Maignart de Bernières and Dugué de Bagnols resigned their posts as stewards of petitions of Parlement to devote themselves entirely to the unfortunate, and came to be known by the fine title "general provisioners of the poor."

The Fronde ended in 1652. The rebel princes were vanquished and the adolescent Louis XIV reconquered his kingdom. Mother Angélique could now return to Port-Royal of the Fields, but before leaving the Paris house, the abbess was present at the deathbed of Anne, one of her younger sisters. On the Day of the Grating, in 1609, Anne had stood at the side of her older brother, Monsieur d'Andilly. Some years later she had entered Port-Royal as a novice, and in 1628 had pronounced her religious vows.

Three other daughters of the Arnaulds died before Anne, all of them religious like herself: first the youngest, Madeleine; then Marie-Claire, who had been directed by Saint-Cyran; finally the eldest, Madame Catherine de Maître. The latter had also entered the convent, but did not survive the death of her beloved son Séricourt, one of the first of the solitaries. Another of her sons, Saci, had been a priest for only a short time when he had to attend his brother and then his mother during their final hours.

"My child," Madame Le Maître said to him, "help your mother, who brought you into this miserable life, to die a good death and gain heaven."

While all around him burst into tears, Saci found the strength not to falter as he recited to the end the prayers for the dying.

Of Monsieur Arnauld's daughters, only Angélique and Agnès remained; the "two olive trees" were destined to face together the great storm that was very soon to break.

The Jesuits first embarked on a war of epigrams against their enemies, calling them "Calvinists" and "frogs from the Lake of Geneva."

One of them, Father Brisacier, published a work entitled Le Jansenisme confondu (Jansenism Confounded). In it he called the religious of Port-Royal "foolish virgins who are impenitent, asacramentary, fantastic." According to this Jesuit, the nuns had made a vow not to receive communion even at the point of death. Father Brisacier hurled insults at the monastery's spiritual directors: "pontiffs of the devil, gates of hell, black and enraged souls, impudent dogs." The Jesuit went so far that Archbishop Gondi of Paris had to censure him for libel.

But the Society of Jesus was to oppose Port-Royal with more formidable adversaries. Since the Holy Office had recognized La Fréquente Communion as orthodox, the Jesuits realized that Antoine Arnauld had escaped them and still retained his spiritual influence. The priest had been too good a theologian to stray into heresy, and it would be the same with him as with

Saint-Cyran, whose numerous writings had revealed no suspect statements under the scrutiny of Richelieu's learned confessor.

Molina's successors therefore modified their tactics by going back to *Augustinus,* that ponderous, arid work by an already forgotten Fleming. This book had been censured by Urban VIII, which was a victory for the Molinists although the bull *In eminenti* was drawn up in such vague terms that it did not explicitly condemn Jansenius. The Jesuits mapped out their objective: a new and completely unequivocal condemnation must be obtained from Rome. If Arnauld subsequently committed the error of defending *Augustinus* his cause would be lost, and with him all Port-Royal inevitably would be involved in heresy. Thus, because of a prodigious piece of trickery, these disciples of Christ would become "Jansenists."

The Society of Jesus knew that it would be useless to submit to the Holy See so enormous a work as *Augustinus:* a new Congregation would be bogged down for years in a study of its text. Perhaps the pope would even refuse to make a pronouncement—as Paul V had done earlier in the case of Molina's book—so as not to risk an excommunication which might involve Saint Augustine and even the Scriptures.

The means used by the Jesuits were extremely clever. On July 1, 1649, Nicolas Cornet, one of the most renowned doctors of the Sorbonne—called by some "the general of the Molinist armies," and a strong supporter of the Society of Jesus—submitted to the Faculty of Theology, whose syndic he was, certain propositions that smacked of heresy. Five of these were to become the weapon that permitted the Jesuits to destroy Port-Royal.

According to the first proposition, certain of God's commandments could not be observed by righteous men, despite their efforts, if grace were wanting.

The second held that the sinner cannot resist grace when it is granted him.

The third affirmed that man is free only insofar as he is not constrained to commit sin.

The fourth said that our will of itself can neither obey grace nor resist it.

Finally, the fifth—the most perfidious—claimed that Jesus did not die for all men.[1]

Only the first proposition figured in almost identical terms in *Augustinus;* the other four had never existed save in the imagination of Nicolas Cornet, Saint Augustine's disciples declared. Later, Louis XIV asked a theological opinion on this point from the comte de Grammont, who had been an abbot. After combing through *Augustinus,* the latter replied: "If the five propositions are to be found in it, they must be there incognito."

---

[1] See Documents: *Text of the Five Propositions* (p. 315).

Most unfortunately, the theologians among Arnauld's friends opposed the examination of the five propositions by the Faculty of Theology, a move which immediately caused these Augustinians to be suspected of Jansenism. They appealed to Parlement in the matter, and, wisely, the first president, Molé, imposed silence on the Sorbonne. Peace would have been reestablished had not certain bishops, at the insistence of Nicolas Cornet, submitted the propositions to Pope Innocent X.

The Jesuits had a powerful ally. Mazarin had sent the Holy Father a letter from Louis XIV requesting a condemnation. Signed on May 31, 1653, the bull *Cum occasione* condemned the first four propositions as insults to divine mercy; the fifth was declared false. The Molinists had won their victory.

As soon as the bull was signed, the Augustinian theologians visited the pope, who "caressed them with extreme fondness" to soften their discomfiture. They anxiously asked Innocent X if he intended to maintain the doctrine of efficacious grace as explained by Saint Augustine.

"Oh, that is certain!" the pontiff replied.

Too easily consoled, the Augustinians left Rome, announcing that they had salvaged what was essential to Christianity. With more reason, the Jesuits were triumphant. In an almanac they represented Jansenius with the wings of the devil; the heretical bishop was shown fleeing from the pope and the King of France, and casting himself into the arms of Calvin. This image symbolized "the downfall and confusion of the Jansenists."

Jansenists! The word was launched and became fixed into the language because Arnauld was about to fall into the trap laid for him. A portrait by Philippe de Champaigne shows this dreamy-faced priest with a deep look in his eyes. Why should so generous and tender a soul, one endowed with such living faith, have been linked to the fate of his family in the posthumous destiny of the somber Bishop of Ypres, a man whose nature, as revealed in his writings, was one of sterile lugubriousness?

It must be admitted that the Jesuits could have found no more inept adversary than the youngest of the Arnaulds. The duchesse de Longueville was to say that if the kingdom of heaven is reserved for the clever, Antoine Arnauld would be excluded forever. He had always been as rich in heart as he was poor in finding ruses; to repudiate Jansenius would have been to abandon the one on whom his master, Saint-Cyran, had founded all his hopes, and to betray the task of reanimating the faith which was undertaken by two young men so long ago. Arnauld refused to do it.

But why after this did Pascal and Nicole—who had "the spirit of finesse" —continue to defend *Augustinus*? Both have explained themselves on this subject.

Were the Augustinians to recognize the Bishop of Ypres as a heretic, that very day they would deny the teaching of Christ which was defended by Saint Paul, Saint Augustine, and then Jansenius—namely that grace, the light of the heart which permits men to unite themselves with Christ in love, opens to them the kingdom of the Gospels. No longer would Christians be called upon to embark on the superhuman adventure of seeking and finding Jesus, of dying and rising again with him. The Molinists taught that one could win eternal life through the observance of certain precepts. Rather than allow this false gospel to lead believers astray, Arnauld would fight. But at this time his enemies had closed him in on the horns of a dilemma: he would be condemned as a heretic if he defended Jansenius, and he would no longer be a Christian if he abandoned him! As Arnauld prepared himself for the struggle, his nephew Saci found fit to reply to the authors of the almanac who represented Jansenius under the aspect of a devil, and devoted to them a satirical poem which he entitled "Highlights of the Jesuit Almanac." The heavy facetiousness of this priest, ordinarily so reserved, revealed the Augustinians' disarray.

Mother Angélique remained apart from these learned disputes, for she considered that a woman should never enter "the impenetrable foray of theology discussions."

"I confess," she said, "I do not understand them at all. . . ." And she added a few words which sum up the whole spirit of the Gospel: "I am content with what our Lord has said: without him we can do nothing."

The straightforward abbess had no premonition of the perils which awaited Port-Royal. "Our community is living in great peace," she wrote. It was from "those outside" that she learned of the latest developments.

As always, Agnès Arnauld was closely united in thought with her older sister. When she learned that the pope had condemned the five propositions, she wrote with disarming candor: "We are not at all anxious about the bull; we condemn what it condemns without knowing what it is."

With the return of peace after The Fronde, the Paris house and that of the Fields recovered their tranquility. Louis XIV was now sixteen years old and had been crowned at Rheims; Mother Angélique prayed God to make "the king a saint."

The Molinists had great difficulty in imposing the bull *Cum occasione* on France; the Church's eldest daughter was slow to obey orders coming from Rome. But Father Annat, the provincial of the Society of Jesus, was determined to take the necessary measures to make everyone bow to the pontifical decision. He therefore undertook the seige of Mazarin.

The cardinal had just lived through the days of The Fronde, which had been made most difficult for him. Around Parlement, then around the princes, a whole people had risen up against Mazarin, "the Italian cad." Between the masses and the cardinal had stood only one woman—Anne of Austria. The high courage of the regent was worthy of her Hapsburg blood, but several times Mazarin had felt that his existence depended upon a heart that loved and at the same time secretly distrusted him.

Finally, in 1652, The Fronde was put down and its leaders exiled or imprisoned. The prime minister recovered his fortune, his works of art, his peace of mind—what, therefore, did theological discussions about grace and *Augustinus* matter to him? But Father Annat evoked a name—Retz—which awakened in the cardinal a memory of past anguish. The Machiavellian Retz had been the soul of The Fronde, and the Paris uprising had been the result of his intrigues. Since then this rebel had been arrested and imprisoned, but he had escaped. Cardinal de Retz was the coadjutor of his uncle, Archbishop Gondi of Paris, with right of succession; should he become the spiritual ruler of the capital, this professional trouble-maker might again stir up the nobility, Parlement, and the populace.

Mazarin had first threatened, then beseeched the imprisoned Retz to renounce the archbishopric of Paris, but had accomplished nothing. Besides, how could he get Rome to accept a resignation wrested by violence from a prince of the Church?

Father Annat offered to act as mediator, but on one condition: Mazarin must immediately offer the pope a sign of his fidelity and obedience by making the French clergy accept the bull condemning Jansenism.

The cardinal came to a decision. On July 11, 1653, he convoked the bishops who were in Paris on that day, and easily assembled twenty-eight of them. All hastened to accept the bull.

One of their number, Pierre de Marca, Archbishop of Toulouse, coveted the see of Paris; he knew that to secure this high position, which would have to be taken away from Cardinal de Retz, it was indispensable for him to have the support of the Society of Jesus, all-powerful in Rome.

Monseigneur de Marca was not a theologian, but something preferable— an excellent jurist. A former magistrate, he had abandoned the subtleties of civil legislation for those of canon law. To facilitate Mazarin's task, this prelate drew up a mandate which affirmed that the five propositions were extracts from Jansenius' book, an important detail which the bull itself had not brought to light.

The Archbishop of Paris, Monseigneur Gondi, who loved and admired Port-Royal, tried to oppose the pope's decision. But Anne of Austria begged him to submit, using a most feminine argument: she had never before asked the prelate for anything—would he refuse his queen's first request? The old archbishop, who had only one more year to live, did not dare prolong his resistance.

Marca, who became more and more zealous, drew up in 1655 the famous formulary which was to be signed by all ecclesiastics: "I condemn by heart and speech the doctrine of the five propositions of Cornelius Jansenius. . . ."

When the day would arrive for imposing signature of the formulary, Saint Augustine's disciples would find themselves with their backs to the wall. In facing this danger, would Antoine Arnauld give proof of great prudence or, on the contrary, would he set fire to the powder-keg? One of his friends, the duc de Liancourt, was refused absolution by a priest of Saint-Sulpice because he had had his granddaughter brought up at Port-Royal and had received Jansenists in his home.[1] The admiration of this myopic duke for the solitaries was so great that when he went to the Abbey of the Fields, he would take off his hat and make a low bow to the least cowherd, asking, "Isn't this one of the Messieurs?"

Liancourt, having refused to make his *mea culpa* despite the commands of his confessor, found himself deprived of the eucharist. When he learned this, Antoine Arnauld was filled with sympathetic anger. Again he took up his pen, as though to justify the strange comparison made three centuries later by the Abbot Brémond in his *Literary History of Religious Sentiment in France* when he described him as "a theological machine-gun in perpetual motion." In defense of the duke, Arnauld wrote a plea entitled "Letter from a Doctor of the Sorbonne to a Person of Condition." The Jesuits were only awaiting such an occasion to resume the combat. They replied from every quarter; nine attacks—one from Father Annat—rained down on Antoine Arnauld. He then wrote his "Second Letter to a Duke and Peer of France," intended for the most faithful of Port-Royal's friends, Monsieur de Luynes. Dated July 10, 1655, this letter was published as a quarto volume of two hundred and fifty-four pages!

Despite the pontifical decision, the man now called "the great Arnauld" continued his struggle in favor of *Augustinus*. In this "Second Letter" he declared that, in his opinion, Jansenius' work did not contain the five propositions condemned by Rome. Even so, he tried to defend the first—according to which a righteous man deprived of grace could not carry out certain of the divine commands—for this did express the thought of Jansenius.

In this connection Arnauld cited an illustrious example, saying that when

---

[1] The defenders of Port-Royal never considered themselves disciples of Jansenius; their master was Saint Augustine. Nevertheless, for the sake of clarity it is preferable here to call them by the name *Jansenists,* whish is better known today than *Augustinians.*

Saint Peter denied Christ he was a just man who was lacking in grace. This argument was extremely dangerous for the cause of Port-Royal: he should have refrained from reminding people that the apostle who founded the Holy See, and whose successors were the popes, had denied Jesus because God had deprived him of grace.

This letter was considered an insult to the sovereign pontiff and suspect of heresy, and on its publication was immediately submitted to examination at the Sorbonne. This celebrated building—established by Saint Louis' chaplain, Robert de Sorbon, to house scholars and students—was the seat of the Faculty of Theology. Its all-powerful head, Richelieu, recently had it entirely reconstructed—today all that remains of his work is the graceful church.

In Antoine Arnauld's time the "Sacred Faculty," composed of doctors joined in a Society, had acquired a high reputation. "The illustrious family of the Sorbonne is an ærie of eagles," wrote a contemporary. However, there were others who reproached the theologians for their tendency to "the quintessential abstractions, quibbling, and sophistries of dialectics."

Antoine Arnauld had not become a member of the Society until after Richelieu's death; so long as the great cardinal lived he had forbidden the entrance of Saint-Cyran. So now the spiritual leader of Port-Royal was arraigned before his peers. Two questions—drawn up, it is said, by the Jesuit provincial, Father Annat—were laid before the doctors. Was not the "Letter to a Duke and Peer" insulting to the pontiff? This was the question of *fact*. Was Arnauld's proposition, according to which grace was lacking in Saint Peter, heretical? This was the question of *right*.

The Molinists did everything in their power to assure their success. Numerous monks belonging to the mendicant orders were added to the doctors; these religious were extremely docile. Moreover, Chancellor Séguier received from the court an order to be present during the debates on the pretext of maintaining order. When this high dignitary, who outranked all the judges of France, came to take his place at the Sorbonne dressed in his robe of red velvet lined in satin and his mortarboard hat trimmed in gold and pearls, preceded by guards bearing halberds, everyone felt that the king had given the weight of his authority to the proceedings.

Already Antoine Arnauld seemed a condemned man. He had been forced to take an oath promising to submit to censure should this be ordered. Moreover, he was not authorized to speak except to explain his own opinions; nor was he allowed to take part in any of the discussions.

From the depths of her enclosure, Angélique sent "her poor little brother" letters filled with expressions of her affection. "Our good mother," she wrote, "who commanded us on her deathbed to suffer for the truth, bequeathed me the tender love she bore her youngest son." Without entering into a debate which was over her head, the abbess expressed her confidence that the youngest son of the Arnaulds would not deviate from the straight path of the Gospels. His elder sister recalled "the joy and tranquility with which she had seen him depart to suffer everything it might please God to ordain in the defense of his grace."

But Antoine Arnauld's firmness had been only apparent. For the first time Saint Augustine's defender felt himself weaken. Alone against all the authorities of the Church and kingdom, he at last measured—too late—the danger that hung over Angélique, Agnès, and the nuns because of him. Was he not bringing down lightning upon a house he loved?

On January 11, 1656, Arnauld resigned himself to sending his judges a written declaration stating "that he would not have spoken as he had in the 'Letter' had he foreseen that it would be considered a crime; that he wished he had not written it."

This humiliation was useless; three days later, on January 14th, Antoine Arnauld was condemned on the question of *fact*. In claiming that the five propositions censured by Rome did not appear in *Augustinus,* the priest had upheld an opinion that was "rash, scandalous, insulting to the sovereign pontiff."

Despite the presence of the Chancellor of France, seventy-one doctors dared vote for Arnauld's acquittal; eighty condemned him. This small majority was increased, it is true, by forty mendicant friars—mostly Franciscans —who had been added to the Faculty when they should never have numbered more than eight.

Antoine Arnauld's friends surrounded him, beseeching him in these terms: "Your cause is lost at the Sorbonne. You will be condemned on the point of *right* as you have just been on the point of *fact*. You must address yourself to honest men. Undeceive them; tell them where the truth lies. The voice of the people will be the voice of God."

Once more Arnauld took up his pen, but on that day he was overcome by great weariness. When he assembled his faithful followers and read to them the far too recondite text he had written, all of them were silent in consternation.

"I see quite well that you do not find this good, and I think that you are right," Arnauld murmured sadly.

Then an event took place with consequences that were to endure for many centuries: the leader of Port-Royal turned to a newcomer who was making a retreat at Les Granges. This man of thirty-two had received no degree from the Faculty of Theology, no dignity from the Church. He was a layman, but he had won great renown because of his astonishing aptitude for mathematics and also for the brilliance of his mind. His name was Blaise Pascal.

"You who are young, you must do something," Arnauld said to him.

The guest at Les Granges was surprised to be entrusted with a task exceeding the powers of a Sorbonne theologian, but he did not try to shirk it. He set to work, and a few days later Pascal read to the solitaries the first of the *Provincial Letters*.

This man was now to take the fate of Port-Royal upon his shoulders.

3

THE PRESENCE OF PASCAL

Blaise Pascal came from the same rugged mountains of Auvergne as had the Arnaulds, and he shared their firmness and stubbornness. Having lost his mother in 1629, when he was only three years old, the child had been most carefully reared by his father, Etienne Pascal. The latter was president at that time of the Cour des Aides of Clermont-Ferrand, a court dealing with matters relating to indirect taxation. He was, moreover, a good mathematician, as were many magistrates of the period. Blaise Pascal soon displayed his talents. At the age of eleven he wrote a treatise on the communication of sound. He even demonstrated to himself, solely through his own reasoning powers, the thirty-second proposition of the first book of Euclid. His older sister Gilberte tells us that on learning of this, her father "was so dismayed that he went to the home of his closest friend and stood stock-still, like a man in a trance."

Etienne Pascal's astonishment was to grow. At sixteen his son wrote an essay on conic sections; at nineteen, he invented a calculating machine. Four years later Etienne Pascal fell and dislocated his hip, and for three months was under the care of two gentlemen from Normandy who were expert in the art of setting bones. They devoted not only their time but their fortunes to the sick, and had even established a hospital. Both had as spiritual director one of Saint-Cyran's disciples, Monsieur Guillebert, Curate of Rouville. This priest had them read the *Lettres chrétiennes et spirituelles* written by the prisoner of Vincennes, and Antoine Arnauld's *La Fréquente Communion.*

Thanks to these gentlemen the same books came into the hands of Etienne

Pascal and his children, revealing to the entire family the realities of a religion which had previously been little more than a ritual to them. Up to that time they had been content merely with accepting Christ as God, and believed that it was enough to recite a few prayers, attend church services, and perform certain charitable works. Now, enlightened by Saint-Cyran and Arnauld, each of them discovered who Jesus was, what he had bestowed, and what he expected of them.

Etienne Pascal and his elder daughter Gilberte tried from that time onward to cross the threshold of Christ's kingdom, but Blaise and his younger sister Jacqueline were of a different stamp. After going back to the sources, reading the prophecies and the Gospels, they went to hear the Abbot Guillebert. Thus they learned what had been taught by Bérulle, Condren, and Saint-Cyran—that God has crucified the flesh and asks us in return to share in his resurrection. Blaise Pascal felt that he had made a tremendous discovery, namely that of a truth which overshadows and explains all others. When he subsequently went to live in Paris, he paid a visit to Monsieur Rebours, one of the priests who directed the nuns at Port-Royal. On that occasion Pascal expatiated on how "well-directed reason" could demonstrate the reality proclaimed by Saint-Cyran. To this, Rebours replied that reason is merely one of the more misleading aspects of pride; that we must humble ourselves before Jesus, and come to him as a little child.

Two worlds were thus brought into opposition. Pascal was disappointed and went away, returning to his science and to his pleasures.

Some have said that this was the period of his first conversion, but nothing could be further from the truth if the word is to be given its Christian meaning. Pascal had considered the supernatural world with the mind of a scientist, and when he learned he could not reach it by intellectual means he had turned away. Other vistas, more accessible, were open to him.

In 1648, he finished his *Traité des sections coniques*. In 1651, after several experiments in atmospheric pressure, he demonstrated the existence of the vacuum in his *De l'équilibre des liqueurs* and *De la pesanteur de la masse de l'air*, thereby proving the theory of Torricelli and demolishing the thesis of Aristotle, which had been accepted up to his day. On this subject he entered into a dispute with Father Noël, a Jesuit—his first Jesuit!—who answered him in a treatise with the curious title: *Le Plein du vide*. That same year Pascal made a speech on science at the home of the duchesse d'Aiguillon, Richelieu's niece, and sent his arithmetical machine to Christine of Sweden.

His renown soon opened all doors to him, and he was called "the new Archimedes." Such learned men as Descartes, Mersenne, and Roberval came to converse with him, and he was received and fêted in the great salons of Paris.

While Pascal performed wonders in the world and moved in the highest circles, his sister Jacqueline, who shared his beliefs, suddenly outstripped him. No one could have foreseen that this young girl would become a mystic. In earlier days, when Blaise was laying the foundations of his daring scientific theories, Jacqueline had been interested only in poetic rhythms and images. Even as an adolescent she knew how to use her gifts to pay court to the great, and at the age of eleven had written a sonnet in honor of the belated pregnancy of Anne of Austria. The queen had received the young prodigy at the château of Saint-Germain, and that same day the king's cousin, the "Grande Mademoiselle," asked Jacqueline to improvise some verses for her, which she did forthwith. Madame d'Hautefort, the celebrated beauty, was likewise favored with an impromptu ode beginning:

> Beautiful masterpiece of the universe
> Adorable subject of my verse . . .

Shortly thereafter the young girl played the role of Cassandra in *L'amour tyrannique* by Georges de Scudéry in a performance given in Richelieu's presence. With anxiety worthy of Cassandra herself, the little actress trembled on the stage. Her father, after selling his post to another incumbent, had taken part in an uprising because the state had deprived him of a quarter of his income. The unfortunate man had been forced to flee the cardinal's anger and to go into hiding in order to avoid being sent to the Bastille.

As Scudéry's play came to its end, Jacqueline advanced toward Richelieu and addressed this petition to him:

> Be not surprised, incomparable Armand,
> If I fail to please your eye or ear.
> My spirit, trembling with unknown fear,
> Forbids me both voice and movement.
> So that I may please you here
> Recall from exile my miserable father.

As the child's voice rose, the minister who terrified all France forgot that one should "close one's heart to pity," and Etienne Pascal received his pardon.

When the repentant rebel came with Blaise, Jacqueline, and Gilberte, to thank the cardinal, Richelieu said to him: "I commend these children to you. One day I shall make them great."

The cardinal was mistaken: his promise had already been fulfilled. The year before, when he had cast Saint-Cyran into the prison cell where he would write his *Lettres chrétiennes,* Richelieu had already opened the highest of destinies to two of these children.

If the prime minister was in poor accord with exceptional minds, he knew how to draw the greatest advantage from more common men. Etienne Pascal, the embittered, impoverished landowner, was to become an excellent civil servant. At that time there was an uprising of the peasants of Normandy, reduced to starvation by taxes; under these circumstances Richelieu appointed emissaries to see that his orders were obeyed. Persons thus appointed bore the title of royal commissioners; Laubardemont filled one of these posts, and Etienne Pascal received a similar one. With another commissioner, a steward of petitions on the royal council, he had to repair to Rouen, make assessments, and see that the taxes were paid by everyone. The cardinal knew that when it came to quelling the revolt, he could place full confidence in the former rebel who had himself been a magistrate.

Arriving in the capital of Normandy as severe measures were being taken to suppress the rebellion, the royal commissioner at first showed extreme severity. But subsequently he gave proof of such fairness and conscientiousness that he came to be loved in a countryside where he had been received as an enemy; the municipal magistrates even offered him money-tokens imprinted with a pascal lamb in his honor.

At Rouen Jacqueline, who was fifteen years of age, met the great Corneille. This bard of the heroic was in private life a good and peaceful man. Moved by Mademoiselle Pascal's poetic efforts, he had her take part in a competition in which she won a prize for her stanzas on the Immaculate Conception of our Lady. Jacqueline was absent from Rouen when the prize was awarded, and Corneille received it for her and thanked the jury in the young girl's name.

In point of fact, Jacqueline sometimes dealt with less devotional subjects, and is known to have exchanged madrigals with Benserade, one of the most celebrated poets at the Hôtel de Rambouillet. One day she sent him "on behalf of a friend, a lady in love with a man who did not know it," these strange verses:

> Her ardor grows by leaps and bounds
> And finally becomes so vehement
> That she can no longer hide it . . .

Surprised, Benserade replied:

> I am ashamed that a girl should be first
> To speak to me of love!

The little muse scarcely seemed destined to the contemplative life, but now, at the age of twenty-three, she pledged herself forever to the Gospel. Jacqueline owed her conversion to her brother: he had guided her through the pages of Saint-Cyran's writings, and had led her first to Rouville to hear the Abbot Guillebert; then, when both were living in Paris, to the church of Port-Royal where Singlin, the nuns' spiritual director, was preaching. Jacqueline's future was determined: after refusing an offer of marriage, she decided to become a religious. In 1648, she was welcomed at the monastery of the faubourg Saint-Jacques by Mother Angélique, who placed her under the direction of Singlin. After several conversations, Angélique had no doubts concerning the young girl's vocation—she would enter the novitiate if she could secure her father's consent.

But Etienne Pascal intended to defend his possessions against God. He did not want his youngest, the dearest of his children, to enter the silent domain where another large family had already been interred. So long as he lived, this daughter should remain with him!

How could she resist the will of a father so deeply attached to his family? In great distress, Jacqueline had recourse to Mother Agnès. But the nun advised her to obey and to be patient: "You must accept the answer given by your father as meaning that God's decree is deferred to another time."

Hearing this voice, Jacqueline bowed her head and obediently returned home. But she already lived another life in secret; she did not cease to correspond with Singlin or with Mother Agnès.

The young girl kept back only one treasure from her past life: her poetry. At the request of a priest of the Oratory, she began translating Latin hymns into verse. Agnès Arnauld, whose counsel she sought in this matter, replied: "You should hate this talent; the world is holding you back and wants to reap what it has sown."

Jacqueline was never again to seek the "satisfaction of her intellect."

On September 24, 1651, Etienne Pascal died in Paris. The sorrow his daughter felt was mitigated by an invincible hope—at twenty-six she was free at last to give her life to God.

Yet a new obstacle arose: Blaise Pascal did not want to lose the companion who had shared his youth and thoughts. "Their hearts were but a single heart," wrote Gilberte, their elder sister. Like his father, Blaise could not resign himself to her decision, and he pleaded with Jacqueline to stay with him one more year before entering Port-Royal. Not wishing to hurt her brother the young girl dared not refuse, but she remained firm in her decision. At dawn on January 4, 1652, she fled to the monastery.

Two months later Jacqueline wrote her brother from Port-Royal, telling him that her intention to enter religion was definite. "I have need of your consent," she added. "Without it I would perform the greatest act of my life with extreme joy mixed with extreme sorrow. . . . Do not take from me what you can never give me. . . . If you do not have the strength to follow me, at least do not hold me back."

Those who have compared Jacqueline Pascal with the Roman Polyeucte were not wrong—she was indeed a heroine after the heart of Corneille.

Blaise gave his consent very reluctantly. He was present with his sister Gilberte in the monastery church of Port-Royal of Paris when Jacqueline was clothed with her habit. She had not concealed from either of them that she would consider them strangers if they were absent on that day. "You may be assured that I will disown you if you are not there," she wrote them.

New difficulties arose when the time came for Jacqueline to receive her dowry. Gilberte and Blaise did not want to turn over to the abbey her share of their inheritance, which she had made over to them. In order to maintain his position among the nobility, Blaise now had financial obligations which he had great difficulty in meeting. Gilberte, who was married, was irritated that Jacqueline "was disinheriting them in favor of strangers."

Learning of this discussion regarding finances, the superiors of Port-Royal declared to the novice that they had decided to receive her without a dowry; but Jacqueline was cruelly humiliated and distressed at the idea of arriving among her companions with empty hands. Her grief was so violent that the abbess had to hold her, Jacqueline wrote later, "leaning upon her bosom and embracing me with the tenderness of a true mother." Jacqueline was never to forget that day when Angélique Arnauld found words to tell her "everything that might sweeten the bitterness I felt." Since the novice had grown to doubt the affection of her family, the abbess reassured her: "They love you very much, but they are still of the world."

Several days later Blaise Pascal came to the parlor to see his sister. She affected gaiety, but her face was sorrowful. The young girl's efforts to appear carefree filled her brother with more remorse than reproaches would have done. His mind was immediately made up; whatever difficulty he might encounter, whatever humiliation he might suffer from those in high places, he would acquit himself toward Port-Royal of what he considered to be a debt of honor.

With this intention, and before his sister made her profession, he presented himself at the monastery in the company of his notary. The abbess, however, could not receive him that day. He was told that because of her scruples she still needed time to reflect and seek advice before she entered into any agreement with him. Both moved and humbled in the presence of such disinterestedness, Pascal did not want to delay in making payment. He was back the following day, and this time Angélique received him with confidence. She realized that Jacqueline's brother was now gladly turning over to the monastery the monies in his possession.

As he was about to sign the deed of gift, she said to him: "See, Monsieur, we have learned from the late Monsieur de Saint-Cyran not to receive anything that does not come to us from God."

The echo of those words and the memory of the next day, when Jacqueline united herself to Christ forever, under the name of Sister de Saint-Euphémie, were to remain engraved on Pascal's heart even as he returned once more to science and to the world.

As though fleeing a danger, Jacqueline's brother renewed his ties with personages of the court and pursued his research more feverishly than ever. He entered into correspondence with Monsieur de Fermat, a remarkable mathematician, and the two men laid the foundation for the calculation of probabilities.

Pascal also prepared an address to the Paris Academy of Sciences, and a treatise on the arithmetical triangle. He was welcomed more and more in high social circles: after being received in the drawing-room of Madame d'Aiguillon, he found the salons of the marquise de Sablé and the duchesse de Longueville opened to him. The duc de Roannez became his friend, and introduced him to the chevalier de Méré; the latter, a frequent visitor at the Hôtel de Rambouillet, opened to this provincial, the son of an austere magistrate, the fine atmosphere of the court, the spirit of the world. The chevalier wanted to make *un honnête homme* of Pascal: one possessing, as he said, "the art of excelling in everything pertaining to life's pleasures and proprieties." Méré, who divided his favors between the duchesse de Lesdiguières and Ninon de Lenclos, knew how to respond to a solemn statement with a smile and how to make the most cutting remarks with an air of nonchalance. A Greek and Latin scholar, able to express himself in Arabic as well as in Italian and Spanish, this gallant Knight of Malta admired the songs of Homer, the imagery of Plato, and the haughty stoicism of Epictetus. He introduced Pascal into the homes of the intimate friends of his cousin, the marquise de Rambouillet, the "incomparable Arthénice." * Another gentleman, Milton, showed the young mathematician the way in which unalterable urbanity enables the well-born man to remain in command of his language when a peasant or ill-bred person shows bad temper, and introduced Pascal to the subtle irony of Montaigne, his favorite author.

Pascal went to Poitu, to the home of the duc de Roannez who was governor of the province. Here he was passed from château to château, from one festivity to another.

When he returned to Paris in 1654, Jacqueline's brother was thirty-one.

---

* Her salon, the Hôtel de Rambouillet, was the meeting-place of intellectuals who exerted considerable influence on the language and literature of the seventeenth century. —*Trans.*

He had absorbed all the intellectual riches of his century and had even fore-seen various discoveries of the future. But one day in the autumn of that year, at the very time when he should have felt only gratification at the fulfilment of all his ambitions, he was sunk in deepest despair.

Was he thinking of his hairbreadth escape from death, when the horses that drew his carriage had taken fright and almost drowned him in the Seine? Was it then that he had become aware of annihilation and infinity? This hardly seems likely in view of his writings, where he clearly describes his misery; above all, approaching the fathomless abyss he contemplated, it is unbelievable that his conversion was brought about by an accident.

Furthermore, there is no need to guess at something that has been fully explained. Pascal's *Pensées* make it possible to follow him along the new road he was about to travel.

After his inquiring mind had led him to absorb all the learning of his time, and even to go beyond, he had cast a glance at vast regions still un-explored. In the heavens he observed a multitude of worlds. Before this vast expanse he was merely a reed, but a "thinking reed." Hence, the awareness that each of us bears within him is separate from and superior to matter.

"All these bodies together cannot succeed in producing one little thought; it is not possible, and is in another order." When the intellect conceives of the existence of the earth and other worlds, it surpasses them: it contains these giant masses within itself.

"If the universe crushes him, man will still be nobler than the thing which destroys him, because he knows that he is dying; the universe knows nothing of this."

Why not, then, go forward to the conquest of the infinite? Pascal thirsted for certainty; he wanted to know, his sister tells us, "the reason and cause of everything." Nothing could escape the sharpness of his intellect.

It was here that the man of science was to meet his first defeat: the mind can imagine the whole earth, but the firmament, "that infinite sphere, the center of which is everywhere, the circumference nowhere," revealed itself as too vast for him. "We may enlarge our conceptions beyond all imaginable space; we produce only atoms in comparison with the reality of things." The author of the *Pensées* then thought of the smallest of insects—the mite. Having mentally divided it into as many sections as possible, he imagined in this "abridged atom" an infinity of universes, each with its firmament, its planets, its earth: in this earth, animals, and finally mites, in which one would find again what he found in the first.

Drawing back from two abysses—that of immensity and that of the atom—Pascal returned to himself.

"What is man in nature? A void in comparison with the infinite, a whole in comparison with the void; a middle point between nothing and all."

His ignorance of the worlds surrounding him made him feel "eternal despair of ever knowing their beginning or their end."

If man must resign himself to live in a mystery, did there not at least remain to him a single fixed point to which he could cling as to an outermost reef? No; he could not succeed even in that.

"We sail within a vast sphere, ever drifting in uncertainty." If we attempt to attach ourselves to a being or to an object, "it eludes our grasp, slips away and flees from us in unending flight. Nothing stops for us."

Borne on this perpetual movement, leaving one unknown to go toward another, Pascal questioned himself concerning his own final end.

"I see these dreadful spaces of the universe which confine me, and I find myself penned into one corner of that vast expanse, not knowing why I am in this place rather than in another, nor anything of the whole eternity that went before me, nor of the eternity that is to come."

What was terrible was "the eternal silence of these infinite spaces," when this silence is the only reply the mind receives. The worlds turn in perfect order—an inhuman grandeur reigns over this infallible and unmeasured operation.

Science had led Pascal to the threshold of the infinite; there it left him stranded. Then it was that the scientist knew terror: "I became frightened, like a man carried in his sleep to a desert island, and who awakens not knowing where he is, and without means of escape."

Becoming aware of reality, the sage returned to the society of other men. He found his friends—the grave Milton, the brilliant chevalier de Méré—engrossed in the thousand details of daily living, and walking with indifference on the edge of the abyss. This attitude suddenly stupefied the future author of the *Pensées*. These men wanted to ignore "an affair which concerns their selves, their eternity, their all." They negligently allowed themselves to be "led to their deaths, in uncertainty of their future condition."

Pascal himself no longer wished to live in this way.

"I do not know what is my body, what my senses, what my soul, or even that part of me which thinks, and expresses what I think.

"It is an indispensable duty to search when one is in such doubt."

Pascal now confronted his future. He had never been deeply concerned with it before, especially when he had lived among sages and gentlemen; now this problem was all that mattered to him.

Then he came back to the enigma presented by man. Miserable as he was, did he not bear within him a prodigious power—namely, thought? Hence in this reed there was as much greatness as baseness; the summit and the gulf were as far removed from each other as the magnitude of the worlds in relation to infinite smallness.

What a chimera, then, is man! What a novelty, what a monster, what a chaos, what a contradiction, what a prodigy!
Universal judge and helpless earthworm.
Depository of truth, sink of uncertainty and error.
Glory and refuse of the universe!

Perhaps for the first time Pascal turned to the Creator in an effort to know his secret.

"They received the Word with all eagerness, daily searching the Scriptures. . . ." These words from the Acts of the Apostles are reproduced in Pascal's *Pensées*. There Pascal tells how he went about his research: after reading and rereading the sacred texts, he realized the way in which they were linked to one another. A whole past rose before him: a past that he would describe one day to the solitaries. He had seen the strange people of Israel separating themselves from other nations in order to adore the unique and invisible God; a people carrying on its shoulders the heavy burden of the "sealed book," passing it on from century to century despite massacres and deportations.

On the threshold of this book appears man's ancestor, Adam. Abandoned to himself because of his sin, he transmitted to all his descendants "the pride which draws us away from God, the concupiscence that binds us to earth"; thenceforth, the Eternal was "a hidden God." Then in succession came Moses and the patriarchs, David and the kings, Isaiah and the prophets; for sixteen centuries these inspired men led the chosen people through deserts and battles. All bore testimony to the presence of the Creator who was to send the Messiah. This deliverer is the manna in the desert who feeds the starving, the rock of Moses from which flows the eternal water, the sovereign whose majesty is praised in David's psalms, the tortured criminal described by Isaiah. The promise was at last fulfilled on the soil of Galilee: Jesus broke the seal on the book, tore aside the veil. His miracles astonished the pagans and his words opened the gates of the Kingdom. A new Occident had appeared on the day of the Messiah's birth.

Since the time of Jesus, the apostles, the evangelists, the saints, and the martyrs have revealed to us from age to age the power of the Redeemer.

Pascal emerged from the darkness; the final destiny of all mankind had been made clear to him. Of the happiness men so avidly seek there remains "only a hollow trace." But united to the Messiah men are again great in the grandeur of God, who wants only to be one with them. This explains the contradiction that makes of man "an incomprehensible monster," at once so noble and so vile. The immensity of space is in no way frightening; it is completely filled by Christ. He is the Mediator, the open road between the inaccessible Father and his lost children. "Apart from him, we do not know the meaning of life, of death, of God, nor of ourselves." All the future is lighted before us. We have not been abandoned in deep sleep at some point of the earth or of the ages. We have been placed on the very ground where we must begin our conquest of the infinite.

Having returned to the religion of his youth, Pascal had only to observe its commandments. Was he finally saved? No. Conversion is a spiritual metamorphosis of the carnal being; it is a new life. Jacqueline's brother knew he had not yet taken a single step forward.

He had made the greatest of his discoveries: he knew the truth. But, he tells us, "truth without charity is not God . . . it is an idol we must not adore."

Pascal saw Jesus dominating the infinite, but how could he succeed in loving him? "It is the heart that feels God and not the reason. The meaning of faith is this: God perceived by the heart."

The domain of which the scientist had just learned was new to him; love does not obey the laws of the mind. "The heart has its reasons which reason does not know." All the material things of earth do not enable us to achieve the puniest thought. But "all bodies together and all minds together do not amount to the slightest movement of charity. This is in an infinitely higher order."

The charity that enables us to reach the Kingdom alone can lift us up beyond all intelligence: it is of a supernatural order. This is the mystery before which all knowledge must bow. Descartes' axiom, "I think, therefore I am," is surpassed by the revelation of the Gospel: "I love, therefore I am."

For the first time, Pascal rebelled against the reason which could show him the straight path but could not open it to him; the false god he had adored was nothingness. It nevertheless remained within him, separating his heart from the superhuman world for which he had been created.

"Humble yourself, powerless reason; be silent, imbecile nature; learn that man is infinitely higher than man and listen to your master. Hear God!"

The scientist fell to his knees; he humbled his talents. Since he could mount no higher, might the Messiah come down to him! "It is good to be tired and weary from a useless search for the true good, so that we may lift up our arms to the Deliverer." Pascal closed the book. He no longer wanted to be anything more than one of those simple men who enter the Kingdom without knowing its height or its extent; he prayed as had so many humble ones before him.

Yet even if we can impose silence on reason, how can we silence our pride? At the moment he abandoned his will to the invisible Master, an instinct to defend himself arose in Pascal; the human being who had earlier guided his thinking wanted to continue to live and rule. As a Christian he began his struggle with this hateful self. "I hate him because he is unjust, because he makes himself the center of everything. I will always hate him."

The new Archimedes exhausted himself in vain: his pride rose up at every moment. He could not remain torn between despair at being nothing and the ambition to be everything. Amuse himself? Go, as did Descartes, from analysis to synthesis? These were mental games, poorly disguising a deathlike immobility. Pascal himself was alive; he wished to go forward; he was condemned to do it. But then the way opened wide to nothingness!

Did the scientist ask too much? The words of Saint Mark's Gospel then took on all their meaning: "Thou hast hidden these things from the wise and hast revealed them to the little ones."

Pascal, who "sought in trembling," admitted his defeat. "How far apart are the knowledge of God and the love of him!"

Pascal had risked losing himself in what Saint John of the Cross called "the dark night of the soul," but a nun was to lead him to a higher abode. Each day Jacqueline found her brother sitting in the parlor of Port-Royal of Paris; taking his place near the recluse behind her grille, he saw on her the mark of eternity. If he still had doubts, the hope that lighted the face of his younger sister told Pascal that he was in the presence of the Holy Spirit.

The penitent confessed to the nun, she later said, "his extreme aversion for the follies and amusements of the world." Chevalier de Méré's friend, Descartes' equal, had arrived at the point where pleasure was folly and science was amusement.

Jacqueline knew that he had placed his highest hopes in her. At that time her brother's visits were so frequent and so lengthy "that I thought I no longer had any other work to do," the nun told her older sister. It was true— the work now to be accomplished required all the strength of the frail young girl. The day after Pascal's conversion she was heard to exclaim: "He was in such a state of abandonment that he felt it was his own reason and his own mind that urged him on, rather than the working of God's will in him."

Pascal had to cast aside all that had made up his previous existence; but when he wanted to abandon his past, it clung to him with such force that Jacqueline surmised the degree to which her brother had formerly given himself over to the world. "In detaching himself from all those things he found within himself," she added, "he must have had horrible bonds to resist God's graces and the movements he gave him."

What was now accomplished did, in fact, require more than human means. To break the chains that still bound the prisoner, the Holy Spirit entered the lists; here we see once more Jacob's struggle with the angel. Torn with compassion, Pascal's sister prayed, beseeching the Invisible to give and give again so that one she loved might be saved.

Finally after long difficult days the young girl's prayers were heard. Lazarus rose, came forth from his tomb, and walked.

Much later, after Pascal's death, a strip of parchment informed his family that on November 23, 1654, a night of inner fire had consumed everything that still bound him to earth. But Jacqueline, as her letter to her sister Gilberte testifies, never asked to know what should not and cannot be put into words; there was only respect and silence on her part.

In announcing the great news to her elder sister, Jacqueline expressed her wonder and joy, her *alleluia;* he who had joined her in his turn had outdistanced her! "I could only follow him as I saw him grow little by little, in such a way that I no longer knew him," she wrote. The nun had seen the growth of a tree which now overshadowed her; the new man had no measure in common with the man he had been. Pascal fled the world and held glory in disdain. Jacqueline saw her brother reach the point, she wrote, "even of distrusting himself." Then she told her sister of the approach of the Eternal: "It clearly appears that it is no longer his natural spirit that moves in him."

What could be expected of him in the future? The nun felt an immense hope rise within her: "That is what he is at this hour; God alone knows what he will one day be."

The *Pensées* can provide the clue. Pascal relates what he discovered when his heart was elevated above his mind. Christ, he wrote, "fills the souls of those he possesses. He makes them incapable of any other end than himself." This hymn was to be continued, from year to year, until he drew his last breath.

For the resurrected man to walk with certainty he had to choose a guide—and this choice was a grave decision on which his whole future depended. A lofty mind could be permanently harmed if directed by someone who was narrowminded or clumsy. As a matter of fact, the choice seemed already to have been made: it was Singlin's words that had led Pascal to the gate of the Kingdom. Nevertheless, the convert was hesitant: this priest, Pascal said, was not attached to the parish in which he himself lived. Should not every Christian have recourse to "his natural pastor?"

Pascal's sister was too shrewd to allow herself to be convinced by such reasoning. If her brother did not go directly to Singlin it was because he dreaded the spiritual power of the priest who alone could control him; in the same way Angélique Arnauld had attempted to avoid Saint-Cyran in other days.

"I saw clearly," Jacqueline wrote, "that this was only a trace of independence concealed in the depth of his heart, which made every endeavor to avoid submission."

The nun did not reveal this thought to her brother, for she had no desire to humiliate him. Such delicacy of feeling would be surprising today. "I did not want to make any advance. . . . I contented myself with saying to him that in choosing a physician for the soul as well as one for the body, it was necessary to choose the best." Her words impressed Pascal, and he conceded. But now his sister had to get Singlin's acceptance, and this she had great difficulty in obtaining. Accustomed as Singlin was to the robust faith of the nuns and solitaries, the priest was little enthusiastic over the conversion of a worldly scientist. "Many more things were needed," Jacqueline said, "to decide Monsieur Singlin, who was remarkably fearful of becoming involved in affairs of this kind." However, when he learned what had happened, the director of Port-Royal was forced to enter on the scene. He felt he did not have the right to abandon someone who had clearly received the effects of grace.

Pascal wanted to go to the Monastery of the Fields, where he could talk at length with Singlin, who was living there at the time. The priest opposed this, saying that the penitent should remain silent, for God was continuing his work. Nevertheless, the presence of another is necessary to one whose eyes have just been opened, and so with sure instinct Singlin made his decision. Jacqueline Pascal was the first refuge to whom the shipwrecked man had turned; she alone must remain beside him to guide his first steps.

The nun received this charge with some apprehension, but her letters show how she carried out her task. Saint-Cyran's disciples never tried to hasten the steps of those advancing on "the royal road"; their freedom should be complete. Jacqueline therefore remained at a distance, as did the women in the Gospel. Pascal, the impetuous spirit, thenceforth showed his younger sister "a humility and submission" which permitted the nun to understand the road her brother had traveled; even so, as soon as Singlin returned to the faubourg Saint-Jacques, the religious urged him to "discharge his dignity." The priest would have liked for her to continue her task, "but I acted in such a way," Jacqueline added, "that I obtained what I desired." When Singlin finally consented to see Pascal, the nun announced her victory in these words: "He received him." The convert and the priest then conversed as two equals; the first revealed his past, the second looked into the future.

The duc de Roannez had just returned to Paris; between this great nobleman and Pascal a relationship which sprang from a common interest in science had ripened into a sincere friendship. But the convert had to renounce all the ties that bound him to his past; Singlin wanted him to leave for the Monastery of the Fields to meditate in peace and silence. Pascal asked Roannez' consent to a long absence. The duke was forced to agree, yet at the moment of parting from his friend he had the feeling of losing so dear a possession that he could not restrain his tears.

Reaching Port-Royal in January, 1655, the new arrival entrusted himself to Monsieur de Luynes, who received him at his château of Vaumurier. But Pascal found too many reminders of his worldly existence there, and moved to the farm of Les Granges, where he was given one of the cells of the solitaries. Only then did he write Jacqueline that he found himself "lodged and treated like a prince." The nun knew the real meaning of these words: the princes of God's kingdom are given two privileges—solitude and poverty.

The spiritual director at Port-Royal of the Fields was Saci, and he became Pascal's confessor. Jacqueline felt completely reassured, for she knew the solid and enlightened faith of this descendant of the Arnaulds. "He comes from a good breed," she wrote. A letter from her brother confirmed this feeling: Pascal was "entirely delighted"; he was finally experiencing real happiness, the happiness of a child, which is the first mark of predestination. Christ had said: "That my joy may be in you, and your joy may be filled."

The convert's enthusiasm was such that Jacqueline wrote smilingly: "I don't know how Monsieur de Saci can adjust to so joyful a penitent."

The author of the *Pensées* had known anguish during his search for the hidden God. Just as he found him he was to risk excommunication for sake of the truth, but always—and up to the day of his death—he experienced that confidence in Christ's presence which illuminates the Gospels.

Saci knew how to receive the man entrusted to him. He was aware of Pascal's fame, but as Fontaine, one of the solitaries, wrote, "the enlightenment that Monsieur de Saci found in Scripture gave him the hope that he would not be dazzled by this brilliant man who charmed and captivated everyone."

The spiritual director of Port-Royal of the Fields was accustomed to talk first of the past with those who came to him, but this he used merely as a point of departure; he would then raise the discussion to the supernatural plane on which they should base their lives.

Pascal spoke of certain philosophers he had admired only yesterday, and Saci asked him who among those sages had attracted him particularly. When Pascal cited Epictetus and Montaigne, the priest said he knew but little about them and expressed the desire to learn more.

The solitaries gathered around the new guest at Les Granges, all curious to hear the learned man who came from a world they remembered and perhaps still regretted. Thanks to Fontaine, the above-mentioned conversation is recorded; the future author of the *Pensées* explained the opinions of the two philosophers. Epictetus exalted men: through strength of will man should triumph over suffering, rise superior to death, equal the gods. Fifteen centuries later Montaigne opposed Epictetus' ideas with the smiling attitude of the skeptic: he derided those humans whom the Greek, succumbing to "a diabolical pride," had raised to the level of divinities. His *Essais* had ridiculed the intellect of the sage who could be annihilated by a grain of sand. But where did such irony lead? Pascal answered his own question with such force of expression that Fontaine reported that Montaigne "doubts whether he doubts, and since he doubts even this last supposition, his uncertainty constantly revolves about itself in a perpetual circle."

Pascal, "still filled with his subject," could not hide the admiration he felt when he found in the *Essais,* "proud reason so utterly routed by its own weapons." He regretted that the author of the book had not been truly a Christian, for, he said, "with all my heart I should have liked the man who was the instrument of this great revenge."

Saci's tranquil faith was shown in his reply to the violence of the new convert: beyond Montaigne he perceived "the omnipotence of grace which had so profoundly humbled an intellect that had risen to such lofty heights."

In Pascal's wake more new penitents arrived at Port-Royal; a man such as he perforce exerted an influence over other lives.

Roannez came to take a place at his friend's side after giving up his rulership of Poitu and his union to a wealthy heiress, Mademoiselle de Mesme. The duke was much sought after, since at that time he was the only peer of France of marriageable age. The members of his family were furious at seeing him ruin his future in this way; one night a porter at their mansion came with knife in hand to the room ordinarily reserved to Pascal, intending to kill his master's evil genius. Fortunately the future author of the *Pensées* was absent on that particular evening.

The duke's sister, Charlotte de Roannez, won over in her turn, no longer aspired to any life save that of a religious; after hearing the nuns chant with a single voice under the arches of their church, she dreamed of joining them. What the young girl experienced is expressed in one of the letters written to her by Pascal: "We do not leave pleasures save for others that are greater still."

One day, eluding the watchfulness of her family, Mademoiselle de Roannez fled to the convent on the faubourg Saint-Jacques. Her mother came to find her, accompanied by a constable; armed with a letter bearing the royal seal, she demanded in the name of the king that her daughter be turned over to her. After the superiors of Port-Royal had interceded in vain for the postulant, the latter appeared, removed her headdress and showed herself to her mother as she wished always to be—during the night she herself had cut off her hair. Her determination had little effect: with the help of the constable, Mademoiselle de Roannez was forcibly removed from the monastery. Mother Agnès would never forget, she wrote, "the strange cries" of the unfortunate girl as she was being taken away. Charlotte de Roannez was later forced by her parents into a marriage with the duc de Feuillade, and her conjugal life was one continual torment. One of her children was born a cripple; the others died in infancy. As long as she was able, the duchess kept the letters which Pascal wrote to sustain and encourage her. But she was not to know peace even at the hour of death: the dying woman was forced to burn these sheets of paper.

The celebrated jurist Domat, whom Pascal had known in Clermont, where both were born, was also to follow in his footsteps. This advocate to the king had been raised by a Jesuit, his granduncle Father Simond, confessor to Louis XIII, and to this priest he owed the wide culture that enabled him to gain his mastery of legal knowledge. Domat's work, *Les lois civiles dans leur ordre naturel*, published late in the author's life, set forth great legal principles. Natural justice existed in man's mind even before the first laws were formulated. Natural justice ordered the development of laws to express its spirit. The jurist also demonstrated how all legal regulations flow from this natural justice. Rigorously subordinated one to the other, they constitute an edifice of which natural law is both the base and the summit. Laws inspired by a tyrant's will betray their origin and have no place in this edifice founded on equity.

"He who masters this work will be the most solid and reliable of jurists in any country," Daguesseau, one of Domat's disciples, was to say. And Boileau affirmed that the lawyer "had restored reason to jurisprudence."

Domat had reached the limits of legal knowledge at the same time that Pascal had discovered the insufficiency of human reason. For the jurisconsult the Creator had been only a sovereign element of order and equity, for there is a god of lawyers just as there is one of "philosophers and scholars." Pascal had destroyed such idols, and Domat had raised his eyes to the Cross.

In January, 1655, Pascal had lived for a month at Les Granges of Port-Royal, in retreat under Saci's guidance. He was drawn to the peace of the Fields, and was there again in October, 1655. His sister Jacqueline writes that he took part in the work of the Little Schools, and that in teaching young children to read he was to invent a new method: words would no longer be spelled out letter by letter, but syllable by syllable—this would give them sound and sense.

Among the older students was an orphan of sixteen, Jean Racine, who had arrived only recently at Les Granges. Thus Pascal and Racine must have found themselves together, one carrying in himself the present, the other the future of Port-Royal. But their ages separated them by sixteen years, and Pascal made only brief stays at the Fields, so their encounters could have been only intermittent.

In January, 1656, Pascal made still another retreat at Les Granges. At that time Antoine Arnauld had just been condemned by the Sorbonne on the question of *fact* and, inevitably, would be condemned on the question of *right*. It was then that the spiritual master of Port-Royal asked the new-comer to defend before the public a cause which had already been lost before the Faculty of Theology.

"You who are young . . ."

In accepting this task Pascal had no illusions regarding the difficulties it presented to a layman. Arnauld and Nicole turned over to him all documents bearing on the trial: their theses, those of their adversaries, the arguments on both sides, and finally the texts that constituted the subject matter of the theological controversies. After examining this voluminous file the guest of the solitaries asked himself how he could interest the good people in so com-plicated a debate. To gain their support he had first of all to divert them with a lively style and a piquant form. Pascal therefore imagined a provincial, one of his friends from Clermont, who was curious to know what was going on in Paris; he would keep him informed of the debates at the Sorbonne. Although these discussions had been followed closely by the court and had fascinated everyone, no one had understood a word of the Latin harangues. To his let-ters Pascal would give the pleasant and sprightly tone adopted by gentlemen of the world and which Antoine Arnauld, a bourgeois, had never acquired. As soon as he had made a fair copy of what he considered to be merely a draft, the guest of Les Granges read to Arnauld and the solitaries his "First Letter written to a provincial by one of his friends on the subject of the present disputations at the Sorbonne."

In a lively and animated style Pascal explained why Antoine Arnauld had been called "presumptuous, scandalous, and injurious" in regard to the question of *fact*; the theologian had dared claim that, despite a careful read-ing, he had been unable to find in *Augustinus* the five propositions con-demned by Rome. Pascal added that he himself was still unable to find any-one who had discovered them, and thereupon shot his first arrow: "The truth is, the world has become sceptical of late, and will not believe things until it sees them."

But the question of *right* to be solved by the Faculty in the days ahead was much more important. Was Arnauld heretical in saying that the righteous could do nothing without grace, and in giving Saint Peter's denial as an example?

"Yes," Molina's disciples replied.

"No," declared the defenders of grace, who invoked Saint Augustine.

Between the Jesuits and the Jansenists were the Dominicans, who appeared as moderates whom both parties wanted to win over to their side. The sons of Saint Dominic were called Jacobins because their motherhouse—which later would shelter Robespierre's Club—was situated on rue Saint-Jacques. The Dominicans wanted to remain faithful to Saint Thomas, the greatest of their doctors, who had proclaimed the omnipotence of grace; but Chancellor Séguier's presence at the Sorbonne left no room for doubt concerning the persecution that would befall those who sided with Arnauld. The Dominicans therefore admitted a compromise: when Saint Peter had denied Christ he had been wanting in grace. Since he had free will, the apostle had had the power not to deny his master, but, according to the teaching of Saint Thomas, this power was so remote that it had necessarily remained ineffective. Molina's disciples maintained, on the contrary, that every man freely disposes of the grace necessary for his salvation; according to them, this power was therefore *proximate*. But since, in any case, it had not been effective, why did the Dominicans and the doctors not now accord it to Saint Peter?

Antoine Arnauld was going to be condemned for not admitting the *proximate power* which could have permitted the Prince of the Apostles not to have denied Jesus. Knowing that Saint Peter, despite this power, had betrayed his master, the sons of Saint Dominic would remain at peace with the Gospel, with Saint Thomas, with the Jesuits, and with the king. They had, unfortunately, counted without Pascal, who went from one to the other under the pretext of informing his provincial friend. He learned how the heirs of Saint Thomas had come to an agreement with those of Molina in favor of the two words *proximate power* about the meaning of which each held a contrary opinion, but which in order to avoid conflict they were careful not to discuss.

Under Pascal's pen, the dialogue became cutting and cruel.

"You must say that all the righteous have the proximate power, abstracting from it all sense," the Thomists and Molinists declared simultaneously.

But the author of the letter to the provincial did not say that he was satisfied. 'This word 'proximate' that I must pronounce in order to avoid being a heretic, is it in the Scriptures?"

"No."

"Is it a word of the Fathers, the councils, or the popes?"

"No."

"What necessity, then, is there for using it since it has neither authority nor any sense of itself?"

"'You are an opinionated fellow,' they told me. 'You must say it, or you shall be a heretic and Monsieur Arnauld in the bargain; for we are the majority.'"

The majority? The majority which condemned Antoine Arnauld was very small and could turn again in favor of the accused when on the morrow the question of *right* had to be solved. But the Molinists had taken their precautions: this majority had been increased, and would be increased again, if necessary, by the presence of monks of the mendicant orders on whom they could call. These were especially the Franciscans known as Cordeliers; when later the revolution came and made their house a hotbed of rioting, their name would be as famous as that of the rebellious Jacobins.

Becoming theologians for the occasion, the Cordeliers arrived to take their places at the Sorbonne and blindly obeyed the orders of the superiors who sent them. The Molinists in the first "Provincial Letter" made no secret of this.

"If necessary we can bring a sufficient number of Cordeliers into the field to carry the day."

Pascal adds: "I took my leave of them on hearing this solid argument."

The guest of Les Granges believed he was bringing his hosts a project that would have to be revised in its entirety; he was astonished at the chorus of praise which arose when he had concluded his reading.

"This is excellent."

"People will enjoy that."

"It must be published."

Arnauld and Saci were delighted; others among the Messieurs who had lived at court—such as Roannez and Luynes—heard the echo of the impertinent laughter of certain great noblemen: the brief phrases which slay an adversary with ridicule. None of the lawyers or theologians of Port-Royal possessed this quality of irony. Pascal knew how to free himself from the heavy tone of bourgeois infallibility which weighted down the style and thought of the solitaries. He had learned that in the world a witty word sweeps all argument aside.

Losing no time, the Messieurs—and particularly one of them, Saint-Gilles—begged money, discovered clandestine printers, had the "Letter" set in type, and came to get the copies as soon as they were off the press. They were distributed at the house of the marquise de Sablé, at the mansion of the Nevers, at Parlement, at court, and among the booksellers of Paris.

Their success was immense. Intelligent people had finally found someone to guide them through the labyrinth of the Sorbonne; all wanted to lay their hands on the "Little Letter"—soon to be called briefly the "Provincial," just as Arnauld's book had been alluded to as *La Fréquente*. In it, readers discovered the secrets of the learned debates of the Faculty of Theology; each now knew the trickery that had formerly been disguised. Deferential silence gave way to smiles.

When the theologians again assembled to solve the question of *right*, many of the Molinists were anxious and irritated; now the public had unhappily been enlightened and would constitute itself the judge of the judges! Chancellor Séguier thought he would choke with anger, and had to be bled. The fury was powerless, for despite all inquiries made by police and spies, despite a search of printing houses and the imprisonment of several booksellers, the "Little Letters" continued to appear one by one, and were passed elusively from hand to hand.

As all informed persons had foreseen, Arnauld's proposition concerning Saint Peter, "in whom grace was lacking," was condemned as heretical by the Faculty of Theology on January 29, 1656, six days after the publication of the first "Provincial." One hundred and twenty-nine votes were cast against the author of the "Letter to a Duke and Peer." Once more the four mendicant orders—Carmelites, Dominicans, Franciscans, and Augustinians—came to give their support to Arnauld's enemies. Pascal's saying regarding these religious was current throughout Paris: "He votes without speaking, like a monk at the Sorbonne."

Seventy-two doctors left the hall where the meeting was held in protest against the violation of the Faculty rule which allowed only two monks of each of the mendicant orders to be present. These theologians were to pay dearly for their show of independence: they were excluded from the Sorbonne by order of the court.

The victory of the Society of Jesus was proclaimed on the same day that the feast of its founder, Saint Ignatius of Loyola, was celebrated. Arnauld was expelled by the Faculty and had to go into hiding; a search was conducted for him night and day. But, hidden in Paris on the rue de Poirées, directly across the street from the Jesuit college, in an inn having on its signboard the image of King David, Pascal held the sling that launched a new attack against Goliath.

With the second "Provincial" we enter into the heart of the debate. The Dominicans, faithful to the ideas of Saint Thomas, had admitted the existence of the *sufficient grace* granted to all men. However, they declared that, contrary to Molina's thesis, none could be saved who did not receive *efficacious* grace, which was a gratuitous gift from God. If this is the case, Pascal asked, in what consists "this grace that is sufficient without being sufficient?" This sufficient grace had the same purpose as *proximate power*: it permitted the Thomists to reach an understanding with the Jesuits in order to avoid again an explanation of the meaning of words. A Dominican confessed this "with such sadness that I pitied him," wrote Pascal. How far removed it was from the time when the monk's order had defended in Rome that efficacious grace which Saint Thomas had placed in its hands as a sacred trust!

The monk explained that since the pope had not wanted to condemn Molina, the weapons of the Dominicans "still sleep in the Vatican." Thereafter, in order to protect themselves, these religious had "to temper the truth of efficacious grace by the apparent avowal of a sufficient grace."

The "Little Letters" now became more violent, and the Society of Jesus turned and tossed at the stings of the gadfly who continually escaped its clutches. In order to discover the identity of the author of the "Provincials," the court sent its spies among all printers, publishers, and distributors. This deployment of force was in vain; as if invisible, Pascal defied the whole kingdom.

The University of Paris, always rebellious, became his accomplice: numerous copies of the "Little Letters" were hidden at the Collège d'Harcourt—later to become the Lycée Saint-Louis-le-Grand—under the benevolent eye of the procurator.

Although Parlement had been requested to act with severity, it gave proof of open indulgence, and the magistrates protected the unknown writer who dared defy the court and the Jesuits. Its first president, De Bellièves, did not hesitate to remove the seals from a bookshop which had been closed down because it was guilty of concealing a large number of copies of the "Provincials"; this leader of Parlement asked only the favor of obtaining a copy of the seditious texts.

Pascal devoted his third "Letter" to the defense of Arnauld. He had just read, he wrote, the censure of the Faculty of Theology and had "expected to find it condemning the most shocking heresies in the world." Now he discovered that the Fathers of the Church, Saint Augustine and Saint John Chrysostom—whose texts he quoted—had affirmed, like Arnauld, that Saint Peter was a righteous man in whom grace was wanting. Would the theologians of the Faculty now condemn those saints? He was fearful, Pascal wrote, "of placing myself in opposition to the doctors of the Church in order to agree too closely with the doctors of the Sorbonne." The Molinists, moreover, were satisfied to condemn without giving any explanation, since, said the author of the "Provincials," "it is much easier to find monks than reasons."

Furthermore, it was not at all a matter of judging the Fathers of the Church, but only of judging Antoine Arnauld. "It is not the sentiments of Monsieur Arnauld that are heretical. It is only his person. This is a personal heresy. He is not a heretic because of anything he has said or written, but simply because he is Monsieur Arnauld." And Pascal concluded, with the fine scorn that was his forte: "Let us leave them, then, to their own differences. These are the disputes of theologians, not of theology."

Just as the defender of Port-Royal was finishing his letter, he gave in to a desire to taunt the enemies who wanted so much to discover who he was in order to silence him. To the last line, reading, "Your very humble and obedient servant," he added ten letters: EAABPAFDEP. The solitaries would recognize what they meant. "Et Ancien Ami Blaise Pascal, Auvergnat, Fils d'Etienne Pascal" (And Old Friend Blaise Pascal, Auvergnat, Son of Etienne Pascal).

The chevalier de Méré read with relish the first three "Letters" which disposed so ably of the Sorbonne doctors; nevertheless, he advised Pascal not to "fall into theological dissertations."

"Why don't you attack the casuists?" he said. "The Jesuits will find themselves in a very unhappy position: they will have to defend themselves."

Pascal had no need of this Don Juan to know what means he should use; he realized that he should now abandon those pale supernumeraries, the Dominican and Thomist doctors, and fight Port-Royal's real enemies: the Jesuits.

To be sure, the casuists were not all members of the Society of Jesus. Certain of them belonged to the Franciscan or Dominican orders. But in casuistry the Jesuits had found a means of satisfying their penitents. Having studied the thorniest cases of conscience, the theologians of the Society of Jesus set down principles to serve as a guide for confessors, and for the use of the latter they had drawn up books in which the scriptural precepts were brought into line with the requirements of the age of the Sun King. Thus, the Jesuits held up to Christians a well-bred Messiah who knew how to adapt himself to the new times.

Bossuet judged these doctors with severity, and one day was to have the Assembly of Clergy condemn what he called "the ordure of the casuists." The Eagle of Meaux lashed out at the new Gospel that Jesus Christ "would not recognize," and expressed regret that he was not the author of the "Provincials."

Like most of the faithful, Pascal had not known the books of the casuists before Arnauld and Nicole had him read them; when he discovered the new Gospel, so cleverly designed to purchase consciences at bargain rates, he felt a great anger that men of religion were using their spiritual power to betray Christ by placing a barrier between divine love and human beings created only for love, thus condemning them to eternal death. In Pascal's eyes no crime could be compared with this.

Later, when the author of the "Provincials" felt he was at death's door, certain persons asked him if he did not repent of having written those pages —what a weapon for the Jesuits, had Pascal weakened on the eve of appearing before the judgment seat of God! But at that moment the sick man's voice rose, and he said so clearly that none could ever forget: "Far from repenting, if I had to do it again at the present time, I would make them still stronger."

"Why," he was then asked, "did you give the names of the authors of all those propositions you cited?"

And Pascal replied: "If I were in a city where there were twelve wells, and I knew with certainty that one of them had been poisoned, I would be obliged to warn everyone not to draw water from that well; and since some might believe this to be pure imagination on my part, I would be obliged to name the one who had poisoned it rather than expose the whole city to death."

"Why did you use a pleasant, bantering, amusing style?"

"Had I written in dogmatic style only scholars would have read the letters, and they did not need them."

Pascal could not afford to give in to indignation: with people of the world he had to maintain his ironic tone.

The "Letters" present a Jesuit who explains the opinions of the casuists of his own Society. The defender of Port-Royal wanted them to be judged on the basis of their own writings, so that the condemnation would be final. The father whom Pascal places on the scene therefore complacently explains the doctrine of the casuists; it calms anxieties, removes remorse, and absolves the sinner when the latter considers himself accursed. To make his point, the Jesuit brandishes the texts of the doctors of his Society, each time giving the name of the book and its page. He then shows the pleasure of a prestidigitator who has just pulled a rabbit out of a hat and enjoys first the amazement and then the admiration of the penitent so easily delivered of his burden of guilt.

In the presence of this cheery wonderworker, Pascal plays the role of the guileless parishioner whose joy knows no bounds because he had never hoped to find so many easy ways out. All roads are made straight; our vilest and even our most savage instincts can have free rein without our salvation being threatened for an instant.

"There are no people like the Jesuits!" Thus begins the fourth "Provincial Letter." Pascal tells his friend that he went to the house of one of the fathers of the Society for clarification, and the priest showed him the treasury of indulgence contained in "The Summary of Sins" by Père Bauny: no one was guilty before God if he were not fully aware of the evil of his action and did not have the firm will to commit it.

Pascal was entranced. "Why, here is an entirely new redemption according to Père Bauny. . . . I see more people justified by this ignorance and forgetfulness of God than by grace and the sacraments!"

The Jesuit next brings out the work of his colleague Le Moyne: only those sins count which were committed with the intention of refusing God's help.

"Oh, what an excellent device for being happy both in this world and the next!" the penitent exclaims. "I had always thought that the less a man thought of God, the more he sinned; but, from what I see now, if one could only succeed in bringing himself not to think about God at all, everything would be pure with him in the future."

This letter surprised and alarmed the Jesuits. The unknown writer was not content with defending Arnauld: he dared attack the Society, to carry the war into the closed preserve of the casuists.

The Society of Jesus did not feel, however, that the threat was serious; the queen mother, who governed France, was on their side. Under the guidance of the fathers, she was to destroy "the Jansenist sect."

Anne of Austria did not share Mazarin's indifference toward religion. Daughter of the Catholic king of Spain, she liked ostentatious devotions and splendid ceremonies. In religious rites she found reassurance of salvation; it was not at all necessary to seek the hidden God when one had a fine, well-lighted church and a Jesuit. Madame de Sévigné relates that the queen used only one argument against Saint Augustine's doctrine.

"Fie, Fie, upon grace!" she said.

Immediately after Arnauld's condemnation, the regent ordered for the second time that the solitaries be driven out of Port-Royal of the Fields. Since Arnauld d'Andilly, dean of the Messieurs, had kept on good terms with the sovereign, he petitioned her for at least a postponement. Anne of Austria, who always had a weak spot for this unambitious courtier, therefore consented for the solitaries to disperse of their own accord, and voluntarily delayed the arrival of the king's men sent to expel them.

After a stay on his property of Pomponne, Andilly obtained permission to return to his wilderness, but all the other solitaries were forced to scatter for the second time. Their pupils, among them young Racine, were either sent back to their parents or to the homes of friends of Port-Royal: Bernières, Bagnols, Luynes.

Mother Angélique had been sorely distressed by the condemnation of her "little brother," who was now a fugitive. Knowing the threat that hung over her monastery—which was at the mercy of a decision from Rome—the former abbess exclaimed: "We await from the Tiber the waters that will submerge us."

Faithful to Saint Benedict's rule, the nuns were silent. "Our sisters live in sorrow but in silence," said Mother Angélique.

The poor nuns did not permit themselves to ask a single question, and learned of the departure of the solitaries only when someone came to the abbey to leave some furniture that had belonged to the Messieurs.

Many of the nuns died around that time, nine of them during the first months of 1656.

At the time the friends of Port-Royal were being dispersed, spied upon, and threatened, Pascal—still in hiding and even more formidable—again made himself heard.

The fifth "Provincial" continues the struggle against the doctors of the Society of Jesus, and mocks their secret sin—pride. "They are a society of men, or rather of angels, predicted by Isaiah in his words, 'Go forth, ye swift angels!' They have the spirit of eagles; they are a flock of phoenixes. . . . They have changed the face of Christianity."

No doubt they had, but in what way? Pascal sets out to tell us, this time in his own words: "Know, then, that their object is not to corrupt morals; that is not their intention. But also it is not their sole aim to reform them. That would be bad politics."

The Jesuits judged it "necessary for the good of religion that their influence extend everywhere, and that they govern consciences." They therefore made use of the teachings of the Gospels "on those occasions when they are favorable to their ends. But, since these same maxims do not fit in with the purposes of a great number of people, they do not stress them in respect to these particular persons, so as to satisfy everyone."

When they considered it opportune, "they suppress the scandal of the Cross." They had succeeded already in India and China, "where they even permitted Christians to practice idolatry itself, by the subtle device of concealing in their clothing an image of Jesus Christ to which they taught them to refer mentally the public adorations which they rendered the idol."

Pascal did not give the casuists a moment's peace, and his fifth "Letter" brings one of them to the fore. He appears holding in his hand Escobar's *Moral Theology*.

" 'Who is Escobar, father?' I asked him."

" 'What! You do not know Escobar, the member of our Society?' "

We then learn that in the preface to his book this theologian compares his work to the Apocalypse, sealed with seven seals; it is Jesus Christ himself who presents Escobar's book "thus sealed, to the four living creatures." These living creatures have become four illustrious doctors of the Society, surrounded by four-and-twenty Jesuits representing the four-and-twenty ancients of the Apocalypse. After this impressive preface, Escobar offers us examples of "easy devotion"; other casuists, not less celebrated, had completed his work.

Pascal is anxious to know what is the authority of these doctors.

"I always believed it my duty," he says, "to take for a rule only Scripture and the traditions of the Church, and not your theologians."

The Jesuit has only a smile of pity for this naive Christian.

"I see very well," says the good father, "that you know nothing about the doctrine of probable opinions."

The priest explains by quoting the casuists themselves: "An opinion is called probable when it is founded upon reasons of some consideration. Hence it sometimes happens that a single very grave doctor may render a probable opinion."

The casuists "often hold different views, but that does not matter. Each renders his own opinion probable and safe." In this way confessors are more at ease, because in these circumstances they have only to follow "the opinion that suits them best."

Pascal asks if priests are obliged to follow the decisions of the casuists. The Jesuit then quotes a passage from the "famous Reginaldus":

"In questions of morals, the new casuists are to be preferred to the ancient Fathers."

At that point the penitent is frightened, and asks if all these people are Christians.

"'What! Christians?' he answered me. 'Did I not tell you that they are the only ones we use in governing Christianity today?'"

On March 30, 1656, just as the fifth "Provincial" appeared, the civil lieutenant, d'Aubray, was sent to Port-Royal of the Fields to make sure all the solitaries had left the valley.

D'Aubray was the father of the marquise de Brinvilliers, famous for her skill with poisons. In fact, he himself was to die ten years later from a draught administered by his daughter.

The civil lieutenant went to the farm of Les Granges, where he found only a laborer. Hoping to learn in what place the "Provincials" were printed, d'Aubray tried to surprise this peasant by saying to him point-blank: "Where are the presses?"

With convincing innocence the good man led the magistrate to the wine-press used at the time of the grape harvest. The only thing left for the disappointed d'Aubray to do was to gather the insignificant evidence of a wine-grower. The latter had such difficulty in signing his statement that the civil lieutenant said to him, "Do the best you can!"

D'Aubray never knew that the laborer was not only a wine-grower but a priest, a former canon.

The magistrate then repaired to the abbey, where he very courteously interrogated Mother Angélique. As the nun made some reference to the sinister Laubardemont, who had preceded d'Aubray some time before, the latter exclaimed: "Madame, for whom do you take me? I am not the devil of Loudun."

However, all his benevolence did not hide the threat that hung over them. Anne of Austria considered the Jansenists heretics and sedition-mongers who menaced the peace of souls and of the kingdom. She was preparing to withdraw the confessors from the abbey, and to expel the pupils as well as the novices so that, slowly but surely, the community would die out. To justify these measures it was enough to compel the nuns to sign the formulary; in that case they would either repudiate their beliefs or become rebels. "The queen," Mother Angélique wrote, "asked the Assembly of Clergy to push us to the wall. She declared it was her own affair."

However, an incident occurred which removed the danger to Port-Royal at the very moment when it seemed most grave.

On Friday, March 24, 1656, the nuns chanted in their church the words of the Psalm: "Lord, show me a token for good, that they who hate me may see, and be confounded." And in the course of that same afternoon they went to pray before a relic which had been lent to the convent—one of the thorns from the crown of Christ.

After the professed nuns and novices, the little pupils approached the reliquary. One of them, Marguerite Périer, Pascal's niece, had on her face a lacrymal ulcer which had caused caries of the bone. The surgeons saw no remedy for it except "to burn it out," to cauterize it. The pupil's father, Monsieur Périer, could not make up his mind to subject the child to such suffering, but the condition was worsening.

As Marguerite Périer brought her face close to the Holy Thorn, the mistress of novices said: "My daughter, pray for your eye."

Immediately afterward, the little pupil said to one of her companions: "I believe I have been cured."

Everyone came to look, and there was great amazement. "One could not tell," Mother Angélique wrote, "which one of her eyes had been affected."

The current abbess, Mother Marie des Anges, forbade anyone to mention the cure. She had the child examined by the surgeon who had attended her, and his astonishment was so great that he declared: "If there has ever been a miracle, this is one!"

Other surgeons, famous physicians, then came to observe the cure. All of them wrote statements saying that "it surpassed the ordinary powers of nature."

Cardinal de Retz, who had become Archbishop of Paris after his uncle's death, was still a fugitive, but his two vicars went to the abbey. They could only confirm the prodigy.

In that period of solid faith, no one doubted that a miracle had taken place. From every quarter the sick were rushed to the faubourg Saint-Jacques and taken into the monastery church to pray to be healed.

Faithful to the dogmas of the nineteenth century, Sainte-Beuve supposed that sharp contact with the reliquary had opened the abscess and the lachrymal canal was "cleared from obstruction." [1] Pascal was more credulous, for since his conversion he had meditated a great deal on happenings that could not be explained scientifically, and which indicated the action of a mysterious power.

When he was asked: "Where is your God?" he replied: "Miracles reveal him—like the lightning flash."

Pascal himself no longer hoped to see God in this life, but now this flash of lightning had passed over the face of one he loved! In order to keep always before him a reminder of this moment, the author of the "Provincials" secretly had a stamp engraved showing the crown of thorns, surrounded by a halo of clouds and rays of light, with these words: *"Scio cui credidi"* (I know in whom I have believed).

Pascal went further. His gratitude inspired him with the desire to help other men to discover God. He decided to write an "Apology for the Christian Religion," which later was to become the basis of his *Pensées*.

Sainte-Beuve found it surprising that the Jesuits did not dare scoff at a cure which had been obtained by the prayers of a child. But the most important priest of the Society, Father Annat, published a work entitled "The Damper on the Jansenists." According to him, God performed this miracle only for the purpose of inviting the heretics to be converted.

Dated April 10, 1656, the sixth "Provincial" continued the struggle against the casuists.

The Jesuit reappears, armed with various books by the theologians of his Society; he tells us how even murder is permitted when it is an expedient considered necessary by great personages, such as royalty.

The good father stupefies his penitent when he quotes this passage written by a casuist: "By the word *assassins* we understand those who have received money to murder in treachery. Therefore, those who kill without receiving

---

[1] Sainte-Beuve, *Port-Royal* (Paris, 1867), I, iii, p. 179.

any reward therefrom, but merely to oblige their friends, are not called assassins." Many probable opinions supported by grave doctors were brought forward to bear up this thesis.

At that point Pascal gives the Jesuit some advice: "If, on one hand, you are the judges of the confessors, are you not, on the other hand, the confessors of the judges? Oblige them to absolve all those who act on a probable opinion; otherwise it could happen, to the great contempt and scandal of probability, that those you render innocent in theory could be whipped or hanged in practice. Without something of this kind, how will you find disciples?"

Two weeks later, the seventh "Provincial" published the opinion of the casuists on duels—these had been forbidden by royal edict, to the great discomfiture of people of quality who prided themselves on their honor. But now these brave swordbearers could be reassured: the doctors of the Society taught that they might slay an enemy, but always on condition that it be done without the intention of committing sin; it was enough for them "to direct their intention." In fact, a man had the right to shed blood to protect his honor, to reply to an insult, or to avoid damage to his property, be it valued at only one crown. The casuist Hurtado allows a son to desire the death of his father, "and rejoice when it happens, provided that it is only for the sake of the profit he will derive from it, and not from personal aversion."

The learned Jesuit scholar Navarrus permits one who wishes to avoid a duel "to slay in a private way to settle the affair; for by this means he escapes both exposing his life in the combat and from participating in the sin which his enemy would commit by fighting the duel."

Pascal exclaims: "Then indeed, Father, we have a most pious assassination! But is this not a manner of treachery?"

"Did I say to you," the father replies, "that he might kill in treachery? God forbid! I told you he might kill privately."

The casuist Tanner did not neglect churchmen: "Ecclesiastics and even monks are permitted to kill for the purpose of defending not only their lives but their property and that of their community."

Pascal allows himself to plead the cause of those who are dispatched in this way, for these unfortunates know nothing of the direction of intention which justifies the crime in the eyes of the Society of Jesus; the victims feel only the blow dealt them.

"I am not sure," adds the author of the "Provincials," "if one would feel less sorry to see oneself brutally killed by an enraged wretch than to find oneself conscientiously stabbed by a devotee."

Although Mazarin had little love for the Jansenists, he laughed heartily when he read the seventh "Provincial." It did not displease the cardinal to see the noble duelists assailed for the first time as Christians. Young Louis XIV had this "Letter" read to him by his chaplain, and the king's confessor was highly vexed when he heard of it.

At Port-Royal, Mother Angélique protested the terrible irony used by Pascal. "Would not silence," she said, "be finer and more pleasing to God? Eloquence amuses more people than it converts."

Singlin shared her opinion: "One should not mix raillery with holy things."

But Arnauld and the Messieurs did not intend to be deprived of the unexpected help they had received, and the combat was to continue. Pascal drew up his "Letters" with the greatest care, and revised them as many as seven or eight times before turning them over to the printer. He cited new examples of the lax morality permitted by the Jesuits: magistrates were allowed to render decisions contrary to their own judgment, the Society of Jesus having regard "only for the repose of their consciences."

Usury is not a sin if the usurer knows how to direct his intention by thinking only of the gratitude the borrower should show him. The property a woman acquires by committing adultery, or a soldier by committing murder," is legitimately possessed and none are obliged to restore it," because, once acquired, all property should be respected.

The casuists of the Society offered to the guilty their method of mental reservation. "A man may swear," writes Father Sanchez, "that he has not done a thing, though he actually did it, meaning within himself that he did not do it on a certain day or before he was born."

Pascal discovers what the casuists call "pious and holy finesses." "It is easy," writes Father Sanchez, "to have two confessors, one for the mortal sins and another for the venial, in order to maintain a good reputation with one's ordinary confessor."

"Oh, father," Pascal exclaims, "how these maxims will draw people to your confessionals!"

"You could scarcely believe how many come. We are crushed under the crowd of our penitents."

Confessors are even authorized to dispense these penitents from the "troublesome and difficult obligation" of loving God. It is sufficient not to hate him—a favor obtained at the cost of the blood of Jesus Christ.

This time Pascal can no longer contain himself, and blames himself for having "allowed to pass by him all this badinage in which the ingenuity of man plays so insolently with the love of God."

"Father, no patience can stand this any longer! That Christ has shed his blood to dispense us from loving him? But this is the very height of impiety!"

The author of the "Provincials" thinks of him who had raised the dead to life and restored sight to the blind. When would he come to these men of religion who professed to carry his cross? "May he fill their hearts with that love of himself from which they have dared to dispense other men!"

The Jesuits replied from every quarter. Like Singlin, they accused Pascal of "mixing raillery with holy things." This time they were answered by a letter addressed, not to the friend in the provinces, but "to the Reverend Fathers, the Jesuits": "In mocking your morality I have been as far from mocking holy things as the doctrine of your casuists is far from the Gospel."

Pascal recalls the words of David: "The just shall laugh at the wicked," and Tertullian's terrible saying: "What I have done is only a little sport before the real combat begins."

Moreover, did not the Jesuits themselves ridicule what is truly holy? On this subject Pascal quotes an ode by Father Le Moyne entitled, "Eulogy on Bashfulness, showing that all beautiful things are red, or inclined to redden." This Jesuit informs us that "The cherubim—those glorious ones/composed of head and plumes/ fly with splendid faces/ ever red and burning high." The ode ends with a gallant verse in honor of a lady named Delphine who often blushed.

"What do you say of this, father?" asks Pascal.

The Jesuits launched out with new libels against their elusive enemy, calling him "buffoon, imposter, heretic, one possessed by a legion of devils."

Pascal, standing alone, replied to them all. "I doubt," he wrote, "that you are good politicians, for the war is waged in your own camp and at your expense."

However, the Society of Jesus continued to wield all its power at the Vatican and at the Louvre. The Inquisition had recently condemned those of Arnauld's writings which had been published since the censure of the Sorbonne; the Assembly of the Clergy approved the formulary which every bishop must have signed in his diocese.

"It is a strange and tedious war," write Pascal, "when violence strives to suppress the truth."

Madame de Sévigné was at Les Rochers. "I have read with much pleasure," she wrote, "the third 'Letter' of the Jansenists. It seems to me very fine indeed." A Jesuit, Father Nouet, published a defense, quoting such casuists of the Society as Father Vasquez, who had condemned murder. "Your interest," Pascal replied, "lay in having doctors of different minds in order to fill all your purposes. To those who wish to kill you present Lessius; for those who do not, you produce Vasquez."

This high degree of dexterity inspired the author of the "Provincials" with a vision of God's judgment that was worthy of Michelangelo: "At the last day Vasquez will condemn Lessius on this point, as Lessius will condemn

Vasquez on another. And all your authors will rise up in judgment one against another, mutually condemning each other for their frightful outrages against the law of Jesus Christ."

The fourteenth "Provincial" is devoted to the subject of murder. Pascal calls on the Jesuits to choose between the God of love and men of blood. "You must be ranked on one side or the other. There is no middle ground. He who is not with Jesus Christ is against him."

Certain of the fathers now took a conciliatory turn. "Lay down the pen you have taken in your hand," one of them wrote. "After a sincere reconciliation with the Jesuits, turn against heresy, against the impious, and against the licentious."

But heresy and impiety threatened the Church only from without; the teaching of the Molinists corrupted it at its heart. The fifteenth "Provincial" quotes the theses supported by the fathers who reserved to themselves the right to calumniate their enemies. "It is only a venial sin . . . to ruin the credit of those who speak ill of us." In this way it was possible for them to cast out from the bosom of the Church, even at the cost of a lie, whoever dared come into conflict with the Society of Jesus.

Nicole came to Vaumurier, to the château of the duc de Luynes, where Pascal had retired, bringing documents that would enable him to proceed with his task.

It was again a matter of defending Port-Royal, that land of refuge. The Jesuit Father Meynier had published a book to prove that the nuns and their directors were Calvinists. The title, "Port-Royal and Geneva in Collusion against the Blessed Sacrament," revealed the deliberate intention of the Molinists to brand their adversaries as heretics.

According to Father Meynier, the Jansenists attempted "to ruin the mystery of the incarnation, to make the Gospel pass for an apocryphal book, to exterminate the Christian religion and erect deism upon the ruins of Christianity."

This Jesuit affirmed that Arnauld, as well as the priests and nuns of Port-Royal, had refused—as did Calvin—to acknowledge the real presence of Jesus Christ in the eucharist.

This was a highly dangerous accusation at a time when Calvinism appeared to Rome, and to every Catholic, as the very image of Satan. To defend those who were closest to him, Pascal wrote his sixteenth "Letter."

If the nuns of Port-Royal did not believe in the eucharist, "why had they bound themselves to have members of their community at all times, night and day, in the presence of the sacred host?"

Father Meynier's slander turned out to be a real blunder. Pascal easily

proved that the nuns did not limit themselves to respecting the eucharist—
they spent their lives in adoration before it. But the author of the "Little
Letters" was not content to plead: he rose up in accusation against the whole
Society.

"It does not matter that the tables of Jesus Christ are filled with abomina-
tions, provided that your churches are crowded with people. Hence make
sure to set down all those who oppose this as heretics on the Blessed Sacrament. This must be done at any cost."

Between Port-Royal and the Jesuits, who was the enemy of Calvin? Those
who honored the eucharist "by so many holy communions," or those who
dishonored it by "so many sacrilegious communions?" Pascal then describes
"the hardened sinners emerging from their debauchery who surround the
altar": a priest sent there by his confessor despite the obscenities he had
just committed, carrying the crucified Victim "with his polluted hands to
mouths as polluted as his own." And these were the men who judged, who
condemned, who claimed to speak in the name of God! The storm, too long
pent up, finally bursts forth:

> Cruel, cowardly persecutors! Must, then, the most enclosed cloisters
> afford no shelter from your calumnies?
> While these virgins day and night adore Jesus Christ in the Blessed
> Sacrament, you do not cease day and night to publish to the world that
> they do not believe that he is in the eucharist or even at the right hand
> of the Father; and you publicly cut them off from the Church. You
> are calumniating those who have no ears to hear nor mouths to answer
> you.

His pen ceased to move; heart spoke to heart. The nuns could not defend
themselves, but the living Son of God had appeared to answer in their name
—one of the thorns which had pierced his brow had healed the afflicted face
of the child in the church of Port-Royal.

"We hear today that holy and terrible voice which confounds nature
and consoles the Church!"

The Jesuits had refused to bow before this superhuman power, and
Pascal threatens them: "I fear, fathers, that those who stubbornly refuse to
hear him when he speaks as God, will one day be forced to hear him with
terror when he speaks as judge."

Now the man is no longer heard, and God himself speaks "through the
voices of the prophets Isaiah and Ezekiel: 'You have placed your hope in
calumny'; 'Your ruin shall be like that of a high wall that falleth'; 'You have
made the heart of the just to mourn . . . you have flattered and strength-

ened the malice of the wicked. Therefore, I will deliver my people out of your hand.'"

In our day these words might seem harsh indeed, but did Christ himself not go farther?

> Woe to you, scribes and Pharisees . . . because you have shut the kingdom of heaven against men. . . . You go round about the sea and the land to make one proselyte; and when he is made you make him the child of hell.
>
> Woe to you, blind guides, that say, "Whoever shall swear by the temple, it is nothing, but he that shall swear by the gold of the temple, is a debtor."
>
> You pay tithes but you have neglected justice. . . . Whited sepulchres . . . full of dead men's bones.

Across the centuries, Pascal's voice had become the echo of the voice of Christ.

On December 9, 1656, following the publication of the sixteenth "Letter," Louis XIV's confessor, Father Annat, came forward personally to combat the invisible enemy in the name of his Society. His book bore an ironic title: *The Jansenists' Good Faith in Quoting Authors as Found in the "Letters" published by the Secretary of Port-Royal.*

Despite all his efforts, the royal confessor did not succeed in convicting Pascal of falsification; actually, Pascal had read with great care not only the passages he had quoted, but also the preceding and following sentences, so as not to distort their meaning. Voltaire, who in his day often got on very happily with the Jesuits, his former teachers, but who loathed the very shadow of Pascal, claimed that the "Provincials" rested "on a false foundation." Joseph de Maistre was to call them "the lying letters"; Chateaubriand called their author an "ingenuous calumniator." Yet not one of them was able to discover a single lapse on the part of this most exact of minds, or to split the rock of his argument.

As for Father Annat, he considered it sufficient to answer the first fifteen letters by repeating fifteen times that the Jansenists "are heretics." And he went on to say that the secretary of Port-Royal should "write comedies and farces, his mocking spirit being better suited to this purpose."

The king's confessor added that one day people would say: "He is as great an impostor and liar as a Jansenist." Unhappily for the Jesuits, this prediction was realized in the future in the exactly opposite way.

Replying to Father Annat meant attacking the court, Mazarin, the queen mother, and Louis XIV. Pascal did not hesitate. On February 19, 1657, he addressed his seventeenth "Letter" to "Reverend Father Annat, Jesuit."

The author of the "Provincials" declared that he was not the secretary of the Messieurs. "I am not of Port-Royal." This was true. Pascal was never considered one of the solitaries, having gone to the Fields only to make retreats. But he belonged to the New Jerusalem even more than did Mother Angélique, more than Nicole, Saci, and even Arnauld: Pascal was Port-Royal incarnate. The imperious yet gentle Christ of the Gospels who filled the lives of Bérulle and Saint-Cyran now animated the future author of the *Pensées*. The torch had passed from hand to hand; one after another, Christians had risen up to defend superhuman love against the princes of the world.

Father Annat ruled the conscience of the king of France, appointed bishops, meted out abbeys, rewarded some and disgraced others, but the priest was defenseless against the unknown author of the "Little Letters."

"All the influence which you can wield is of no avail in my case. I have nothing to hope from the world, nothing to fear, nothing to desire. . . . You may concoct assaults on priests and doctors, but not against me, who am neither the one nor the other. And thus you have perhaps never had to do with a person so completely out of your reach."

Pascal then put forward his strongest point. Arnauld, a priest and theologian, remained strictly submitted to the Church; a layman, the author of the "Provincials" could not be compelled to obey the hierarchy. Moreover, he could attack and no one would have the power to silence his voice; he said plainly to the king's confessor: "You feel you have been smitten by an invisible hand."

Pascal intended to reply once for all to Father Annat's charge that "they are heretics." The five propositions had been condemned by Rome, and the author of the "Little Letters" accepted this—in fact, he "detested them with all his heart." But were they to be found in Jansenius' book? We were now outside the field of dogma, and were dealing with a fact that could easily be verified. If Jansenius had taught the condemned propositions, he was a heretic and no one could defend him. But had he really done so?

"The pope, as pope, and even as the head of a universal council, may err in particular controversies of fact which depend principally on the information and testimony of men."

Who was the author of this text quoted by Pascal? None other than a Jesuit, one of the most illustrious, Cardinal Bellarmine, and his opinion was that of the whole Church. It would take two centuries and another council to bring about the recognition of papal infallibility extending not only to dogma but to all facts connected with it. In the seventeenth century an ecclesiastic could not be compelled to say that he condemned the five propositions "in the sense of Jansenius" without knowing whether or not they were contained in his book. It was Nicole who first had the idea of distinguishing between *right*—that is to say, dogma—which all must accept when Rome had spoken, and a question of *fact* in regard to which it was enough to observe "a respectful silence."

Pascal adopted this thesis which was to become the Jansenists' main argument. "Few people are disposed to sign a blank confession of faith," he wrote. The theologians of the Society of Jesus would have been quick to take advantage of such a signature. "It would leave you free to interpret the unexplained sense of Jansenius as you see fit." What an unhoped-for occasion, in fact, for the Molinists to destroy, by means of an ingenious syllogism, the "doctrine of Jansenius," that omnipotence of efficacious grace which had so greatly impeded the activity of the Society. "Here we have another case of your *proximate power*," wrote the author of the "Provincials." Sufficient grace—which would suffice at last—would then abound in all Catholics, and *proximate power* would reassure consciences.

For this purpose, the trap into which the Jansenists were to fall had already been laid: the formulary had been produced. Questions of dogma and questions of fact were cleverly intertwined. Pascal thought of the anxiety of the nuns and ecclesiastics whose signatures would be required: knowing that Molina's disciples wanted them to condemn the precepts of the Gospel under the name of Jansenism, these religious and priests would have to endanger their eternal salvation.

"Would it not be, then, a monstrous tyranny to place them in the unhappy dilemma that they must either make themselves culpable in the sight of God by signing this condemnation against their consciences, or be treated as heretics by refusing to sign it?"

And Pascal concludes: "If these signatures are exacted, they will fall into a trap, whether they sign or do not sign."

The whole drama of Port-Royal is contained in these two lines. It was to be played out as its defender had predicted. Inevitably the Society of Jesus would win, but what was a victory of this kind worth? Pascal suddenly retired to a distance and looked down upon this human triumph from the height of the cross: "How well I know you, father, and how sorrowful I am to see that God has abandoned you so far as to allow you such happy success in such an unhappy enterprise. Your good fortune deserves pity and can excite envy only in those who know what good fortune really is."

On February 9, 1657, a decree of the Parlement of Provence, rendered at the request of the procurator general, ordered that the first sixteen "Letters," filled with "calumnies, falsehoods and defamations against the Faculty of the Sorbonne, the Dominicans, and the Jesuits," be delivered to the executioner and burned by him on the pillory of the Place des Prêcheurs in the city of Aix. But the judges did not want to be deprived of the "Little Letters" they so greatly enjoyed and kept in their libraries, so on the day of the execution the hangman had to be content to throw into the flames . . . an almanac!

Nevertheless, Father Annat published a reply to this man whom he still considered as "the secretary of Port-Royal," and this time the king's confessor stated very clearly why, in his opinion, *Augustinus* was heretical.

There were, Father Annat explained, two ways of defending efficacious grace. The Jesuits and Thomists asserted that man remains free to resist grace—these are orthodox. Calvin held, on the contrary, that the righteous are compelled to do good when grace is imposed on them. Jansenius shared this opinion, an opinion that denied man's free will. Therefore, the Jansenists were heretics.

On May 24, 1657, Pascal addressed to Father Annat an eighteenth "Letter," intended to be his last. He was happy that the spiritual head of the Society had finally set forth his position so clearly.

"What a necessity there was for this clarification! What difficulties it removes!"

Freedom? The power to resist grace? Those Father Annat called Jansenists had never doubted either; on the contrary they affirmed, together with the whole Church, that "God transforms the heart of man by infusing a heavenly sweetness into it." Therefore the righteous man, "finding his greatest joy in the God who charms him, is drawn to him infallibly by a motion entirely free, voluntary, and loving, so that it would be a torment and punishment to be separated from him."

Here Pascal did no more than to summarize the ideas of Bérulle, Saint-Cyran, and Arnauld. However, he had never gone so far in expressing his own deepest sentiments; he knew—from his own experience and because he lived it each day—that when Christ comes to dwell in a man's heart, this man desires and loves to be sustained by his presence.

"The free will, which always may resist grace, turns to God with a movement as free as it is infallible, when the same God is pleased to draw it to himself by the sweetness of his efficacious inspirations."

Here Pascal places himself beside Saint Augustine and Saint Thomas. How far was the somber Calvin from any conception of this mystical marriage! The Christian soul surrenders to the Spouse who calls—a perfect union in which freedom is preserved by love.

So finally everything becomes clear. The adversaries are reconciled and found to be in complete agreement. The error for which Molina's successors reproach the Jansenists becomes, in Nicole's words, "an imaginary heresy."

Unfortunately, Father Annat had only to say a few words for Port-Royal to be thrown back into anxiety. Pitilessly he pronounced them: "Recognize that *Augustinus* is heretical!"

To repudiate the book containing an essential part of Saint Augustine's doctrine would have been to deny grace purchased at the price of the divine blood.

"Jansenius," Father Annat stated, "has distorted the saint's thought. He has denied free will and maintained that man cannot offer resistance to grace."

Had this been so, Pascal would have abandoned *Augustinus*, but he did not believe he had the right to do so because he himself had read what Jansenius wrote: "We always have power to resist grace. Free will may always act or not act, will or not will, consent or not consent, do good or do evil" (vol. III, book VIII, chapter xx).

This time the decisive words of the Bishop of Ypres are set before us— indisputable.

Moreover, why should anyone pronounce the name of Jansenius if his name was the cause of all the discord? Pascal would consent very willingly to its being banned if it meant that Christ's children could finally live in the joyous union of the Gospel. But the author of the "Provincials" was not so naive as to abandon himself for one moment to such a dream.

"Father," he writes, "you consider it of no consequence to condemn errors unless you condemn the individuals to whom you impute them."

The Society of Jesus replied by invoking the authority of Rome. The pope had spoken: he had said that the five propositions were to be found in *Augustinus* in the heretical sense.

Then sadly Pascal was forced to proceed with the discussion: "What had you to do about this except to cite the page where you had actually found the words?"

No one was able to reply; the pope had therefore been mistaken about the question of fact, or, more exactly, he had been deceived by the Jesuits.

Several times earlier the Holy See had committed similar errors. Father Grassi, a Jesuit, had persuaded Urban VIII, in 1616, to impose on Galileo a condemnation which remained a blot on the memory of the papacy.

"It was in vain that you obtained against Galileo a decree from Rome condemning his opinion regarding the motion of the earth. It will never be proved by this that the earth remains stationary. All men put together will not prevent it from revolving, nor themselves from revolving with it."

By means of an excommunication, Pope Zacharias had annihilated belief in a New World situated at the antipodes. Nevertheless the King of Spain had done well "to give more credence to Christopher Columbus who came from the place than to the judgment of the pope who had never been there."

As the son rails at the father, his irony becomes painful. But whose fault was it?

"It would render the pope's authority contemptible to refuse the name of Catholic to those who do not believe that certain words were in a certain book where they were not to be found, for the reason that a pope has mistakenly declared that they are."

Even admitting that Jansenius was the author of the condemned propositions, "would they be more severely censured because they said that Jansenius maintained them? . . . What interest has the state, or the pope, or bishops, or doctors, or the whole Church?"

The arrow then shot home: "It does not affect them in any way, father, and it is only your Society which would really derive some pleasure from the defamation of an author who has done you some injury."

Before closing his letter, Pascal's mind went to the people of Port-Royal who kept silence while he became angry: Singlin, Saci, Mother Angélique, Mother Agnès, and so many others who waited humbly for God's will to be done. "I see them religiously bent on silence to an extent that is, I fear, excessive. As for myself, father, I do not believe that I can maintain this silence."

Even so, the author of the "Provincials" proceeded to express his greatest hope: "Leave the Church in peace, and with all my heart I shall leave you as you are."

Anne of Austria had been greatly moved when, at Compiègne with the court, she learned of the miracle of the Holy Thorn.

Racine, in his *Abridged History of Port-Royal,* tells us of the conduct of the queen mother at that time:

> It was difficult for her to believe that God had so particularly favored a house which for a long time had been represented to her as infected with heresy. She placed no confidence either in letters written her on the subject by pious individuals or in public rumor, or even in the affidavits of the Paris physicians. She sent Monsieur Félix, chief royal surgeon, to the place of the miracle, charging him to bring back to her a faithful account of all he could learn at first hand. Monsieur Félix carried out his commission with the greatest exactitude. He interrogated the nuns and surgeons, had their reports on the onset, progress, and end of the ailment, examined the pupil carefully, and finally declared

that neither nature nor the remedies used had played any part in the cure, and that it could only be the work of God.

As soon as she was convinced that a real miracle had taken place, Anne of Austria, as a good Catholic, ceased to persecute Port-Royal. Not merely was it no longer a question of sending away the novices and nuns who were there, but the religious were authorized to receive as many more as they wished.

During the year 1657, the solitaries recovered the farm of Les Granges. Singlin was appointed superior of the two houses, that of Paris and that of the Fields. Mazarin ruled France, but he was not anxious to oppose the wishes of the queen mother.

Port-Royal had been saved by a child. This occurred none to soon, for the dreaded signature of the formulary was about to be imposed on the nuns. Already Pascal had begun a nineteenth "Letter," addressed to Father Annat: "Be consoled, father; those you hate are in distress."

The Jesuits could be reassured; this "Letter" and a twentieth which was to follow never appeared. Pascal abandoned a campaign that had lasted for fourteen months, from January 23, 1656, to March 24, 1657.

The author of the "Provincials" would never have fled from a fight which he considered sacred, and which would continue so long as the world lasts. But he did not want the writings which Father Annat attributed to the "secretary of Port-Royal" to constitute a danger for the nuns, those silent victims who had been granted peace because of the miracle of the Holy Thorn.

Pascal's desire had been to explain to honest men the way in which the casuists betrayed the Gospel, and he had fully succeeded. "Could anyone have adopted a more perfect style, or finer and more delicate raillery?" wrote Madame de Sévigné. Later, James II of England, living in exile at the château of Saint-Germain, took great delight, along with members of his court, in reading the "Little Letters."

Father Pirot, a Jesuit and professor of theology at the College of Clermont, replied to Pascal in December, 1657, with "An Apology for the Casuists." The author of the "Provincials," he said, "used his natural powers as an ape to mimic the manners of a Jesuit priest, so that by such buffoonery he might amuse simple souls and make the feeble-minded laugh."

Not confining himself to insults of this kind, which he considered to be on the lighter side, the theologian recalled how the Jesuits had interpreted in their own way the words of God to Noah: "At the hand of every man . . . will I require a reckoning of the life of man."

On this subject, Father Pirot wrote: "We believe we have reason to except from this precept those who kill to protect their honor, their reputation, and their property." After this, those individuals who had not read the casuists and who wondered if Pascal had accurately quoted the texts could no longer harbor the least doubt in the matter.

Several members of the Society of Jesus attempted to prevent publication of the unfortunate "Apology," but it was authorized at Rome by the general of the order.

The parish priests of Paris closely examined the passages of the casuists which were quoted in the "Provincials"; they found them correct word for word, and even discovered others more scandalous, sometimes obscene, which Pascal had had the decency not to cite. Therefore, they were greatly disturbed when they read Father Pirot's "Apology" in defense of these doctrines. Assembling in synod, these priests decided that a petition should be made to the Church and to Parlement to condemn such a book, and they asked Arnauld, Nicole, and Pascal to draw up a letter in support of their request. Arnauld would have liked this letter to be written in Latin, so that it would reach only theologians and not cause a violent backlash of public opinion, but his counsel did not prevail.

The first "Paper of the Priests of Paris against the Apology of Father Pirot" was published in French in January, 1658, and was written largely by Pascal. Nine similar letters followed up to October, 1659; the second and fifth were completely drawn up by the author of the "Provincials." In them, the Molinists were called to account with biblical violence: "God's anger threatens us on one side, and the audacity of these men on the other." The cry of Jesus' disciples when they were in danger of drowning in the waters of Lake Tiberias was heard: "Save us, for we perish!"

But were not the Jesuits themselves God's children? Pascal was torn between anger and charity, as the fifth "Paper" testifies. "They are our brothers; they are in the unity of the Church; they are members of our body."

The author of the "Provincials" had never given up hope completely. Certain Jesuits had expressed their disapproval of Pirot's "Apology," and Pascal foresaw a time when the whole Society would condemn the book. But this mirage faded; the Society declared that it could not take sides either for or against the "Apology." In the sixth "Paper of the Priests of Paris," Pascal did not hide his disappointment: "What, fathers, the whole Church is in an uproar! The Gospel is on one side and the 'Apology for the Casuists' on the other. The Jesuits, urged to make a choice, declare that they cannot take sides in this war. Criminal neutrality!"

Pascal's voice was heard from province to province. Now the priests of Paris were joined by the parish priests of Rouen, Nevers, Amiens, Lisieux, and Evreux. All requested their bishops to condemn the casuists of the Society of Jesus. They were heard, and in many a diocese episcopal pronouncements censored "the audacity of these men." Up to the day of his death, the Bishop of Cahors cursed the Jesuits as "the scourge and ruin of the Church." Rome finally pronounced against them. On August 21, 1659, the Holy Office forbade the printing and sale of the "Apology for the Casuists." Later, in 1679, Pope Innocent condemned sixty-five of the propositions which had scandalized Pascal.

Would the Church allow the "Provincials" to be freely circulated? They were published in 1657 under the name of Louis de Montalte; perhaps, with this pseudonym, Pascal was thinking of his native city, Clermont, built on a "high mountain." In any case, his choice of pseudonym maliciously furnished a new enigma for the king's men, who were still looking in vain for the author of the "Little Letters."

What should he do now? Separate himself from Rome as Luther had done? Never in the world! The body of the Church could not exist without its head. "Were I to separate myself from her," Pascal wrote, "I should be lost forever." Christians ought to surround, to besiege Saint Peter's successor, until the truth would be proclaimed.

"We must cry out all the louder the more unjustly we are censured and the more that violence is used to stifle our words."

How long?

"Until there comes a pope who listens. . . . Thus good popes will still find the Church in turmoil."

But the evil was there, lying in wait for Pascal, threatening even his innermost thoughts. "Let truth not perish in my hands, and let no falsehood. . . ." When the fragment of paper on which this was written was later found, it was possible to read this unfinished sentence—how fragile the truth that depended on the breath of so fragile a man!

The Jesuits lost no time in resuming the battle, convinced that they acted for the greater glory of God. "Never is evil more fully and gaily accomplished than when it it is accomplished for conscience's sake," wrote Pascal. And Racine was to add in his Abridged History of Port-Royal: "It is the vice of people in a community to believe they can do no harm when they defend the honor of their corps. This honor is a kind of fetish to which they believe they are allowed to sacrifice everything—justice, reason, truth."

In 1658, the "Provincials" were published in Latin at Cologne, thus reaching a vast public of intellectuals and theologians beyond the French frontier. The translator was Nicole, who, under the Flemish pseudonym Wendrock, also wrote the commentary on the letters.

Knowing that he could not obtain from the Paris Parlement the condemnation of a work that had already met with such success, Louis XIV had it examined by carefully chosen prelates and theologians. The latter declared that the book "deserved the penalties provided by the laws concerning defamatory and heretical libels." Monseigneur de Péréfixe, Bishop of Rodez and future Archbishop of Paris, was one of the first to sign the results of this consultation. The Council of State—at that time the king's own council—expressed the sovereign's will: the Latin book was to be burned by the executioner in Paris as the French text had been in Aix-en-Provence.

Peace had not been restored to the Monastery of Port-Royal. The miracle of the Holy Thorn had brought only a temporary truce.

On March 2, 1657—shortly before the publication of the last of the "Little Letters"—the papal nuncio delivered to Louis XIV a bull of Alexander VII which admitted of no equivocation. The five propositions, the sovereign pontiff declared, were contained in *Augustinus* and, in the form in which Jansenius explained them, were to be condemned.

Shortly afterward, the Assembly of the Clergy took formal note of the papal decision and added it to the formulary, asking the king to compel all ecclesiastics to sign. But the magistrates of the Paris Parlement, who admired the Jansenists, refused to register the bull. To force them to do so Louis XIV, at that time nineteen years old, had to go in person to the law courts and pronounce judgment. Mazarin, who still governed France in the name of the young king, could see his past anxieties returning: had not The Fronde begun under similar circumstances? Since Anne of Austria had made her peace with Port-Royal, she could scarcely be counted on to stand against Parlement if it were to revolt again. When Father Annat returned to see the prime minister, he found himself in the presence of a man whose patience was at an end.

"Your Society," Mazarin declared, "gives me more worries than all the rest of the kingdom put together; His Majesty has already done more for you than he should."

The Jesuit understood it would be better to retire into the shadows. Furthermore, his Society had lost some of its prestige since the publication of the "Provincials." In his book, Father Pirot admitted that the Jesuits had suffered greatly "from the poisoned sweets of a cruel prankster." After the unfortunate publication of the "Apology for the Casuists," it was wise to lie low; the storm was brewing not only in Parlement, but among the clergy. The Society, therefore, gave up the struggle for the time being.

At the end of three years, however, the Jesuits gained a fresh victory. In March, 1660, the civil lieutenant received an order to disperse the pupils of the Little Schools for the third time. This measure was final, and never again would the teaching of the Messieurs cause anxiety to the Society of Jesus.

But this was only the beginning. The young sovereign for whom the nuns of Port-Royal had offered so many prayers now entered on the scene. At the end of 1660 Mazarin's health was failing, and his death was not far off. On December 13th, seated beside the cardinal's bed, Louis XIV received the leading members of the Assembly of the Clergy, and the king—who was now twenty-two—made known his will. "Exterminate Jansenism entirely," he said. "It is necessary for three reasons: the first, my conscience; the second, my honor; the third, the welfare of the state."

Coming from so high a source, these words put an end to any hope. The solitaries and the nuns could no longer count on the amiable skepticism of an Italian adventurer or on the devotion of a queen disarmed by a miracle.

Mazarin had no thought of contradicting the king who had suddenly become his master. The prime minister spoke up from his invalid's bed, but merely to give loud approval to what had just been said. Several moments later, however, he confessed to the great Condé that Louis XIV's speech had not been inspired by himself nor by the queen mother. He admired, he added with veiled irony, "His Majesty's ability in a matter that is purely ecclesiastical."

The history of the young king who was to decide the fate of Port-Royal is illuminating. For more than twenty years of marriage Louis XIII and Anne of Austria had remained childless; then, however, a downpour of rain forced the king to take shelter in the Louvre, where he and his wife shared the delights of an ardor that was to prove fruitful. When nine months later, on September 5, 1638, the future Louis XIV was born, all France was transported with joy. Cannons were fired, fifes resounded, and the people prayed in thanksgiving to God for this unexpected blessing—in fact, during all of the dauphin's childhood the good people referred to him as Dieudonné (gift of God).

At the time of the child's birth, Louis XIII renewed a vow he had made a year earlier: to place his kingdom under the protection of the Virgin. Anne of Austria made another vow, and when her son was seven she laid the cornerstone of the Church of Val-de-Grâce, dedicated to the "Infant Jesus and the Virgin Mother." Such was the enthusiasm of the nation that the juxtaposition of the royal family with the Holy Family did not seem exaggerated, and only certain Protestants were concerned enough to make jokes about it—for which Dieudonné would make them pay dearly one day.

The dauphin's childhood was dour. Having lost his father at the age of four, he saw Anne of Austria madly enamored of the handsome Mazarin.

The child's life was uncomfortable and anxiety-ridden beside this strange couple—a Spanish queen and an Italian prince of the Church. France was suffering the harsh consequences of Richelieu's warlike policies, and had scarcely avoided total occupation by foreign troops. The soldiers of the king of Spain occupied Corbie in Picardy, and their advance forces had crossed the Somme and reached Pontoise, but had been beaten back at Rocroi by the duc d'Enghien.

France would then have been at peace, had not the Paris Parlement instigated The Fronde. The queen and Mazarin lived through days of revolution during which the famous coadjutor, Paul de Gondi, the future Cardinal de Retz, abetted by the magistrates, became master of the capital. The arrival of Condé's victorious troops enabled the queen, young Louis XIV, and Mazarin to escape from Paris.

After an effort to subjugate the royalty he had just rescued, Condé in his turn was arrested at the order of Anne of Austria. This was the beginning of The Fronde of the Princes, the last effort of the nobility to restore feudalism. For four years the adolescent Louis XIV led a precarious existence, going from town to town, homeless, sometimes lacking food and clothing. He had to win back his kingdom; the rivalry of the princes who were unable to come to an agreement was the salvation of his monarchy. Louis XIV was acclaimed by the provinces and then by Paris, for the majority of men of good will united in his name to bring the civil war to a close.

Mazarin, who had been forced to go into exile in Germany, then returned to the side of Anne of Austria. Their mutual dream was realized when he signed the peace of the Pyrenees which, completing the treaties of Westphalia, ended the struggle against the Hapsburgs. The kingdom was thereafter to enjoy years of prosperity on the frontiers and throughout the provinces. Louis XIV lived in the shadow of the cardinal-minister who was now all-powerful. But the young king listened and learned. When authorized, he took his place in the council, "reasoning alone on all events," he later said, and opposing his opinion to that of the ablest statesmen. Mazarin taught him "to consider the nobility as lower than the grass," and "to keep absolute secrecy concerning state affairs."

By the time the cardinal lay dying, the king was ready to rule France. Anne of Austria had instilled in him the pride that Louis XIII lacked: the young sovereign was told that he was "a visible divinity"; his penmanship master frequently made him copy the famous phrase: "Homage is due to kings; they do as they please." Having determined never to show any of his father's weaknesses, Louis XIV for the rest of his life was to exercise what he called a "profession that is great, noble, and enjoyable." He fulfilled his duties with the assurance of a man who had learned in advance that he was superior to everyone. "It seemed to me that I was king and was born to it," he wrote. This monarch who had removed the spectre of civil war from France had become the living symbol of national prosperity; thereafter his power was absolute.

We know how he was preparing to use this power in regard to Port-Royal. Could it have been otherwise? The Jansenists had been so imprudent as to place themselves under the patronage of Cardinal de Retz, the organizer of The Fronde, and had gone so far as to offer him subsidies. Other rebels had gathered around the monastery, among them the duchesse de Longueville and Monsieur de Sévigné, whose nephew was married to the celebrated marquise. Finally, while the Jesuits proclaimed the king's absolute sovereignty, the solitaries adored God alone, and placed every human being redeemed by the cross on the same level—hence in Louis XIV's eyes they were "a seditious sect."

The king was quite willing for the revolution that had almost swept him from his throne to be called The Fronde, or sling-shot, after a children's toy. But woe to anyone who reminded him of this past history! The former rebels who assembled around Port-Royal showed their hostility by contrasting the purity of the nuns with the corruption of the court. Reared by the devout Anne of Austria, Louis XIV felt toward religion neither Richelieu's haughty lack of deference nor Mazarin's skepticism; he recited his prayers, told his beads, assisted at the offices, listened to sermons, and went regularly to confession and communion. When his mother saw that he was involved in a scandalous affair with Louise de Vallière, she remonstrated with him. The heavy young man with the sensual lips replied "with tears of sorrow that his passions were stronger than his reason, and were so violent that he could not resist them, and did not even desire to do so."

Louis XIV went from mistress to mistress, still in fear of the hereafter and bowing his head when certain preachers fulminated from the pulpit. His religion consisted in what Angélique Arnauld had long before called "a horrible and servile fear of hell." The abbey in which the Gospel was followed in its purity was a constant irritant to the king.

Mazarin died on March 8, 1661, and the king immediately announced that thenceforth he would be his own prime minister. A month after the cardinal's decease D'Aubray, the civil lieutenant, arrived at the faubourg Saint-Jacques and announced to Mother Agnès, who was again abbess, the orders of the king: the Paris monastery and the one of the Fields must receive no more novices nor pupils, and any pupils already in either place must leave immediately.

This decision deeply distressed the nuns, and some of them believed the day of their execution had arrived.

"Mother," one of them said to the abbess, "when the executioner comes to lead us to martyrdom, should we not wear our big veils?"

When relatives came to take the pupils away, the children threw themselves at the feet of the religious, weeping and begging them to obtain permission for them to remain.

"Sister," said one of them, "you know I will be lost if I return to the world."

Exhausted and near death, Mother Angélique had to leave the house of the Fields to help her sister restore courage to the nuns of the Paris monastery.

She found them in tears. "What!" she exclaimed, "I find you crying here! Have you no faith, my children? Men are moving about? Ah, well, they are flies. Are you afraid of them? You hope in God and yet you are afraid?"

The former abbess had to lead to the grill one of the pupils, Mademoiselle de Luynes, whose grandmother, the famous duchesse de Chevreuse, had come to take her home.

The duchess told Angélique Arnauld how surprised she was to find her so calm and firm.

"Madame," the nun replied, "when there is no longer a God, I will lose courage. But until then I place my hope in him."

Then, after embracing Mademoiselle de Luynes, she tried to instill in her some of her own hope. "My daughter," she said, "we will meet again elsewhere, in a place where men no longer will have the power to separate us."

As the novices had not yet been expelled, eight of the pupils received permission to join them. Learning of this, Louis XIV ordered the white veil to be taken away from them, and the girls to be sent back to their families. The abbess, Mother Agnès, then wrote to the sovereign, begging him not to annihilate a monastery "established for the purpose of giving servants to Jesus Christ down through the ages."

Louis XIV knew that he had read "the most beautiful letter in the world," yet he repeated his order. Mother Agnès had to inform the new novices of this: although forced to leave the convent, they went away clothed in their veils and habits, and swore never to wear anything else.

At this time Angélique and Agnès Arnauld suffered another great blow: their superior, Singlin, was forced to go into hiding to avoid arrest, and was succeeded by Father Le Bail, a declared enemy of the Jansenists.

The nuns were separated from everyone who could have encouraged them in their resistance. In August, 1661, the civil lieutenant and the royal procurator visited all the houses constructed in the vicinity of the Paris monastery by the friends of Port-Royal; on the order of the king, all doors and windows opening on the monastery were walled up. Madame de Sablé was no longer able to observe the services from her home.

The new superior, Le Bail, intended to combat the evil doctrines that "infected" Port-Royal.

"The devils of hell," he said to the nuns, "rage particularly against the spouses of Christ; Satan considers them his most delicious food and favorite meat."

The superior added that in Spain and Italy heretical religious were dressed as devils and burned at the stake. Then this medieval priest proceeded to question the nuns one by one, in order to find out by what means Satan had seduced them.

The eldest daughter of Arnauld d'Andilly, Sister Angélique de Saint Jean, expressed her surprise. The religious did not know, she said, that such a grave suspicion hung over them. "A clap of thunder right over my head at the moment I least expected it could not surprise me more."

"Why do you say that?" Le Bail asked.

"Well, Monsieur, what could be more surprising to nuns who live here in deep peace and forgetfulness of the world in general? People come and talk to them of anathemas, and tell them they are on the brink of, or have already fallen into, the precipice of heresy. Who would not be frightened?"

Realizing that he had gone too far, Le Bail tried to soften the effect of his words: "It is sometimes better to surprise people at the start so as to awaken them."

The superior took it upon herself to make this stern reply: "Monsieur, remedies which have no other effect than to awaken are often very dangerous."

Le Bail put this question to Jacqueline Pascal: "If Jesus Christ died for all men, how does it happen that so many are lost forever?"

Should she allow him to understand that Christ's blood had been shed only for the predestined, the nun would affirm her belief in one of the five condemned propositions. Pascal's sister avoided the trap with all innocence, and with a frankness that showed how human she still was.

"I confess to you, Monsieur, that this often troubles me. But when such thoughts come to me, I reject them because I do not believe I should probe the secrets of God. That is why I content myself with praying for sinners."

Each day, despite his prejudices, Port-Royal's adversary found himself a little further disarmed. Monsieur de Contes, the vicar-general, had said to him: "There is not one of those nuns whose joy is not written on her face."

Father Le Bail had now seen this joy, and when he had finished his inspection of the Paris monastery, and the one of the Fields, the priest loyally admitted that he had uncovered "nothing contrary to orthodox faith and the doctrine of the Catholic Church." On the contrary, he stated, he had found "great simplicity and no curiosity regarding controversial questions; they were not discussed by the religious, their superiors having taken care to forbid it."

The bishops now had to require that the formulary be signed. This was ordered by a decree of the Council of State dated April 13, 1661, which gave legal force to the propositions of the Assembly of the Clergy.[1]

In the absence of Cardinal de Retz, Monsieur de Contes, the vicar-general who was favorable to Port-Royal, reached an agreement with the Messieurs to draw up the order imposing the signature. The text allowed it to be understood that the ecclesiastics who signed could in conscience make reservations on the point of knowing whether the five condemned propositions were actually to be found in *Augustinus;* in this way, they would avoid associating themselves with the condemnation of Jansenius and of efficacious grace. This adroitly worded mandate seemed strangely subtle to the nuns because the reservations, as one Jansenist said, "were included in slightly veiled terms, and some attention was needed to recognize them." Reassured by this text, every word of which, it was whispered, had been weighed by Pascal himself, the religious of the monastery of Port-Royal resigned themselves to signing the formulary. Even so, they felt great anxiety, because even if the mandate was obscure the formulary was very clear. Consequently, the nuns had their signatures preceded by several lines saying that they confessed their inability to understand the theological decisions they were asked to approve.

"Our directors," Mother Angélique had written shortly before, "took particular care never to discuss with us the contested matters which are far beyond our sex and our profession. For this reason alone, we were never told to read these books, not even the one on 'Frequent Communion.' "

Now the nuns must declare before God that they "condemned" the doctrine in the five propositions of Cornelius Jansenius contained in his book entitled *Augustinus.* These religious, who had never read, nor even seen, this book, were being compelled to affirm that the doctrine it contained "was in no way that of Saint Augustine which Jansenius had ill-interpreted, and was contrary to the true meaning of the Doctor."

A vain effort was being made to transform the poor women into theologians. All they knew was that Monsieur de Saint-Cyran had told them of God's love and that Monsieur Arnauld had fought in defense of grace. Now they were being required to renounce their beliefs.

---

[1] See Documents for text of the formulary (p. 315).

At Port-Royal of the Fields one of the nuns in particular, Pascal's sister, who was sub-prioress and mistress of novices, was filled with anguish. At the moment she was about to sign the formulary after reading the reservations obtained by the Messieurs, Jacqueline Pascal's mind revolted at what seemed to her a kind of trickery.

The nun wrote to the sub-prioress of the Paris monastery, Angélique de Saint Jean, to tell of her anxiety. She would have desired "the mandate to be worse, because in that case one could reject it in complete freedom. . . . Certain persons would embrace it through sheer cowardice and as a means of placing their persons and consciences in safety. But I am persuaded that neither one nor the other will be made secure by this means. We are really delivered by truth alone."

The nun thought that one must have "the courage to expose oneself to suffering." Before God, the clever are condemned; therefore "either renounce the Gospel or follow the maxims of the Gospel."

But would not the rebels be cast out of the Church? Jacqueline answered: "No one can be cut off despite himself." United with Christ, "we can be deprived of the marks but never of the effects of this union." The mistress of novices did not want to rebel against the Church, yet she could not consent to a lie. Certainly she admired the skill of those who had drawn up the mandate; only it was with God that one was dealing. Those who knew the truth were not permitted "to use dissimulation and evasion." Pascal's sister feared that the wisdom of clever men who disguised their thoughts did not come "from the Father of lights," but was "only the revelation of flesh and blood."

For a moment the nun was astonished at her own audacity. Did a young religious have the right to enter the discussion and look toward a time when it might become necessary to hold her own against prelates of the Church? But immediately there came to her mind the words of Saint Bernard, founder of her order. Every Christian, he said, not only might but should cry out with all his strength when his pastors were asleep and the entire flock in danger of being devoured by wolves.

Then Jacqueline found words similar to those that gave such impressiveness to the writings of Pascal. "I know it is not the place of nuns to defend the truth," but "since the bishops have the courage of nuns, nuns must have the courage of bishops." Suddenly her voice took on a tone of humility; if a nun is too insignificant to have the right to defend Christ's teaching, she still has the duty "to die for the truth."

Jacqueline Pascal could not seek shelter behind an admission of weakness. "Now is the time to remember that the timid are placed on the same level as perjurers," she said.

Her cry of anguish found no echo. The great Arnauld himself abandoned a resistance which could only lead Port-Royal to its ruin. He beseeched the nuns to sign the formulary; their scruples should be removed by the mandate, which had been obtained with great difficulty. Mother Agnès, the abbess, and after her all the professed nuns, had signed. What would Jacqueline Pascal, isolated as she was in the Abbey of the Fields, accomplish alone? She obeyed in turn, but she saw her end approaching. "I speak," she wrote to Angélique de Saint Jean, "in the throes of a sorrow to which I feel I must succumb."

Four months had not elapsed from the day her letter was sent when the nun died, broken-hearted, at the age of thirty-six years.

As could have been foreseen, the martyrdom suffered by Pascal's sister was in vain. The court made known that it considered as an offense the authorization given by the vicars-general to make reservations in submitting to a decision of the Holy See. A decree of the Council of State declared the mandate null and void; as for the pope, he declared in a brief that the interpretation given to his thought by the authors of the mandate was mendacious. Terrified, the vicars-general replaced their text by an order requiring signature pure and simple of the formulary, without any restriction or reservation.

One day Pascal was to write: "The false justice of Pilate only served to make Jesus Christ suffer, for he had him scourged and then slain. It would have been better to kill him outright." Like Pilate, the vicars-general prolonged the torment of the nuns they claimed to protect but did not save. The resistance of these poor women who were asked to give up their only sustaining hope became so strong that Arnauld and Nicole feared they would revolt. Therefore they advised them to place a "preamble" above their signatures:

"Considering that we are ignorant of all the things which are beyond our profession and our sex . . . we sincerely and wholeheartedly subscribe to the decision of His Holiness."

Pascal protested against what he felt compelled to call "this Jesuitry." The letter written by his sister Jacqueline had been sent to Angélique de Saint Jean, but was really intended for Antoine Arnauld, and it had been turned over to the latter; the lines she had written were, therefore, read by the defenders of Port-Royal. Pascal, who had taken part in "the pious finesses" concocted by the Jansenist advisers, was undoubtedly touched to the core when he learned his sister's opinion of these "dissimulations and evasions." A thought he had expressed long ago at the time of his father's death then took on its full meaning: "One of the most solid and useful charities we can show the dead is to do what they would have done were they still on earth."

Jacqueline now spoke through the voice of her brother, and never had she been more alive. She who had opened the gate of the Gospel to Pascal again guided him with all the inflexibility of love. No, there should be no compromise whatever when a wholehearted condemnation was made before the eyes of God. The daughters of Port-Royal did not have the right to plead ignorance when approving a text that rejected Saint Augustine, belied Saint Paul, and denied grace. To advise the nuns to make such an abjuration was again to inflict on the purest of souls the moral torture that had killed Jacqueline. Pascal would have no part in this crime against consciences, and never again would he play the rôle of Pilate.

At a gathering of the Port-Royal theologians and solitaries in his room, the author of the "Provincials" declared that the attitude they had taken was "so timorous that they did not appear worthy of the true defenders of the Church."

"But one can quite well bend a little," Antoine Arnauld said.

Many of the Messieurs wanted to abandon Jansenius who, after all, was only a biographer of Saint Augustine. This opinion was expressed in a memorandum drawn up by Monsieur de Barcos, the nephew of Saint-Cyran. Pascal brushed this aside, and even rejected the distinction between *fact* and *right* so dear to Nicole and Arnauld.

"There is no difference at all," he said, "between condemning Jansenius' doctrine on the five propositions and condemning efficacious grace." Those who entrenched themselves behind a "respectful silence," in order not to attribute the condemned propositions to the Bishop of Ypres, were taking "a middle way which is abominable in the sight of God, contemptible in the sight of men, and entirely useless for the persons it already has been decided to eliminate" The propositions should be defended at no matter what cost, in the way Saint Augustine had intended them.

Pascal's fight was as unsuccessful as had been his sister's. "If the nuns refuse to sign," replied the Port-Royal theologians, "they are in revolt against the king, which is grave; against their archbishop, which is worse; and against the pope, which is unthinkable. They will become heretics and find themselves excommunicated. Port-Royal will be rejected by the Church."

Pascal was carrying the meaning of the Gospel to its ultimate conclusion, but his thinking was too drastic for other men. Priests, doctors, and solitaries fell in with Arnauld's opinion, now much sobered, and of Nicole, who had always been on the side of prudence.

The author of the "Provincials" was crushed; the last defenders of the truth were abandoning it and taking shelter behind pitiful artifices. Pascal looked on their grave faces for the slightest glimmer of hope, but there was none; he felt himself isolated beside one who no longer lived in this world. In his despair he descended into the night of Gethsemane and fell unconscious to the floor.

The Messieurs saw lying at their feet the warrior who had dared enter the lists against the confessors of Louis XIV. After they had revived him, Arnauld, Nicole, and his friends went away in silence, unable to meet his eyes. Only two faithful friends remained in the room—Roannez and Domat. They, at least, shared Pascal's convictions.

Domat was even more stern. "Will I ever have the consolation of seeing a Christian pope in Saint Peter's chair?" he had said one day.

Before these two, Pascal spoke freely: "I must confess I felt such sorrow I could no longer bear it, and I had to give way to it." Once more we hear Jacqueline's words coming from the lips of her brother.

The future proved Pascal to have been right. Obeying their spiritual directors after painful hesitation, the nuns signed the formulary for the second time, preceding their signatures with the "preamble" drawn up by the theologians.

When the vicar-general received this document he read it over and murmured: "I am satisfied." But the court was not.

Mother Angélique was the only one dispensed from questioning by Le Bail and from signing the formulary, for she was already so close to death that no one dared approach her.

"We needed," she said, "those things which have happened to humiliate us; they are talking about us everywhere."

And she added: "Affliction, pain, and suffering are more necessary to us than bread."

What she feared was the old enemy—pride. "The best part of persecution is the humiliation it brings, and humility is best preserved by silence."

Mother Angélique was about to die deprived of the comfort of Singlin, the spiritual director bequeathed her by Saint-Cyran. The abbess did not want to admit how heavy this cross was for her to bear.

"I hold Monsieur Singlin in great honor," she said. "But I put no man in God's place."

The dying woman shrank from the admiration of the nuns, who already spoke of her as a saint, and scolded them in her brusque language.

"I beg of you to bury me in the courtyard, and after my death, don't go in for so much banter."

Mother Angélique gathered her last strength to dictate a letter to Anne of Austria, who loved and revered the Arnaulds, and in it the former abbess once more defended Port-Royal.

When her last hours came Angélique, who had ruled with such a rod of iron and gone through so much struggle, was terrified at the idea of appearing before God—she would have to answer for all the souls that had been entrusted to her.

Her feeble voice was heard saying: "I am like a criminal at the foot of the gallows, waiting for the execution of the judge's sentence."

Some time before Singlin had been able to reassure her. She had promised him "to fear God no longer," but now her eyes were opening on infinity.

"All I had imagined is less than nothing," she said, "in comparison with what it is, what I feel, and what I understand."

Agnès Arnauld put her whole heart in trying to help Angélique. As her older sister's life drew to its close, Agnès meditated and prayed. In a letter to her brother, Antoine Arnauld, she wrote: "God wants to try her to the last."

The quiet Agnès was never to know terror of the same kind, for she was one of those "imbued with Christ's goodness and mercy who are filled with great joy and great tenderness." At this time the distance that separated her from her sister was apparent. Hope in God's goodness "is in conformity," she said, "with human understanding and gives us greater consolation," but the fear her sister felt before God's holiness was "something greater, since it was the state Jesus Christ chose for himself. It seems that it is the lot of stronger souls."

In these words Mother Agnès paid homage to the vigorous spirit of one she admired so greatly to the very end.

On Saturday, August 6, 1661, the feast of the Transfiguration, Angélique Arnauld went to her rest.

"Die to everything and await everything!" she murmured, finally at peace. Then followed the last words of one who was the most "Jansenistic" of all the religious of Port-Royal: "Lord, have pity on us all. I say upon all, my God, upon all."

Left alone, Mother Agnès carried on the duties of abbess for several months. She was succeeded by Madeleine de Ligny on December 12, 1661.

It then seemed that the nuns were to be granted a ray of hope. A month after Mother de Ligny assumed office, a cure took place which was reminiscent of the miracle of the Holy Thorn. One of the nuns, Sister Catherine de Sainte Suzanne, had been unable to walk for over a year. The doctors found no cure, and Mother Agnès had spent many hours praying for her.

One day during January, 1662, on coming from vespers, the former abbess knelt down beside this nun to ask once more God's mercy on the invalid. Then, as the latter related, "I felt a glimmer of hope for my cure." A few hours later Sister Catherine rose up and walked.

Her father, Philippe de Champaigne, the painter of Port-Royal, has left us the picture of Mother Agnès in prayer beside the young nun. Catherine sits with her paralyzed legs stretched out before her, her hands joined, her face thoughtful. Kneeling at her side, Agnès gazes on her in silent contemplation; from high above, a ray of light is seen descending upon her.

We are indebted to Philippe de Champaigne for many moving portraits of the personages of Port-Royal which reflect their inner lives in their faces, but none of his works was painted with so loving a hand.

It was far from the day when a miracle caused Anne of Austria to stop her preparations to strike at the monastery. Louis XIV, unlike his mother, was not sensitive to the supernatural. A month after Sister Catherine's cure, he asked if the religious had signed the formulary; on learning they had done so only with reservations, he declared: "Very well! But we won't let matters stand there!"

In order to destroy the "Jansenist sect," the king turned more and more to Father Annat. The latter now felt closer than ever to his objective, for the religious had reached the extreme limit to which they could consent. Father Annat therefore had additions made to the formulary of so precise a nature in regard to the question of *fact* that it would be impossible for the cleverest theologian to find a loophole.

A visit by Madame de Guémené to Le Tellier had no effect; the minister told her that his master's mind was definitely made up.

At that point the princess said: "Sir, the king does as he pleases; he makes princes of the blood, he makes archbishops and bishops. He will also make martyrs."

Even so, Port-Royal still had allies at the Paris archbishopric, where the vicars-general were as favorable to them as was the archbishop, the fugitive Cardinal de Retz. However, on February 26, 1662, de Retz, after lengthy haggling, decided to offer his resignation to the king. Thereupon the author of the formulary, Monseigneur de Marca, Archbishop of Toulouse, was immediately appointed to take his place. After finally obtaining the see of Paris which he had so greatly coveted, this prelate never occupied it, for he died on June 29, 1662, two days after receiving the pontifical bulls conferring his new dignity on him.

After the occasion on which he lost consciousness in the presence of the Port-Royal sages, Pascal suffered from heart trouble, as had his sister Jacqueline. Upheld by Domat and Roannez, he blamed his former companions in the struggle who had become casuists in their turn. Arnauld and Nicole were hurt, and could not hide their bitterness in replying to him.

Pascal had only a few more months to live, and he gave up the fight. Since his advice had been rejected, he could not carry on the work he had felt compelled to do; nothing remained for him except to prepare himself for death.

The sick man, who had not spent a single day without suffering since the age of eighteen, added voluntarily to his ills by wearing a belt studded with iron points which pressed into his flesh. We would be at a loss to understand this excessive hardship if we did not know that every instant of suffering brought Pascal into closer communion with the Man of Sorrows and led him in this way to the source of his love. In his "Prayer to ask God for the good use of sickness," written several years earlier, he says: "I praise thee, O God, and all the days of my life will I bless thee, that it has pleased thee to place me in a condition where I am incapable of enjoying the sweet things of earth and the pleasures of the world." Christ had given him the example: "O God, who became man that you might suffer!"

Pascal's room was bare, all its contents having been sold at his orders for the benefit of the poor. He had an unbounded respect for these witnesses to Christ, and had installed in his house a poverty-stricken family of whom he took care. He was the godfather of one of the children, and had no wish to separate himself from these unfortunates.

Pascal read and reread the sacred Scriptures and found everywhere in them the God for whom he had searched in earlier days. Nevertheless, he continued his scientific research. At the time of his conversion he had given up publication of his studies on the equilibrium of fluids, and on atmospheric pressure, as also his "Treatise on the Mathematical Triangle." Even so, he was unable to make up his mind to halt his labors, and had written a work entitled "History of the Roulette" on the problem of cycloids, wherein he studied the curve made by a nail on a moving wheel. Roannez had decided to publish this work in 1658 because, said the duke, it was necessary to show free-thinkers that faith, far from being opposed to science, was conducive to it. The following year, in January, 1569, Pascal sent Huygens his "Letter on the Dimension of Curved Lines," and continued his correspondence with Fermat. Now he was organizing in Paris the first means of public transportation, "the five-sou carriages," for the sole benefit of the poor.

In July, 1662, Pascal was afflicted with a severe intestinal disorder; his older sister, Gilberte Périer, who came every day to take care of him, learned that the children of the family he was sheltering had smallpox. Fearing to carry the disease back to her own home, she persuaded her brother to leave his house and come to live with her not far from the Church of Saint Etienne du Mont in Paris. There Pascal gave the guidance of his conscience into the hands of the pastor of the parish, Father Beurrier.

When interrogated by the Archbishop of Paris, three years after his penitent's death, Father Beurrier stated that Pascal had cut himself off from Port-Royal "because he saw that the Messieurs went too far in matters of grace and seemed to show less submission than was proper to our Holy Father the Pope."

More than pleased to have this retraction, the archbishop, Monseigneur Péréfixe, divulged this confidence despite his promise of secrecy in its regard. Pascal's friends—Nicole, Arnauld, Roannez, Domat—who had remained in touch with him to the end were indignant, and affirmed that, on the contrary, the author of the "Provincials" had ceased his collaboration with the theologians of Port-Royal because he considered them too weak in defense of their beliefs.

Father Beurrier then wrote Gilberte Périer, admitting that he had been mistaken in quoting the dead man's words. Later in his memoirs the priest re-established the truth—Pascal had never impugned Port-Royal but only had said that, insofar as he himself was concerned, he had given up the discussion about grace and submitted to the pope. Such was, in fact, the attitude of this Christian who for a time had been close to revolt, but who had abdicated when his companions abandoned what he considered to be a fight on the side of God.

With all confidence Pascal had placed his soul in Father Beurrier's hands, and the latter said of him in wonderment: "He was a child. He was as humble and submissive as a child."

Science had led Pascal to the threshold of the Gospel, and the grace had been given him to pass within. So now we see him like the little ones whom Jesus loved.

The sick man wanted to be taken to the hospital for incurables, in order to have the happiness of dying among the poor, but the physicians opposed this move. Neither did they permit him to receive communion despite his pleas, pronouncing him in no condition to endure the fast. During the night of August 17, 1662, Pascal suffered violent convulsions; they ceased when Father Beurrier arrived carrying the Host.

"Here is the One you have wanted so much," the priest said.

With a tremendous effort, the dying man half rose from his bed to receive his Savior. After receiving extreme unction, Pascal expressed his highest hope in these words: "May God never abandon me!"

As soon as he had ended his thanksgiving, the convulsions returned, and gave him no moment of rest. He died in the throes of this struggle on August 19, 1662.

With him, Port-Royal lost the greatest of its defenders. Mother Agnès called Gilberte the sole heir "of a brother and sister who were rich in the goods of God." And the former abbess added that Pascal "had immolated his life" to divine love.

In days gone by, Nicole had considered the author of the "Provincials" a "collector of sea-shells," a man who had met with great successes but who would scarcely be remembered by posterity. Now the theologian rendered him justice. The day following Pascal's death he wrote: "The one we mourn was a king in the kingdom of the intellect."

Upon the advice of his Council of Conscience, Louis XIV designated Hardouin de Péréfixe de Beaumont, Bishop of Rodez, as successor to Monseigneur de Marca in his capacity as Archbishop of Paris. Despite his imposing nomenclature, this prelate was of humble birth. His father had been house-steward at Richelieu's residence. A former instructor to the king, de Péréfixe was one of those prelates later called by Saint-Simon "cads in violet."

The king presented the new archbishop to the Holy See under conditions that could hardly be called favorable, for a conflict had developed between the pope and Louis XIV. Following a quarrel, the soldiers of the pontifical guard had fired on the French embassy, the Farnese Palace, and one of the pages of the king's ambassador, the duc de Créqui, had been killed. Louis XIV made loud complaint "at an outrage without a parallel to this day, even among barbarians." Pope Alexander VII had to present apologies through his nephew, Cardinal Chigi. But long and difficult discussions were necessary before any compromise could be reached, and Monseigneur de Péréfixe had to wait two years for the bulls permitting him to occupy the see of Paris.

During these two years the vicars-general continued to administer the diocese, but they were no longer Monsieur de Contes and Monsieur de Hodencq, regarded as favorable to Port-Royal. Their successors drew up a mandate requiring the signature pure and simple of the formulary.

This time, in justification of their refusal to sign, the nuns found an excellent excuse by invoking the absence of the archbishop whose consecration was awaited from day to day. Thus the Roman incident gave Port-Royal a respite of two years, and its defenders attempted to take advantage of the delay to save the monastery.

The Bishop of Comminges, Monseigneur de Choiseul—a friend of Arnauld's—learned that a Jesuit, Father Ferrier, had been instructed to negotiate with him, since the Society of Jesus now considered itself strong enough to offer peace to the Jansenists if they would consent to a complete repudiation of their errors. Monseigneur de Choiseul arrived in Paris in December, 1662, and met with Father Ferrier; Louis XIV granted permission for Antoine Arnauld to leave his hiding-place and personally take part in the discussions.

Jacqueline Pascal had imposed on her brother the yoke of the Gospels, both so heavy and so light; it would appear that after his death the author of the "Provincials" handed on to the great Arnauld the task of continuing his work. Saint-Cyran's successor, who had weakened to the point of proposing "subterfuges," recovered the intransigent purity of his earlier days and refused Louis XIV's offer, well knowing that agreeing to a discussion with the Jesuit under the glowing aegis of the Sun King would be the first step to betrayal.

In a letter Arnauld wrote at this time, we recognize the language of Jacqueline and of Pascal. It would be, he said, "to abase oneself in a cowardly manner to accept the distinctions proposed by the negotiators"; he did not consider it permissible "to make use of counter-letters in a religious matter."

Like Pascal, Antoine Arnauld had witnessed the suffering of the noblest souls around him when he had attempted to save the community by directing the intention in the way of the casuists. He did not want to give the nuns of Port-Royal a false sense of security, and thenceforth would never forget the counsel given him by Saint-Cyran: "We must go where God leads us, and never do anything cowardly." Sharing the same belief, various of the Messieurs, among them Nicole and Saci, now took their place at the side of Arnauld. At this time, too, a new generation of nuns entered the struggle. Refusing the humble obedience imposed by Mother Angélique, and rejecting Mother Agnès' peaceful ways, these religious were inspired by the memory of the martyrs and decided to go out to meet persecution. One of their number, Angélique de Saint Jean, the daughter of Arnauld d'Andilly, was at the head of this movement.

"Everything about her was lofty," wrote Fontaine, one of the solitaries who knew her. Angélique de Saint Jean encouraged her uncle, Antoine Arnauld, to remain firm; he must not hesitate for fear of exposing either her or her sisters to danger.

"Venture forth," she said to him. "Perhaps we can be the servants of the princes of Ahab's army who were first to enter the fight and win the battle."

However, certain of the spiritual directors of Port-Royal—Singlin, among others—considered that they had no right to reject the last chance of peace held out to them. Despite Arnauld's opposition, five of them appeared before Father Ferrier and declared they were ready to condemn the five propositions, and to adopt a "respectful silence" regarding their attribution to Jansenius.

This ultimate concession was useless; when it was submitted to the king's Council of Conscience, Father Annat stated that it was not acceptable. Disappointed, Monsieur de Choiseul returned to his diocese; the negotiation had been in vain and never could have met with anything but failure.

They now had to expect persecution. At the request of Angélique de Saint Jean, Mother Agnès, her aunt, drew up a "Notice to the religious of Port-Royal on the conduct to be followed in case of a change of government in the community."

Removal, exile, deprivation of the sacraments—all the hardships soon to befall the monastery were foreseen. The "Notice" instructed the religious to accept them with humility, as comes from God, but without ever lending themselves to "traffic in souls." In the last words a new voice could be discerned—that of Angélique de Saint Jean.

Singlin, the former superior of Port-Royal, who, like Arnauld, had to live in hiding in order to avoid arrest, came in secret to bring spiritual aid to the nuns. The priest had to put aside his ecclesiastical garb and disguise himself in the dress of a physician to prevent being recognized. Consequently he compared himself to Jacob, who clothed himself in the skin of an animal so as to be taken for Esau. "But I must try," said Singlin with a smile, "always to have the voice of Esau despite this clothing."

Exhausted by his fugitive existence and the feeling that he was being followed everywhere like a criminal, the most peace-loving man of Port-Royal died on Easter Sunday, April 17, 1664.

Shortly before, on April 10th, Monseigneur de Péréfixe had finally received from Rome the bulls enabling him to occupy the see of Paris. Outspoken, clumsy, and muddle-headed, the new archbishop hid a kind heart beneath apparent rudeness. Even his language was not always seemly for a prelate: Boileau relates that he was frequently heard to swear, after which he would do penance by disciplining himself; but then each stroke would elicit another oath. At least there were in his life no scandalous escapades such as those that showed the skepticism of certain high-born prelates; chaste, and a believer in his faith, he declared himself "a Jansenist as regards morals." This modest man felt much closer to Port-Royal than to the Louvre, but because, unhappily, his rise was due to the king's favor, he had to pay the price of his ambitions.

The queen mother, who by this time had quite forgotten the miracle of the Holy Thorn, said to the archbishop when he went to visit her: "Monsieur de Paris, remember on what conditions you have received your see. Now that you occupy it, we will see how you conduct yourself."

One of the solitaries, Lancelot, was charged with presenting the compliments of the community to the new prelate in the name of the Abbess of

Port-Royal. Monseigneur de Péréfixe's reply was touching but saddening, coming as it did from the lips of a prince of the Church. The nuns, he said, "should resolve to find means to satisfy the king."

The popes, he continued, had spoken: the bishops, the sacred Faculty of Theology, and the religious communities had obeyed. "It is not at all proper for a single house to lay down the law to others," the archbishop ended.

Lancelot was quick to reply: "As these nuns answer only for themselves, they do not believe they need consider what others do."

The solitary hastened to soften his words by expressing his respect for the nuns whose scruples he well knew, saying: "Monseigneur, spare their tenderness of conscience."

Archbishop de Péréfixe had not understood Lancelot and never would. "Oh," he replied, "it would be better to call it their stubbornness.."

Then with instinctive masculine scorn he added: "Women should never go so far when the pope and bishops have given a command. What do they know?"

Nevertheless, the archbishop declared he would prefer to convince rather than to conquer. "Assure them that I respect their virtue and would shed my blood to get them out of the awkward situation they are in, but let them see what they themselves can do to this end."

Then the good de Péréfixe pleaded with Lancelot: "Think about it yourself. See what expedient they can use. Find me some means of escape, I beseech you."

The solitary remained silent, for there was nothing he could do; no expedient could ever place a Christian's conscience beyond the reach of God.

To the chaplain who showed him out, Lancelot confided a message that summed up the whole future of Port-Royal:

"These nuns know that whatever respect they owe the pope and hierarchy, it is better to obey God, who will require an exact accounting for a deceptive signature and false testimony. Monsieur de Paris must not expect anything else."

One of Port-Royal's former confessors, Sainte-Marthe, now suspected and threatened, dared to write the archbishop in defense of the nuns he had directed for a considerable period of time. "I am a priest, Monseigneur, like yourself, and committed to the guidance of certain souls; perhaps this has given me more experience in human misery and weakness." Sainte-Marthe asked "that there not be exacted something which serves only to trouble us and take away our peace of soul. Concede this little to our weakness and to the peace of the Church."

It was too much to hope for; the day Monseigneur de Péréfixe had been appointed Archbishop of Paris he had lost the right to be generous.

After much reflection the prelate believed he had found an "expedient." He issued a mandate imposing the signature but establishing a distinction: the five propositions should be condemned with *divine faith*, but on the point of knowing whether they were held by Jansenius it was sufficient to subscribe with *human faith*.

In this the simplest of men came together with consummate theologians, since the latter actually admitted the two kinds of faith. But what distinguished them? Where did one begin and the other end?

The nuns of Port-Royal refused to accept this subtlety, for it strongly resembled a trap. They had been led into similar labyrinths and already had suffered too much.

Nicole wrote with sad irony: "This must be an entirely new sort of human faith: its absence makes one a heretic!" The means of escape offered by the archbishop was rejected, and the bridges were burned.

On May 20, 1664, Monseigneur de Péréfixe went to Port-Royal of Paris at seven o'clock in the morning. Received with the chanting of the *Te Deum*, he gave his blessing to the nuns at the choir grill. In the parlor he talked with the abbess, Mother de Ligny, and informed her that she must sign the condemnation of Jansenius "with trust." When Madame de Ligny acknowledged that she did not have this trust, the archbishop accused her of audacity and presumption.

On June 9th, Monseigneur de Péréfixe returned to the monastery and exhorted the community to sign, questioning the religious one by one and passing from entreaties to threats.

"Hold your tongue! Listen to me!" he said to one of the nuns who tried to explain her position.

The prelate showed such violent anger that she was frightened and begged his pardon.

"And I beg you to excuse me," replied Monseigneur de Péréfixe in return, disarmed by her humility. After this he cheerfully bestowed his blessing on the rebel.

Before Angélique de Saint-Jean, whose loftiness of mind intimidated him, the archbishop showed his clumsiness.

"You should make an effort," he naively said, "to withdraw from all this regrettable business."

Thinking to honor the daughter of Arnauld d'Andilly, the prelate drew on his store of memories. The late Cardinal de Richelieu had said to him when he had Saint-Cyran arrested: "This priest has peculiar and dangerous opinions which could one day bring on a row and division in the Church."

Angélique de Saint-Jean was indignant at hearing Richelieu's opinion of one whose memory she venerated. "I heard with horror," she said, "this injurious accusation against a man attached to the Church with charity so strong and deep that it could have been called his only passion."

Monseigneur de Péréfixe realized he was on the wrong track—the shadow of the great cardinal should not have been evoked at Port-Royal.

The archbishop was more fortunate in his choice of words when he talked with Sister Christine Briquet, the daughter and niece of parliamentary magistrates. Alert and enthusiastic, this young nun of twenty-three discussed theology with him. The prelate smiled when she broached the problems of human destiny; here at last was a religious who expressed herself with confidence.

"When one finds a person who reasons," said Monseigneur de Péréfixe, "it is a pleasure to talk with her."

Even so, he reproached Christine Briquet with stubbornness.

"How is it possible for God to listen to you? You are saying to him, 'God, give me grace, but I do not want to sign. I will take care not to do so despite everything that is said to me.' After that, how is it possible for God to hear your prayers?"

The archbishop ended his visit without winning over a single rebel. The daughters of Port-Royal could not hesitate in a conflict between Saint-Cyran, Arnauld, and Singlin on the one hand, who had taught the nuns Christ's meaning, and on the other, a prelate who came bearing the orders of the court.

The Archbishop of Paris had granted the nuns a delay of three weeks in which to reflect and come to a decision. He gave the abbey a confessor, Chamillard, a doctor of theology, who was to restore the rebels to obedience.

Despite his learning, this priest could not gain a single victory, for the road he opened to the religious did not seem to them quite straight.

"You should say: 'I submit in heart and speech to the pontifical decisions.' The submission of heart is for the *right* and the submission of speech for the *fact*."

The theologian seemed surprised at the blind faith of these religious.

"What have you done with your reason?" he said.

"I hold it captive to believe God's words and those of the Gospel," replied Sister Christine Briquet. "I never try to reason about divine things."

Suffering from a touch of fever, Monseigneur de Péréfixe had to delay his return to Port-Royal. The community began a novena to ask God for the archbishop's recovery, but also to implore Christ, the Virgin, and the saints to protect them. The nuns wrote down requests—one addressed to Saint Lawrence, another to Saint Mary Magdalen, and a third to the apostles Peter and Paul—which they slipped beneath the altar-cloth when mass was celebrated in commemoration of these saints. A letter was carried to Clairvaux and placed on the tomb of the greatest of Cistercians, Saint Bernard.

On August 21, 1664, Monseigneur de Péréfixe had recovered, and he went to the monastery on the faubourg Saint-Jacques. He had decided to act energetically; the king's confessor, Father Annat, had come to reproach him for showing an indulgence which the court was beginning to consider suspect.

The prelate had the community assembled in his presence. The hour had come, he said, to obey; the nuns must sign the formulary. Hoping that some of them would weaken, he questioned them one by one. They were still unanimous in refusing.

What the Jesuits had hoped for had come about: since it was impossible to take refuge in any compromise, the nuns found themselves in conflict with their archbishop.

Anxiety in the abbey ran so high that Mother Agnès opened the New Testament in the hope of finding some words of consolation. But what she read were the words spoken by Jesus to those who came to seize him in the Garden of Olives: "This is your hour, and the power of darkness."

Darkness! It gathered around the head of the prelate who had earlier shown such benevolence. It was another man entirely who rose up suddenly before the silent community, a man powerful in his authority.

"I today declare you to be rebels to the Church and to your archbishop. As such, I judge you unworthy to receive the sacraments. I forbid you to approach them."

After pronouncing these words, Monseigneur de Péréfixe went out, leaving the nuns in tears.

The archbishop might perhaps have taken advantage of their disarray to make the religious bow to his will, since they were accustomed to obedience. But now he saw at the monastery entrance some friends of Port-Royal— among them the princesse de Guéméné—who had come to plead the cause of the nuns. Wishing to avoid any incident with the ladies of the court, Monseigneur de Péréfixe returned to the parlor where the community were still assembled. At sight of the nuns who had caused him such torment, and who might raise powerful enemies against him, he felt the violent rage of a plebian. When Mother de Ligny tried to say a few words, the prelate cut her off brusquely.

"Hold your tongue! You are nothing but a saucy little woman!"

Astonished but regally calm, the abbess thereafter remained silent. Hearing one of the religious murmur that justice would be rendered Port-Royal in heaven, the archbishop shot forth a reply worthy of Molière:

"Yes, yes. When we get there, we can see how things are going."

Thus, after casting an anathema in the manner of a prelate of medieval times, Monseigneur de Péréfixe became the regent of a college scolding his recalcitrant students. He might cause them anxiety, but never again would he terrorize them.

However, the archbishop had to leave and this time he could not avoid Madame de Guéméné, who still stood waiting. As soon as she saw him, the princess told him of the high esteem in which she held the nuns.

The archbishop then delivered his celebrated reply: "They are pure as angels but proud as devils."

Between these religious, who lived in the light of grace, and Louis XIV's former instructor, who saw only a ridiculous pride behind their resistance, there existed a gulf that never could be bridged.

The prelate's rage enabled even the most timid of the nuns to regain her composure. Truly, the Holy Spirit did not speak from the lips of the archbishop! As soon as he had left, they drew up a protest against the punishment inflicted on them, the most cruel possible: namely, forbidding them to receive Christ in communion. "One hundred poor religious who left everything to cleave to Christ are snatched from the foot of his altars, banished from his holy table—those who have devoted themselves day and night to adoration of the Blessed Sacrament."

As her sisters expressed their distress, Angélique de Saint-Jean tried to console them.

"We are," she said, "ranked among the dogs who eat the crumbs that fall from their master's table; from that place we cannot be driven away."

Since they were judged unworthy to receive the host, the religious thereafter prostrated themselves on the floor during the prayers at communion.

Drawn into the struggle despite herself, Agnès Arnauld saw God's will in all that had happened. But why had he permitted so cruel a blow to those she loved? "God's will is inscrutable, and unsearchable his ways." Were not the pope, the archbishop, and the theologians merely the instruments of grace who tested the religious so that they might gain eternity?" With recovered serenity, Agnès concluded: If God has chosen this way for our salvation, what else matters?"

The archbishop determined to act. If simple nuns dared disobey him, it was, he thought, because the superiors and their predecessors had induced them to rebel. Let these be removed from the monastery and peace would be restored!

Monseigneur de Péréfixe then visited several convents which might receive the religious. Learning of this, Arnauld d'Andilly went on the morning of August 26, 1664, to the parlor of the Paris monastery to warn his sister

Agnès and bid her farewell. Far from engaging in lamentations, the two old people recited together the words of the Psalm: "This is the day the Lord has made. Be glad and rejoice!"

Early in the afternoon the archbishop arrived, vested in rochet and cape, preceded by his cross-bearer, and surrounded by the vicars-general, the ecclesiastical judge, and the principal pastors of Paris. In addition, Monseigneur de Péréfixe had himself accompanied by the civil lieutenant, the provost, the knight of the watch, and a large troop composed of four police commissioners, twenty subordinate officers, and two hundred soldiers carrying muskets. The prelate believed he could intimidate the nuns in this way, but succeeded only in strengthening their courage. In the eyes of Port-Royal's daughters the approach of armed men was a reminder of the Passion—here were the princes and the priests surrounded by warriors and swords.

"Ah, Mother," said one of the nuns to Agnès Arnauld, "how splendid this is!"

Andilly was waiting at the door of the monastery. Kneeling before the archbishop, he expressed his sorrow at seeing the house where his sister and his daughter lived in God's service besieged in such a manner. Monseigneur de Péréfixe raised him to his feet, said a few words, and then started for the chapter hall where the community had assembled. Far more moved than he wished to appear, the archbishop first of all deplored the severity he was being compelled to show; after this he read the names of twelve nuns who were to be expelled from the monastery. Among them were Madame de Ligny, abbess, Mother Agnès, Angélique de Saint-Jean, and the other two daughters of Arnauld d'Andilly.

Mother de Ligny did not lose her calm. "Monseigneur," she said, "we believe ourselves obliged in conscience to appeal against this violence and to make protest."

Around her the voices rose: "We appeal! We protest!"

"Don't make me laugh!" replied Monseigneur de Péréfixe.

He personally led the twelve religious he had designated to the door of the cloister. One of them did not walk quickly enough to suit him, and he asked her "if she wanted him to take her by the feet and head."

The archbishop was so flustered that he did not see the door and passed it by. One of the nuns to be exiled, Angélique de Saint-Jean, had to point out the way to him. Nevertheless, at the moment of crossing the threshold, she requested an order in writing to leave the house, since the rule forbade her to go without the Church's authorization. Monseigneur de Péréfixe agreed to this willingly, satisfied to grant a request so modest.

"This is real obedience," he said. "It is to leave as a good religious should."

When the exiles went out into the faubourg Saint-Jacques, they were given one consolation: Arnauld d'Andilly had stayed to receive "the queens" and accompany them to the carriages provided by the archbishop.

The old knight of Port-Royal first guided the steps of his sister Agnès, who, at the age of seventy-one, was feeble and moved with great difficulty. After this he gave his blessing to his three daughters, and before their departure took them into the monastery church in order to commend them to God and offer them to him for the second time.

Finally the patriarch led the religious one by one to their conveyances, thereby doing his best to give the abbey the assistance due it from the Arnauld family in its day of trial. This time Monseigneur de Péréfixe dared not intervene to hasten the departure—Andilly was too well liked at court. So that the exiled religious could not encourage one another, the archbishop dispersed them among several convents where they were immediately placed in solitary confinement. They were to receive neither visits nor letters, and were to be deprived of the sacraments.

Of all the "Communications" written by the captives to exhort their sisters to be courageous, that of Angélique de Saint-Jean is the finest. Well instructed in theological matters, this religious, now forty years old, had lived at Port-Royal since the age of six, when she entered as a pupil. When she was a young girl her aunt, Angélique Arnauld, said of her: "She is too strong-minded and precocious; she will do much harm if she doesn't do good."

A novice at seventeen, Angélique had been moved to turn her thoughts to eternal things by the letters written her by the imprisoned Saint-Cyran from his dungeon at Vincennes.

When the civil lieutenant asked her name, she gave him the one she bore in religion: Angélique de Saint-Jean. But when the magistrate wanted to know the name of her family, the nun could not master her sense of pride. Had not several generations of Arnaulds consecrated themselves to God?

"I said it very loudly," she acknowledged, "for it was almost like confessing the name of God to confess the name of Arnauld."

She was taken to the Monastery of the Celestial Annunciades, close to the Hôtel Carnavalet. The Annunciades, who were called "Blue Sisters" because they wore azure-colored mantles over their white robes, were under the direction of the Jesuits; one of their confessors was Father Nouet, who had earlier attacked Port-Royal with such violence. When night fell over this hostile house, Angélique de Saint-Jean felt alone, separated for the first time from her superiors and her sisters, her daily existence completely changed. "I felt," she said, "as though my spirit had been suspended up until that time and that suddenly it had fallen from a great height."

After two days the nun received permission to adore the Blessed Sacrament exposed in a chapel.

"I trembled as I entered." Before God's majesty, Saint-Cyran's spiritual descendants were always torn between fear and love.

Nevertheless, Angélique de Saint-Jean had enough confidence to "draw near to Jesus."

"In his presence I poured out my heart together with my tears."

Yet immediately thereafter she reproached herself with weakness: "At great moments we should not lower the eyes we have raised toward the mountains."

Recovering her strength, the nun made an effort to forget her mother house. "It seemed to me that I carried my soul in my hands in the way a governess carries a child who is being weaned: she diverts it as best she can to prevent it from thinking of its wet nurse."

Angélique felt two persons living within her. "One had enough strength to support the other in her weakness; my spirit rejoiced in those things that afflicted my senses."

In subduing the pride which separated her from Christ at the very time when the nun believed herself in union with him required an inner turmoil more violent than the first. Angélique de Saint-Jean became deeply depressed and was haunted by the words of the Psalm: "They mount up to the heavens, and they go down into the depths; their soul pined away at the sight of evil."

This evil was always feared by the Christians of Port-Royal: it was the one Saint-Cyran confronted in his cell, and the mere thought of which had terrified Pascal—namely, the absence of the Spirit, who withdraws from the presumptuous soul because his power over it is no longer supreme.

Angélique de Saint-Jean gave up the attempt to describe what she suffered at that time: "No one who has not been through it can imagine this anguish and abandonment."

Did God exist? Had past centuries been filled only with a dream? Such words as redemption, grace, kingdom—were they only words?

Angélique de Saint-Jean was one day to acknowledge to her uncle, Antoine Arnauld, that she suffered a temptation which is the worst of blasphemies—the temptation to the sin against the Holy Spirit.

"It is a kind of doubt of all the things of faith. . . . I am frightened even to write that much about it."

At the time when she felt the threat most dangerous, the nun could no longer find within herself the means to combat it.

"I would have preferred," she said later, "to be delivered up to all the demons."

In her shame at falling so low, the unhappy nun dared not even open her eyes. Like Eve, driven by God from Eden, "I thought only of hiding myself from him," she wrote.

Angélique now discovered the truth for which she was being persecuted: "God has only to turn his face away and we are left with empty hands."

In vain the nun reread the most beautiful passages of Scripture, those she had cherished the most; the voice of the prophets and evangelists no longer sustained her, "for God had taken away the power of the bread."

During this period, which seemed without beginning or end, Angélique de Saint-Jean underwent a new temptation—to despair. What would it be to surrender, finally to be given peace! The nun almost "allowed her lamp to go out."

But it was here, at the bottom of the precipice where her powerful spirit lay broken, that she found grace. Christ suddenly made himself known; he was at the heart of the suffering experienced by Angélique, and he had shared its pain with her.

At the dawn of this discovery, the nun made "her prison into a church"; there she chanted the *Kyrie eleison* and *Gloria in excelsis,* and followed the words of the office in a missal. Slowly she walked back and forth in her narrow room, holding a cross in her hand; at night she awakened to say matins.

However, a fresh trial was in store for Angélique de Saint-Jean. The superior of the Annunciade convent where she was held prisoner told her that her two younger sisters, expelled from Port-Royal the same day as herself, had signed the formulary. Angélique lived in a nightmare: "As far as my eye could reach, I saw only a vast, unknown land from which it seemed impossible ever to escape by any road which would not take as long as I lived."

Some time later, the Annunciades told Angélique that Mother Agnès herself was preparing to sign. This was the most cruel blow of all. Again for an instant the supreme temptation rose: to deny God. How could he have abandoned the best, the most faithful of his servants? "I feared the shipwreck of my faith . . . I imagined horrible things. . . . Like Saint Peter, I was about to drown."

The Annunciades, thinking that the rebel was now ready to give in, advised her of the latest signature: that of another exile, Sister Françoise Marie, held captive in the house of the Ursulines. The following day Angélique de Saint-Jean learned that the unhappy woman was dead—her signature had been obtained during her last agony.

"Cruel, cowardly persecutors!" But the Jesuits could be reassured—Pascal lay in his tomb and his voice was no longer heard.

But from that moment onward, no one could do anything to affect Angélique de Saint-Jean. At each new trial she bowed beneath the load, and always a superhuman power raised her up again. The nun was saved. "God has clothed me inwardly in the habit of joy." This joy, born in anguish and so closely linked to sorrow, would be, said Angélique de Saint-Jean, "a cluster of grapes which I bring back from the land of captivity."

One of the leading nuns at the convent of the Annunciades had formerly been a Lutheran—Madame de Rantzau, the widow of a marshal of France. Imbued with the zeal of the neophyte, she had already made several converts, and the Archbishop of Paris had high hope that this great lady would be able to convince Angélique de Saint-Jean of her errors and persuade her to sign.

"They are equals in intellect and learning," said Monseigneur de Péréfixe. "This should work out well."

Madame de Rantzau was surprised that a religious deprived of the sacraments and a spiritual director could sustain herself by will power alone; she therefore embarked on a theological debate with Angélique de Saint-Jean.

"I know everything you may have to say," announced the marshal's widow at the start of the conversation.

She cited the Origenists, who themselves were compelled to anathematize Origen when he became heretical. Angélique countered with a reference to Saint Jerome. Madame de Rantzau "wanted to buttress her remarks with the decisions of the fourth Council of the Church," but the prisoner "cited the fifth and sixth Councils."

The Annunciade religious returned with renewed vigor to the fray.

"I am quite well versed in Church history; I can give you an answer to all those questions!"

"And I, Mother, know nothing," replied Angélique. "The discussion would be quite unequal. Please allow me to pray to God."

Nonplussed, the marshal's widow dared not continue the theological debate. But she still tried to find an opening wedge into the rebel's mind. After careful consideration, she thought she had found it: it would be enough to ask the exile from Port-Royal to give her an account of recent events in that abbey. Angélique would not be able to avoid becoming angry and saying imprudent and condemnable things.

"Tell me your whole story," asked Madame de Rantzau.

The reply was quick and ironical. "Please wait, Mother, for it to be finished, for we have now come to the best part."

Disappointed, Madame de Rantzau decided to retreat to more solid ground.

"Don't you fear excommunication for disobedience to the pope?"

"I have one consolation," the prisoner replied. "It sometimes happens that

Saint Peter's successors imitate his hastiness in drawing the sword and striking too soon, without waiting for Christ's permission. But Jesus came forward
and healed the ear."

Madame de Rantzau was indignant at hearing the nun speak so freely of
the head of the Church, and gave up her attempt to convert her.

The rebels in the other convents were similarly harassed. Called on to
confess "the secrets of the Jansenist heresy," one of them, Sister de Saint-
Candide, ended by saying:

"The secret of the 'Jansenists' is the secret of Saint Paul: Jesus Christ
within us." The whole spirit of Port-Royal was contained in her words.

Mother Agnès was held in the Monastery of the Visitation, on the faubourg
Saint-Jacques. Because of her advanced age and infirmities, the archbishop
allowed her to have with her a niece, Marie-Angélique, daughter of Arnauld
d'Andilly, also a religious of Port-Royal.

Knowing he could get nowhere with Agnès Arnauld, Monseigneur de
Péréfixe decided to convert the young nun. He went to see her, taking with
him Bossuet, not yet a bishop at that time although he had already acquired
a high reputation.

"He is a learned man and one of the gentlest in the world," said the archbishop to Marie-Angélique. "He is just the one you need, for he belongs to
no party."

Bossuet visited the nun on several occasions, but she did not know how to
reply to his arguments.

"He often embarrassed me," she said.

The illustrious priest represented the signature as a duty easy to fulfill, and
one that in no way would endanger her salvation; on the contrary, to refuse
would make her a heretic.

Monsieur Chéron, a doctor of theology, came to back up Bossuet's words
with exhortations that mingled threats with overtures for peace. One day
Monseigneur de Péréfixe brought her a declaration signed in advance; to
remove, he said, any remaining scruples that Arnauld d'Andilly's daughter
might have. He solemnly affirmed that the signature would constitute neither
a lie nor false testimony on her part.

The poor girl went through days and nights even more difficult than those
inflicted on Angélique de Saint-Jean, for she did not have her elder sister's
strength of mind. She asked her aunt to clarify matters for her, but Mother
Agnès did not believe she had the right to bring pressure to bear on the tortured heart of her niece. As she wrote to Henri Arnauld, Bishop of Angers:
"May God prevent me from dominating another's faith. Souls belong to
God, and it is for him to give them the sentiments they should hold."

"Will you always love me?" the young nun asked Agnès, and was assured of the latter's whole-hearted affection.

The day finally came when Marie-Angélique decided to sign. But after doing so, she experienced the same suffering as had Jacqueline Pascal; far from feeling relief, the nun was weighed down with a burden that grew heavier as time went on.

She begged God to let death come. She no longer dared to look at her right hand, and for the rest of her life hid it with an instinctive gesture, as though covering up a sacrilege. "This signature in which the hand wars with the mind cannot bring peace to consciences," Mother Agnès wrote sadly. The young nun was seized with a fever from which she was to suffer for the rest of her life. In tears she told her aunt that she wanted to retract. Agnès Arnauld found in her heart the words to comfort her: "God," she said, "allows his child to be cruelly wounded because he wants to heal her himself."

Madame de Sévigné gives a light-hearted account of how it was that Marie-Angélique had come to obey: "Monsieur de Paris gave her a certain form of counter-letter that won her heart; that is what obliged her to sign that deuce of a formulary."

The marquise had learned of the event at the Visitation monastery. The Visitandines said to her in triumph: "At last, God be praised! He has touched the heart of the poor child and set her on the road of obedience and salvation."

Curious to know how the news had been received at the nearby Abbey of Port-Royal, Madame de Sévigné rushed over; there she met the nun's father, Andilly, who said to her with the usual abruptness of the Arnaulds:

"Well, the poor gosling has signed! God has abandoned her; she has taken the leap."

The conflicting views of two Christians concerning the same person and the same act greatly amused Madame de Sévigné, who "thought it was killingly funny." She herself, thank God, was a stranger to such conflicts. "I believe," she wrote, becoming serious again, "that the happy medium between two extremes is always the best." Between Golgotha and the Jesuits, Madame de Sévigné chose the middle course to be followed by reasonable people.

Agnès Arnauld had not only to console her niece but to face her own suffering. Deprived of the eucharist, she felt she had lost everything; consequently she wrote to the archbishop pleading with him to allow her to approach the communion rail: "I want to live and die as a daughter of the Church." If she refused to sign, she said, it was "through fear of offending God by affirming a controversial fact which I am not capable of judging."

All Saints' Day had gone by. Then came Christmas, the day when Jesus, Agnès wrote, "asks with his blood for his Father to reconcile men." Monseigneur de Péréfixe remained deaf to her entreaty. Again at Easter, the former abbess implored the archbishop "to give her back her Savior," but it was still in vain.

Madame de Sévigné returned to the Visitation convent to meet the prisoner about whom she had heard so much. She wanted to have a talk with Mother Agnès so that she might describe the nun to her daughter and friends. But her plan went awry: the Visitandines kept Agnès Arnauld away from the inquisitive marquise. However, she was able to catch a glimpse of Mother Agnès at prayer, and told the Marquis de Pomponne: "I saw your aunt, who seemed to be lost in God. She was present at Mass as though in an ecstasy."

The Abbess of Port-Royal, Mother de Ligny, had less to suffer than the other exiles. The Archbishop of Paris dealt with her gently, for she was the niece of the all-powerful Chancellor Séguier. She was placed in the custody of her brother, Dominique de Ligny, Bishop of Meaux, who lodged her with the Visitandines in that city; moreover, the prelate never importuned his sister to sign the formulary. Since in exile she was not under the authority of the Archbishop of Paris, the abbess was not denied the sacraments.

Monseigneur de Péréfixe had thought it most important that the superiors and influential religious be removed from the monastery. The prelate thought that he could then prevail with ease over the other nuns.

The very evening the principal rebels were taken away the archbishop sent to Port-Royal five Visitandines, among them one of the oldest members of the order, Mother Eugénie de Fontaine, who was to take over the duties of the former abbess. With sadness the religious of Port-Royal saw as their jailers the sisters of the Visitation, the spiritual daughters of Saint Francis de Sales and Madame de Chantal. The oldest among them remembered the time when the two founders of that order had been Angélique Arnauld's best friends.

As Monseigneur de Péréfixe presented the Visitandines to the nuns, a cry arose, one the archbishop had already heard:

"We appeal! We protest!"

At this the prelate tried to win the religious over to his side by declaring that he was forced to act as he was doing: "Listen to reason; do this for love of me. Receive Mother Eugénie—she will not be here long. We had to give in this much to the violence of your enemies."

Shortly after the arrival of the Visitandines, the queen mother mounted her carriage and said to her equerry: "To Port-Royal!"

The officer was surprised. Was Her Majesty going to visit the Jansenists?

Anne of Austria reassured him: "It is not they I am going to see, but Mother Eugénie."

On arriving at the monastery, the queen had a long conversation with the new superior, who was a friend of hers. As she left, one of the Port-Royal religious threw herself at her feet asking for the Blessed Sacrament and for the return of the exiles.

"Then obey!" replied Anne of Austria. "What! Nuns disobeying their archbishop? This is horrible."

Monseigneur de Péréfixe wanted at any cost to win over the nuns in the absence of their superiors. Over a period of weeks he came time and again to Port-Royal to present the formulary and demand signatures, but he obtained only seven.

Those called "the signers" were for the most part very simple nuns. Mother Agnès wrote in regard to them: "God's flail separates the chaff from the wheat; the chaff is carried away by the wind, for it is not capable of resisting it."

Two of the signers, however, made their choice deliberately. Sister Flavie Passart and Sister Dorothée Perdreau wanted higher positions, and each eventually wanted the abbess' chair. After signing, they received the principal posts and carried out their duties under the control of the Visitandines.

Even before signing, Sister Flavie Passart had gone over to the camp of the enemies of Port-Royal. She had spied on the religious constantly, and it was thanks to the information she sent Monseigneur de Péréfixe that he was able to select the nuns to be exiled. The fact that she had lived at the side of the sisters while betraying them cast a Judas-like shadow over the monastery and made the period of waiting even more depressing.

During one period Monseigneur de Péréfixe tried a gentler method, and authorized the nuns to receive communion. But since this did not lead to any further signatures, the archbishop deprived the religious of the eucharist for the second time.

Several of them envied those who had won God's crown of martyrdom. But even on this point there still existed a painful uncertainty for the nuns— in refusing to obey their pastors, were they not damning themselves?

The daughters of Port-Royal were surprised at the rather servile obedience imposed on the Visitandines by their Jesuit directors, for they themselves were accustomed to a certain independence of mind and attitude. Now they saw Mother Eugénie, the acting abbess, prostrating herself face downward on the floor as she listened to the words falling from "the holy and sacred lips of Monsieur the Archbishop." One of the Visitation sisters declared that "we must not believe anything of the Gospel except what the pope tells us."

Torn between the authority of the new arrivals and the memory of their own superiors, several of the excommunicated nuns suffered the same torments as their captive sisters, but were sustained by the example of certain of their number who now resisted as strongly as the exiles. The courage of these nuns was often accompanied by that wit which made Port-Royal so human and so French. One of the vicars-general said to Sister Christine Briquet that his own idea of obedience was such that should the archbishop say that the white steps leading to the altar were black, he would sincerely believe this.

"Your belief, Monsieur, would not change their color," the religious replied.

Now aware that the numbers of rebels would be little diminished, and not daring to inform the court of his lack of success, Monseigneur de Péréfixe decided to have recourse to further and harsher measures.

On November 29, 1664, he removed three more religious from the Paris monastery. Again the prelate had been well informed: one of the new exiles had defended the truth with such energy that her mother, the comtesse de Brégy, after an unsuccessful attempt to make the nun obey, said angrily: "I have a daughter who leans only on God and on his sword."

The following December 19th, Sister Christine Briquet was exiled in her turn and taken to the Visitandines.

In the Monastery of the Fields, complete authority rested in the hands of the prioress, Mother d'Angennes du Fargis. Daughter of an ambassador, cousin to Cardinal de Retz and to the marquise de Rambouillet, related to the duchesses de Longueville and de Lesdiguières, she had renounced the world where a great fortune awaited her against the wishes of her family.

In other days Angélique Arnauld had been surprised at the firmness with which Mademoiselle du Fargis, still only a postulant, resisted the appeals of her family. Fearing for her salvation, Mother Angélique had said to her: "Humble yourself, my daughter. You are too strong!"

This calm but steadfast strength Mother du Fargis was to bring to the defense of Port-Royal. Without putting herself forward needlessly, she never weakened in the slightest. Her rule of life consisted in a maxim that she owed to Mother Angélique. "I have no fear of anything that is not eternal."

The archbishop went to Port-Royal of the Fields, taking the formulary with him, just as he had done at the faubourg Saint-Jacques. He was very courteous to the prioress, whose father he had known at court, and spoke familiarly of the Cardinal de Retz, hoping to win her confidence in this way. Monseigneur de Péréfixe next questioned her religious, but as soon as he saw his efforts were in vain, the prelate lost his temper and raged as he had done in Paris. Highly dissatisfied both with the nuns and with himself he departed, after depriving the entire community of the sacraments. At his order, the two confessors at Port-Royal of the Fields were compelled to leave the monastery, as was also the physician, Monsieur Hamon, and even the sacristan. Shortly thereafter, in order to avoid arrest by orders under the royal seal, all four had to go into hiding in Paris. Subsequently, Monseigneur de Péréfixe sent Monsieur Chamillard as superior to the Abbey of the Fields. Knowing that this priest had made many derogatory remarks about their nuns in Paris, Mother du Fargis forbade him to enter Port-Royal of the Fields, saying that she could not recognize his authority because he had not been appointed superior of the monastery under the regular conditions.

The archbishop still went several times a week to the Paris monastery in an effort to obtain new signatures.

The humble people of the neighborhood, mindful of the kindness of the nuns who had always come to their aid, began to grumble each time the prelate appeared. Soon he was forced to change carriages so as not to be recognized in the faubourg Saint-Jacques. He successively persuaded several more religious to sign, but three of these were devoured by remorse and retracted soon afterward.

Monseigneur de Péréfixe now knew that he could obtain nothing more. The court was beginning to tire of the whole affair, for the royal treasury had to pay for the upkeep of the prisoners in the other convents, and at a time when Colbert was trying to reduce expenses. Despite his minister's reproaches, Louis XIV was more lavish than ever in his expenditures. On May 8, 1664, the king arranged at Versailles, for the amusement of his mother and wife and especially of his mistress, the gracious La Vallière, the festival of "Pleasures of the Enchanted Island," which lasted nine days. It was the height of voluptuousness.

Molière, in a chariot, played the role of the great god Pan; his comedy The Princess of Elis was presented before the château. In the prologue, Aurora appears as a radiant young girl, singing this verse:

> When Love presents a charming choice
> Respond to his flame, O youthful fair!
> Affect not pride that cannot be subdued,
> Even when told this pride becomes you well.
>> When one is of a lovable age
>> Nothing is so fine as to love.

The king did not want to forego any of his pleasures, but was highly displeased at having to pay for the upkeep of the captive nuns, modest as was this expense. In full agreement with Colbert, the sovereign said one day to Monseigneur de Péréfixe who happened to be at the château of Saint Germain: "Why not send these nuns back to their house of the Fields where they can eat up their own revenues?"

Away from the capital, lost in the solitude of the valley, the nuns would soon be forgotten and the royal treasury would have to disburse nothing further. Actually, payment was already being made with such irregularity that the communities housing the prisoners were often forced to feed them at their own expense.

For the archbishop, the king's wishes amounted to an order. Immediately on returning to Paris, Monseigneur de Péréfixe took measures for the exiles to be taken to Port-Royal of the Fields. He likewise decided to send with them the Paris religious who had refused to sign, for the prelate quaked at the idea that these rebels might persuade the few nuns who had obeyed him to retract their signatures.

On July 2, 1665, at nine o'clock in the evening, Angélique de Saint-Jean saw the superior of the Annunciade convent enter her cell. She had come to tell her that a carriage awaited before the monastery—she was to leave at once.

The nun was carried in a conveyance that rolled through the night along streets lighted only by the candles in shop windows. A lady who had been awaiting her in the carriage, and who was now sitting beside her, explained that the archbishop had returned very late from Saint Germain, and this was the reason he had been able to carry out the king's wishes only after nightfall.

"It is just and right, Madame," replied Angélique de Saint-Jean, "that we should be as ready to carry out God's orders as some are prompt to execute those of the court."

The carriage stopped on the Place Royale, and there Arnauld d'Andilly's daughter saw climb into it another captive, Sister Christine Briquet. The nun's face was invisible in the darkness, but Angélique recognized the voice of the one she called "her child."

The carriage continued on to the Saint-Jacques gate, which had already been shut for the night and had to be opened to them. Finally at eleven o'clock they reached the Visitation convent on the faubourg Saint-Jacques. The two exiles were now very close to their own abbey, and could hear a familiar sound—the clock of the Carthusian convent sounding the second stroke of matins.

At the Visitation convent, where they had to spend the night, Angélique found her two younger sisters. The "poor goslings" had signed the formulary. They threw themselves at her feet, asking pardon for a weakness they would mourn all their lives even though they had atoned for it by retracting.

"A new day dawned for me," said Angélique in recalling this moment.

Now closely united, the three daughters of Monsieur d'Andilly went to the room where they found their ailing aunt, Agnès Arnauld, lying on her bed. She showed immense joy at seeing her three nieces gathered around her. Although Angélique de Saint-Jean was anxious to save the strength of the former abbess, she could not resist her desire to know whether the latter had denied her beliefs, as the Annunciades had given her reason to fear. In fact, in one of her petitions to the archbishop poor Agnès, who could no longer live apart from the eucharist, thought she could write that she was "indifferent" insofar as the formulary was concerned, "and had not yet decided not to sign," whereupon the archbishopric had immediately proclaimed her submission. Agnès reassured her niece—she had not signed.

Thus relieved of her greatest worry, Angélique felt that she was reliving, as she said, the words of the Psalm: "My flesh has flourished again, and with my will I will give praise to him." She experienced, she wrote later, the feeling of "coming out of a tomb in which she had been buried for ten months"

The night was spent almost entirely by the four religious in telling what had happened during this separation and in reassuring one another. At dawn they learned that a conveyance awaited them, ready to depart.

Angélique asked her aunt to open the Bible at random so that they might know the will of God. Agnès read this passage from Jeremiah: "I will gather together the remnants of my flock . . . and I will make them return to their own fields." Thus was the existence of Port-Royal marked by the voices of the prophets.

The conveyance left, bearing the nuns away, but soon the coachman had to stop because a horse had lost its shoe. Then in succession five more carriages appeared. Behind the glass panes could be seen familiar figures: the white habits, the red crosses. Almost the entire community of Port-Royal was on its way to the Fields! Each carriage was hailed with cries of joy and answering voices. Angélique de Saint-Jean describes the nuns standing upright in the carriages, stretching out their hands to their sisters: "It was like the resurrection of the dead."

The carriages stopped before the Abbey of Port-Royal of the Fields. There was no such ringing of bells nor lighting of bonfires as had welcomed Mother Angélique Arnauld years before, but Angélique de Saint-Jean found even more beautiful the sight of the church filled with the nuns, reunited at last.

In the absence of the abbess, who was still unable to come to the convent of the Fields and was at Meaux, the new arrivals were received by the prioress, Mother du Fargis. Several days later, the newcomers celebrated with their sisters the anniversary of the dedication of the church of the Fields, and with their whole hearts joined in singing the words of the hymn: "This is the house of the Lord, which is built with solid unity. It is well founded upon a firm rock."

The transfer of the community to the house of the Fields caused a great upheaval. The nuns from Paris, most of whom had never been in the valley, felt lost in the heart of "this wild and inaccessible desert."

As for Mother Agnès, she found the silent reminders of her youth in each hall of the abbey, each path of the garden. "This house is so hidden and enclosed it makes you feel you have just entered the religious life," she said to her sisters.

Nevertheless it was agreed that the measures taken by Monseigneur de Péréfixe could not be accepted, for in that case the community would definitely lose their Paris house.

"It was necessary," said one of the nuns, "for a storm to cast us into Port-Royal of the Fields, for it was not our own choice."

Furthermore, the seventy-two religious and fourteen lay nuns who had to live in the valley soon learned that their reunion was not due to royal benevolence. An officer arrived at the abbey with a corps of guards; the soldiers' duty was to see that no one communicated with the nuns. The guards occupied the inner gardens and permitted the religious to breathe the fresh air for only a few hours each day; even then they were subject to surveillance by soldiers, either mounted or on foot. The recluses could not speak to anyone; not even to the gardeners, who were threatened with hanging if they accepted or transmitted a single letter.

The court hoped that the nuns, deprived in their solitude of any moral support, would not long delay in making their submission. However, they were accustomed to live "at sword's point," as they expressed it. They used every sort of stratagem to correspond with their former spiritual directors; the hollow measuring rod of a stonemason or a piece of fruit sufficed to send messages thrown over the wall and furtively picked up by someone outside. Antoine Arnauld, Nicole, Saci, and Sainte-Marthe received letters in this way and replied to them. All of them asked the religious to answer persecution only with humble love, as Christ had done. One of the priests sometimes went to Port-Royal at night, and from the top of the wall the religious could hear a familiar voice addressing them with words of consolation.

Later, when Saci was arrested, the police found among his papers several confessions written out by the religious, to whom he then sent messages containing absolution. At times he was even able to attach consecrated hosts so that the nuns might receive communion.

The abbess, Mother de Ligny, reached Port-Royal three weeks after her sisters, and held a chapter meeting. Three nuns who had retracted after signing came to rejoin their sisters; these made honorable amends and renewed their retractions.

The good Mother Agnès accused herself of having used lightly the word "indifferent" in regard to the formulary.

"I confess my fault," she said, "and I do not want to seek any excuse for it."

Thereafter, the former abbess put herself under the authority of the younger nuns who had been firmer than she had, saying: "Please command me in regard to what I should do in the future."

Learning of all this, Monseigneur de Péréfixe increased his severity. Not only were the choir religious denied the sacraments, but they were forbidden to chant the office or ring the bells. The peasants in the country would look with fear in their eyes at the monastery buried in silence.

Agnès Arnauld could not resign herself to living without holy communion. Knowing that the lay sisters, who had been dispensed from the obligation to sign, were receiving the eucharist, she hid herself behind the veil of one of their number in order to receive the host surreptitiously.

The new director sent to Port-Royal of the Fields by the archbishop was a young Savoyard, pretentious and ignorant, who constantly harried the consciences of his penitents. Nevertheless they were to receive some unexpected aid in this connection. Marsh fever, especially increased by the lack of medical attention and fresh air, was a daily danger to women already in delicate health, and the superiors had to ask for a physician to be sent to them. Only one doctor could be found who was willing to share the exile of the religious and to live imprisoned as they did. This was the doctor of the Abbey of the Fields, Hamon, whose gentle smile and intelligent eyes are shown in his portrait by Philippe de Champaigne.

Although he had driven him away earlier, the archbishop was forced to call Hamon back. The conditions imposed on him were extremely harsh: he must always speak to the sick in a voice loud enough to be heard by an extern sister charged by the archbishop to watch the community. The guards were to search his pockets and examine the food served him.

The doctor accepted all this. Earlier, after making a brilliant record as a student and with a fine future before him, Hamon had felt irresistibly drawn to God. He had placed his destiny in the hands of Singlin, who sent him to the Abbey of the Fields. There the physician worked as a laborer, for each of the solitaries had to do manual work in order to supply the needs of the community.

Later on, when the solitary who attended the nuns died, Hamon succeeded him. At first it had been difficult for him; many of the nuns believed only in the efficacy of quack medicines distributed by Antoine Arnauld and the duc de Luynes; all Saci's authority had been needed to get them to follow the prescriptions of the new doctor. But now they welcomed as an old friend the discreet man who had learned to use few words in speaking to them, as provided in their rule.

A new role awaited Hamon in the Monastery of the Fields. Not only was he erudite, versed in Greek and Latin as well as in Spanish and Italian, but he was the author of a fine exegesis of the "Song of Songs." The Messieurs asked him to write out meditations as circumstances inspired him, for he would represent the last hope of the poor nuns. Hamon was frightened—they wanted him to do the work of a priest, he, a simple layman! Even so, he decided to obey.

Unable to speak freely with the religious because the extern sister was always on watch, Hamon gave them his writings, which were passed from hand to hand and gave great consolation to the recluses. Almost despite himself, the physician of the body became the physician of souls.

The members of the community suffered because they were deprived of priestly guidance. Their confessors, Hamon wrote, "were formerly between God and ourselves; at present God himself is between us and them. . . . We have spoken to his ministers so many times; let us now speak to Jesus Christ."

The nuns had to live without the eucharist, yet, wrote Hamon, "who separates us from the invisible altar where we ourselves are the priests? Who separates us from our hearts? Let us revive within us the grace of past communions. A crumb of this bread will be enough to feed the whole world."

Often in her last hours a dying nun would confess her despair at being deprived of the help of the Church. Hamon, who was to assist at five deathbeds, wrote these lines: "The Spouse has come; it is he who knocks at the door. You will see Jesus Christ as he sees you."

Burials were conducted in the presence of a priest, but he did not have the right to say the Mass for the Dead. The silence around a bier was heartbreaking to the survivors; Port-Royal's doctor consoled them with words worthy of Saint Francis of Assisi: "No human being will chant at your burial. The angels will be singing there."

Hamon had to conduct himself in this manner at the time of the death of Madame de Saint-Ange, whose name in religion was Sister Anne Eugénie. The poor woman's signature had been wrested from her, but once at the Fields she had retracted it.

Madame Le Febvre, the extern sister charged with watching the nuns, appeared at the bedside of this dying woman. Despite his kindness, Hamon could not refrain from expressing his feeling against this spy. "She was," he said, "one of those instruments whom God holds in reserve among his treasures of snow and sleet."

Strong in the authority conferred on her by the archbishop, the extern put a limit on the time the doctor could devote to Sister Anne Eugénie because she did not want to waste a whole hour watching over a single bed.

"Each person has his own work to do," she said.

At the moment of the nun's death, Hamon asked her to pardon her enemies. She did this so willingly that the physician murmured: "Have you nothing to say to Madame Le Febvre?"

"Ask her to come closer so that I may embrace her," said Sister Anne Eugénie.

She did this with so much tenderness that the extern sister, Hamon wrote, stood there "frightened and confused"; this enemy of the Jansenists was forced to recognize that she had been completely disarmed.

"She could not defend herself against the charity of the dying nun," the doctor said.

Hamon himself was overwhelmed; watching Madame de Saint-Ange die, he had seen a believer victorious over death: "Charity so pure as this took the place of the communion refused her. To receive such love as this is to receive God."

For another twenty years Port-Royal was blessed with the gentle attentions of this man. In later years the country people would watch as the old doctor passed by on a donkey, knitting so that his hands would never be idle.

Confronted with royal proclamations and pontifical bulls, the majority of the French hierarchy obeyed. However, four prelates refused to give in. First and foremost was Henri Arnauld, Bishop of Angers, the brother of Antoine and Angélique Arnauld; in his own diocese he revived the faith of Port-Royal and with calm courage gave his moral support to the persecuted nuns. Buzanval, Bishop of Beauvais, Caulet, Bishop of Pamiers, and Pavillon, Bishop of Alet, showed themselves as determined as did Henri Arnauld.

Pavillon, who was considered a saint, quickly became the hero of the resistance. This prelate, a disciple of Saint Vincent de Paul, owed his bishopric of Alet in Languedoc to Richelieu. As a priest he had not wanted dignities and had always dreamed of becoming a country pastor, so as "to teach religion," he said, "to simple men." But Monsieur Vincent had persuaded the great cardinal to entrust a diocese to the man he considered the ideal priest. Alet was only a village lost in a wild, poor countryside, and there Pavillon went about as a simple pastor trying to win the souls of a rustic people.

When, to satisfy Louis XIV, the Assembly of the Clergy requested the signature of the formulary, the Bishop of Alet said quite loudly that he did not recognize the right of this "uncanonical assembly" to make laws for the Church. The day a royal proclamation ordered the signatures to be handed in, Pavillon expressed his indignation at seeing a layman impose his will on the clergy in a matter dealing with dogma and faith. He was daring enough to address remonstrances to the monarch from his bishop's residence in Languedoc: "No truly Christian prince," he wrote, "has ever attributed to himself the authority to make laws for the Church." After sending this letter out, Pavillon forbade any of the priests in his diocese to sign the formulary.

In a country where royal power was absolute as it then was in France, everybody was stupefied. Chancellor Séguier declared that "Monsieur of Alet has wanted to spit in the king's face." Advocate-General Talon, who was commissioned to carry out the sovereign's wishes, requested Parlement to condemn the bishop's audacious protest. The magistrates had to yield, but the language of their decree was extremely moderate. The first president, Lamoignon, consented to sign only after long delays and at the instance of the king.

Determined to stamp out any resistance, Louis XIV procured a new condemnation of *Augustinus* from Pope Alexander VII, on February 15, 1665, together with a brief ordering the signature pure and simple of the formulary. This time Pavillon had to obey the authority of the Holy Father, but did so only with express reservations. On June 1, 1665, the bishop published a mandate making a distinction between the condemnation of the five propositions—to which he submitted—and the one attributing them to Jansenius; to Rome's affirmation contained in the last he replied by a respectful silence, as Antoine Arnauld had done.

A decree of the Council of State condemned this mandate, yet it was difficult for the king to engage in a theological disputation with a bishop who had great moral prestige and with whom three other bishops had declared themselves to be in agreement. Louis XIV was again compelled to request support from the Vatican. The pope answered with two briefs, one revoking the mandate of Pavillon, the other providing for the appointment of prelates to sit as a pontifical commission to judge the four rebel bishops.

Only then did the monarch realize he had gone about things in the wrong way; after sharply defending his authority against Rome, he had placed himself in the position of a suppliant. The pope was already making his power felt; were the bishops chosen by Alexander VII to be commissioned to pronounce final judgment on French soil, a grave blow would be struck at royal power and at the Gallican Church. Several ministers—Colbert, Lyonne, Le Tellier—showed their concern, the latter declaring that the affair "had taken a bad turn." But death restored order in everything: Alexander VII died just as he was designating the nine prelates to judge the four bishops. Clement IX succeeded him on June 20, 1667. The new pope was reputed to be a conciliatory man; he was to be the pope of peace.

Louis XIV had won victory after victory in his struggle with the Hapsburgs. Turenne had conquered Flanders and Condé the Franche-Comté. In
May, 1668, the king signed the peace of Aix-la-Chapelle, which assured him
of eleven strongholds; all that remained for him to do was to bring concord
into his kingdom's internal affairs.

Now Jansenism had become a real danger, for nineteen prelates had
signed a letter stating that the doctrine of the four bishops was the doctrine
of France. Was there to be a schism? Furthermore, a student had been so
bold as to present to the Sorbonne a thesis on the following subject: "Can
Parlement depose an adulterous king?"

Le Tellier and Lyonne counseled Louis XIV to take advantage of the
new pope's election to recover France's dominant position at the Vatican. On
his side, the nuncio, Monseigneur Bargellini, was determined to use every
means to reconcile the Church and the Jansenists.

The Jansenists themselves were tiring of the fight. Arnauld and Nicole
were living in hiding at the residence of the Longuevilles; Saci had been
arrested and incarcerated in the Bastille on May 13, 1666.

Then, without the knowledge of the Jesuits or of Monseigneur de Péréfixe, the ministers and prelates intervened. Le Tellier wrote that it was
necessary "to find honest means to disassociate the king from the measures
taken at Rome."

The greatest obstacle was presented by Pavillon, who would have to be
forced to retract his mandate, for the intransigence of this prelate was known
to everyone. In the hope of facilitating negotiations, certain personages
urged that the Bishop of Alet be ordered to come to Paris. Le Tellier opposed this plan. "Pavillon," he said to the king, "is regarded as a saint.
Everywhere he passes crowds will come to ask his blessing; all Paris will
march along with him. He will arrive at court in the midst of a triumphal
parade."

It was then agreed to leave the Bishop of Alet in his remote diocese; he
would only be requested, as would the other three bishops resisting the pope,
to send a letter of submission affirming respect for the authority of the
sovereign pontiff, their own desire for peace, and their promise to sign the
formulary. But a tacit reservation would now be permitted; it was agreed
that the signatures could be preceded by a statement allowing it to be
understood that the question of *fact* was only the subject of deferential
silence.

The Archbishop of Sens, Monseigneur de Gondrin, and the Bishop of
Châlons, Monseigneur Vialart, were the principal negotiators. With great
difficulty they drew up a letter which had to satisfy the pope, the king, the
nuncio, the four prelates, and Port-Royal. Still hidden at the house of the

Longuevilles, Arnauld and Nicole sent messages to assist them in bringing about a reconciliation. Nicole was already completely satisfied; as for the great Arnauld, he wanted to protect the nuns from a storm similar to the one he himself had provoked earlier. The text to be sent to the four bishops was submitted to Louis XIV, to his ministers, and finally to the nuncio. After obtaining the agreement of all these, the Archbishop of Sens signed the letter in the name of the four prelates, since Antoine Arnauld had promised that they would accept its terms. On August 9, 1668, Monseigneur Bargellini, who had received full powers from Rome, apposed his signature in turn. Had peace finally been made? The Archbishop of Sens and all the negotiators wanted to think so. In succession the bishops of Angers, of Beauvais, and of Pamiers gave in.

Alone, as might have been expected, the Bishop of Alet held back. To courier after courier sent to urge and beseech him, he merely replied: "We must think this over in the presence of God." The bishop never reached an important decision without long prayer and reflection, and he thought of those who were forgotten by everyone—the nuns and defenders of Port-Royal who must be restored to their place in the Church.

"How is it possible," he exclaimed, "to give the name 'peace' to a compromise that abandons those who have waged the best fight? As for myself, I would prefer to remain alone and expose myself to every kind of suffering rather than to abandon them."

The court ended by giving in; peace was extended to all the men and women under the protection of the Bishop of Alet. So after three messages from the Archbishop of Sens who "fell to his knees before him," and at the entreaty of the Bishop of Pamiers, his faithful companion in the struggle, Pavillon was the last to sign a letter of submission to the pope, on September 10, 1668.

There was great jubilation among those who had worked for peace. The bishop of Comminges wrote Arnauld: "At last, Monsieur, you can serve the Church without being obliged to hide; the light that burns so brightly in your books no longer need proceed from the midst of darkness."

Not having been advised of the preliminaries for peace, the Jesuits could do nothing when they learned it had been concluded. The most important of them, Father Annat, expressed his bitterness to the nuncio, accusing him "of having ruined by a quarter-hour's weakness the work of twenty years."

As his protests were in vain, the father confessor addressed himself to Louis XIV. Did the king forget that the Jansenists were a danger to the state as well as to the Church? But the penitent sovereign was keeping his distance from the Society of Jesus, and drily replied:

"Insofar as religion is concerned, it is the business of the pope; if he is satisfied, you and I should be satisfied. Insofar as my state is concerned, I advise you not to distress yourself; I shall know how to do what is necessary."

In other days Father Annat had met with a similar refusal in the office of Mazarin; today the king's confessor again realized that he could not have the bad grace to insist.

On October 8, 1668, Pope Clement's brief proclaiming "the peace of the Church" was brought to Paris. The Holy Father declared that the four bishops had agreed to the signature pure and simple of the formulary; he did not know, or at least he did not want to know what attenuations were contained in the statements that preceded these signatures.

"It was a sort of conjurer's game," one priest described it crudely.

In his joy, Monseigneur de Gondrin, Archbishop of Sens, went to seek out Antoine Arnauld and present him to the nuncio. Earlier the latter had sarcastically compared the learned theologian to the famous Athanasius, the fiery patriarch who during the fourth century had engaged in a merciless struggle against Emperor Constantius; yet in the presence of the defender of grace, the Roman emissary found words to flatter Arnauld in his secret pride as a writer.

"You have a golden pen," the nuncio told him.

When the king learned that the Port-Royal theologian had paid a visit to Monseigneur Bargellini, Louis XIV also expressed a desire to receive him. The marquis de Pomponne, the French ambassador to Holland and Arnauld's nephew, rushed to find his uncle at the Hôtel de Longueville where he was in hiding and to accompany him to Saint-Germain. There Antoine Arnauld was welcomed by his friends Luynes and Condé, and then by the king. He thanked His Majesty "for suffering him to appear before him," and, naively convinced that his cause must appear to everyone as the cause of God, he added, with a touch of pride, "that nothing was greater than the protection given by His Majesty to the Church in this instance."

Louis XIV was accustomed to dealing with men of varying mentality, and knew how to win them all. He replied to Arnauld "that he was most pleased to see a man of his merit," and hoped that he would henceforth "use the talents given him by God for the defense of the Church." Actually, the king wanted to make use of this "golden pen" against the Protestants.

Like a litigant unable to forget his lawsuit, Arnauld could not resist slipping in a word about the recent "disputes." But Louis XIV stopped him, saying: "That is in the past; we must not speak of it any more." The king added that one should never write anything "that might embitter people." Here was the grandson of Henri IV in his role as sovereign—conciliating, appeasing, healing over wounds.

As the interview came to an end, Louis XIV turned to his ambassador with a radiant smile, saying, "Monsieur de Pomponne, I think you are very happy to see this happening."

The uncle and nephew left the king's presence in triumph. A crowd of courtiers, always on the alert for some newsworthy incident, pressed curiously around the Jansenist. Each of them wanted to see "a person so well received by the king after having been invisible for so many years."

Monseigneur de Péréfixe, hastening to join the victorious side, had no difficulty in obtaining pardon for Saci, who was still imprisoned in the Bastille. Pomponne, who had become the master of ceremonies, arrived at the prison armed with the royal order. After having his cousin liberated, he conducted him to Monseigneur de Péréfixe. Saci asked the archbishop for his blessing and the latter, who had always really admired Port-Royal, humbly replied: "Ah, it is I who should ask you to bless me!" Only a few minutes later Saci was led into the Louvre by the archbishop and the ambassador and received by Louis XIV.

After so many effusive exchanges, thought had to be given to the nuns, for the sovereign was now determined to put an end to quarrels which had been so detrimental to royal authority. He therefore urged Monseigneur de Péréfixe to be as conciliatory as possible in regard to the nuns. It was proper, said the king, "to be no more difficult than the pope himself, and to be satisfied with having the religious do the same as the four bishops."

The prelate bowed to the monarch's will with more relief than he cared to admit. But, unlike the people of the court, the nuns did not assume several attitudes and several faces; their anxieties returned when the signature was once more requested of them.

Nicole saw the danger: if the unfortunate women were stubborn, they were going to be cast off by the entire Church. They must concede, but first someone would have to calm them down.

"They are accustomed to regarding the formulary," Nicole wrote, "as a frightful monster bearing the mark of the Beast."

Arnauld shared Nicole's opinion. But, understanding how deeply the tender consciences of the religious had suffered from the dispute, he arranged that signature pure and simple be not required of them. They were to send Monseigneur de Péréfixe a petition assuring him of their obedience. The terms of this document were long debated between the archbishop and the Messieurs; the five propositions were condemned without reservation; their attribution to Jansenius was received with deference. Antoine Arnauld then wrote to the nuns asking them to sign a petition which had been prepared with so much care. If peace is broken, he told them, you will be blamed for it, for simple nuns who had no access to the domain of theology would be accused "of conducting themselves according to their own opinions and without taking the advice of any ecclesiastic. . . . Do not stand apart on a road by yourselves."

As Monseigneur de Péréfixe believed it wise not to put in his appearance at the monastery, it was the Bishop of Meaux, Monseigneur de Ligny, who brought the formulary. Arnauld and Saci arrived at the same time, and after a long talk with the religious, finally persuaded them to sign.

The Bishop of Meaux received the signatures of the whole community on February 15, 1669; on February 18th the sentence raising the interdict was read by the vicar-general to the assembled religious of Port-Royal of the Fields. With the exception of one nun, who was seriously ill, all were present in their stalls, wearing their mantles and long veils.

As soon as the words of pardon were spoken, the whole abbey came back to life. An order from the king withdrew the men-at-arms who had forbidden anyone to approach; the church was alight with candles; bells were rung, calling the peasants, who came from the fields and hastened to stand before the doors, open at last. With tears in their eyes they heard from behind the grill the nuns' clear voices rising beneath the echoing arches. The song was a song of deliverance—the *Te Deum.*

Shortly afterward, on Sunday, March 3rd, Antoine Arnauld, again able to walk about in broad daylight, arrived to celebrate mass at Port-Royal. Just as he came to the consecration of the host, a hymn was heard at the entrance to the church as the villagers of Magny, led by their pastor who had always defended the nuns, began to sing the words of the office of the Blessed Sacrament: "All of us who partake of the same bread and of the same chalice are but one bread and one body. . . ." Hearing these words, Port-Royal's daughters looked at one another in silence; in the Abbey of the Fields all were indeed one, and all shared a single thought.

But coming back, as was necessary, to terrestrial things, one shadow remained. The house on the faubourg Saint-Jacques, acquired so long before by Madame Arnauld, was lost to her descendants. Only the "signers" were privileged to remain; they were now but ten in number, for among them had been two lunatics who had to be confined.

Monseigneur de Péréfixe ordered the meager community of the faubourg Saint-Jacques to elect an abbess. Sister Dorothée Perdreau was chosen by the Paris nuns and received her expected reward: her rival, Sister Flavie Passart, fell ill with vexation, for she had thought she would be made the abbess.

Mother Perdreau's election was irregular, for each religious had formerly bound herself not to take part in voting except in the company of all her sisters. The nuns of the Fields protested without success; Louis XIV would not allow Parlement to hear their complaint.

On May 13, 1669, a decree of the Council of State expressing the king's will proclaimed the separation of the two communities. In future the abbess of the Paris house would not be elected by the nuns but appointed by the king; in this way, Louis XIV again acquired the power relinquished by Louis XIII. The house in the valley became the Monastery of Port-Royal of the Fields, and there the nuns retained the right to elect their abbess every three years.

The separation was made final by a brief from the pope confirming the decree of the Council of State. This decree bestowed all property on the Paris monastery; the ten signers had only to turn over a modest pension to each of their sisters in the Fields.

What did it matter? "Times are better, for we have been permitted to live," wrote Angélique de Saint-Jean. "All they want is the purse which, God be praised, contains neither our treasure nor our heart."

The Bishop of Alet was still mindful of the fate of his flock. "God is impoverishing you so that you may be filled with the riches of his grace," he wrote to Mother Agnès.

The old nun was completely happy to be in her valley and able to receive communion. Her sisters, freed of anxiety, enjoyed the sweetness of peace. Postulants and novices arrived to assure the future of the monastery; young boarding pupils could once more be received. The first to arrive were the daughters of Pomponne. "The whole community," wrote Mother Agnès, "shares the joy of having these little doves, who come bearing the olive branch."

The solitaries returned to the valley, where the former confessors of Port-Royal took up their old posts. Saci still lived in Paris, but came frequently to the Fields. Madame de Ligny was succeeded by a new abbess, Mother du Fargis, who appointed Angélique de Saint-Jean prioress.

Death came to many of those who had taken part in the struggle. Father Annat died in June, 1670. Several months later Monseigneur de Péréfixe expired in his turn; on February 19th of the same year the last Arnauld daughter, Mother Agnès, followed to the grave the archbishop who had caused her such great torment. Up to her last hour she found strength to smile tenderly at her sisters gathered around her.

"Her last gesture," wrote her niece, Angélique de Saint-Jean, "was to try to raise her arm in order to bless the whole community."

Agnès' burial mass was said by her brother, Antoine Arnauld. As the nuns chanted the *In exitu* for one who had shed the light of sweetness and gentleness over Port-Royal, their voices broke, and their weeping prevented them from going on with the hymn. At that moment the grave voices of the solitaries were lifted at the rear of the church, and the Messieurs continued the office to its end. Listening to this, the recluses were consoled in the best possible way—by the promise of undying loyalty.

After leaving Port-Royal of the Fields, Andilly lived on his estate of Pomponne. The amiable old man was often favored with the company of such brilliant women as Madame de Sévigné and Madame de La Fayette. With them he liked to play the role of the Jansenist, telling the marquise that she was nothing but a "pretty pagan" because she made an idol of her daughter, Madame de Grignan.

Since peace had been made and the solitaries had returned to the Fields, Angélique de Saint-Jean wished for her father's return. But he lingered on in the beautiful domain of Pomponne which had been left him by his dead wife. When his son, who had adopted the name of this estate, was appointed Secretary of State for Foreign Affairs, Louis XIV allowed it to be understood that he would appreciate a visit from Monsieur d'Andilly if he saw fit to come to thank his king for the favor shown his son. This awakened the courtier slumbering in the breast of the old solitary, and the eldest of the Arnaulds hastened to leave his lands in response to his sovereign's call. The people of the court showed no displeasure at the arrival of this sage of eighty-two, who had not put in an appearance for so long and was coming on his last visit—here was a man who did not constitute a threat to anyone.

"The king," Madame de Sévigné wrote her daughter, "chatted an hour with the good Andilly, as pleasant, simple and agreeable as anyone could possibly be; it was easy for him to be himself with this good old man."

Louis XIV, who liked to be beguiling, expressed to Andilly his satisfaction at having the latter's son at this side, and added that he would not leave his minister's father in peace, for he wanted to see him again.

"When the good man," Madame de Sévigné continued, "assured him of his loyalty, the king said he did not doubt it; that when one serves God well, one also serves his king." The marquise then recounted "the marvels" that followed the conversation: Louis XIV took care that Andilly be served with dinner and that he be driven around in a barouche.

Touched by all these favors, the patriarch of Port-Royal feared he would succumb to the sin of pride. "He was in raptures," wrote Madame de Sévigné, "and felt that he must say to himself from time to time, 'We must humble ourselves.'" Later, in giving his own account of the way he had been received, Andilly confessed that he had lost all notion of time. "My memory was as though suspended," he wrote.

What a distance between this and Pascal! But it was good to be at peace.

Back at his estate of Pomponne, Andilly lingered nearly two years more. Finally, having paid his tribute to the world, with good grace he decided to return to his place in the valley.

Although he had left his friends, the solitary found them coming to him. Madame de Sévigné could not resist her desire to visit him in his retirement in the "desert"; when she went she ran into her husband's uncle, Renaud de Sévigné, and came away charmed by the surroundings.

"This Port-Royal," she wrote, "is a desert place, a paradise; its holiness spreads over the whole countryside for a league around. The nuns are as angels on earth; all those who serve them, down to the wagoners, the shepherds, the workmen, all are holy."

Monsieur d'Andilly died, surrounded by his family, on September 27, 1674, at the age of eighty-five. The community prayed for him night and day, and, although a layman, he had the privilege of being buried with ceremonies reserved to the religious. His brother, Antoine Arnauld, pronounced the funeral oration.

After Madame de Sévigné, many prominent personages visited the "desert." Cardinal de Retz came to dine, and other prelates and members of the nobility followed his example. The road leading to the monastery was often blocked with carriages; the solitaries had the greatest difficulty in remaining alone, and the nuns were disturbed at seeing their parlor invaded.

One of the visitors, the Franciscan Father Comblat, told how moved he had been by the chanting of the nuns. "The one who begins the Psalms has an entirely admirable voice; she starts and ends each one in a wailing, mournful way that pierces your heart. . . . Their chant is a veritable prayer."

Ladies came to the valley to make retreats, as certain of them had done at the monastery of the faubourg Saint-Jacques. One of them, the duchesse de Longueville, had a house built for herself in the shadow of the Abbey of the Fields.

Before her conversion, this illustrious penitent had led a turbulent life. She was thirteen years old when her uncle, the duc de Montmorency, revolted against Richelieu; he was condemned to death and beheaded at Toulouse. Several years later the young girl entered a world which was immediately enraptured by her beauty. "Her light hair and other marvelous features gave her the look of an angel. No one could see her and not love her," Madame de Motteville wrote. The brilliant company at the Hôtel de Rambouillet admired the princess' grace and the strange languid air that added to her charm. Her marriage to the duc de Longueville was almost a misalliance for, as daughter of Henri de Bourbon, prince de Condé, the duchess was cousin to the king.

For her sake, Coligny was killed in a duel. François de Marsillac—the future duc de Rochefoucauld—later became her lover. The liaison of the author of the *Maxims* with Madame de Longueville provoked so great a scandal that her husband asked her to join him at Munster, where he had gone to take part in the negotiations that ended in the Treaty of Westphalia. Turenne was charged to escort the unfaithful wife to Germany. Captivated in his turn, the marshal became violently enamoured of the duchess, but his love was not returned. After joining her husband at Munster, Madame de Longueville continued to lead her gay life, but ardently defended the Jansenists in the name of a brand of religion which she adopted to suit herself. One of the ladies of her entourage expressed surprise at seeing her "at table, settling with great ease questions which the Fathers and Councils of the Church discussed only in trembling."

Extremely well read, the duchess gave the laurel crown to Voiture but withheld it from Benserade. Her passion for La Rochefoucauld led her to take part with her lover in The Fronde; at that period Cardinal de Retz led the beautiful rebel in triumph to the Hôtel de Ville, where she was acclaimed by the populace. The great Condé, Madame de Longueville's brother and hero of the battle of Rocroi, became the leader of The Fronde of Princes, and the duchess persuaded first her second brother, prince de Conti, next her husband, and finally Turenne to join in the revolt.

When they were defeated, Madame de Longueville had to flee to Normandy and then to Holland. News of the death of her mother, the princesse de Condé, arrived to overwhelm the lady in her defeat.

Shortly afterward, La Rochefoucauld seized on one of the pretty woman's flirtations as a pretext to break with her. Following this, he was indelicate enough to make public in his *Memoirs* certain details of his liaison with the duchess. Deeply wounded by this, she began to feel "a secret torment," and thought of entering a Carmelite convent. "If I had attachments," she wrote, "they have been broken." So at the age of thirty-four, after many twists and turns of the road, Madame de Longueville felt disgust for the world.

At Moulins, where she had been exiled by the king, she discovered at the Visitation monastery "the road that leads to life. . . . The faith that lay as though dead and buried beneath my passions was revived," she said. "I was as a person who awakens from a deep sleep." The duchess then became the friend of Mademoiselle de Vertus, the descendant of an old Breton family, whose conduct atoned for the scandalous life of her sister, Madame de Montbazon. Mademoiselle de Vertus' health was too poor for her to become a religious, but she wore the white habit of a novice and remained in the novitiate all her life. It was she and the marquise de Sablé who led Madame de Longueville to Port-Royal. The latter "identified her sentiments with those of her two friends to such a degree that she could no longer recognize her own," wrote La Rochefoucauld who observed his former mistress' conversion with curiosity.

As soon as she discovered the Monastery of Port-Royal the duchess wished to go to its aid. It did not displease the *frondeuse* to place herself on the side of "angels," and in this way teach a lesson to a king who went from adultery to adultery.

Shortly before her death, Mother Angélique Arnauld had been touched by the sentiments of Madame de Longueville, whose faith was then showing itself to be as strong as her passions of other days. "All I have seen of this princess seems to me to be pure gold," the former abbess said.

Mademoiselle de Vertus begged Singlin to take charge of the new penitent's conscience which, she said, "could find no rest." The priest hesitated, as he had done in the case of Pascal, because he feared that her conversion would be short-lived. But on rereading the story of the Samaritan woman in the Gospel, he was reminded that Christ did not scorn a woman from an alien land. He consented to listen to Madame de Longueville and to talk to her. After her conversation with the spiritual director of Port-Royal, she told Mademoiselle de Vertus "that she was like another person." On November 24, 1661, Singlin heard the duchess' confession, and at that time she obtained what she had been denied for years: "a ray of hope."

Madame de Longueville meditated on her past life. The memory of civil war and of her adulteries frightened her less than the sin which had dominated her life as it had that of Angélique Arnauld—the sin of pride. The duchess had thrown herself body and soul into The Fronde to escape her condition as a woman; she had so wanted to play a role "in great affairs."

After her conversion, the temptation was stronger than ever. "My pride is transformed into an angel of light, so I have something to live on," she said. Nevertheless, she inflicted on herself the harshest of humiliations, namely, that of recognizing her own faults. Even here she had no illusions. "We would rather say bad things about ourselves," she confessed, "than not talk about ourselves at all"—words which inspired one of the maxims of La Rochefoucauld.

Singlin had to moderate the austerities practiced by the duchess, for they could easily have ruined his penitent's health. She took up residence at the Hôtel d'Epernon, rue Saint-Thomas-du-Louvre, and during the Jansenist persecution hid Nicole and Saci in her house. Sometimes the latter would fall asleep in her presence after rolling down his garters in front of her, "which made her suffer somewhat." The duchess preferred Nicole, who was better bred. It was in her home that the two theologians translated the New Testament into French; Saci was arrested on his way to Madame de Longueville's to work on this project. The rebellious noblewoman continued her fight against the king, but this time it was under divine aegis.

The princesse de Conti, Madame de Longueville's sister-in-law and the niece of Mazarin, was also a fervent friend of Port-Royal. The two women wrote in defense of *Augustinus,* with the collaboration of Mademoiselle de Vertus. La Rochefoucauld sarcastically referred to them as "the Mothers of the Church."

In 1668, the duchesse de Longueville played an active role in the peace concluded between the Jansenists, the Holy Father, and the king. She did not fear to write to Louis XIV and then to the pope in support of the cause of the nuns and the solitaries.

It seemed that God wanted to test this woman who was on the way to him. Stricken first in her loves and her ambitions, Madame de Longueville now had to suffer through her children. Her husband was the descendant of Dunois, the Bastard of Orleans, Jeanne d'Arc's companion, and in his honor one of the duchess' children was called the comte de Dunois. Although this unfortunate young man was unbalanced, holy orders were conferred on him at the command of Louis XIV. "This young man must be launched on the road of the priesthood," said the king.

The duchess' other son, the comte de Saint-Paul, was born of her liaison with La Rochefoucauld. Born during The Fronde, the child was named Paris by a mother who at that time was the idol of every Parisian. The count was killed at the age of twenty-three, during the crossing of the Rhine, at the side of his uncle, Condé. La Rochefoucauld had to hide his suffering, but "his tears," we are told by Madame de Sévigné, "flowed from the depths of his heart."

Madame de Longueville, who had placed all her hopes in this son, never recovered from her grief. She retired from the world and lived sometimes in the convent of the Carmelites on the faubourg Saint-Jacques, sometimes in the house she had built near the Abbey of Port-Royal of the fields. After Singlin's death, Saci became her spiritual director. She died on April 15, 1679, before reaching the age of sixty-five.

The terror that formerly devoured her had been replaced by complete confidence in the mercy of Christ. When her last hour came, and as Condé wept at her bedside, Madame de Longueville lifted her arms to heaven and expired.

Combining her recollections of La Rochefoucauld with those of the duchesse de Longueville, Madame de Sévigné wrote: "They died the same year; there is much to ponder in the story of these two souls."

The persecution had ended, and the valley bore its fruit. Andilly translated Sacred Scripture and published his "Christian Instructions Extracted from the Letters of Saint-Cyran." Arnauld and Nicole wrote a defense of the perpetuity of faith in the Catholic Church as a measure against the Calvinists. Saci, working with Arnauld and Nicole, finished his translation of the New Testament and began the publication of his Bible; his *Essays on Morality,* in which he showed his deep knowledge of the human mind, were published. "Methods," Lancelot's textbook for learning languages, was revised.

But Pascal, who lay in his tomb, continued to tower over Port-Royal. After his death his elder sister, Madame Périer, together with his nephew and friends, found the key to the world in which the author of *Provincial Letters* had lived and meditated. They discovered a testimonial sewn into his clothing, the existence of which no one had suspected.

Pascal had spent from September to November, 1654, in his search for the hidden God. Though he was anxious at first, his hope grew stronger and stronger. But even his young sister Jacqueline, who sustained and led him at that time, did not know at what moment this light had appeared. Pascal never spoke to anyone of that moment, but he wanted to remember it for the rest of his life. Should he meet the only misfortune he henceforth feared—separation from Jesus—he would put his hand over his heart, feel the leaf of parchment, and recall that fiery night, "Monday, 23rd November, from about half past ten at night until half past twelve."

After her brother's death, Madame Périer often meditated before the parchment on which the beloved hand had hastily traced each letter, always writing the name of Jesus in large letters. The document was wrapped in a thin sheet of paper, which also contained a copy of the testimonial and several addenda. Such was the pact concluded between God and Pascal, and the relatives and friends of the dead man called it the "Memorial."

FIRE

This word, standing alone on the first line and which would be recopied in capital letters, proclaimed the miracle.

When night had fallen over the house near the Luxembourg where Pascal lived, and doubtless as he was reading the Scriptures, he felt his whole soul embraced in the bright radiance of God's presence. In days of old, God had set this fire on the burning bush before the eyes of Moses; this fire descended upon the apostles on the day of Pentecost. At Emmaus it had entered the hearts of the disciples of the risen Christ: "Did not our hearts burn within us while he talked to us on the road?" Pascal had seen the fulfillment of the words of the Precursor: "He will baptize you with the Holy Spirit and with fire."

The One adored by the patriarchs and prophets had revealed himself to the author of the *Pensées*:

God of Abraham, God of Isaac, God of Jacob

Pascal's whole past rose up before him. He remembered the god of "philosophers and scholars" laboriously constructed by reason; he himself had followed this mirage at first and had run the risk of being lost. The Creator "is not the God of the dead, but of the living," says the Gospel. On his parchment Pascal wrote the name of the New Covenant, the symbol of pardon and grace:

God of Jesus Christ

All the man of science had explored, learned, and conquered was now as nothing:

Forgetfulness of the world and all things, except only God

One road remained, and there was only one: the road opened to man so that he might reach the beyond. Never before had Pascal been so fully aware of this progression toward the world of the supernatural.

He transcribed these words:

Greatness of the human soul

There had been an infinite distance between God and the author of the *Pensées,* but none of this remained. The vast space was annihilated, consumed by fire.

Joy, joy, joy, tears of joy

Yet at the very moment when Pascal came to the possession of God, he was overcome by remorse: in other days he had rejected Jesus:

I have fallen away from him

This must never happen again! Eternity was here, visible, and must he live without him?

My God, wilt thou forsake me?
Let me not be separated from thee for all eternity

Snatched back from the abyss, Pascal cleaved to the Messiah; in large letters he wrote the name that now embodied his every hope:

Jesus Christ

Yet remorse was still there, and it became more and more painful. At court were those who were quick to scoff at the beliefs of humble men, and the friend of chevalier de Méré had laughed along with the libertines. Doubtless carried away by high spirits, his own irony had surpassed theirs. "Nothing is so cowardly as to swagger before God," he was to write. But now, on this night, he was torn with anguish; like so many others, he had denied his Master:

I have fallen away from thee; I have denied thee, crucified thee

Christ's words were terrible: "He that shall deny me before men, I will also deny him before my Father." And now the guilty man, even after committing the sin against the Holy Spirit, expected everything from the mercy that knows no bounds and resumed his prayer:

May I not be separated from thee for all eternity

He humbled himself, surrendered his pride, his learning, and even his reason. What sudden relief to cast these vain treasures into the void!

Renunciation total and sweet

Pascal's older sister now knew more than the younger had known when Jacqueline told her of their brother's conversion, when she saw him "grow in such a manner that she no longer recognized him," he had received the revelation of a superhuman presence.

With pious hands the dead man's kinsmen put the "Memorial" back into the sheet that enveloped it; thanks to them it was to be preserved.[1]

Other writings were found which proved to Pascal's relatives and friends that the abyss of nothingness never again opened before him. "I am with

---

[1] See Documents, original text of the Memorial (p. 316).

you all days until the end of the world," Christ said, and his promise had been kept.

Those who read what was written on these sheets of paper entitled it "The Mystery of Jesus." A Christian stands before the Garden of Olives at that hour when Christ was abandoned by every one and delivered to the worst of torments. Love inspired the words that have been repeated down through the centuries: "Jesus will be in agony until the end of the world; during that time we must not sleep."

Pascal had not slept. He had risen and cried out when evil shepherds had tried to lead believers astray.

"The Mystery of Jesus" is couched in the sober poignancy of the Gospel language; in it we hear the voice that encouraged the new man as he advanced blindly along the straight road of the Kingdom: "Be comforted. You would not be seeking me if you had not already found me.

"I love you more ardently than you have loved your own uncleanness."

When a great many scraps of paper covered with fine handwriting, some tied into bundles, and others loose, were discovered, all who admired Pascal knew that among these documents they would find the outline of a book under the dead man's seal.

The day following the marvel of the Holy Thorn the defender of Port-Royal had written down his thoughts on miracles, "which revealed God like the lightning flash." Other ideas then came to him, and he embarked on a vaster enterprise. At that time, his sister tells us, he was thirty-four years old; his physical sufferings, though constantly growing more intense, still left him moments of respite. Pascal remembered the time when, although he had not yet succeeded in loving God, the limitations of science had inspired him with the desire to set out on the discovery of the infinite. He had struggled, suffered, and would have fallen into despair had not this young sister come to his help.

The author of the *Provincial Letters* wondered if he should not make the way he had traveled known to others who might follow along the same path. This was to be the purpose of his book *Apology for the Christian Religion*.

When he wrote the *Provincial Letters*, Pascal knew what tone to adopt in addressing honest men; when he began to write the *Apology* he was familiar with the language of skeptics—grave ones like the enigmatic Miton, or gallants of the ilk of chevalier de Méré. Everyone fled from the saccharine effusions and insipidity of many devotional works, and ridiculed the subtleties of the theologians. Many persons concealed a vague fear of religion beneath this contempt. "They hate it, and fear to find that it may be true," Pascal was to write.

On the other hand, he recognized the distrust created by affectation and false eloquence. Only those things a person would have liked to write himself are read with interest; each wants to find in an author's style what is natural to him. Then, says Pascal, "we are astonished and delighted, for we expected to see an author and we find a man."

This time it was to be the man who spoke to other human beings; Pascal wanted to grip his readers' attention in order to compel them to recognize themselves. Doubtless he ran the risk of irritating and revolting them, but he wanted to avoid the most formidable barrier of all—boredom.

Pascal tried everything to induce his readers to follow him. At one moment he even thought of appealing to the gambler who lies hidden in each person. "A game is being played at the extremity of this infinite distance where heads or tails will turn up. What will you wager?" Some people will try not to risk the play, but this is in vain. "You must wager. You are committed." Why, then, would you hesitate? If eternity awaits you and you have wagered on it, you will win everything; if after death you are reduced to nothingness, what will you lose? Nothing.

But he abandoned the idea of the wager. The *Apology* should guide Christians in a more worthy way. Moreover, having learned from his own experience, Pascal did not want to appeal to reason: "proofs convince only the mind," but he knew "there were demonstrations of another kind which are as certain as those of geometry." They reach the heart, move and transform it. If reason makes its way slowly, "feeling acts in an instant."

On learning that Pascal was about to lay the groundwork for this project, the solitaries begged him to divulge its plan to them. His nephew, Madame Périer's son, tells us that Pascal did not have the courage to disappoint them. Etienne Périer gives us no inkling of the place where "the discourse" took place, or who was in the audience—the peace accorded the Jansenists remained precarious and prudence was necessary. But we know that during the peaceful days at Les Granges, Pascal had taken part in discussions with Arnauld, Nicole, and the solitaries.

The plan described by Etienne Périer is similar to the one traced in more detail by Filleau de la Chaise, an intimate friend of the duc de Roannez. After recalling the time when the future author of the *Apology* told the Messieurs what the book would be, Etienne Périer adds: "From one who was present we know what can be added to the little I have just reported." Very likely this information was given by Roannez, who had been Pascal's confidant during the most important moments of his life; to him, more than to anyone else, we owe the first edition of the *Pensées*. The preface to this book was written by Etienne Périer, and includes the plan of the *Apology*. This plan would not have been accepted by the solitaries had it not faithfully followed Pascal's own outline.

Further information on this subject comes not only from Filleau de la Chaise and Madame Périer, but from the *Pensées* itself, which contains two fragments of the "discourse."

"Man's misery": Pascal wanted first to make his readers experience the terror he himself had known. He shows himself as he was at the time of his conversion, contemplating "nature in her grand and full majesty." She assumes again the place she had formerly held for him, an unstable equilibrium between infinity and the atom. He wanted to explain how absurd is the egotism in which we take refuge, to denounce the illusions of our senses, of our imagination, of our passions, of our falsehoods.

"Greatness of the human soul": weak and miserable as we are, we are able to have a concept of the world and to know our own weakness. These two states, one brutelike, the other divine, cannot leave man indifferent.

"If he praise himself, I humble him; if he humble himself, I praise him; and I always contradict him until he understands that he is an incomprehensible monster."

Man must be obsessed by the stupendous contrast he carries within himself in order to be willing to pay any price for an explanation of his own enigma: "Let man now know his value . . . let him love himself, let him despise himself."

After recalling the astonishment and anguish he had personally experienced, Pascal would attempt to persuade his reader to follow him. The author of the *Apology* wanted to show the contradictions presented by philosophers as he had done during his conversation with Saci. The skeptics describe the weakness of man condemned to live in the world of appearances; the stoics, on the other hand, exalt the will in all its pride. Thus the sages condemn man either to despair at being nothing or to the absurd pretension of being everything.

The *Apology* then would study the religions that preceded and followed Jesus, in order to show that all worship is sterile when the believer is deprived of the light of the Gospels. Then it would describe the strange people of Israel, condemned to carry through the centuries the Bible that tells of the fall of Adam, of the hope of David, of the visions of Isaiah before the coming of the Messiah.

"Man's happiness with God": here the work should reach its summit—the order of the heart.

"I am the vine, you are the branches. Abide in my love," Jesus said.

The *Apology* would open the ears of its readers to this voice, and lead to the hidden God. Finally, it would show the apostles, the saints, and the martyrs gathered around Christ.

A new horizon opened up for two hours as Pascal explained his plan. The solitaries, who spent their lives meditating on the Scriptures, confessed, wrote Etienne Périer, "that they had never heard anything so beautiful, stronger, more touching, or more convincing."

In the peace of Les Granges, these men dreamed of the future destiny of Port-Royal: the *Apology* would make fully effective the divine love revealed in the *Spiritual Conversations* of Saint-Cyran and in Arnauld's *Frequent Communion*. Jesus would again proclaim to men that there was only one truth. The most rebellious spirits would be touched by this book; it would be the Bible of future ages.

Now, in a house depopulated by death, the survivors looked with consternation at the scraps of paper which must serve them to finish the book. In haste Pascal had jotted down half-finished sentences, words scarcely legible—the scythe had passed over before the time for reaping had come!

Pascal's elder sister asked herself if his century were worthy of such a gift. In an age of pride and splendor would not the living water be lost in the sand? Madame Périer thought that many prayers should be offered so that a Christian might one day write the book which had fallen from her brother's hand.

Fate was indeed cruel to Port-Royal. Jansenius could dwell only on the curse of Adam. Saint-Cyran, Arnauld, and Nicole lacked the genius to lead men to contemplation of the Resurrection. Pascal alone could have done this, but he was struck down when, after leading us to the threshold of despair, he was on the point of bringing us to life again.

No wonder the Jansenists seemed stern and pitiless on the day they assembled their forces to lead us to the highest of all experiences.

After the first moments of discouragement, patience won and the struggle was resumed. Pascal's family and friends assembled all the writings discovered after his death, and the ones to be included in the *Apology* were recopied. These fragments turned out, Etienne Périer tells us, to be "so formless and disconnected" that their publication seemed impossible. Moreover, how could they contemplate such a step when the persecution against Port-Royal was being renewed more violently than ever? The cooperation of Arnauld and Nicole was indispensable, and they were in hiding at that time.

Nevertheless, on December 27, 1666—several months after Saci's arrest—Florin Périer, Etienne's father, obtained a licence from the king to publish the "Pensées de Monsieur Pascal." Thus four years after the death of the author of the Provincial Letters, his brother-in-law gave notice of his intention to make his "thoughts" public.

More than two years elapsed. Finally, in October, 1668, when peace had been concluded between Rome, the Louvre, and Port-Royal, Arnauld, Nicole, and the solitaries found each other and assembled. One copy of the Pensées was submitted to them by the Périers so they might consider in what form the drafts could be presented to readers, and a committee was formed to examine these texts. It was presided over by Pascal's friend the duc de Roannez, who had known him better than anyone. Arnauld, Nicole, and Filleau de la Chaise, as well as three friends of Port-Royal—Du Bois, Tréville, and Brienne—took their places beside him. Etienne Périer was to follow the work of the committee closely and represent his father and especially his mother, Pascal's elder sister, both of whom resided in Auvergne.

A difficult task confronted the Messieurs. In turning over "formless" writings to the public, were they not betraying the wishes of the most exacting of authors?

Roannez wanted to reorganize the Apology according to the plan outlined by its author. In the duke's opinion, the Pensées should be presented in the order which he knew better than anyone, and then filled in with words which he remembered as having come from the lips of Pascal. The committee approved this proposal and began its execution, but Madame Périer sent word from Clermont that she opposed the reorganization of material: she did not want the texts left by her brother altered in any way. The Messieurs deferred to her quite understandable feelings; nevertheless, since what Pascal wrote down has been faithfully preserved, it is regrettable that a version of the Apology, clarified by the addition of all that Roannez knew, was not made available.

In obedience to the wishes of Madame Périer the committee limited itself to choosing the thoughts "that were clearest and most complete." They were published in January, 1670, under the title for which Florin Périer had obtained a licence: Pensées de M. Pascal sur la religion et sur quelques autres sujets. This is known as the Port-Royal Edition.

The order conceived by the author was not respected. Following the passages concerning atheists, others on proofs of the Christian religion were grouped; everything concerning man's weakness and greatness was relegated to the second part of the book. The Messieurs did not want readers to find that terrible description of a human being lost in immensity right at the beginning, and judged it wiser to deal in the first chapter with the things of religion. Their prudence led them even to set aside every text that might be considered "Jansenistic," for, in order to safeguard the nuns, they felt they must not endanger the hard-won peace.

Madame Périer had written "The Life of Monsieur Pascal," which she intended as an introduction to the *Pensées*. The Messieurs did not dare to include it, for a timid allusion to the *Provincial Letters* and certain details on the author's spiritual rigorism made them fear the renewal of discussion and attacks.

One of the members of the committee, Filleau de la Chaise, would have liked the work to be prefaced by his "Discourse on the Thoughts of Monsieur Pascal," which set forth the plan and purpose of the *Apology*. This was also the desire of the Messieurs, but Madame Périer, her husband, and her son did not find, they said, in Monsieur de la Chaise "any of the things we want to say, and several things we do not want to say." It was then that Etienne Périer decided to write the preface to the *Pensées* himself. It contains an overall description of the *Apology*, briefer than the one of Filleau de la Chaise but certainly very faithful to the spirit of Pascal. Etienne Périer tells, moreover, of the conditions under which the *Pensées* were written, what their purpose was, and how they were being presented; finally, he gives certain details regarding the author's life.

So as not to offend Roannez and Filleau de la Chaise, Pascal's nephew did not reveal the fact that he himself had written this preface, and presented it to them as a text drawn up by his parents.

Brienne, a member of the committee, had to confess to Madame Périer that not only had the *Pensées* been cut, but that he had added "small embellishments." These were, however, of a discreet kind: certain cutting expressions were softened and startling ellipses were briefly explained.

By giving due consideration to the requirements of their times, the Messieurs realized their objective: the work aroused a lively interest but did not offend their yet unappeased enemies. Arnauld obtained the approbation of several bishops and theologians, permitting the *Pensées* to be published in full light of day.

As the years rolled on, all the combatants were united in death. Later, in 1842, Victor Cousin pointed out to the French Academy the importance of Pascal's manuscript. Learned men have since made careful studies of these "papers." In our own day a study was made of a copy which allowed, at least in part, the restoration of the original order.

Reading the "Memorial," the "Mystery of Jesus," and certain pages of the *Pensées* today, a hymn of love more fervent in its evangelical simplicity than is the "Song of Songs" in all its splendor can be heard. Pascal had the genius to resurrect a voice that had been silent for seventeen centuries, but which he heard within his own heart.

Of this treasure there remains only a distant echo, and Pascal, in his turn, is a hidden god. Men are still haunted by his despair before the infinite, by his denunciations of blindness; he seems inexorable because, after attempting to destroy the old man in man, he did not live long enough to lead him to the Kingdom.

Nevertheless, the author of the *Pensées* never wished to lend himself to the odious blackmail that tries to impose faith through evoking the tortures of hell. "To wish to instill it [faith] in the soul by force and threats is not to instill religion, but fear," he wrote. Pascal startles and harasses only for the purpose of opening the road to happiness. "He believed we should never distress another without consoling him," his elder sister said.

In relation to Pascal, men are like the Jews of the Old Law, who knew only Jehovah's anger, and were ignorant of Christ's love.

Among the *Pensées* are some which offend, especially this one: "We understand nothing of God's works if we do not accept the principle that he wishes to blind certain people and give light to others."

But Christ was just as severe when he showed the crowd to his disciples, and said: "I speak to them in parables, because seeing they see not, and hearing they hear not, neither do they understand."

Pascal must be pardoned for "so arrogantly attacking our self-respect," since his violence was in proportion to the passionate love he left. He wanted not only to comfort his companions in misery, but to rescue from shipwreck those of the same race as himself.

"Love one another as I have loved you." Pascal is perhaps the only man who completely fulfilled this commandment. He emptied out his last strength for others, and ended in exhaustion, in Gethsemane. No one except Christ has ever offered such a gift to men.

After the Gospel proclaimed in the shadow of Calvary, the *Pensées*, written on the threshold of death, contain the highest titles of nobility that man has ever received.

Cornelius Jansenius, Bishop of Ypres and author of the Augustinus.

LA R.MERE CATHERINE AGNES DE S.PAVL ARNAVLD *cy deuant*
Abbeſſe de Port Royal. Elle est morte le 19.Feurier 1671.en odeur de tres grande piete.
Os ſuum aperuit ſapientiæ, & lex clementiæ in lingua ejus.   Prouerb.31.

Reverend Mother Agnès Arnauld, Abbess of Port-Royal; died in 1671.

Angélique Arnauld.

Pascal. In the background of this portrait of the author of the Provincial Letters *can be made out the outlines of Port-Royal of the Fields.*

Racine.

Port-Royal of Paris. The buildings exist today as a maternity hospital.

Port-Royal of the Fields.

Port-Royal of the Fields in ruins. The property is now owned by the French government, and is to be restored as a national monument.

4

RACINE, THE PRODIGAL SON

During the years of peace, Port-Royal saw the return of its prodigal son, Jean Racine, who, after having cruelly offended the solitaries, was to become the most devoted of their followers.

Once again it is necessary to go back, for little understanding of the poet is possible without following his career up to the moment when he took his stand for the rest of his life before the ramparts of the new Jerusalem. This journey across a stormy existence leads quickly away from the valley where righteous men lived in serenity and back to the world where the prodigal son was to meet with temptations of every kind before returning to his father's house.

It would seem that Racine was destined to become the spiritual son of the solitaries from his birth. In 1638, when the solitaries were dispersed for the first time after Saint-Cyran's arrest, Le Maître and Séricourt, led by Lancelot, were given refuge at La Ferté-Milon, in the home of the Vitarts, the great-uncle and great-aunt of Racine. The couple did not want to be separated from their guests; when, at the end of the summer of the following year, the solitaries regained the valley, Monsieur and Madame Vitart came to join them. Another of Racine's great-aunts was at that time a religious at Port-Royal; his father's sister had been a pupil there and later had made her profession as one of the religious. Thus, like the Arnaulds and Pascals, the family of Racine found itself involved by a kind of predestination in the fortunes of this high-minded group.

The solitaries had been gone for several months when Jean Racine was baptized at La Ferté-Milon on December 22, 1639. Losing his mother, and then his father, he was an orphan at the age of three, and was given a home by his grandparents.

It appears that when very young the child was admitted to the Little Schools of Port-Royal at the request of his grandmother, who had retired to the house of the nuns of the Fields, after being widowed, to engage in humble household work. There he also found his aunt, whose name in religion was Agnès de Sainte-Thècle Racine. At fourteen the youth was an intern student at the College of Beauvais, but two years later he was again in the valley. Almost sixteen, he was at an age when the mind is being formed and impressions received are indelible. Nicole gave him an appreciation of the harmony and forcefulness of the Latin tongue; to Lancelot young Racine owed a knowledge of Greek perfect enough to enable him to read Homer, Sophocles, and Euripides with ease. The lines of these poets, light and resonant as the song of the cicada, unveiled to him the distant light of the Aegean isles. It was doubtless at this period that the pupil of the solitaries learned by heart fragments of Heliodorus' Greek romance, *The Love of Theagenes and Chariclea,* an idyl that gave him his first glimpse of the world of the passions.

Le Maître still possessed a very beautiful voice, a reminder of his oratorical gifts. To his pupil he revealed the enchantment of Virgil's rhythm, of Cicero's rounded sentences, of Tacitus' imagery.

If the child's grandmother and aunt were able to make him forget that he was motherless, the orphan received a father's affection from Le Maître. The former lawyer dreamed of seeing his disciple embarked on the profession of which he retained memories more vivid than he cared to confess, and to this end taught him the secrets of style and rhetoric.

In a letter addressed "to little Racine, at Port-Royal," the solitary asked his pupil to take care of certain books he had to leave behind when again he was compelled to quit the valley after Antoine Arnauld's condemnation by the Sorbonne.

For Le Maître this second dispersion was a portent from on high. "We must try to profit from this persecution," he wrote Racine. "May it serve to give us detachment from the world." His letter ended with the much-quoted words: "Good day, my dear son, always love your papa as he loves you." The solitary died just as his pupil was leaving Port-Royal for Paris, and bequeathed him a part of his library, his sole possession.

Hamon was as proficient a guide to the study of Italian and Spanish as to the dead languages. He imparted his knowledge to the young man with so much patience and devotion that in his will Racine was to ask the favor of being buried at his tutor's feet.

Thus we have a young boy living in a "desert" where thoughts and actions were centered on the invisible Ruler. In the middle of each night Fontaine, Saci's secretary, went about the corridors ringing a little bell to awaken the Messieurs to say matins in the monastery church; their pupils' day began at six o'clock. Racine had his bed in a dormitory which he shared with one of his teachers and several fellow students. He saw the solitaries returning from the fields where they worked on the abbey lands. Some of them devoted their spare time to reading the Scriptures, others to translating the sacred texts. "When they are together," wrote one witness, "they discuss only the news of the other world."

In the church beside the solitaries, or sometimes serving mass before the altar beside the priest, young Racine assisted at the sacred mysteries. Behind the grill he could see the white scapulars and scarlet crosses of the nuns, and hear them raising their voices beneath the lofty stone arches as they offered mankind's miseries to God. His very first verses were devoted to the beauty of these "holy dwellings of silence," where biblical song mounted, died away, and was then resumed:

> There a thousand mortal angels
> In an eternal plaint
> Wail at the foot of the altar.

Remote, almost invisible and yet making their presence deeply felt, Christ's spouses instilled in Racine a respect for women and an awareness of the supernatural that was never to be effaced. Sometimes he was granted the favor of a talk in the parlor with his aunt Agnès, and the nun would emerge from the semi-darkness and appear behind the grill to instruct her nephew in the lessons of the Gospel.

When the young man returned to Les Granges his teachers continued to remind him of the reality of the supernatural; they taught him that without grace we are as bits of chaff blown toward the abyss. The solitaries showed him in the best of Greek and Latin literature the image of the ancient world before the coming of the Savior: in those days, fate weighed men down, pursued them, bent their steps to the moment when the idols they had made into gods, who were but the mirrors of their human passions, led them to their death.

To tell the truth, although he was born in an age following the Redemption, this disciple of the solitaries did not feel grace dwelling in him; in the land of saints he remained an outsider, apparently docile but aloof. Perhaps it was in an effort to change that he began to translate into French verse the hymns of the breviary:

Beneath the pale sun, the shadows flee away.
O chaste and blessed day, arise in our hearts.

It was easy to inspire confidence in the good solitaries who, like Saint-Cyran, saw each child as the living temple of the Holy Spirit. Jean Racine's secret domain lay in the world of human beings, susceptible to the attractions of the flesh and of pleasure. He was ready to embark on a future still unknown but full of promise; captivated, he surrendered in advance to a still distant conqueror.

When the solitaries had to leave the Chevreuse Valley the pupil of the Little Schools followed his tutor Lancelot to the château of Vaumurier, where he was made welcome by the duc de Luynes. Close to the deserted monastery, Racine carried on his studies together with the duke's son, Monsieur de Chevreuse, under the guidance of their common teacher, Lancelot. Later when the Messieurs returned to the valley, this life was resumed at Les Granges.

During his sojourn in the Little Schools, Racine heard the rumors raised by Arnauld's condemnation at the Sorbonne, then by the miracle of the Holy Thorn. He nonchalantly recounted these great events to his father's cousin, Antoine Vitart:

> Here one hears of the censure,
> The shame, and discomfiture
> Of the poor Augustinians
> Known as Jansenians.
> Others cry out, on the contrary
> The verdict of the vicar-general,
> The hymn, the story, and record
> Of the miracles of Port-Royal.

At this time the "Provincials" were launching their attacks one by one on the Company of Jesus. In the presence of their pupils, however, the solitaries guarded the silence that permitted Pascal to escape the search being made by the king's men.

Racine, now nineteen, had to complete his studies by taking a course in philosophy. In 1658, he left the valley of the Chevreuse to attend the Collège d'Harcourt in Paris. This choice was doubtless due to the Messieurs, who counted devoted friends on the faculty of the college, where numerous copies of the "Provincials" were being hidden in the cellars.

By 1661, Racine was twenty-two and living "in the world." Filled with youthful desires and joyous at his escape from the desert, he was leading the unrestrained existence of which he had dreamed. At last he felt himself free, and he filled his lungs with the Paris air.

The persecution of Port-Royal increased in violence and Singlin had to leave the Paris monastery in haste. Racine told this to one of his friends, Le Vasseur, a gallant priest who composed madrigals, was everywhere, and was in love with "a darling little miss of fourteen." Indeed, the former pupil of the solitaries spoke mockingly of "madame our holy aunt, who believes she cannot enjoy anything since she has lost her holy father." These words referred to Singlin, "who is no longer in the shadow of Saint Augustine's throne; by wise retreat he has avoided the unpleasantness of receiving an order from the king sending him to Quimper." In the same ironical vein, Racine told Le Vasseur of the way a new spiritual director had been imposed on the nuns: "The post was not vacant for long; from what I hear, the court —without consulting the Holy Spirit—elevated Monsieur Bail to this position. The entire consistory fell into schism when this new pope was created."

But the young man had ideas on other matters. A mysterious beauty inspired his "Stanzas to Parthenice." He had come under the spell of an unknown woman, perhaps imaginary: "Though I felt myself a slave, I believed I was happy." Racine went before Parthenice as though he were entering a new universe: "In you I saw nothing that was not lovable,/Within myself I felt nothing but love."

He also wrote a sonnet in honor of the birth of a little cousin, but, not forgetting the great ones, he sent another to Cardinal Mazarin on the conclusion of the peace of the Pyrenees. When he addressed some words of praise—and they were very moderate—to an enemy of the Jansenists, "excommunication after excommunication" rained down upon his head. However, the poet was forgiven, and made good use of the connections he owed to the Messieurs. The duc de Luynes, who had received him earlier at his residence of Vaumurier, opened to him his château of Chevreuse which was managed by one of Racine's relatives, Nicolas Vitart.

"I have the bedroom of a duke and peer," the young man wrote as he watched from a distance the building ordered by Monsieur de Luynes.

Shortly thereafter, ensconced in the Paris house of this Jansenist noble on the quai des Grands-Augustins, Racine became friendly with Madame de Longueville's brother, Condé, who became his protector. There he also met such celebrated contemporary writers as Perrault and Chapelain. The latter had Racine awarded a hundred *louis* for his ode "The Nymph of the Seine," written in honor of the marriage of Louis XIV. This nymph sang in praise of the peace secured by the king when he triumphed over The Fronde: "After the long winter, comes spring with its charms!"

Racine drank of every pleasure; at the side of La Fontaine and several gay companions, he haunted the cabarets and engaged in various amorous adventures.

At one time there was great danger that Racine's escape would be short-lived. In 1661, his uncle, Canon Sconin, asked him to join him at Uzès so that he might obtain for him an ecclesiastical benefice; his dashing nephew could take the tonsure and be made a prior. At Port-Royal his grandmother and aunt breathed a sigh of relief: the young Joas they had raised was saved, and was to be consecrated to God.

Racine decided to seize this opportunity to establish himself in an honorable position. Certain pressing debts helped convince him that such a step was necessary; a religious career would lead him, if not to God, at least to stipends. The example of the gallant priest Le Vasseur showed that one could live in the bosom of the Church without abandoning the worship of the muses or even the adoration of mortals. Clothed in black, assiduous in his attendance at religious services, the would-be prior played a devout role in the streets of Uzès and in the shadow of his uncle, the canon; once again he was the pupil of the Little Schools. Ostensibly studying Saint Thomas and the Fathers of the Church, he found secret consolation in the poems of Homer, Pindar, Virgil, and Horace, and only then did he discover the "Provincials" and their attacks on the Jesuits. Slyly his eyes devoured the young provincial beauties who were, he said, "dazzling," and admired their robust bodies "bursting with vitality." The soft skies inspired him to write, for the benefit of one of his father's cousins, Nicolas Vitart, the famous verse: "And our nights are more splendid than your days."

At least appearances were saved. "You see," Racine wrote Fontaine, "one must be regular with the regulars, just as I was a wolf running with you and your companions, the other wolves."

However, he did not hide his feelings when he wrote Vitart, whose indulgence he knew and who had become his confidant; the correspondence he kept up with his grandmother and "the holy aunt" had become a burden to him. "It is enough," he wrote, "to play the hypocrite here without becoming one in correspondence, for I call hypocritical those letters which deal only with devotional matters and do nothing but ask others to pray for the writer."

In the end the clergy of the *grand siècle* did not have to count one more bad priest in their midst—Uncle Sconin did not obtain the hoped-for benefice for his nephew.

In 1663, disappointed and happy at the same time, Racine returned to Paris after an absence of a little less than two years. He sought out his comrades, and was careful not to forget Chapelain, who had received from Colbert the order to commemorate in some way the recovery of Louis XIV, who had triumphed over measles. Racine hastened to compose an "Ode on the

King's Convalescence," and in addition wrote a poem dedicated to "Fame," in which the muses were invited to come down from heaven and contemplate the noblest of all kings.

This time Racine was rewarded with a pension of six hundred livres. He made his entry into Versailles and had the honor of assisting at the king's levee, and there he met Molière.

Spurred by this initial success, ambition raised its head. Since the Church had refused Racine, why shouldn't he turn to the theater? Earlier, Heliodorus' romance, *The Love of Theagenes and Chariclea*, had inspired him to write a play, *Amasia*. This beginning work was never performed on the stage, but during his sojourn at Uzès, Racine had started to write a tragedy, *The Thebaid, or the Enemy Brothers*. When it was finished Molière read the script and entrusted it to his own troupe, the Company of the Royal Palace. Relieved of the restraint that would have been imposed by an ecclesiastical life, snatched from the monotony of the provinces, Racine saw the future open up before him.

However, the thought of Port-Royal cast a shadow over his rejoicing. The theater was banned by the Church because it drew hearts away from God by depicting passions that were sinful. Actors were excommunicated, and when they died could not be buried in consecrated ground.

At the time he was about to embark on a new life so remote from the one for which he had been prepared, the poet wanted to renew his ties to a past he both loved and feared. He let it be known that he intended to visit Port-Royal, but, just as he was about to leave for the Abbey of the Fields, he received a letter from his aunt telling him that the doors of the monastery were closed to him.

I am writing in the bitterness of my heart. I have learned with sorrow that you are consorting more than ever with those whose very name is abominable to everyone who has even a little piety.

I implore you, my dear nephew, to have pity on your soul, to think seriously of the abyss into which you are casting yourself.

I hope that what I have been told is not true, but if you are so unfortunate as not to have broken off relationships that dishonor you before God and men, you must not think of coming to see us.

Sister Agnès could not refrain, however, from expressing her affection in these final lines: "I pray God constantly to grant to you his mercy, and to me for asking this of him, for your salvation is very precious to me."

The young man's heart was torn, yet never for a moment did he consider casting fame aside. Le Maître had buried only a lawyer's speeches in his cell; Racine was too talented and ambitious to dream of imitating him.

The narrow piety of his time condemned theatricals which in other days had been welcomed before cathedrals even on Good Friday. So be it! The bridges were burnt between Port-Royal and Racine; he was cruelly but finally liberated from an unbearable tutelage. Obeying a firm desire to forget, he went out in search of "those whose very name was abominable." He loved the strange individuals who tried to surpass themselves each evening as they took on the flesh of kings, heroes, murderers. Actors had the power to create life and even to surpass it; the poet was happy to entrust his future to their voices, their gestures, and their hearts.

On June 20, 1664, Molière had his troop perform *The Thebaid;* the leading actress in the cast was his young wife, Armande Béjart.

The characters in this tragedy (inspired by Euripides and also by Rotrou's *Antigone*) killed themselves on the stage without the audience's being moved in the slightest, for they lacked the warmth of flesh and blood. In this play Racine revealed his Jansenistic training, for he showed that in a world deprived of grace, Oedipus' family—born of incest and with murder in the heart—was pursued by the wrath of the gods.

Racine's second tragedy, *Alexander the Great,* was presented to the public by Molière in 1665, not without courage, for *The Thebaid* had been a failure. This time the solitaries' former pupil desired to liberate himself from his past. The fates that pursued Antigone and her brothers no longer figured in the poet's play—he wanted to live among the living.

The Sun King presided over a France at peace, and feeling that the young ruler should be shown in all his majesty, Racine compared him to the Macedonian conqueror: "The fire of his glance, his lofty majesty/Bring Alexander to our minds. . . .

Louis XIV, who liked to adorn himself with illustrious names and ancient breastplates, was highly satisfied when he viewed his ennobled image on the stage. From that time on, Racine enjoyed the favor of his sovereign.

Tall and slender as Diana the huntress, the marquise du Parc played the role of Queen Axiana—and she yielded to the conquering hero.

Too young and too ambitious to have regrets, Racine was overjoyed at this conquest of the greatest of kings and of the most beautiful of actresses. He would finally have attained the perfect serenity that surpasses fugitive moments of joy had not Nicole, one of his former teachers, suddenly brought to his mind a world he had tried to forget. Impressed by the success of the "Provincials," this theologian had in turn published some "Letters" in an effort to prove that Jansenism was merely an "imaginary heresy." These new epistles, "The Imaginaries," were also anonymous and secretly circulated, but, as they were much less brilliant than the "Provincials," they aroused but little public interest. Far from being discouraged at his lack of success,

Nicole decided to publish new "Letters" in reply to attacks made by one of Port-Royal's adversaries, Desmarets de Saint-Sorlin.

This poet was a former protegé of Richelieu, who had granted him one of the first seats in the French Academy. He had become very religious after leading an extremely rakish life. He had seriously proposed to Louis XIV that the king raise a militia of a hundred and forty-four thousand righteous men—the number of the elect in the Apocalypse marked with the seal of God and for these pious soldiers to round up and exterminate heretics.

From the height of the Apocalypse, Desmarets came down to the Jansenists and decided to assume personally the role of the sacred militia in regard to them, believing that God had inspired him to do so. After sending a "Warning from the Holy Spirit" to the king, demanding that the Messieurs be handed over to the secular arm, he placed himself at the disposition of the Archbishop of Paris to spy on them, seek them out, and turn them over to the police.

To his "Imaginaries," Nicole therefore added some new letters, the "Visionaries," intended to hold Desmarets up to ridicule. His title alluded to one of Desmarets' plays attacking the Jansenists, and to alleged miracles which the academician believed had been worked in his favor. Incapable of writing at length in ironical vein, the solitary lapsed into anathemas against Desmarets, who had authored plays and novels.

"A novelist and a poet of the theater," Nicole wrote, "is a poisoner of the public, not of bodies but of souls. He should consider himself guilty of an infinite number of spiritual homicides."

With that incomparable ineptitude never lacking in the Messieurs, Port-Royal's defender thus aroused the hostility of the whole writing confraternity.

Desmarets replied to the "Visionaries" in a very bungling manner, but Racine took up the gauntlet. From the long, solemn sentences of his former teacher he detached three words: "poisoner of the public." The wound inflicted on the poet when his aunt forbade him to reenter the domain of his childhood had been reopened. Now for the second time he was rejected by those closest to him, and with what harshness!

No one was more sensitive than Racine to tribulations of the heart, but no one knew better than he how to respond to pain with violence, to strike blow for blow, to cauterize the sorest wounds in the fire of combat. The author of *Alexander* knew how hard it was to endure insults from persons of high rank to whom a commoner had no right to reply, but he could not agree that Nicole, who like himself had risen from obscurity, could excommunicate people at the very time when the pope had condemned the Jansenists and the king was preparing to put them behind bars.

Already Racine's pen was gliding over the paper as he replied to his former tutor in a letter that would be read by all Paris, and would even reach the court. Should he sign it? The young poet did not dare engage openly in a polemic against the Messieurs. He would run the danger of being accused of ingratitude by the duc de Luynes, to whom he owed his introduction into society, and by Condé, so favorable to Port-Royal. It was better to remain anonymous.

Racine was, moreover, very careful not to give free rein to his anger; when he wanted to, he could be both clever and witty. The Messieurs had drawn no lesson from the style of the "Provincials," and to these scholarly bourgeois dons the poet replied in the free and easy manner of a gentleman of the world.

At the beginning of his letter he refused to take part in the quarrel between Desmarets and Nicole. "I will leave it to the world to judge which of you two is the visionary," he wrote. He nevertheless expressed surprise at seeing the Messieurs compromise themselves with so miserable a personage as Péréfixe's spy. "Where is your pride which stood up to the pope, to archbishops, and to the Jesuits?"

Endowed with the acumen that discerns the shortcomings of even the noblest of minds, Racine saw in Nicole a desire to rival the "Provincials" which had brought such extraordinary celebrity to one the solitary had once considered a "collector of shells." Racine therefore crushed Port-Royal's Latin scholar beneath the giant shadow of Pascal. "I note that you pretend to take the place of the author of the "Little Letters," but at the same time I note you are quite inferior to him, and that there is a great difference between a 'Provincial' and an 'Imaginary.' "

Thus cut down to size, Nicole found himself "mocked in the most cutting manner," to quote the words of one of Racine's sons.

"You could have employed gentler terms than the words 'poisoner of the public.' Do you think that people will believe this because you say so? No, no, sir, no one is accustomed to taking your word so readily. For twenty years you have been saying every day that the five propositions are not to be found in Jansenius; nevertheless, people still do not believe you."

After this arrow was sped, the solitaries were given a stern lecture:

"We know how austere are your morals. We do not find it strange that you damn poets, for you damn many others as well. . . . Eh, sir, be satisfied with assigning places in the other world, and do not try to mete out rewards in this one. You left it long ago; allow it to judge of the things that belong to it."

Behind Nicole, Racine was attacking all his former teachers: he showed them desiring to make a name for themselves, which was perhaps their great secret weakness.

"What do you want? Everyone can't write against the Jesuits. Fame can be won in more ways than one." Was the theater the most dangerous of these ways? If so, hadn't the Messieurs themselves taken part in the devil's work—hadn't they published the comedies of Terence? "So couldn't you yourselves be numbered among the poisoners?"

The solitaries had been depicted in glowing terms by Mademoiselle de Scudéry in *Clélie,* the most famous of her novels. Not one of them had protested. "I have heard people say," Racine added, "that you patiently suffered yourselves to be praised in that horrible book. . . . This work mentioning you was ordered from 'the desert,' and quickly passed from hand to hand, for each of the solitaries wanted to see the passage describing him as a famous person."

Carried away by his feelings, the former pupil of the Messieurs hammered away at those he once had felt obliged to admire. He was so bold as to attack the most venerable of all the nuns, Mother Angélique Arnauld, who had died five years before. In a vein foreshadowing Voltaire's *Candide,* Racine told a story which had amused Paris and the court.

One day two Capuchin friars came to ask hospitality at the Monastery of Port-Royal. At first they were served with white bread and the wine reserved for the Messieurs when they honored the abbey by taking a meal. However, on learning that one of the Capuchins had played a part in obtaining the bull condemning Jansenism, Mother Angélique—so the tale ran—replaced the white bread by bread given the servants, and the wine by cider. The good fathers, Racine wrote, could not but admire "the care taken to see that they did penance."

Fortunately, added the author of *Alexander,* all this was due merely to an error. It was repaired the following day when the abbess learned the suspected monk "was an extremely good religious and, in his heart, even friendly enough to truth." (How well "little Racine" had come to know the language of Port-Royal!) Immediately Mother Angélique gave orders countermanding those of the previous day. "The Capuchins were led with honor from the church into the refectory where a fine meal awaited them; they ate with good heart, blessing God who had not made them eat their white bread first."

Next Racine attacked Le Maître, who had been dead for eight years, saying that in former times this solitary had not scorned to write on profane matters. "He made speeches, he made verses. . . . In a letter he confessed he had retired to your house to mourn his crimes. . . . He spent two entire years digging in the garden, reaping the field, and washing dishes. That is what made him worthy of the doctrine of Saint Augustine."

This ruthless letter reached Port-Royal in 1666, just as it was staggering under other blows. Arnauld and Nicole had to go into hiding; Saci was about to be arrested. The bells had been silenced at the Monastery of the Fields; the excommunicated nuns lived in anguish, watched day and night by the police. Only by unbroken silence did they reply to the letter in which Racine ridiculed a dead woman whom they honored as a saint.

But rebuttals came from two of Port-Royal's friends—Du Bois and Barbier d'Aucourt—who were one day to take their seats at Racine's side in the French Academy. Barbier d'Aucourt's letter, which the writer tried to make witty, was frankly bad. A more serious epistle by Du Bois seems a little bombastic, but it contains a severe censure of the former pupil of the Little Schools who heaped ridicule on a nun and on a solitary both of whom had passed into eternity. "Your hatred disinters the dead!" Du Bois wrote. Some time afterward, Nicole published the writings of his defenders in a collection that included the "Imaginaries," and at that time he himself replied to his former disciple: "Everything in that letter was false and contrary to good sense, from beginning to end. It had, nevertheless, a certain flashiness suited to those mean minds with which the world is filled."

Thus revived, the quarrel continued. Racine drafted a second letter addressed to the two writers who had defended the cause of the Messieurs. "I can assure you," he wrote, "that the melancholy one made me laugh and the joker made me pity him."

To divert his readers, the poet informed them that "the melancholy one" thought he should go back to the Romans and had depicted them in a naive way "at the head of an army and the tail of a plow."

But Racine abandoned these obscure men of letters to face more worthy opponents—the solitaries themselves. Again the poet accused them of a desire for fame, an idea that had become an obsession with him.

> The number of those who condemn Jansenius is too great—how does one find the means to stand out in the crowd? Cast yourself among the small number of his defenders; take it into your heads that people are talking only about you, and are looking for you everywhere so as to place you under arrest; change your lodgings often, change your names if you have not already done so—or rather, do not change them at all, for you could not be less well known except among yourselves.

Then Racine raised the debate to a new level and dared to criticize the dead man who represented the supreme bastion of Port-Royal—Pascal. The Messieurs, he said, considered the theater as a danger to religion, and condemned it in the name of the Church. But had not the "Provincials," with their harsh attacks on the Society of Jesus, worked infinitely more harm to Catholicism than all the plays taken together? Besides, their author himself was being theatrical.

Do you think that the *Provincial Letters* are anything other than comedies? Tell me, sirs, what goes on in a comedy? There are the rascally man servant, the avaricious bourgeois, and the extravagant marquis. . . . I admit that the Provincial makes a better choice of characters: at times he brings onto the stage some Dominican friars, at others some theologians, and always the Jesuits. And how many roles does he make the latter play? Sometimes there is a good-natured Jesuit, sometimes a disagreeable Jesuit, but always a Jesuit who is ridiculous.

With the gift of prophecy often found in great minds, Racine concluded by saying that if the Church forbade plays "we will stop going to them, and wait patiently for the time when we can put Jesuits on the stage." The whole of the eighteenth century of Voltaire, of Diderot, and of the Encyclopedists was voiced in these words.

After mounting to these heights, the adversary of Port-Royal suddenly descended, and returned once more to Le Maître. The former lawyer had permitted his legal speeches to be published, but not without revising them to include "more spirituality." But shouldn't a repentant man forget all he had done in the world?

The dead man's influence over Racine was still powerful. The first of the solitaries had dreamed of a brilliant future for his disciple among the members of the court, and Racine was constantly haunted by the memory of his affection. Le Maître's example, the nobility of a life devoted to meditation, his tenderness for the orphan harbored at the Fields, were reminders of a lost paradise; laughter was his pupil's only weapon against the reproach on the face of one who was no more.

Since he enjoyed the royal favor, the author of *Alexander* believed everything was permitted him, and he intended to add a second "Letter" to the first and to publish them both with a preface. Before doing so, however, he read the second letter to his friend Boileau.

"That is very smartly written," the latter said, "but remember that you are attacking the most honorable people in the world."

Louis Racine, who reports these words in his *Memoires,* adds: "This remark immediately brought my father back to his senses. . . . His obligations to those gentlemen passed before his mind. He suppressed the second letter and withdrew from circulation as many copies of the first as he could."

Such, no doubt, was the version of the affair given by Racine to his family. Today the reason for his retreat is better known.

Racine's anonymity had been quickly pierced. Vitart, his first cousin once removed, was the steward of the duc de Luynes, and when the first "Letter" was published in January, 1666, he asked for explanations on behalf of the

Messieurs. The erstwhile pupil of the Little Schools was disturbed by this and said that he did not know anything about the libel, even confirming this in a short letter which Vitart turned over to Nicole. Shortly afterward, knowing that Racine was no longer making a secret of his authorship of the "Letter" and was planning to publish another, Lancelot, one of the Port-Royal solitaries, charged Vitart with this warning to his cousin: "Since he was not honorable enough to give an unqualified 'yes' or 'no' as to this affair, let him beware, for he will do more harm to himself than he can do to others. . . . True honor is not served in this way." When he read these lines, Racine recognized the Messieurs' style, and realized that he was about to discredit himself with honorable men. Only then did he decide to abandon the dangerous polemic.

The Jesuits were disappointed, for the first "Letter" had whetted their appetite for more. They were happy to see the arrival of an ally with talents they themselves did not possess; only Racine could make fitting reply to Pascal's "scathing" irony.

The fathers' hunger was not appeased. The author of *Alexander* deliberately turned his back on his past and concentrated on the brilliant future before him. During the next years, from 1667 to 1677, Racine's fame rose to such heights that it even added luster to that of his king. *Andromache, Britannicus, Berenice, Bajazet, Mithridates* and *Iphigenia* aroused the admiration of a new generation—the new court.

As *The Litigants* was being played in December, 1668, the marquise du Parc died. Her lover saw her entering that unknown land upon which the solitaries had taught him to gaze with open eyes. Nothing of yesterday's triumphs and ephemeral scepters remained on that bed of pain but a tortured creature who would have to stand before the judgment seat that very night. In terror, Racine rushed to the pastor of the parish and led him to the actress—she could not receive the sacraments unless she denied her past. Before the author of *Andromache,* and under the eyes of the priest, the dying woman summoned strength to sign the act of renunciation: "I promise God with all my heart and in full freedom of mind never to take part in plays for the rest of my life and even if it pleases his infinite goodness to restore me to health." Marquise du Parc had also to renounce her lover, confessing with a sigh that the last was the greater sacrifice.

As Racine followed his mistress' funeral cortège, he appeared "half dead," in the words of one newsmonger. But sorrow was quickly dispelled by a restless mind constantly occupied with bringing to life heroes and heroines of the past: the poet made Nero, Agrippina, Junia, live again. While *Britannicus* was being played at the Hôtel de Bourgogne, Racine was writing *Berenice.* Effortlessly and without a false note, Racine depicted the torments of a woman losing all hope and light as she saw herself separated from the man she loved.

It was to his new interpreter, La Champmeslé, that the author of *Berenice* owed a good part of his great success. Several months earlier he had seen this actress, then twenty-six years of age, playing the role of Hermione in a performance of *Andromache* at the Hôtel de Bourgogne. In the beginning La Champmeslé had appeared rather colorless, but as her passion manifested itself Racine was more and more impressed by the actress' portrayal of the woman whose love for Pyrrhus was not returned. Filled with admiration, Racine paid a visit to the young actress in her dessing room, and decided that very day that Champmeslé should play Berenice. He expected far more of her than he had of du Parc: this new tragedienne would not only depict the shadowy queens of the past in the throes of violent emotion, but would bring them closer to the audience by revealing their innermost thoughts. At last Racine had in his possession the marvelous instrument on which he could play with a sure hand. His new pupil was just as docile as her predecessor, but more intelligent and sensitive. She had, indeed, much to learn. Her teacher had to make clear to her the emotions she was to express; to teach her the secrets of poetry; to explain how to distinguish long syllables from short, giving each line its proper volume and rhythm, and stressing its melodiousness. La Champmeslé learned the value of a pause to emphasize the full meaning of the following words; to modulate her voice; at times to lower her tone to a whisper. Finally, she acquired an ease of bearing and attitude that was the envy of many a princess. Doubtless this actress did not possess the tall figure or beautiful features of the marquise du Parc, but Madame de Sévigné revealed the secret of her charm: "At close range she is ugly, but when she recites her lines she is adorable."

This actress was married to Charles Chevillet, called Champmeslé, an actor without talent. In any case he was always the most obliging of husbands, for it was due to his wife that he had been able to remain in the troop of the Hôtel de Bourgogne when there was a question of dismissing him. His career was assured when his wife gave herself to the author of *Berenice*. A sarcastic verse then ran about the theater wings which served as the setting for this household of three:

> Champmeslé, that happy mortal
> Will never have to leave the Hôtel;
> His wife holds Racine captive there.

The poet consented to the shame of favors shared. Racine was obliged to become as philosophical as La Champmeslé's husband, and to close his eyes to her successive liaisons. Nevertheless, his attachment to her was deep and strong.

Berenice, as depicted by the tragédienne, was the wraithlike and pathetic creature the poet had imagined her to be. "When she appears on the stage, one hears a murmur," wrote Madame de Sévigné. "Everyone is in raptures and weeps at her despair."

The king's favor grew and the poet's pension became larger and larger. Did he finally know peace? No, the gods were never to grant him an instant's respite. Shortly after his triumph, the author of *Berenice* met with one of the most cruel humiliations of all.

La Champmeslé decided to console Madame de Sévigné's son, Charles, when this young gentleman was dismissed by Ninon de Lenclos, whose lover he had been, following in the steps of his own father. Racine's mistress arranged for him a series of after-theater suppers, where prominent people sat side by side with actors and poets. The obliging husband and the illustrious lover and friend of Boileau were the life of these parties. "There is a little actress and Despréaux and Racine with her," wrote Madame de Sévigné. "These suppers are delicious: that is to say, they are deviltries."

The generous Champmeslé was quick to offer herself to Charles de Sévigné. The marquise deplored her son's misconduct, but not without a modicum of satisfaction at his success. "He drinks up sin like water," wrote Madame de Sévigné in reluctant admiration.

Was Berenice less inspiring to Charles than Ninon had been? At the decisive moment he was incapable of receiving La Champmeslé's favors. What was worse, he was so ungallant as to make no mystery of this failure. "His cockhorse ran short at Lerida," Madame de Sévigné wrote with ribaldry. The most famous of horsemen, Condé, had hastily raised the seige of Lerida on June 17, 1647, under conditions that surprised his companions-at-arms; Charles de Sévigné felt himself disarmed in the same way before the conquered citadel. "He was like a horse overstuffed with oats," his mother added.

This misadventure greatly amused the friends of the marquise. "We had a good laugh," she wrote. At court no one dreamed of blaming Madame de Sévigné for her lack of reserve in regard to her son. An actress in no way deserved the respect of a wellborn woman; wasn't it permissible to joke about creatures of light virtue who lived under the public gaze?

La Champmeslé broke off her liaison with Charles de Sévigné, saying, "He has the heart of a pumpkin fried in snow"—which could have been true.

This anecdote was bandied about the anterooms, causing much hilarity among the gentlemen. It was impossible for Racine not to be deeply mortified. He had accepted many compromises, but now his future was tied to a girl of the theater of whom wellbred people made fun. Port-Royal had taught the poet the dignity that should be maintained by every thinking man, an idea that had become the heaviest of crosses to an ambitious, proud, and humbly born courtier.

Writers, however, had a means of healing their wounds: they could publicize them. Racine wrote *Bajazet,* identifying himself completely with the voice of the jealous Roxana.

Flouted, if not in love at least in his self-respect, Racine nevertheless saw one of his greatest ambitions satisfied. When he was only thirty-three, Colbert opened to him the doors of the French Academy, where he was received on January 12, 1673.

The following day his play *Mithridates* was performed for the first time at the Hôtel de Bourgogne. La Champmeslé, who took the role of Monime, made herself more appealing than ever before. Racine had metamorphosed the actress who had so miserably betrayed him into a princess radiantly pure and infinitely chaste even in her thoughts about love. When the voice of Monime was heard, it was almost as though one were behind the grill and beneath the cloister arches, in the presence of the nuns and pupils of Port-Royal.

The following year was consecrated to *Iphigenia.* Agamemnon's daughter bears an even closer resemblance to the virgins of the monastery. Renouncing the promises of youth, she consents to the sacrifice of her life in obedience to her father and the gods. As incarnated by La Champmeslé, the victim appeared in all her sweetness and grace, her white robe and veils symbolizing the sad fate she goes out to meet with sadness but resignation.

A deep hush fell over the audience when La Champmeslé spoke in the melodious voice of the daughter of Agamemnon, as Boileau's famous verse confirms: "Never did Iphigenia in Aulis immolated/Draw so many tears from the assembled Greeks."

The author of *Iphigenia* knew that he could not count on talent alone to keep the favor of the king. He had lost his protectress, Henrietta of England, during the tragic night that "reverberated as a clap of thunder" in Bossuet's words. But Racine did not linger in vain regret. As soon as Madame de Montespan became the king's favorite, the poet laid his talents at her feet, and in this new sovereign found an admirer almost as fervent as Queen Henrietta had been. Doubtless the haughty descendant of Montemart was little moved by Junia's charm or the gentleness of Berenice and Iphigenia, but she recognized her own likeness in the imperious Roxana.

Thereafter Racine had to fear only one rival: Corneille (or rather his partisans, for the author of *Le Cid* was coming to the end of his career). In reality, the confrontation was that of two generations, not of two poets. The comparison—so often made—between Racine and Corneille on the literary plane must be considered under a different aspect—political, social, and religious.

Corneille had been trained by the Jesuits just as Racine had been formed by the Messieurs of Port-Royal. Loyola's sons had given him a solid Latin culture, but, on the other hand, his study of Greek was wilfully neglected. The fathers of the Society considered the liberty-loving Democrates and the poets and philosophers of Athens dangerous to the peace of the realm. Moreover, they felt they must rule out the ideas of Sophocles and Euripides about man's helplessness before the forces that govern the world and those that dwell within him.

If Corneille did not know the Greeks, he was perfectly familiar, thanks to his instructors, with the genius of Rome. He had learned that the Latins had triumphed by force of courage and will-power, and that, like them, every man could conquer if he would but master himself.

The lessons of the Jesuits are found in their entirety in Corneille's verses: as a good pupil of the fathers, he mocked the Jansenists as human beings reduced "to a freedom that leaves them nothing to choose."

A disciple of Molina, the poet naively proclaimed his self-sufficiency vis-à-vis God. Heaven, he said, "should offer us its aid and then let us act."

This proud attitude enthused the old soldiers who, under Richelieu, had defended the French frontiers. The tragedies of Rotrou and Corneille permitted these retired heroes, who had been so dangerous at the time of The Fronde until put down by Mazarin, to live on in their dream world. When they listened to Le Cid, they felt the peace of conscience which the Society of Jesus held out to its penitents; wise, brave, generous, and at times sublime, the wellbred man casts temptation aside and responds to his noblest impulses.

But when Racine appeared on the scene a new and disappointed generation was beginning to transform the spirit of France. The sons of the rebels knew that the exhausted kingdom wanted only peace; that the day of feudal lords was over. Those who did not want to perish of boredom and poverty in their dismantled châteaus had to find a post in the king's household, and already noblemen rivalled one another in servility to their master. When Louis XIV rose in the morning or went to bed at night, they stood by waiting for a word or a smile; each feared that he might fall from favor. All took part in intrigues, no longer for the purpose of winning power, but to attain a kneeling-bench in the royal chapel or a folding chair at the Louvre.

To these down-at-the-heels noblemen, Racine revealed the harsh reality that justified their abdication: man is but a plaything, the victim of passions that lead him astray and of the destiny allotted him.

The solitaries had not kept their disciple ignorant of the lucid pessimism of the Greek thinkers and poets. They told him that the powers of darkness that spread over the ancient world still hovered over every place where Christ has not taken up his abode. Now the Messieurs' former pupil was teaching the downtrodden aristocracy how to accept the blows of fate.

Like Pascal before "his night of fire," the author of *Andromache* knew inward despair. From the first to the last act, Racine's dramatic characters are shown as the victims of fatality. In his work on the poet, Thierry Maulnier shows how in each case the characters are led inexorably by their passions.[1] Andromache is haunted always by the memory of her husband and the image of her child. Pyrrhus is filled with desire for his captive. Hermione burns with the same hopeless love for the king of Epirus that Orestes feels for her. Britannicus is marked for death by the will of Nero, who has inherited a proclivity for crime. Berenice lives for Titus, and is parted from him forever when he is made king. Iphigenia is led to the sacrifice by a father already condemned by the hatred of the gods.

Chained together, and yet strangers to one another, men march along the road to death. The fate of these predestined beings is fulfilled at one time and in one place.

Such was the fruit of the tree of knowledge that Racine had tasted. Beneath the rigorous form of the Greek tragedies and the starkness of the scriptural accounts he discerned the secrets of the human heart. Actions are but appearances; in the presence of the drama that takes place within ourselves, time—immutable and simultaneous in its unity—is suspended; it is one of the dimensions of space.

"Every invention," wrote the author of *Berenice*, "consists in making something out of nothing." This "nothing" is the mind and heart; it is what we have within ourselves.

Racine's visions of enchantment were more appealing to his audience than Corneille's grandiloquent heroism. Before such frailties masks were removed as each individual recognized his own likeness.

"Poisoner of the public!" The day was to come when the poet would confess that he had been the most dangerous, among "those guilty of spiritual homicide." His princesses appeared on the stage fitted out with every seduction. The beautiful captives Andromache and Junia, coveted by Pyrrhus and by Nero, reveal the powerful attraction of the flesh; Roxanna exhales a sensual ardor; Berenice's words recall pleasures of the most intimate nature. Kings and warriors betray their weakness in the presence of these too-lifelike idols, and, succumbing to the most burning impulses, fall victim to their passions. This last word was again given the meaning it held in other days— namely, suffering.

---

[1] Thierry Maulnier, *Racine*. Paris, 1947.

The audience felt itself so close to these queens and sovereigns that it experienced their desires and shared their hope and despair. They were, Bossuet said, "real emotions that set fire to every seat and box in the theater."

Drowned in waves of exegesis, mutilated in quotation, Racine has undergone the wear and tear of time, but imagine the feelings of those who heard for the first time his hymns to sensuality and death. Certain ones among them would never forget those siren voices . . . and when the false piety of the *Grand Siècle* had been swept away, Racine's tragedies were to become the delight of the Regency rakes.

When he wrote *Phaedra,* Racine had not only been disappointed in love, but apparently had also lost a child born of his union with the marquise du Parc.

His work was being subjected to the harshest criticism; rivals of little talent revenged themselves for their lack of success by comparing his reputation to the glories of old Corneille. Around Fontenelle, Corneille's nephew, gathered a group of literary people who professed a mad admiration for the author of *Polyeucte* and saw Racine as a danger to their future. Segrais, the favorite of the Grande Mademoiselle, an affected individual whose insipid pastoral poems were the delight of the Hôtel de Rambouillet, and Benserade, Ménage, and Boyer united their efforts against the common enemy. Saint-Evremond, trained as was Corneille to admire the grandeur of Rome, considered the latter much greater than Racine. And finally the author of *Le Cid,* seeing the public turn aside from him, gave vent to his anger. In his struggle against his rival he allied himself to Molière who, in 1668, produced a comedy, *The Foolish Quarrel,* intended as a parody of *Andromache.*

Racine never succeeded in disarming his enemies, and there were mutterings in the "old court" against *Andromache, Berenice,* and *Bajazet.* In a desire to defend herself against impure temptations, Madame de Sévigné forgave Corneille for "some bad verses, because of those other godly and sublime beauties that enrapture us." The marquise added: "Beware of comparing Racine with him."

When *Bajazet* was performed, Madame de Sévigné wrote: "Racine writes comedies for La Champmeslé, and not for posterity."

With a lucidity inspired by jealousy, the poet's enemies sneered at his romantic warriors who mooned about in the same way as in D'Urfé's old-fashioned romance, *Astrée.* Saint-Evremond deplored insipidities that made one yearn for the noble vigor of the Latins. It would take two more centuries for Euripides' savage power to be discovered beneath its trappings. Racine's contemporaries admired only one of its aspects—the delightful frailties that sent so many women into raptures.

For years the critics—especially those who wrote in the *Mercure Galant*—

were cruel. The poët replied to his enemies in the prefaces to his plays with bitter words that betrayed the anger of a wounded swan.

From *Andromache* to *Phaedra*, Racine had come a long way; there was a wide gulf between the two. The story of Phaedra, as told by Euripides and Seneca, is transfigured in the second play. The daughter of Minos and Pasiphae carries her love for Hippolytus like a hidden cancer; her premeditated crime is all the more hideous in that it is never committed but lives and grows, absorbing Phaedra's whole soul despite her despairing struggle against it.

Formerly, Racine's protagonists had gone to their fates after blindly surrendering to their inner passions: the gods had dominated them from on high. But in this case Phaedra tries to resist her desires, but a goddess comes down from Olympus, grasps the rebel, and throws her at Hippolytus' feet.

Cruelly humiliated, Theseus' wife renounces all things, one by one, until she approaches the dark hour of her death, for to save herself she is forced to commit suicide. None of Racine's heroines appears so carnal, so palpitating with desire as this woman haunted by a shameful passion.

> I feel my whole body freezing, burning.

> .   .   .

> I pined, I drooped, in fiery torment and in tears.

> .   .   .

> When under a shameful yoke I could scarcely breathe.

This is far from the comfortable optimism of Corneille and the Jesuits. At Port-Royal Racine had learned that it is useless to hide inner corruption beneath fine sentiments. The poet knew from experience at each moment of his life how easily man is overcome by evil when deprived of grace.

> In vain my hand burned incense on the altars;
> Even when my lips invoked the goddess' name
> I adored Hippolytus!

Thus every man, with the exception of those predestined to be saved, is created only for contamination and punishment!

> I knew Venus and her dreaded flames
> The fatal torments of a race she loathes.

Phaedra's anguish and horror of death are accusations cast by the victim against the cruelty of the gods.

Jesus had saved his children in the past and would save them in the future. But Racine saw a horde of libertines and bad Christians hastening toward their own destruction—the actress he loved, the king he admired, the friends who surrounded him; finally, he saw himself as already judged and already condemned.

It was to no avail that transgressors felt sterile remorse springing from disgust with their exhausted flesh:

> I have a fitting horror for my crime;
> I hate this passion and I loathe my life.

Before Hippolytus, Phaedra accuses Venus:

> The hapless victim of heaven's vengeance,
> I loathe myself more deeply than do you.
> The gods are witness, they who in my breast
> Have lit the fatal fire in all my line.

The day he wrote these lines Racine's thoughts were lifted to a realm higher than Olympus, and went out to the Christ he had forsaken for deceptive love affairs and earthly vanities. After the first "Jansenist" of Port-Royal who revealed his miseries in the *Pensées,* the second now emerges. While Pascal lived in the world he experienced for weeks and months the feeling of a blind man groping for light in the midst of darkness. When Racine wrote *Phaedra* he lacked even the first movement of grace which would have enabled him to take a step toward the Beyond.

At these moments of their lives each of these two Christians knew a terror which his genius enabled him to describe in a way that would reverberate across the centuries. Pascal was not able to hand down the second part of his message, telling of the consolation that follows despair. Racine, for his part, presents the image of Phaedra, who is vanquished before she has even begun to fight.

Isn't it dangerous to face men with a fatality that consigns them to the abyss? A hero would confront it, as Pascal did, and even dare tempt the Almighty so as not to fall into the void. But how many weaker souls might be tempted to give up the struggle, to abandon themselves to inevitable defeat? Here is the very heart of the danger inherent in Jansenism. A generation with the leisure to discover its ills, following in the magician's steps, and inebriated by an amazing pessimism, the new court took Racine to its heart.

Racine was now very near his return to Port-Royal, but he did not know it. He still felt that he belonged entirely to the strange world where each evening the heroes of old came to tell men of their inner struggles. Hearts were touched, tears were shed. The poet was more than a king: he was the god who unveiled mysteries, made each man aware of unsuspected delights and torments in the secret fibers of his own being.

Other bonds, less glorious, chained Racine to the theater. La Champmeslé returned to her lover when her interludes did not come up to her expectations. After each of these escapades the poet would find the actress as pure as if she had never failed him, as appealing as when his genius first created her. Again, despite himself, Pygmalion would become enamoured of Galatea.

On January 1, 1677, the first performance of *Phaedra* took place before an audience of tradesmen, shopkeepers, and lackeys. It is said that the duchesse de Bouillon, who was hostile to the poet, had bought up all the seats and filled the hall with an audience of this kind. Three days later, the *Phaedra* of Racine's rival, Pradon, was played before the great personages of the court.

Meanwhile, at the Hôtel de Bourgogne, La Champmeslé was being forced to play a role she found humiliating, for she had to confess the love of a mature woman for the young Hippolytus. Racine had taken this way of striking back at his cynical mistress, who was too susceptible to the charms of youthful noblemen.

> . . . I know my baseness, Oenone,
> I am not one of those who in their crimes
> Enjoy a tranquil peace, and know the art
> Of keeping blushes from their countenance.

In vain did La Champmeslé ask the author to take out these lines: the injured lover wanted to shame the woman unfaithful to him in the measure he himself had been made to suffer shame.

The momentary failure of Racine's play discouraged the actress. Not a woman to remain long in the camp of a loser, she abandoned her role and broke with her lover. Then, yielding to a passion similar to those she had portrayed on the stage, La Champmeslé forsook the theater and devoted herself entirely to the amorous life.

A young man of twenty-six, who bore one of France's greatest names, the comte de Clermont-Tonnere, had fallen under the siren's spell. Phaedra fled with this rather tame Hippolytus, and all over Paris La Champmeslé was ridiculed in this epigram:

> Le Tonnere est venu qui l'a déRacinée.[1]

And now the poet was deprived of the interpreter who brought his dreams alive—Orpheus had lost his Eurydice.

Racine had met with too many humiliations in his pursuit of fame and too much anguish in his amorous affairs not to feel overwhelmed.

---

[1] A play on the two proper names. Literally: "Came the thunder which uprooted her."—Trans.

He had already begun a new tragedy—*Iphigenia in Tauris*. In this play Agamemnon's daughter is rescued by Diana from the death to which her father has condemned her, and is carried away to Tauris, where she becomes a priestess of the most chaste of the goddesses. Diana demands the sacrifice of all strangers who approach her shores; among the victims Iphigenia discovers her brother Orestes, accompanied by Pylades. The ensuing conflict takes place between the pitiless huntress and the young girl determined to save one to whom she is bound by ties of blood.

Venus had cast Phaedra at Hippolytus' feet to drive the guilty woman to suicide, but in that play the goddess remained an offstage allusion. Now Racine wanted to go further: to introduce a deity on the scene. Diana watches as the priestess vowed to her worship rebels against her. No longer does the poet curse Venus, the pagan voluptuary, but instead the virgin Diana. Against the implacable goddess he turns the most formidable of all weapons—the pity in the heart of a woman, as expressed in Iphigenia's gentle complaint.

When he began the outline of this tragedy, Racine had wearied of living under the eyes of God; the guilty Adam felt himself followed by silent but incessant reproach. Behind the bright crescent of Diana he would hide the hatred mingled with remorse felt by the lover of Du Parc and La Champmeslé for the master of men. Iphigenia's heart-rending cry would be launched against the pitiless love that condemns everything not superhumanly pure to the fires of eternal death.

But, immediately following *Phaedra,* the daring archer was so cruelly wounded that this last arrow fell from his hand. Having humiliated him in his vainglory, God had taken from him the beloved mistress who could bring his heroine to life. Then, in the way of Pascal, the poet bowed his head, joined his hands, and came, or rather returned to the Spirit to whom all must be given. In his turn he now wanted to cast the world aside, to annihilate everything he had become.

Racine was only thirty-seven, but at this age any failure is an omen of defeat. Formerly the passions had appeared to the poet as an inexhaustible source of riches; to them he had sacrificed a seemingly inaccessible religion and had surrendered to sensuality and ambition. But now the edifice of his happiness lay in ruins about him.

Racine had nothing more to hope for in the domain of sensual love or in the theater. He had everything to win on the ways of eternity, and he accepted the wager Pascal would have offered him.

Carried away by his new passion, the poet wanted to enter one of the strictest religious orders—the Carthusian. His confessor, the pastor of Saint-Landry—the priest who had in days gone by received Du Parc's adjuration—

dissuaded him from this plan. Brought about by disillusionment, Racine's conversion was too human in its motivation to lead him to the peace of the cloister. The author of *Phaedra* must abandon the theater, but his spiritual director thought he should remain in the world in order to give the good example of a Christian life after having jeopardized so many souls. Racine then turned to his lost paradise—Port-Royal—yielding to the attraction that had led the Arnaulds, the Pascals, and the members of his own family to that mysterious valley. He was dominated more than ever by the grave faces of the men and women who had been the guides of his youth; far from the intrigues and desires of the world, the solitaries meditated under the eyes of God. What pace and what horizons they opened to him!

When he wrote the preface to *Phaedra*, Racine held out his arms to his past. He wanted forgiveness not only for his old offense against the solitaries, but for his last tragedy, all the more loved because it had been attacked. Pasiphae's daughter would be the messenger of the prodigal son. He said he had written no other tragedy "in which virtue is given greater prominence; the slightest transgressions are severely punished. The very thought of crime is regarded with as much horror as the crime itself." The author further confesses his desire "to reconcile tragedy with a host of people famous for their piety and their doctrine, who have recently condemned it."

Would the solitaries listen to the appeal of their former disciple? More than ten years had gone by since Racine had published the "Letter" which so cruelly ridiculed his former teachers.

In March, 1677, Clement IX's peace had reigned for eight years. In the Monastery of the Fields hymns and the sound of bells could again be heard. At Les Granges the Messieurs were publishing translations of the Scriptures and of the writings of the Fathers of the Church.

It was in this climate of peace that Racine approached Port-Royal. A distant relative, the Abbot du Pin, took him to see Nicole, who pardoned him with all his heart. However, although the author of the "Visionaries" and the "Imaginaries" opened his arms wide to his most beloved disciple, Arnauld himself was less pacifically inclined.

Racine had "caricatured" the Messieurs. The spiritual leader of Port-Royal did not refuse to relent because of this, but he could not forget that the poet had represented Angélique Arnauld as a small-minded person capable of showing bitterness toward religious who came to ask her hospitality. Years had passed since then, but Antoine could not forget the offense against his great older sister.

At that point Boileau, Racine's most faithful friend, intervened. After a riotous youth, the former had become a fervent Christian and he, too, had fallen under the spell of Port-Royal. To Antoine Arnauld he had dedicated his third "Epistle" on "False Shame," in which the poet confesses his misery to the Augustinian theologian:

> Thus am I ever sliding, giddy, and in doubt,
> I've always a foot in the slough of vice.
> So soon as I timidly get one out
> The other sinks into the mire.

Boileau took to the faubourg Saint-Jacques a copy of *Phaedra* which Racine had asked him to present to Arnauld on his behalf. After reading to Arnauld the preface in which the author expresses his desire to reconcile the theater with Port-Royal, Boileau tried to explain how Phaedra's example might lead Christians to grace.

Arnauld read *Phaedra* the following day. Not without trepidation Boileau awaited his verdict, but he had good reason to be hopeful: the Arnaulds were never unreceptive to the good qualities of a masterpiece.

"That is perfectly beautiful," pronounced the theologian when Boileau returned to see him a few days later.

Arnauld had only one criticism: "Why did he have Hippolytus fall in love?" Euripides had presented Theseus' son as impervious to the charms of women, but, fearing that his hero might be suspected of abnormal leanings, Racine had concocted an idyllic love affair between the untamed hunter and the gentle Aricia.

Arnauld admired the portrayal of Phaedra's devastating passion—this expressed the ideas of Port-Royal. But he feared that the amorous dialogue of Hippolytus and Aricia would increase the lure of carnal temptations.

Despite this reservation, Boileau understood that his friend was forgiven. Rushing out to find the poet, he accompanied him to Arnauld's home. When Racine found himself before the man he had earlier wounded in his affection for the dead, the poet was speechless and fell to his knees. His son, Louis Racine, tells how Arnauld himself knelt down and the two men embraced. Such a scene may seem surprising, but it can easily be explained: Arnauld, as Saint-Cyran's disciple, could not allow a son of Christ, redeemed by the sacred blood, to humiliate himself before him; by kneeling he showed in his turn the respect due to any Christian.

From that day forward the spiritual leader of Port-Royal treated the author of *Phaedra* as a friend and equal.

That same year, 1677, Racine married, in the Church of Saint-Severin, the daughter of a Treasurer of France, Catherine de Romanet. This good, simple woman of the middle class knew nothing of the theater, never read her husband's works, and gave him seven children. Le Vasseur, the gallant priest, who had now settled down, was one of the witnesses to the marriage.

It is possible that Louis XIV was afraid that Racine would bring publicity to the "desert" of Port-Royal by going into retreat there, as Le Maître had once done. In any case, he quite willingly granted Madame de Montespan's request that the poet be granted the position of court historiographer; Pellisson, Fouquet's friend who had formerly held this post, had been so unfortunate as to incur the displeasure of the king's favorite. Thus the author of *Alexander* was entrusted with the task of chronicling for posterity the great deeds of his sovereign, and his salary was six thousand livres. At Racine's request Boileau was given the same position, for the poet did not want to be separated from his companion. The author of *Phaedra* now began to lead a double life: though a courtier at the Louvre, at Versailles, and at Marly, he lived piously at the side of his wife and especially at Port-Royal, where he went to make retreats as Pascal had done earlier.

Serving both his God and a king who showered him with favors, Racine finally enjoyed two peaceful years. But in 1679 he was suddenly confronted by a specter rising from his past.

The "Poison Affair," discovered through an anonymous denunciation made in a Jesuit confessional, began to cast a growing shadow over the court. Among the names mentioned was that of Racine. Through this affair the strange creatures among whom the poet lived when he was du Parc's lover have been recorded for history. One of his mistress' friends had been a woman known as La Voisin, the poisoner.

During the whole course of the illness preceding her death the marquise had called constantly for this shrew, and she on her side made vain attempts to gain admittance to the dying actress. But Racine had prevented the two women from coming together. Now La Voisin declared before judges of the court that the poet had poisoned the marquise du Parc out of jealousy, and had even stolen her jewelry.

The charge seemed serious, and on January 11, 1680, Louvois wrote Bazin de Bezon, the magistrate charged with investigating the affair: "Orders of the king . . . for the arrest of Sieur Racine will be sent immediately on your request."

Bezon never asked for these orders. He was a state counselor who sat beside the poet in the French Academy, and, moreover, he probably did not consider the evidence against his colleague to be sufficient.

Nevertheless, Racine must have known hours of anguish. François Mauriac [1] thinks it was at this time that he wrote the ode inspired by David's psalms: "My ruin was inevitable. . . ."

---

[1] F. Mauriac, *La vie de Jean Racine*, Paris, 1928.

But, like the psalmist, the poet was saved by a power more than human: "Thy hand has drawn me back from the pit/Dug for me by evil men."

The disciple of the solitaries, the grandson and nephew of two saintly women, had known not only the intrigues of the world of the theater but a sordid underworld of vagrants. For thirteen years his violent passions had held him suspended above the abyss, and it must have been with a great sense of deliverance that, after the cabal surrounding *Phaedra,* he sought out the pacific Nicole, the loyal Arnauld, and especially the nun awaiting him beneath the arches of Port-Royal—his aunt Agnès.

For Louis XIV himself the whole Poison Affair was a great trial. Four years earlier the case of the marquise de Brinvilliers had shown the king the first symptoms of the evil. Now debates in the criminal courts drew his attention to crimes being plotted in the slums of his capital while great ceremonies were taking place at the Louvre, Saint-Germain, and Versailles.

The sovereign had given free rein to his subjects. Knowing that one must divide in order to rule, he had encouraged ambitions, jealousies, and hatreds. Now, confronted with the mounting wave of crime, he was appalled. To satisfy their passions and eliminate certain rivals, women in whom the master of all France had placed absolute confidence were roaming the slums of Paris in search of philters and poisons.

When it was a matter of maintaining order in the state, Louis XIV acted as king: punishment was meted out only to Voisin and her obscure accomplices. Reckoning better than Louis XVI at the time of the "Necklace Affair," the monarch wanted no scandal to touch his court: it might even involve the throne, over which the gentlemen of Parlement maintained an ever-watchful eye. But almost imperceptibly the king began to bring about a palace revolution—the reign of royal mistresses was coming to an end. Madame de Montespan was to be definitively dismissed, and Fontanges, "the beautiful idiot," to die in childbirth at a convent. The reign of the pious Madame de Maintenon would soon begin.

Born a year earlier than Racine, Louis XIV knew at the same period as the poet the joys of freedom rewon, of successes in winning fame and love. Three years later than the poet the sovereign, who had suffered the same disillusionments, began in his turn to lead a devout life which would continue until his death. And so the distance separating the most powerful of kings from the man of obscure birth was abolished.

During this interim the Monastery of Port-Royal, like a person who is happy, had no history; it was living at peace.

Monseigneur de Péréfixe died on January 1, 1671, at the time *Berenice* was meeting with such success on the stage. The king appointed the Archbishop of Rouen, Francis de Harlay, to succeed Péréfixe in the see of Paris.

Defenders of the Church had unsuccessfully urged the nomination of Monseigneur Vialart, Bishop of Châlons, whose moral qualities placed him well above many of his colleagues. Louis XIV preferred the brilliant and worldly prelate for whose ability, subtlety, and above all pliability he had a high regard.

The scion of a great family of lawyers, Monseigneur de Harlay was only forty-five years of age, a very handsome man, and one who carried himself with an air of distinction. His exquisite courtesy and cleverness in negotiations made this prince of the Church a consummate diplomat. Those who came into his presence were struck, they said, by "his majestic bearing, his eloquent and flowing manner of speaking, a certain ingratiating and pleasing quality in his voice." His charm, mindful of Racine's own, made Francis de Harlay particularly seductive. Saint-Simon lauded "his courteous and lordly manners," and expressed for the prelate a measure of admiration he seldom accorded anyone. "He had infinite graces of body and mind," he wrote.

The author of the *Memoirs* could not conceal, however, what he discreetly called De Harlay's "gallantries." Despite all his qualities—or perhaps because of them—Monseigneur de Harlay was unworthy of the priesthood. In Rouen, his liaisons with two abbesses had caused scandal. In Paris, when night fell the archbishop could be seen on his way to the house of a woman of light virtue who lived on the island of Notre-Dame now known as the Ile Saint-Louis. The belle's lover, a captain of the guard, did not dare molest the prelate, but one evening he had him accompanied back to the archbishop's palace by two officers who were his friends, both carrying lighted torches. On this same island the prelate made visits to another tender friend, Madame de Bretonvilliers. The Parisians—who could always find a witty epithet for anything—added to the archbishop's titles that of "Visitor to the Island of Notre Dame."

Louis XIV willingly closed his eyes to this weakness, even seeing in it an advantage: he had at his mercy an archbishop whose "gallantries" called for pardon. For the same reason, the Jesuits received Monseigneur de Harlay very favorably, knowing he would not dare take a stand in opposition to the Society.

The prelate held no animosity toward Port-Royal. If earlier he had commanded the signature of the formulary, it was solely to advance his own career. He had coveted the Paris archbishopric, and now he wanted the post of guardian of the seal. "He would have made a great chancellor," wrote Saint-Simon. "He could not have been mediocre at anything."

In 1671 it was no longer good form to persecute the Jansenists, and, since peace had been concluded, the archbishop wanted to maintain it in the common interest of Church and state. Unfortunately, the Arnaulds liked to fight. Earlier they had bowed their heads, but a few years of peace had been sufficient to revive their desire to defend an immortal dream.

Antoine Arnauld's brother Henri, Bishop of Angers, published, in 1678, a mandate which restored the distinction between *fact* and *right* in regard to *Augustinus*. Henri Arnauld went so far as to forbid in his diocese the signature pure and simple of the formulary—to which no one any longer gave thought—because he wished a reservation made as to the question of *fact*. The members of the Faculty of Theology denounced the mandate as contrary to papal decisions.

Louis XIV was with his armies in Flanders when he heard the dispute had been renewed, and was immensely irritated.

"Those Messieurs!" he said. "Always those Messieurs!"

On May 30, 1676, the king rendered in Council a decree known as "from the Ninove camp," which did away with all equivocation. If some persons in the Church had been authorized to sign the formulary with reservations, this must be considered "only as a favor granted certain individuals to ease their scruples."

Calm was restored by the authority of Louis XIV, but the Arnauld name had been unfavorably called to his attention.

In 1677, the following year, it was the bishops of Arras and Saint-Pons who resumed hostilities. These prelates had experienced the same reaction as Pascal when they read certain casuistic treatises in which Jesuit authors sought to assuage their penitents' remorse. The two bishops decided to submit these books, which they considered dangerous to salvation, to the judgment of the pope. However, since neither of them felt he was sufficiently learned to draw up the letter to Rome, they asked Nicole to do this in their names. At first the theologian refused for reasons of prudence, but Madame de Longueville begged him not to shun the task. Nicole dared not displease the most powerful of Port-Royal's defenders. Hadn't the princess given refuge to himself and to Arnauld when a search was being made for them to throw them into the Bastille?

In the fine Latin he knew so well, Nicole wrote the accusing letter; it was signed by the two prelates and sent to the Vatican. Pope Innocent XI gave satisfaction to the bishops by condemning the casuists, but it was soon learned that Nicole was the real author of the letter sent to the Holy Father. When the Jesuits discovered the adversary who stood behind the prelates, their ire was carried up to the throne. The marquis de Pomponne—whose functions as Secretary of State made him a hostage—warned his uncle that he, too, was suspected of having had a hand in drafting the letter to the pope. The king, who formerly had been quite satisfied with Arnauld's behavior, and with Nicole's, no longer took the same attitude toward them. At court one heard complaints about the quarrelsome disposition of the Messieurs; did Arnauld forget his sovereign's strong recommendation to do nothing "that might embitter people?"

The theologian himself had been imprudent. He had written to the superior of the Visitation convent in Angers, declaring that Monseigneur de Harlay was "the minister of Antichrist." The letter fell into the archbishop's hands—and so now Francis de Harlay knew what Port-Royal thought of him!

Thus once more the storm clouds gathered. The danger was averted by Madame de Longueville, who was of royal blood; wishing to maintain intact the prestige of the crown, Louis XIV did not want to take measures against personages related to him except in case of extreme danger. He therefore waited—but not for long. The duchesse de Longueville died on April 15, 1679, and Louis XIV's hands were freed.

On May 5th of the same year, Pomponne went to the home of his uncle Arnauld to inform him of the wishes of the king. The latter had always been opposed to "the assemblies at the home of the late Madame de Longueville; Monsieur Arnauld must take care to hold none in his own, because this would seem to be setting up a party." The king wished for Monsieur Arnauld to live "as did other men."

Four days later, on May 9th, Monseigneur de Harlay sent a priest, Abbot Fromageau, to Port-Royal of the Fields. The new abbess, who had succeeded Mother du Fargis on August 3, 1678, was Angélique de Saint-Jean. Although Nicole admired the fine mind of this religious, he had earlier found her "rather exacting and not liking to be contradicted," and the nuns had reproached her with having "some haughtiness, and a certain coldness in her conduct." But since she had been made abbess, Angélique de Saint-Jean had carried out her duties with a gentleness and simplicity that none of the religious had thought she possessed. Arnauld's niece realized that to sustain her sisters she must place herself on the level of the humblest among them; one of them said how much she had been impressed by the "respectful manner" of the new abbess when she received the girls entrusted to her care.

When Angélique de Saint-Jean received the archbishop's emissary, Abbot Fromageau asked her a great number of questions. How many professed nuns were at the Abbey of the Fields? How many novices? How many pupils? What was the number of the solitaries living at Les Granges? Having known persecution, Angélique sensed the approach of danger, and after giving the abbot the information he requested, she told him of her fears. In a conciliatory manner, he replied:

"Madame, what have you to fear under so benevolent a government? The king loves peace and Monsieur the Archbishop is the enemy of scandal and does everything gently."

It was not, in fact, without great unction that Monseigneur de Harlay proceeded to execute the king's orders. In a conversation with the Port-Royal superior, Father Grenet, the prelate discreetly verified the accuracy of the information furnished by Abbot Fromageau after his visit to the Monastery of the Fields. Thus, in two different ways the archbishop was in possession of details that would make it impossible, when the time came, to conceal the presence of a single postulant or pupil in the monastery.

On May 17, 1679, Monseigneur de Harlay went to the abbey. It was the first time for, not wishing to compromise himself, he had not visited the monastery during the eight years he had headed the Paris archdiocese. He arrived at the hour of the high mass, and as soon as he appeared the religious brought in a rug and cushion to place before him, and prepared to sing the customary *Te Deum*. But Monseigneur de Harlay merely cast a brief glance over the church where the community had assembled, and went out again. He then asked for Saci, who was attending mass in the choir of the church, to come to him. When the priest arrived, the archbishop covered him with praises—his life and conduct were examples of piety, he was told; his fine writings were consolations to the Church. Still, Monseigneur de Harlay slipped in a thorn among the flowers: he had, he said, just read with some surprise an epitaph in the cloister lauding a priest for never having said mass. Had this priest by any chance been a Jansenist? Saci replied that the priest had previously lived in the world, and had not considered himself worthy to ascend the altar.

Monseigneur de Harlay intended to avoid discussion, for he had better things to do. Lowering his voice, he became confidential and revealed the intentions of the king. The postulants and pupils, who represented the future of the monastery, must leave and never return. Monsieur de Saci was asked to warn the abbess.

As the priest left in consternation, Monseigneur de Harlay sent for Racine, whom he had seen in the church when he entered it earlier. He received the poet as an equal—were they not both members of the French Academy? Monseigneur de Harlay had not voted for the author of *Andromache* at the time of his election, but then it was not fitting for a prelate to give his suffrage to a man connected with the theater. Now that Jean Racine had given up writing plays—he was married, leading a devout life and, better still, was the king's historiographer—wasn't he, a man on good terms with the court, just the one to help smooth things over? And wasn't he the nephew of one of the oldest of the nuns, and the best friend of the Messieurs since his reconciliation with them?

Beneath the portico of the church of the Fields, Monseigneur de Harlay chatted with Racine in the easy, courteous tone he reserved for those he honored with his confidence. Without in any way concealing his mission from the poet, he let it be understood that certain circumstances had contributed to break the peace of the Church. The Jansenists had unfortunately obtained from the Holy Father the condemnation of the sixty-five propositions of the casuists. The Society of Jesus would never forgive Port-Royal for this victory.

Meanwhile the mass had ended, and Mother Angélique de Saint-Jean, after a brief word with Saci, had gone to the parlor to await the archbishop. When he entered, she knelt to receive his blessing.

Monseigneur de Harlay said he had wanted Saci to speak to her before he himself did, because "what we hear from the lips of a friend softens what in itself could not be pleasant." Yes, the king wished the monastery to receive no more novices; the postulants and even the little girls who were only pupils must be sent away. In all this Madame the Abbess should see only a measure of wise economy; the number of religious must be decreased because since the division of property there were too many of them in the monastery in view of its modest resources.

Overcoming her emotion, Angélique de Saint-Jean pleaded the cause of the community. She said she could not see the necessity of sending away the pupils, who were not an expense to the monastery but who brought in a modest revenue. Monseigneur de Harlay was careful not to contradict her. He replied "with a show of gentleness and pity" that her reply had merit, but, he added, "a sovereign's will is law, and there is no need to go into his reasons."

The archbishop always took this attitude. The religious always found themselves in the presence of a plaintive and desolated man over whom no one had a hold. Angélique de Saint-Jean now knew that, despite all her intellectual resources, there was nothing she could do. Nevertheless, she reminded the executor of the royal orders that he was a prince of the Church and would have to answer to God for what he was about to do. Her words failed to move Monseigneur de Harlay, who confined himself to renewing his expressions of regret.

The nun deplored the fact that the archbishop's first visit to the monastery should bring it such sorrow.

"Alas!" exclaimed Monseigneur de Harlay.

He then excused himself for not having come earlier to Port-Royal with so much humility that Angélique de Saint-Jean was embarrassed. She recovered herself sufficiently, however, to tell him how saddened her nuns would be by the news she must give them.

"Alas!" repeated Monseigneur de Harlay. "I can understand it very well, and I feel it already."

The abbess then expressed the wish that the tears of her sisters might serve before God for the salvation of the archbishop who had caused them. Her words provoked no show of emotion in the prelate, who continued to play the role of a man distressed at being the bearer of bad tidings.

"I am deeply grieved," he said.

The abbess, however, did not consider herself beaten. She asked what was wrong. Was the king suspicious of the education given their young pupils by the nuns?

Monseigneur de Harlay realized that he owed Angélique de Saint-Jean some explanations. Since he could not avoid them, he gave in with good grace.

The sovereign's displeasure was not caused by the nuns—they were irreproachable. But Louis XIV had heard too much talk about the Messieurs of Port-Royal. He did not like their secret meetings, or favor a sect with no visible leader; finally, he accused them of secretly governing the Monastery of Port-Royal of the Fields.

"A body without a head is always dangerous to a state," the archbishop concluded.

He then came back to the condemnation of the casuists by Rome. It showed what could be done by "cabals and secret assemblies." The monarch —who never forgot The Fronde—intended to put an end to such intrigues.

The boarding pupils? Well, they formed a link between Port-Royal and the great families to which they belonged. This identity of interests could not be tolerated.

To Mademoiselle de Vertus, who was still living at that time, the archbishop repeated the civilities he had heaped on the abbess. Angélique de Saint-Jean said later that the Jesuits greatly admired the cleverness of the prelate because, "having accomplished all he came to do, he left us quite satisfied with him."

Even so, Monseigneur de Harlay had not yet struck the harshest blow of all: he had been instructed to remove the spiritual directors and confessors from Port-Royal. The elegance with which the archbishop carried out this task must be admired: "On the way to his carriage he said in a pleasant way to Monsieur de Saci that the king did not intend for him to remain here any longer, nor any of the other ecclesiastics."

Before the priest could reply, the archbishop had swept away, having carried out his mission without engaging in any dispute or even raising his voice. What a difference between him and the good de Péréfixe—so choleric, so plebian, and so human! Monseigneur de Harlay had demonstrated the distance that separates the wellborn man from the upstart.

One of the nuns died on the day of the archbishop's visit, and in the hands of the dead woman Angélique de Saint-Jean placed a handwritten prayer to Christ: "Lord, we appeal to thy tribunal! Thou art our justice and thou wilt render justice to us."

In the silent cloister the abbess meditated on the fate of the monastery under her charge. What the king called Jansenism had become, according to him, "a party dangerous to the state." His words surprised Angélique de Saint-Jean. "Who would believe," she wrote her uncle, the Bishop of Angers, "that under a prince who makes all Europe tremble there is cause to fear our little troop of children and the four or five priests who guide the community?" How could one explain the mysterious apprehensions of Louis XIV, the absolute master of France, who in the year before, 1678, had seen all his victories consolidated by the Treaty of Nijmegen?

The nuns were vowed to silence, and their monastery lay hidden in the folds of a valley. Yet, the abbess wrote, "the thunder always falls on our bell tower." She saw a supernatural design in the incomprehensible hostility of the monarch. Angélique de Saint-Jean felt the pride of the martyrs— God's finger pointed out Port-Royal to its persecutors. The Lord, Arnauld d'Andilly's daughter wrote, willed that "however hidden, we are sought out and pursued everywhere." Yet, like Pascal, Angélique de Saint-Jean considered that one must fight; Christian resistance had a place marked on the plan of predestination.

The abbess intended to defend to her last breath the daughters entrusted to her, and wrote to Innocent XI: "We are condemned without being accused of anything whatsoever, and Monsieur the Archbishop of Paris gives us only praise the while he imposes penalties on us."

The sovereign pontiff was quite favorable to Port-Royal, but he could do nothing against Louis XIV. The affair of the *Régale* was soon to create a barrier between Paris and Rome.[1] The only prelates in France who at that time dared to defy the king were those who had defended the Jansenists— Monseigneur de Pavillon, the Bishop of Alet, and Monsiegneur Caulet, the Bishop of Pamiers—thus the king always found the same "sect" in opposition to him. The purely moral support of Innocent XI prevented none of the harsh measures which were to be taken against Port-Royal.

---

[1] The *Régale* was the right by which the kings of France upon the death of a bishop drew the revenues of the see and made appointments to benefices until a new bishop had registered his oath in the Court of Exchequer.—*Trans.*

The scenes Angélique de Saint-Jean had witnessed earlier were repeated. Postulants about to be admitted to the novitiate had to leave the abbey forever; again the little pupils were led to the parlor and turned over to their relatives. As soon as they were back in the world, they were surrounded by curious people who wanted to see children who had lived at Port-Royal.

One of them, a girl of eleven, the daughter of the comtesse de Grammont, was taken to call on Madame de Montespan. The latter—who was to remain the king's favorite for yet a while longer—had asked to see the child. Candidly, the little girl blamed Monseigneur de Harlay for having come to Port-Royal "only for the fine affair he carried out."

Louis XIV entered the room just at that moment and Madame de Montespan said to the child: "There comes the king, your enemy."

The little girl did not fall into this trap. "I don't believe," she said, "that he is our enemy, because in our house we always prayed God for His Majesty."

Mademoiselle de Grammont's good manners and engaging personality won many new friends for Port-Royal. Yet nothing tempered the severity of the king's orders. "All this is my affair and affects me personally," he declared.

Again the confessors, Saci and Saint-Marthe, and the solitaries, Tillemont and Luzancy, had to leave the valley. More compromised, Nicole and Antoine Arnauld were forced to flee to Flanders.

In an effort to avert his uncle's exile, Pomponne begged him to state publicly that he had nothing to do with the letter sent to the pope by the bishops of Arras and Saint-Pons to obtain the condemnation of the casuists. It was useless to expect Arnauld to make the least concession. Although innocent, he wished he were guilty!

"I should go myself," he replied, "and make such a cowardly declaration? To say that I had no part in what those saintly bishops did in the best cause there ever was? This is, in truth, a thing so shameful that I cannot understand how anyone would dare make me such a proposal."

The Abbey of the Fields kept only its physician, Hamon. None of his colleagues would consent to live in a desert so marked by the king's displeasure.

The archbishop had great trouble in finding new confessors: in succession, twenty-two ecclesiastics were called in and refused the charge. In the end two ill-educated and mediocre priests were sent to the monastery.

Father Grenet, the superior of Port-Royal, was distressed to see so blameless a community condemned to abandonment. He went to see Monseigneur de Harlay, and was glad to hear the prelate speak of the nuns in very kindly terms. Telling Angélique de Saint-Jean of this conversation, Grenet said:

"He promised me, swearing on the cross he held in his hands, that he would do you no harm; he would have to be the most knavish and detestable of men if he did not speak the truth."

Alas!—to quote Monseigneur de Harlay—a friend of Port-Royal, Madame de Saint-Loup, learned that among his intimates the prelate's words were quite different from those Père Grenet had heard.

"It is necessary," he said, "to set the axe to the root and to eradicate Jansenism. I hope to see it completely destroyed."

The archbishop was waiting for the return of the king, who had gone to the frontier to welcome the dauphiness. "There are still," Monseigneur de Harlay added, "some frogs croaking in the marshes of Port-Royal, but we need only a little sun after the king's return to dry up the whole thing."

At that same time Antoine Arnauld's nephew, Pomponne, was relieved of his post as secretary of state for foreign affairs. The king considered the position too exalted for him. "Everything that passes through the hands of this minister," said Louis XIV, "loses the importance and force necessary for executing the orders of the king of France." There are strong reasons to believe that the real cause of this sudden fall from favor was to be found at Port-Royal. The monastery was losing an ally who, however timid, had afforded it protection because of his high office.

Angélique de Saint-Jean, sister of the marquis de Pomponne, looked on this event, grave as were its effects on her abbey, as a sign from Providence. The nun had been saddened by the thought that one so close to her held a place at court, where he ran the risk of losing his soul. "Nothing is easier than having a high position; nothing is more difficult than living as God would wish," Pascal had written.

On learning of her brother's disgrace, the abbess wrote her relatives a letter in which she thanked the Lord for having opened the road of salvation to her brother. Madame de Sévigné read with astonishment and admiration the contents of a letter which has now been lost. Fortunately, she found them so fine she made a copy to send to her daughter and added words of her own which are enlightening in regard to the false piety of the grand siècle: "This is the first time I have seen a religious speak and write as a religious."

Louis XIV was too absolute a monarch to be content with assisting at the slow agony of Port-Royal of the Fields. He wanted to change the spirit of the convent, which was located quite close to Versailles and cast an unpleasant shadow over court festivities.

The king thought of Colbert's sister, the abbess of the Monastery of Lys, near Melun. By putting her in charge both of the house in the faubourg Saint-Jacques and the one in the Fields, he would give satisfaction to the

most hardworking of his ministers. Above all, he would see the disappear-
ance from the Chevreuse Valley of the authority of "those Messieurs."

To dismiss Angélique de Saint-Jean from her post he had only to renew
the charge of Jansenism against her. But unfortunately the Paris monastery
was directed by Mother Dorothée Perdreau, who held on all the more firmly
to her dignity as abbess because she had obtained it at the cost of disloyalty.
Despite the most earnest solicitations, she refused to resign.

As he was still in difficulties with Rome, the king did not see how he
could remove Mother Perdreau without provoking an incident. On the other
hand, he could not offer Colbert's sister only the Abbey of the Fields. How
could he deprive Madame Colbert of the house in the faubourg Saint-
Jacques and compel her to live in exile in the desert?

So, due to a nun who had betrayed Port-Royal, the community in the
valley was safe for a while longer; but it continued to lead a difficult existence. One of the confessors sent to the Fields by the archbishop, a Breton
priest named Poligné, heaped invective on the nuns. On Good Friday and
Easter in 1680, his sermons were so abusive that Angélique de Saint-Jean
begged Monseigneur de Harlay to deliver the community from his presence.
The prelate, too wellbred to condone in a man of humble birth an attitude
which he considered in bad taste, sent Poligné away from Port-Royal. He
replaced him by a priest named Le Moine, recommended to him by the
pastor of the parish where the "Visitor to the Island of Notre Dame," carried
on his nocturnal adventures.

Monseigneur de Harlay had once boasted that he recognized by instinct
those persons who were dangerous, and so could remove them from his
path. "I am a good hunting dog," he said. "I know where to point."

But this time His Majesty's pointer had mistaken the scent. Abbot Le
Moine, former superior of the Alet seminary, was a fervent disciple of
Monseigneur Pavillon and a friend of all those who had joined that prelate
in opposing the king. When the Bishop of Pamiers, Monseigneur Caulet,
was deprived of his benefices because he refused to submit to the *Régale*
and could no longer help the poor of his diocese, Abbot Le Moine had
obtained important assistance for the prelate from a wealthy man, Monsieur
des Touches.

Better informed than the Archbishop of Paris, Louis XIV had the new
confessor of Port-Royal of the Fields come to Saint-Germain, where the court
was residing. A minister, Châteauneuf, interrogated the priest. After obtaining a promise that Monsieur des Touches would not be molested, Abbot
Le Moine admitted having been able to help the Bishop of Pamiers thanks
to the generosity of this rich man. Not considering himself bound by his
promise, the minister submitted to Louis XIV for his signature an order for

the imprisonment of Monsieur des Touches. This the sovereign refused to sign, and his words on this occasion were spoken in regal tone:

"It shall never be said that under my reign someone was sent to the Bastille for having given alms."

Unhappily, the king's benevolence went no further. Le Moine, who had been welcomed to the Fields as a savior, lost the right to return, and on February 17, 1681, sent the abbess a letter containing his farewell.

"Monsieur the Archbishop has ordered me to return to my diocese and does not even permit me to go back to Port-Royal to collect my poor belongings. I write with stricken heart and tears in my eyes at being separated from a place that was an earthly paradise to me. I regard myself as having been driven out of it for my sins, as was Adam from the one he was in."

Several days later Angélique de Saint-Jean had new cause for anxiety. The three years for which she had been elected abbess were drawing to a close. Would the Archbishop of Paris allow the community to proceed with another election? When the request was made to him, Monseigneur de Harlay replied that he would think the matter over. On August 1, 1681, the abbess spoke to her religious as they were on the way to matins, telling them of the threat that hung over them. The relics of the saints, the abbey's last remaining treasures, were then exposed, and during the night Angélique and her sisters prayed to the dead for the protection of the monastery.

On August 6th, a faithful friend of the nuns, Madame de Saint-Loup, sent Mademoiselle de Vertus a victorious letter: "Joy, joy, joy! You will have your election tomorrow."

Monseigneur de Harlay had given in, and the monastery was to survive. Angélique de Saint-Jean was elected for three more years, for her religious knew she was the only one who could defend them.

The amiability of the archbishop—who with his customary courtesy had hastened to congratulate the abbess—encouraged her to request authorization to accept more novices. She asked the prelate to grant his servants "the same blessing God gave at the beginning of the world: to increase and multiply." She met with a refusal but one couched in the usual desolated terms. However, new hope was offered the nuns when, on All Saints' Day, Le Tourneux, a priest beloved by all who knew him, was authorized to come as confessor to the Monastery of the Fields. His disdain for oratorical effects and his deep faith impressed all who listened to him.

"Who is that preacher named Le Tourneux?" Louis XIV asked Boileau. "They say everyone is rushing to hear him. Is he clever?"

"Your Majesty knows that people are always looking for novelty—he is a preacher who preaches the Gospel," was the poet's bold reply.

Shortly afterward, Mademoiselle Vertus was taken ill and asked for Saci to be allowed to come to Port-Royal to hear her confession. But the arch-bishop dared not consent without the permission of Louis XIV, who was at Saint-Germain. When the king replied that he left the matter to the prelate, the latter immediately granted the requested authorization with the habitual demonstrations of benevolence. On this occasion he even received Saci, who came from his retirement at Pomponne. The former confessor of Port-Royal than went to the Monastery of the Fields where the whole com-munity gathered to receive his blessing. Saci was permitted to remain in the valley for eight days, and during that time some of its happiest days were relived.

Le Tourneux, too, brought much consolation to the monastery. But neither the king nor Monseigneur de Harlay wanted certain spiritual cur-rents revived, and it was not long before this priest was ordered to leave Port-Royal of the Fields. Angélique de Saint-Jean begged the archbishop that this confessor be allowed to remain in her abbey, for she feared the effect of his departure on her sisters. "We remain," she wrote Monseigneur de Harlay, "as destitute of spiritual assistance as we have been for the past three years."

Angélique de Saint-Jean was so anxious to win her cause that she had recourse to an innocent ruse. She let it be understood that Le Tourneux would be able to create between Port-Royal and the archbishopric a tie which the prelate wanted to see established in order to keep the nuns under better surveillance.

But all the abbess' efforts ended in failure. The archbishop never gave in except on details; when hope revived in the condemned monastery, he immediately quenched its flame.

Two years after Le Tourneux's departure, in 1684, Port-Royal suffered a new blow when Saci died at his Pomponne retreat. In accordance with his last wishes, he was brought for burial to the monastery whose soul he had been. Clothed in his sacerdotal vestments, the body of the priest who had welcomed Pascal was for the last time surrounded by all the nuns. During the office of the dead the former solitaries, back in the valley for the day, sang the *Dies Irae* and *Requiem*. But their voices broke as had those of the nuns when they laid Agnès Arnauld in her tomb. This time it was the daughters of Port-Royal who took up the hymns and continued them to the end of the office. The voices of two alternating choirs rose up, died down, and rose again, sustaining one another—this was the secret of their peaceful but unshaken resistance.

Meanwhile, the person most afflicted, Angélique de Saint-Jean, remained impassive. Replying to a nun who expressed regret that Saci's remains had been buried so quickly, she said:

"We must hide in the earth what is only earthly, and return to nothingness what is, of itself, but nothing."

Yet the unshed tears of this descendant of the Arnaulds flowed within her soul, and helped to kill her. Two weeks after her cousin's death, the abbess stood for a long time before his grave, and then this woman who had struggled so long returned to her cell and lay down on her bed, never to rise again.

As heartbroken as she was her brother Luzancy, who came to assist the nun during her last hours, and expired in turn only a few days later. Fontaine, one of the solitaries who was present, said that the love of the Arnaulds "was as strong as death."

Mother du Fargis was again elected abbess and came to occupy the position left vacant by Angélique de Saint-Jean. Agnès de Saint-Thècle Racine, the aunt of the poet, was made prioress and later succeeded Madame du Fargis when the latter became infirm and almost blind.

During these years the community, deprived of its novices and pupils, constantly diminished. The *De Profundis* rose more and more feebly in the church as one by one the voices of the nuns were silenced. Death came also to their physician Hamon, their old confessor Sainte-Marthe, and their friend Mademoiselle de Vertus. The religious who survived were, for the most part, old and sick.

Even so, Port-Royal still represented the Jerusalem of which Angélique Arnauld had dreamed. Behind the ramparts and towers built long ago by the Messieurs to resist the storms of The Fronde silence still reigned; pervaded by prayer and meditation, it was broken only by hymns. When the community gathered for the celebration of the offices, the sound of plain chant rose beneath the stone arches; it was psalmody as Saint Bernard desired, in the rhythm of a long, soft supplication. Afterward the nuns would walk in procession and with lowered veils around the cloisters and along the paths of the garden where their dead lay buried.

Racine now had before Louis XIV the most powerful of protectresses— Madame de Maintenon. He had won the friendship of this pious lady as easily as he had that of the introspective Henrietta of England, and later of La Montespan.

After the death of Queen Maria Theresa, Madame de Maintenon became the king's morganatic wife. She owed a very sure taste in artistic matters to her first husband Scarron. She had *Andromache* played under her direction by the young ladies of the Saint-Cyr school. Unhappily, they expressed far too well the passions portrayed in this tragedy. "They will never play it again in their lives, nor any other of your plays," the wise Maintenon told Racine.

Nevertheless, the directress of Saint-Cyr wanted her pupils to be instructed and at the same time entertained. "I wish," she wrote, "for our girls to learn fine poetry. They come to us babbling in their frightful provincial accents. The one from Britanny mixes Breton jargon with her speech and we cannot understand very well what the young lady from Provence is saying." How could she prepare these young daughters of good families for their place in society when they betrayed their provincialism so plainly?

Madame de Maintenon then told Racine of her plan. "I want to have them learn the rhythm and harmony of our language. When we constantly correct them, they hesitate over everything. They must have something quite different from the lessons they stumble through every day. . . . We must open up to them a new garden."

One of the mistresses at Saint-Cyr, Madame de Brinon, had written some pious plays for her students. "But those plays are stupid," Madame de Maintenon said to Racine, and she asked him to compose "some sort of poem, either moral or historical, from which any mention of love is banished."

At first the poet hesitated; Boileau was of the opinion that Racine was willing to risk falling from Madame de Maintenon's favor. However, the king deigned to support his wife's request. "Refusal was impossible," wrote Madame de Caylus.

Racine resigned himself with good grace. Perhaps he thought the moment had finally come to reconcile the theater with religion. The author of *Andromache* therefore searched Scripture for "a pious and moral subject in which singing and recitation could be combined." Madame de Maintenon, in fact, wanted the pupils of Saint-Cyr not only to correct their diction but to be taught to sing agreeably.

The poet chose one of the most charming episodes in the Bible—the story of Esther. Living in the sight of the Lord, this daughter of Israel became queen only in order to defend the chosen people; throughout the centuries she has taught, in Racine's words, "great lessons of love of God and detachment from the world, while living in the world itself."

These lines pointed to Madame de Maintenon: humbly and quietly Scarron's widow had supplanted "the haughty Vashti." Here Racine had in mind Madame de Montespan to whom he owed his appointment as historiographer; now, however, he cast her into the past.

Like Esther, the directress of Saint-Cyr fled from the world and shunned fame; her only desire was to lead to God an Ahasuerus too long under the influence of Vashti's philters. The king's wife also wanted to protect her people—the "timid doves" from distant châteaus who gathered around their queen in the royal house of Saint-Cyr; in the way of Esther, she devoted herself to "these young, tender flowers."

> I make their training my chief care and study.

These virgins make up a chorus similar to the ones in the ancient Greek tragedies of Sophocles and Euripides. This chorus expresses the reaction of the humble to events in the lives of the great, thus permitting the voice of the people to be heard. Mainly, the young girls sing the sorrows and joys of the Persian queen. United more discreetly to Louis XIV than she would have wished, Madame de Maintenon did not obtain the royal crown; but the young Israelite maidens surrounding Esther do not hesitate to offer it to her:

> It is the Queen! . . .
>   Hasten, sisters, let us obey.
> The Queen is calling us.

The Ahasuerus of the Bible—known in history by the name of Darius— now becomes the King of France. The idyl between a reformed Louis XIV and an Egeria three years older than himself is ennobled by Racine's art. Esther remains quite humble in the presence of the monarch who has come down among mortals for her sake.

> My lord, I have never looked with aught but fear
> On the majesty stamped upon your brow.

Ahasuerus admits the chains that bind him to his subject:

> In you alone I find the nameless grace
> That never palls nor loses its attraction,
> That noble modesty in every act of yours
> Bestows a value above purple or gold.

Madame de Maintenon is not only the beloved wife, but a source of inspiration. Having spied on his ministers without their knowledge, she counsels Ahasuerus. Indeed, he himself wishes her to do so:

> Come, and behind a curtain hear what is said
> Help me with your clear judgment.

According to the song of the girls of the chorus Louis XIV, anointed by the Lord, is a paragon of virtue:

> . . . a wise king and one who hates injustice
> Is the finest gift heaven can send.

Unhappily, Ahasuerus is misled by an evil adviser, Haman, but in the end the latter is vanquished by Esther.

The directress of Saint-Cyr had in mind merely the discreet performance of a pious play written for school girls. But when, at Versailles, Madame de Maintenon, seated before the king in her big chair of red damask, heard Racine read *Esther,* she could not make up her mind to bury so touching a portrayal of the finest Christian virtues in the obscurity of a student class-room. No one had yet depicted her so faithfully in her hermitage of Saint-Cyr.

> There, fleeing the pride of a diadem,
> Weary of vain honor, and retiring within myself,
> I humble myself at the feet of the Lord,
> And taste the bliss of self-forgetfulness.

As for Louis XIV, after being compared to Alexander and Titus, it did not displease him to be reincarnated as Ahasuerus.

When Madame de Sévigné came to attend one of the performances and had the honor of a conversation with the king, he told her how deeply he was touched by the homage paid him by the poet. "What a fine mind Racine has!" he said.

Nothing was spared in lending regal splendor to the performances in the great hall of Saint-Cyr, which usually served as a dormitory. Moreau, the choirmaster, composed the music for the words sung by the young maids of Israel. Louis XIV offered them theatrical jewelry—the same illusory emeralds and false pearls that had glittered on the shoulders of dancers when they performed in airy ballets in the groves of Versailles. The scenery was that used in *Iphigenia.*

Madame de Maintenon's young cousin, Madeleine Le Valois, who was shortly to become the comtesse de Caylus, played the role of Piety. The duc de Saint-Simon did not conceal the emotion that swept over him as he watched the performance of this young amateur actress. "Never," he wrote in his *Memoirs,* "has there been a face more spiritual, more touching, more expressive; never such freshness or such grace and spirit; never a creature more seductive!"

The curate of Versailles observed with some anxiety the enthusiasm aroused by the young ladies of Saint-Cyr, and said: "Knowing them to be virtuous, the courtiers are incomparably more moved by them than by real actresses."

In the wings, choirmaster Moreau had the young ladies repeat for one last time the verses to be sung by the chorus; before going on the stage they recited the *Veni Creator,* so that God would make them worthy of their noble audience. One of them, Mademoiselle de la Maisonfort, who played the role of Eliza, had a lapse of memory and was suddenly struck dumb. Racine reproached her for "spoiling his play," and then wiped away her tears. The king laughed heartily when he heard that the poet had succumbed to theatrical fever to the point of forgetting decorum.

In succession, everyone of any importance at court and even in the Church attended the performances of *Esther.* Louis XIV, cane in hand, checked on those admitted. Here came the King and Queen of England; the dauphin; Father de La Chaise, leading in "from twelve to fifteen Jesuits"; here came Bossuet, Fénelon, and even Louvois.

Among the spectators were not only princesses of royal blood, but also the most brilliant women of the kingdom—Madame de Sévigné, Madame de La Fayette. The latter, the declared enemy of "Madame de Maintenant," said that *Esther,* "which should be regarded as a convent play, has become the most serious business of the court." After observing the happiness of the directress of Saint-Cyr at seeing herself represented on the stage wearing the royal diadem, the author of *The Princess of Cleves* slipped this remark into her *Memoirs:* "The chief difference is that Esther was a little younger."

When they read *Esther,* the defenders of the Monastery of the Fields easily saw what the author had in mind. Racine lived at court, where his mind was still animated by ambition; but his heart dwelled in the valley. This was his way of carrying out "detachment from the world while living in the world itself."

Madame de Maintenon came to her retreat at Saint-Cyr to seek shelter from the world, but the author of *Esther* flattered himself that he knew a refuge more hidden and more secure. From the moment in the prologue of his play when Piety begins to speak, we are carried back to the Abbey of the Fields:

> From the divine Creator's blessed abode
> I descend to this dwelling-place of grace.

The chorus presents the nuns of Port-Royal hidden beneath the veils of the virgins of Israel, and is reminiscent of the days when the best of these nuns were carried away from their homeland and languished in convent jails.

> Fertile valleys, holy hills
> Marked by a hundred miracles!
> Must we be exiles still
> From the sweet land of our ancestors?

Whereupon the voice of one of the young girls is heard expressing hope

of a triumphant return to the monastery, where the doors will be flung open
to the crowds:

> When, Zion, shall I see thy ramparts raised,
> Thy lofty towers rebuilt in all their pride?
> By festal throngs pressing from every side
> When shall I hear the God of Israel praised?

But what, indeed, could the poor religious do against their persecutors?

> Frail lambs 'mid ravening wolves we stand,
> Our sighs to Heaven are our only arms.

But the Lord is watching and will save his children:

> The God we serve is the God of battles.
> No, no, he will not suffer
> Anyone to slay his innocents.

The enemies of the Gospel join with darkness in the battle against light.
The treacherous Haman boasts that he has won the sovereign's trust:

> I know ways to push him forward, to stop him,
> To make calm or storm as it pleases me.

The chorus beseeches the sovereign to beware of Haman:

> Turn away, mighty king, close your ears
> To all inhuman and false advice.
> The time has come for you to awaken.

Obviously, Racine hoped to win Madame de Maintenon to the cause of
those dear to him. His whole play was designed to persuade the king's wife
to protect the Jansenists, who had been represented to Louis XIV as "rich,
powerful, and seditious." With the help of the Almighty, she could save
Port-Royal; in ancient times had not the Persian queen's prayer to Ahasuerus
been enough to change the fate of Israel?

Mordecai, Esther's uncle, unfailing in his defense of the people of Israel,
Racine had known since his youth—he was Antoine Arnauld. In the play
he is shown as inflexible. He alone refuses to humble himself before Haman,
who says: "This insolent dog will never bow before me." When Esther tells
Mordecai how dangerous it would be for her to approach the throne, he
replies in words spoken by Arnauld's sister Angélique when she was trying
to give heart to her nuns: "God speaks, and you fear the wrath of a man!"

The Almighty is described by Mordecai as Arnauld saw him, thanks to
Saint-Cyran:

> At the sound of his voice the sea recedes, the heavens tremble.
> The whole universe he sees as a void.

Accompanied by Eliza and the virgins of Israel, the queen enters the forbidden domain of the greatest of Asian kings. When he sees his subjects crossing the threshold of the hall where no one dares to appear without being summoned, Ahasuerus shows his anger:

> Who enters unbidden?
> Who is this insolent mortal who courts destruction?
> Guards! . . .

Angélique Arnauld had fainted in her father's presence on the Day of the Grating; in the same way, Esther loses consciousness before Ahasuerus' throne. Like the nuns who rushed to the side of their abbess, Eliza and the young maids of Israel go to the help of their queen:

> My daughters, support your distraught queen.
> *I am dying.*

Then was re-enacted the scene that had disarmed Angélique's father and decided Port-Royal's fate. Ahasuerus began to speak gently and calmly:

> Live on! the golden sceptre held out by this hand
> Is the secure pledge of my clemency.

But the danger had not passed. The virgins who worshiped God had seen Haman,

> Trying to force their unwilling lips
> To blaspheme the Almighty's name.

Like the nuns threatened by their archbishop in days gone by in the name of the king, the young Israelite maids ask one another:

> Perhaps Ahasuerus, trembling with anger,
> If we do not bend our knee
> Before a dumb idol,
> Shall give command that we be slain.
> Dear sister, which will you choose?

One of the maidens in the choir answers: "I—could I betray the God I love?"

To save her people, Esther now begins her struggle against Haman. She denounces the barbarous Scythian who, she tells Ahasuerus:

> . . . with lies that appear as zeal in your eyes
> Arms your virtue against our innocence.

By words from the lips of the Persian queen Racine let Madame de Maintenon know what she ought to say to her husband—that the Jansenists, represented to Louis XIV as troublemakers, were in reality his faithful subjects:

> Were there slaves ever more submissive to your yoke?
> Adoring, in their fetters, the God who chastises them
> While your hand bears down on them,
> Delivering them inexorably to their persecutors,
> They beseech the same God to watch over you.

The new Esther could have cited examples as impressive as those which determine Ahasuerus to revoke the edict of persecution: Antoine Arnauld, exiled in the Low Countries, had defended the rights of his king against William of Orange; the nuns of Port-Royal prayed each day for the life of their king. Unfortunately, Louis XIV had allowed himself to be misled by the enemies of truth. The justice meted out by even the greatest of kings could be mistaken.

> Incapable of deceiving
> They had trouble escaping
> The snares of guile.

The danger is overcome by Ahasuerus' wife. The entire chorus proclaims: "Gentle Esther has done this great deed."

If only on the morrow the "queen" would dare speak to the sovereign, God would act! "She has spoken. Heaven has done the rest."

Racine's disgrace did not permit him to pursue his objective, which was Louis XIV's reconciliation with Port-Royal through the mediation of Madame de Maintenon. When, after the poet's death, the latter read the letters discovered among the papers of Father Quesnel and learned that her protégé was "the procurator general of the Jansenist order in Paris," she trembled at the thought of the danger she had courted.

Racine did not know that he had nothing to expect from Madame de Maintenon's intervention in favor of the "chosen people"; in reality she had no power over the Jesuits, particularly over the king's confessor. Had the directress of Saint-Cyr undertaken to defend the Jansenists, she would have run grave danger of compromising herself. In the near future, her friendship with Madame Guyon and the Quietists would bring down on her the strong remonstrances of Louis XIV.

Had the new Esther been influenced by Racine as she was to be by

Madame Guyon—if she had dealt with the Messieurs—would Louis XIV have forgiven her? Nothing is less certain. In the king's eyes Quietism was only a heresy, whereas Jansenism always appeared to him a conspiracy.

On April 11, 1704, Madame de Maintenon was to write to Mademoiselle de Glapion, one of her former pupils at Saint-Cyr, who had played the role of Mordecai in the performances of *Esther*, and who had later become a nun: "In the world you would have been lost; Racine would have involved you in the cabal of the Jansenists."

But, to return to the poet when he still believed he was protected by Madame de Maintenon: carried away by his dream, he proclaimed Port-Royal's victory. He saw Louis XIV welcoming Arnauld back from exile in the way Ahasuerus welcomes Mordecai:

> Mortal beloved by heaven, my salvation and my joy!
> Thy king is no longer prey to evil counsel;
> My eyes are opened, the crime has been confounded.
> Come, shine close to me with the rank which is thy due.

The poet imagined the Jansenists, yesterday imprisoned and exiled, returning to a monastery re-established in its former glory:

> Rejoice, Zion, and rise from the dust.
> Cast off the clothing of thy captivity
> And return to thy first splendor.
> The roads of Zion are open at last.
> > Break your fetters,
> > Captive tribes.
> > Fugitive troops,
> Pass back over mountains and seas
> Assemble from the ends of the earth!

A voice is heard announcing the return to the valley: "I will see those beloved fields."

There the exile will find again the earth where sleep the nuns and solitaries who have died: "I will go to weep at the tomb of my fathers."

Then Christ will come to find his children again: "God descends and returns to abide with us."

The poet forgot his former rebellion; for Christ he now felt the same passion he had devoted to human creatures in the past. "Racine has surpassed himself," Madame de Sévigné wrote after attending a performance of *Esther*. "He loves God as he loved his mistresses." It was indeed a Canticle of Canticles that arose. Racine had returned to his wellsprings, to his pious youth lighted by intermittent love for heavenly things:

How good is the Lord, how light his yoke!
Happy the man who has known his sweetness since childhood!

Before, the author of *Esther* had turned to the world and had nearly been lost; but how generously the Father of All Men had welcomed the prodigal son on his return to the valley!

He is appeased, he forgives.
He awaits the return
Of the ungrateful heart that abandoned him.
He pardons our weakness.
He even hastens out to meet us.
A mother has less tenderness
For the child she brings to life.

The orphan's words tell us how humane Jansenism really was. Founded on love, it has a message for our times.

When Racine told Esther's story, he was rediscovering the sphere of Port-Royal. In the eyes of the solitaries, the Bible was not only the history, transfigured by the Messiah, of the Hebrew people: the men and women who lived and died in it, persecutors or persecuted, criminal or innocent, represented all humanity. The Jansenists wanted to relive biblical times; when they communicated with each other they called themselves the "sons of Israel." Had they not been dispersed throughout provinces and nations as the Jews had been? The hill of Zion and Jerusalem, the holy city, symbolized the Abbey of the Fields. The name Haman was applied to the enemies of *truth*.

Racine himself revealed this thought in his *Abridged History of Port-Royal*. The disciples of Saint Augustine, he wrote, felt for the Cistercian monastery "the same love the Jews of old retained throughout their captivity for the ruins of the Temple of Jerusalem."

With gratitude the Jansenists received the gift offered them. From Flanders, Arnauld wrote to say how much he liked *Esther;* he appreciated the art with which Racine had combined his talent with the scriptural text to express, as Arnauld wrote, "God's greatness and the vanity of what men call happiness."

Another Jansenist, Duguet, said: "The courage of the author is even more worthy of admiration than his inimitable talent."

Madame de Sévigné praised the manner in which the poet made bold to speak to the king through Esther's lines and those of the girls in the chorus. "I felt extraordinary pleasure," she wrote, "that someone could entertain and sing and at the same time utter such solid truths."

All these allusions certainly did not escape the notice of Louis XIV, who knew of Racine's ties to the valley but was prepared to ignore the "truths" so long as they remained in the domain of the theater. The poet was granted new favors: he was invited to the Maintenon château, and into the intimacy of the sovereign and his wife; in addition, he was given quarters at Marly. Louis XIV liked listening to Racine's voice: after the king retired at night, the historiographer was privileged to read to him the *Lives* of Plutarch and the *Commentaries* of Caesar, remaining beside the bed until sleep overcame the master of France.

At that time Racine did not hesitate to pursue the task that he had begun with so much promise. For the schoolgirls of Saint-Cyr he wrote his second religious play—*Athaliah*.

Even though human love was banished, the passion underlying the poet's lyrics appears as strong as in the days of *Andromache* and *Phaedra*. Born of an accursed race, Athaliah persecutes believers in the true God and is slain by the swords of pious men. At every instant the Almighty frustrates the wicked queen, who hastens toward her downfall and in the end is vanquished by a child.

The poet no longer rises as accuser: reconciled with heaven, he portrays certain humans as fated to advance toward the heights, while others descend to the abyss.

The queen's vain fury crumbles before the majesty of the invisible Creator who arms the avengers. This time Racine sought inspiration in his past, and in Joas' reply to Athaliah's questions the poet was describing his own childhood:

> I am an orphan, so they say,
> Thrown into the arms of God since birth.
> I never knew my parents.

Disturbed at this, the queen wants to know from what country Joas has come. The child points to the sanctuary, a symbol of the monastery that had been the poet's first home and was destined to be his last: "The temple is my home; I know no other."

The orphan had been taken in by the righteous men of Israel just as Racine had been given a home by the solitaries. When Athaliah asks Joas: "But in your earliest years who took care of you?" the descendant of David answers:

> Has God ever left his children in want?
> He feeds even the smallest birds.

He then brings his childhood again before his listener's eyes:

I worship the Lord; I learn of his laws.
I am taught to read his holy Book.
And already I've begun to copy it.

Athaliah then asks, "What says this law?" and Joas answers, "God wishes to be loved."

Anxious to forestall any disturbance, the queen wants to know what all these silent people are doing. Joas' answer reassures her: "They praise and bless the Lord." Such a life seems to her very harsh for a child: "What are your pleasures then?"

Joas is reminiscent of the young Racine, serving mass in the church of the Fields amid the singing of the nuns:

> Sometimes I hand
> The high priest salt or incense;
> Listen to songs of the infinite greatness of God.

Port-Royal's enemies are represented by Mathan, the apostate priest who offers sacrifices to Baal:

> You, sitting on the plague-ridden throne
> Where falsehood reigns and spreads its poison!
> You, reared in imposture and treachery!

Mathan dreams of tearing down God's dwelling-place:

> . . . I shall be happy
> If wreaking vengeance on his temple,
> At last I prove his hate of no avail.

This bad priest bears a strange resemblance to the Jesuit of the *Provincial Letters,* and also to Father de la Chaise, the king's spiritual director, who was so quick to absolve his august penitent that he was known at the Louvre as *la chaise de commodités* (the chair of convenience).

> I gave my soul entirely to the court.
> By slow degrees I gained the ear of kings,
> And soon I rose to be an oracle.
> I studied their hearts, I flattered their caprice
> I sowed with flowers the precipice's edge;
> Nothing save their passions was sacred to me.
> I changed both weight and measure at their whim.

Around Mathan are seen the confessors who dispense believers from loving God and cause them to fear only hell:

> You who know nothing but servile fear,
> Ingrates, can such a God not conquer you?
> Is it, then, so difficult for your hearts
> And so painful to love him?

Joad, the high priest of Israel, enters and faces these wicked men. Antoine Arnauld, no longer in the guise of the obscure Mordecai seated at the gate of the king's palace awaiting the hour appointed by the Lord, appears now in his priestly vestments. Abner, the honest man, warns Joad against virtue, which many sinners find offensive: "Do you think you can be just and holy with impunity?" It is too easy to consider the believer who defends his God a trouble-maker:

> Long has your deep devotion to religion
> Been treated as sedition and revolt.

Racine, inspired by the memory of the wonders that moved Pascal, has the high priest reply by testifying to the power of the One he serves:

> When did such miracles abound as now?
> When has God shown his power to such effect?

However, men must go to the aid of heaven. Arnauld speaks through Joad's lips:

> A coward race indeed and born for slavery,
> Brave against God alone!

Who remains to defend the truth? Several priests and some children reared in the shadow of the temple:

> These then, eternal Wisdom, are the avengers
> Armed for your quarrel—priests and children!
> But if you uphold them, who can make them quail?

These Christians do not have the pride of Molina's disciples, who believe only in themselves:

> They do not trust in their own merits
> But in thy name, invoked so many times.

A year had passed between *Esther* and *Athaliah*. Racine now knew he could hope for no benevolence for Port-Royal, neither from his protectress nor from Louis XIV. So, ceasing to hide "solid truths" beneath the songs of the chorus, the poet proclaimed them courageously and sadly. The high priest warns Joas, the royal child, of future dangers:

You do not know the heady joy of boundless power
Or the beguiling voices of cowardly flatterers.
Soon they will tell you that the holiest laws
Though rulers of the rabble, must bow to kings;
That a king has no bridle save his own will,
That all should be sacrificed to his greatness;
To tears and toil the people are condemned
And must be ruled with scepter of iron,
If not oppressed, they will one day oppress.

Then he tells of the presence of dangerous counselors:

From snare to snare and from abyss to abyss,
Corrupting the shining purity of your ways,
In the end they will make you hate the truth,
Painting you virtue in a hideous guise.
Alas, they have led astray the wisest of kings!

Racine had never gone so far as this. Disappointed in his sovereign, he turned to the Lord, described by Joad in all his power:

You strike and heal; you destroy and resurrect.

The high priest is inspired by the gift of prophecy:

My eyes are opened
And the dark centuries unroll before me.

The Almighty, who has come down among men, speaks through Joad's lips. Did Racine, through his intimacy with the sovereign, know that Port-Royal was condemned? Or did he only have a presentiment? The prophet foretells the ruin of the holy place of Israel and of the monastery:

God no longer wills men to come to your solemnities.
Temple, collapse! Cedars, burst into flame!
O Zion, the object of my sorrow,
What hand has ravaged all your loveliness?

Silence falls over this vision of horror. But again Joad's voice is heard, firmer and more triumphant: no, truth will never die. Over the ruins of the temple a kingdom will one day rise—the kingdom of the Gospel.

What new Jerusalem rises now
From out the desert, shining bright,
Eternity upon her brow
Triumphing over death and night?

> Sing, peoples, Zion is more
> Lovely and glorious than before.
> Whence come these children manifold
> She did not carry at her breast?
> Lift up thy head, O Zion, behold!

This poem tells of the source from which Port-Royal derived its hope: the stones of the church of the Fields, rejected by men, would be used one day to rebuild the City of God.

The voices of the choir magnificently prolong the prophet's vision:

> Founded upon His eternal word
> Zion will be protected by the Lord.
> . . . My eyes behold her glory disappear.
> . . . I see her brightness spreading everywhere.
> . . . Zion has fallen into the abyss.
> . . . Tow'ring Zion and the heavens kiss.
> [. . . How sad her downfall!
> . . . What glory immortal!]
> [. . . Ah, what cries of woe!
> . . . What songs of victory!]

These voices, echoing back and forth over the centuries, express the finest hymns inspired by Jansenism. But, returning to flesh and blood, the book of Kings is rife with murder. Behind the Ark of the Covenant, behind the gold of the Holy of Holies, hide the armed men who are to slay Athaliah—for this is the will of God.

"On our side stands the Angel of Death," sings the high priest.

Everything must be accomplished according to God's plan. To the queen, who suddenly finds herself surrounded by swords, the patriarch of Israel says:

> Your eyes search in vain; there is no escape,
> And God has hemmed you in on every side.

Mathan, the apostate priest, has been slain, and the soldiers charged to defend him have fled.

> Even as smoke is scattered in the air by wind
> The Almighty's voice has dispersed that army.

Vanquished, Athaliah raps out a curse, the last Racine ever addressed to heaven: "Relentless God, you have brought everything to pass."

About to die, she expresses the conflicting emotions that have led to her downfall: her hate for Joas' race is in conflict with her pity for this child and

with the illusion of a power she cannot grasp. Athaliah discovers the identity
of her invisible enemy:

> Luring me on with easy vengeance, thou hast
> Set me against myself twenty times a day.

Here is the uncertainty of a tormented soul still beating its wings beneath
the trapper's net. The simplified heroes of Corneille have receded into the
distance; instead, an inextricable knot is unraveled—the inexhaustible riches
of the human heart, as revealed by the mystics of Port-Royal.

Never again did Racine rise so near to Jehovah in his glory. Doubtless he
had tried to climb too high—his century did not understand him.

Madame de Maintenon, already called "the new Esther," did not recognize
herself in any of the personages in *Athaliah,* and Louis XIV looked in vain
for an Ahasuerus worthy of himself. He took no pleasure in the appearance
on the stage of Joas, the young sovereign who would one day forget his religious duties, and even go so far as to commit crime: "How can pure gold be
changed to vilest lead?"

The final words of the high priest, which close the play, were certainly not
agreeable to the monarch's ears:

> . . . Kings have in heaven a judge severe,
> Innocence has an avenger, the fatherless a father.

Consequently, the Louis XIV who had held *Esther* up to the admiration
of his court gave no support to *Athaliah.*

Racine had to contend with a number of enemies in having this work
accepted: the most implacable was the Bishop of Chartres, Godet des Marais.
This prelate was Madame de Maintenon's spiritual director and owed his
miter to her; his penitent had to account to him in writing, on fixed dates, for
the state of her conscience, and now he reproached her for introducing
theatricals into Saint-Cyr.

The young actresses were intoxicated by their success and had great difficulty returning to their roles as pious and industrious students. Their directress remonstrated with them: "You sang the songs in *Esther* so well. Why
don't you want to sing the Psalms?"

Madame de Maintenon's cousin, the comtesse de Caylus, found herself
compared to Champmeslé, because her impersonation of Piety on the stage
had been so sensual. In the audience was a page who developed the same
feeling as Saint-Simon toward one of the young girls in the chorus, and a
note written by this cherub was discovered in the young lady's hands.
Madame de Maintenon received letters reiterating the reproaches of the
Bishop of Chartres from the mothers of some of the pupils; the provincial

ladies were disturbed on learning that their daughters had appeared on the stage before the public.

Louis rallied to the opinion of his wife, who suddenly became more prudent, and decided that *Athaliah* should be played discreetly, without costumes or scenery, in one of the classrooms at Saint-Cyr, and then later, at Versailles, in the presence of only a few intimate friends in the private rooms of Madame de Maintenon. Racine's work was therefore to become, in Madame de La Fayette's words, "only a convent play."

What was worse, the Messieurs of Port-Royal were disconcerted. In their view the Bible had only symbolical meaning when it recounted the bloody history of a primitive age; their Christian equanimity was somewhat disturbed by Jehovah's cruelty. Perhaps, also, the scarcely veiled allusions to the Monastery of the Fields and the villany of its enemies appeared dangerous to them. In his exile, Antoine Arnauld read *Athaliah* with interest, but he preferred *Esther.* "I will say frankly," he wrote to one of Racine's friends, "that the charm of the younger sister does not prevent me from preferring the older one."

The poet's discomfiture was such that this time he abandoned the theater forever. Moreover, neither the king nor Madame de Maintenon asked him to write any more plays for the students of Saint-Cyr.

Several weeks after the performance of *Athaliah,* Louis XIV bestowed on his historiographer a favor that a man of the middle class, even though he was a poet, should have highly appreciated. Racine was appointed one of the twenty-four gentlemen ordinary of the chamber of the king. To fill a post of this importance at the side of the sovereign at least four quarters of nobility were required; no doubt *Berenice, Phaedra, Esther,* and *Athaliah* were judged worthy to supply these. A few years later Jean Racine had his armor decorated with "a silver swan against an azure background, with sable beak and feet, linked by blue threads to a broad silver shaft. Three sable chevrons decorated the shaft, and on either side gold-armed lions faced each other."

This coat of arms was tarnished before its time, by this epigram:

> Racine, for thy Athaliah
> The public cares but little.
> It has made thy family noble
> But does thy name belittle.

The duchesse de Bouillon was highly amused when she learned of the new title bestowed on the author. "Racine," she said, "is not an ordinary gentleman, but rather a gentleman extraordinary."

Mazarin's niece had no idea of how prophetic her words were. Deciding to ignore his enemies, the historiographer devoted himself to his duties and followed the king and the army to Flanders. But he had not lost his poetic talent, and at the request of Louis XIV and Madame de Maintenon he wrote the *Spiritual Canticles,* which the young ladies of Saint-Cyr sang to airs composed by Moreau. These were the majestic and flowing poems which aroused the admiration of Fénelon.

Here are echoed the words of Saint Paul when he told the Corinthians that unless they opened their hearts to God they would become as "sounding brass":

> In vain would I speak the tongue of angels
> In vain, my God, would I fill
> The whole universe with thy praise;
> Without love, my glory would equal
> Only the tinkling of the cymbal
> Beating the air with vain sound.

To extol the power of grace, Racine combined the words of Isaiah and Jeremiah, making these words of the prophets into a hymn of infinite sweetness:

> The soul, happy in its captivity,
> Finds peace beneath thy yoke,
> And drinks of the living water
> That flows forever.

One day the poet read to his king and his patroness a canticle inspired by the Epistle of Saint Paul to the Romans, which ran:

> My God, how cruel is this war!
> I find two men within me;
> One, filled with love for thee,
> Wants my heart to remain ever loyal to thee.
> The other rebels against thy will
> Makes me revolt against the law.

On hearing this, Louis XIV turned to his wife and murmured these simple and moving words: "Madame, those are two men that I know well!"

The sovereign always had a great predilection for the *Spiritual Canticles,* and had them sung in his private chambers.

Racine now filled his position at court with the ease of a nobleman. Formerly his manner had been too affected and obtrusive, and it was easy to identify him as a man of the theater. But in contact with wellborn people he returned to the sober and distinguished demeanor of the Messieurs. Like

Pascal, he knew how to behave as a man of the world, pleasant and discreet.

Spanheim, a German diplomat sent to Versailles by the Elector of Branden-burg, describes in a few words the author of *Alexander* as he had been and had now become: "For a man risen from obscurity, he easily assumes the manners of the court. His association with actors had given him an air of falsity; this he has corrected. He goes everywhere, even to the bedside of the king, and sometimes has the honor of reading to him—something he can do better than anyone."

It was during this time that Saint-Simon knew Racine. He found the his-toriographer lacking in the naive vanity usually displayed by makers of tragedies and sonnets. "Nothing in him denotes the poet," wrote the duke in his *Memoirs;* "everything an honest man, a modest man, and above all, a man of integrity."

Even so, the author of *Phaedra* carried the weight of his past. A regent of the Jesuit College of Louis-le-Grand made a speech at that institution in which he asked the questions: "Is Racine a poet? Is he Christian?" In his opinion the writer was unworthy of either appellation.

The news was no longer fresh when it penetrated the walls of certain col-leges. Better informed, the most eminent religious of the Society of Jesus, Father Bouhours and Father de La Chaise, protested loudly against the re-gent's impoliteness. For this they received the thanks of Racine, although he said he had to agree with the regent's criticisms.

At one of the sessions of the French Academy, the poet showed the same humility when Abbot Tallemant reminded him of his earlier insulting be-havior toward the solitaries of Port-Royal.

"Yes, Monsieur, you are right," was Racine's reply. "That is the most shameful part of my career, and I would shed my blood to wipe it out." At this, everyone stopped laughing and a silence fell over the assembly.

In Brussels, Arnauld found Nicole, who also had been forced to flee from France. But the latter did not have the courage to endure exile to the end, and at the price of certain concessions was allowed to return to his native land. As for Arnauld, he was to carry out one of the sayings of his master, Saint-Cyran: "When it is a matter of defending truth, fight until you die."

Since he no longer resided in his native country, the spiritual leader of Port-Royal knew the nuns of the Fields could not be held responsible for what he did, and could not be suspected of following his advice. He therefore expressed his views with complete freedom. He published a paper defending the bishops who refused to submit to the *Régale*. After thus definitively mak-ing an enemy of Louis XIV, Arnauld dared to defy Rome, where until that time he had been so respected that the pope had considered offering him a cardinal's hat. The author of *Frequent Communion* publicly gave his approval to the Four Articles voted by the Assembly of the Clergy in 1682 to limit the authority of the Holy See over the Gallican Church. The bridges were broken between Arnauld and the Vatican.

Arriving in Holland, the exile published a "Defense of Catholics," which was a violent attack on the Protestant inhabitants of the United Provinces. One of them wrote about this work: "It calls for carrying the war even into people's homes."

Worthy of Mordecai and Joad, the indomitable old man of seventy-seven did not stop there: he defended the rights of the Catholic king of England, James II, against William of Orange, who had dethroned him; he represented the latter as "a new Absalom, a new Herod, a new Cromwell, a new Nero." This time the cup was full; for his insults against the ruler of Holland, Antoine Arnauld had to leave that country and return to Belgian Flanders.

All of his writings reached France and were widely read. Numerous arrests were made when persons were found possessing them but although this saddened the old fighter, it never disarmed him.

Despite his many disillusionments, Arnauld remained always the faithful subject of a king who in his eyes personified France. According to him Louis XIV, the Lord's anointed, had never wished to silence consciences of his own accord. The sovereign had been deceived by evil counselors: Haman, Mathan, and the worshipers of Baal.

Each time he learned of a new injustice, Arnauld exclaimed: "Ah, if the king only knew!" In the alien land where he had to live, he was reproached "for being too passionately fond" of his king.

The marquis de Pomponne almost succeeded in arranging for the exile's return, but his uncle would have had to promise never to publish any work on a religious subject. This Arnauld's conscience did not permit him to do. He also would have had to ask for the support of Monseigneur de Harlay. The proscript refused. "How can I see him after all that has happened?" he wrote. "I am the last man in the world to make myself say what is not in my heart."

The old man was never able to return to his fatherland. Pointing out the melancholy landscape of Flanders to his last remaining friends, he said: "It is here I must die!"

He expired in Brussels on August 8, 1694, at the age of eighty-two. His faithful companion, the Oratorian Father Quesnel, also an exile, wrote: "He gave his soul into God's hands with admirable peace and tranquility, without effort; he simply went to sleep, as a child of the Resurrection."

Of all the epitaphs written for Antoine Arnauld, the most celebrated is the one composed by Boileau:

. . . He crushed Pelagius, struck Calvin down
The morality of the false doctors he confounded.
But, as reward for his zeal, we see him rejected
In hundreds of places oppressed by the black cabal.
A wanderer, poor, banished, their still burning fury
Would never have left his ashes in peace
Had not God hidden here the bones
Of this holy ram from the devouring wolves.

Antoine Arnauld's body was buried in Brussels, safe from the "devouring wolves." But friends carried his heart to the home his thoughts had never left—the Monastery of Port-Royal of the Fields.

During the office of the dead celebrated by the nuns before Arnauld's heart, Racine took his place in the abbey church. That day he had left his king to come to meditate on the life and the death of a Christian.

The following year, in 1695, Lancelot and Nicole died in their turn. During the latter's final hours, in the vain hope of saving the life of his former tutor, Racine again left Versailles to bring Nicole an elixir, "English drops," given to him by Madame de Grammont.

During all these years the Monastery of Port-Royal remained in the shadow. When the abbess, Mother Dorothée Perdreau, died in 1685, Monseigneur de Harlay's sister succeeded her. The Archbishop of Paris wished this house to become one of the fiefs of his family, and, reverting to the project of Louis XIV, he wanted to increase its importance by adding the Abbey of the Fields to that of the faubourg Saint-Jacques. However, the new abbess of Port-Royal was the opposite of her brother—fragile, delicate in health, and extremely pious. It was only with regret, after trying to avoid the new appointment, that she left her convent of the Nuns of the Virginity in the diocese of Mans. She never consented to the expulsion of the nuns of the Fields in order to take over their house.

When Madame de Harlay died, in 1695, the archbishop had one of his nieces, Marie-Anne de Harlay, appointed abbess of the faubourg Saint-Jacques. This religious intended to carve out a career for herself in the Church, and was in full accord with her uncle on the combination of the two houses of Port-Royal under one direction—her own. Racine's aunt, Mother Agnès de Sainte-Thècle, was at that time abbess of the Monastery of the Fields; in electing her, the nuns hoped the favor her nephew enjoyed at court would constitute a protection for them. When Father Quesnel learned that the Archbishop of Paris had congratulated and commended the new abbess, he remarked that such praise was due the aunt of a man "it was not wise to offend."

Lost in the wilds of Flanders, the exiled Oratorian was ill informed. Louis XIV had attached Racine to his person because he considered him a first-class servitor, but the sovereign was displeased at the poet's loyalty to Port-Royal. Spanheim said bluntly what one should think of the favor enjoyed by Racine: "He wanted people to believe he was able to render them services, but he had neither the desire nor the power to do so; it was quite as much as he could do to keep his own head above water."

Risking disgrace daily, the poet became the last defender of the Monastery of the Fields. Spanheim could not understand Racine's motivation, and said he acted as he did in order to be looked on as a saint, adding: "This became obvious, and it did him harm."

For a long time Monseigneur de Harlay had delayed the appointment of a superior for the abbey after the resignation of the last incumbent in that difficult position. Now the nuns feared the archbishop would drive them away one fine day if they had no superior to defend them.

Meeting Monseigneur de Harlay at Versailles, Racine asked him to come to some decision in this matter. As was his habit, the prelate tried to temporize.

"Why don't you yourself speak to the king?" he said.

The author of Athaliah realized that in advising him to take this step the archbishop was trying to compromise him.

"The King," the poet replied, "would ask me since when had I become the superior of Port-Royal of the Fields."

The Bishop of Soissons, Monseigneur de Silléry, was at Versailles at the time and was present during this conversation. Aware that the cause of the nuns would be lost if Monseigneur de Harlay ruled the diocese of Paris much longer, the bishop took Racine aside and said, with a glance at his colleague:

"Have patience and don't press him. Don't you see the mark of death on his face?"

Five months later, in fact, on August 6, 1695, the archbishop of Paris was struck down by apoplexy, and was unable to receive the cardinal's hat which Louis XIV had obtained for him. A great lady, the duchesse de Lesdiguières, was with the prelate at the time of his attack.

"It is said quite loudly in social circles," said a priest, Abbot Blache, "that Monsieur the Archbishop wished to end his days gloriously; that he was ashamed of having shared the good graces only of waiting-maids and seamstresses or, at most, those of certain ladies of the upper middle class. He finally succeeded in having a duchess open her door to him and believed he would reach the height of happiness if he could die in her arms—this desire was fulfilled."

Monseigneur de Harlay died without being able to receive the last sacraments. Louis XIV was much affected when he learned that a man with so heavy a past had appeared before his Judge without confessing his sins and receiving absolution.

"This is terrible!" the sovereign muttered.

The archbishop was given a sumptuous funeral. In the cathedral, lighted by a forest of candles, the words of the *Requiem* were sung: "May perpetual light shine upon him"; one of those present expressed the thought in every mind: "In the case of the deceased there is rather more cause to fear perpetual darkness."

Several prelates in succession refused to preach the funeral oration of Monseigneur de Harlay. "Two things keep me from doing so—the life and death of this personage," one of them replied.

The archbishop's demise occurred just in time to prevent him from carrying out his plans. Had he lived a few days longer, the nuns who would not consent to live under the direction of Abbess de Harlay at the faubourg Saint-Jacques would have been imprisoned in various convents; the carriages to take them away had even been hired. All the property of the Abbey of the Fields would have been turned over to the Paris house; as for the monastery itself, it would have been torn down for the greater satisfaction of the king.

The scandals raised by the prelate's amorous life determined Louis XIV to appoint a successor worthy of the most important ecclesiastical post in his kingdom. At the request of Madame de Maintenon, without the knowledge of the Jesuits, he designated Louis Antoine de Noailles, Bishop of Châlons and brother of the maréchal duc de Noailles.

The new archbishop, a Sorbonne director forty-five years of age, was a solid theologian and, moreover, a prelate known for the dignity of his life. The city and the court applauded the choice. But Monseigneur de Noailles had one defect—one which, however, helped him to obtain the see of Paris: he was unable to stand up to the king. Fénelon reproached him with having a heart that was "weak and wavering," and a "limited and confused" mind. At first Monseigneur de Noailles refused the archbishopric, but in the end felt compelled to accept.

Racine was commissioned by his aunt, the Abbess of the Fields, to visit the prelate and convey to him the respects of her community. When he wrote to Mother Agnès immediately after this interview, her nephew told her he had been received "with extraordinary kindness." And he added that the archbishop had charged him "to assure your house that he holds it in particular esteem."

The poet made Monseigneur de Noailles a request close to his heart, saying that the Monastery of the Fields was still without a superior and that in order to obtain one the abbess was waiting for the prelate to receive the papal bulls granting him his powers. Monseigneur de Noailles replied with a smile that Mother Agnès de Sainte-Thècle was right to place her confidence in him, and that when the time came he himself would watch over the future of the abbey.

Even so, Racine warned his aunt against "the indiscreet jubilation of certain of her friends," who were already hailing a victory as if Monseigneur de Noailles had been won over to their cause! Let the community beware! Clumsy allies of this kind ran the danger of placing the prelate in a position where he could not come to the help of Port-Royal.

The nuns lived in prayer and silence, but how could one silence the Jansenist theologians and, above all, prevent them from writing? After raising a storm they could disappear, whereas the community remained vulnerable to every attack.

"There are only these poor recluses on whom the storm will fall," Monsieur de Bernières, one of the most faithful but also one of the most discreet supporters of Port-Royal, had written many years before.

Racine's anxiety was soon justified. Saint-Cyran's nephew, Monsieur de Barcos, had reiterated his uncle's ideas on *Augustinus* and grace in a work entitled *Exposition of the Faith*. This book had remained in manuscript during Monsieur de Barcos' lifetime, but at his death his friends thought the time had come to publish it.

This unfortunate publication broke the silence that had reigned since the peace of the Church in regard to the writings of Jansenius. Barcos' posthumous work was submitted by the Molinists to Monseigneur de Noailles, who adopted the ambivalent position that was too often to be his. His mandate of August 20, 1696, censured the book but at the same time defended Saint Augustine's teaching on grace. Fénelon said it "blew hot and cold." Boileau exclaimed, on reading it, "Here we have Jansenius condemned and Jansenism placed on a pinnacle!"

Nobody was satisfied. The friends of Port-Royal considered the censure unjust, and the Molinists regarded Monseigneur de Noailles as a disciple of Saint-Cyran. To Bourdaloue, one of the members of the Society, the archbishop said that "he wished to be the friend of the Jesuits, but not their valet." When this remark was repeated to the fathers, they took it as an insult.

Nevertheless, on receipt of the pontifical bulls canonically establishing him Archbishop of Paris, Monseigneur de Noailles at last gave a superior to Port-Royal of the Fields. He appointed one of his vicars-general, Monsieur

Roynette. The priest was well known to Racine, who had discreetly guided the archbishop's choice. The new superior was in poor health and feared it would be difficult for him to go often to the valley. To calm his anxiety on this score, the poet told him it would be sufficient for him to attend the next election of the abbess in three years' time, "assuming," Racine added sadly, "that this poor community, which properly speaking is only an infirmary, is to last another three years."

The author of *Esther* had still another task to accomplish. Monseigneur de Noailles wanted to know under what circumstances the Monastery of the Fields, formerly an unknown convent, had become what it was; not having the leisure to study the abbey archives, the prelate asked Racine for an account of the reform instituted by Angélique Arnauld and of the events that followed. It seems quite probable that it was on this occasion the poet undertook the writing of his *Abridged History of Port-Royal*, on which he worked up to the time of his death. In these pages Boileau admired "the most perfect piece of history we possess in our language." In purity of style and the sustained emotion it reveals, the *History* is indeed worthy of Racine.

The author of *Esther* tried to reconcile the worship of God with the cult of the king. At the same time he knew how difficult it was for a Jansenist to remain in good favor at court; if he had to choose between his admiration for the man who governed France and his love for the little flock in the Fields, he would not hesitate. "I would not worry," he wrote, "about being disgraced and coming to a cropper if Port-Royal could be restored and flourish anew."

Unhappily the poet was to fall from royal favor without the consolation of seeing the valley flourish anew. Saint-Simon—who considered himself well informed about everything—attributed Racine's disgrace to an unfortunate remark on his part.

One day the poet was, as frequently happened, in the intimate company— the *privance* as it was called—of the king and Madame de Maintenon. When Louis XIV asked the question, "Why are dramatic performances at such a low ebb?" the poet replied by blaming Scarron—according to him the bad plays of that writer had done much harm to the theater.

This reference to her dead huband gravely perturbed Madame de Maintenon and antagonized the sovereign. Saint-Simon tells us of the unfortunate effect produced by mention of Scarron's name: "At this word, the poor widow became red, not because of the attack on the reputation of the legless cripple, but at hearing his name spoken before his successor. The king was embarrassed, and the silence that fell made the unfortunate Racine realize what he had done."

The author of the *Memoirs* adds that on pretext of getting back to work, Louis XIV dismissed his historiographer and Racine went out "with a distracted air."

It would be surprising for so reserved a courtier to have committed a blunder of this kind; in fact, it is known from Louis Racine's memoirs that Saint-Simon was mistaken. It was the most inept of flatterers, the good Boileau, who—perhaps not without malice—mentioned Scarron's name before Madame de Maintenon and in the king's presence. Despite his boldness, the author of *Lutrin* was not disgraced at all: trained in the school of Mazarin, Louis XIV was too good a politician to hold an unfortunate remark against a writer.

Racine fell from royal favor for a far graver reason. When the poet forsook the glittering world of the Louvre, Saint-Germain, and Versailles to make retreats at Port-Royal, he discovered what had so astonished La Bruyère: the frightful misery of peasants reduced to the condition of animals. The solitaries and the nuns devoted the greater part of their revenues to these starving people. On returning to court, Racine no doubt spoke to Madame de Maintenon of this distressing state of affairs. She had always been very generous to the poor, but it was no longer a question of giving aid to certain indigent individuals—all France was exhausted by wars and asking for relief. The king's wife was touched, and asked the poet to write a memorandum concerning the plight of the people; she would submit it to the sovereign when she considered the time favorable.

Louis XIV often entered his wife's room unexpectedly; one day, coming upon her suddenly as she was reading the pages written by Racine, he demanded to see them. Madame de Maintenon had promised not to reveal her protégé's name, and attempted at first to keep it secret. But as the king insisted on complete frankness, she felt it impossible not to reply and named the author of the memorandum.

Louis XIV had no need for a poet to tell him of the condition of his kingdom, for he was kept far too well informed by the reports of his intendants. The idea that Racine was carrying on a correspondence with Madame de Maintenon, and presuming to take part in state affairs, irritated the sovereign.

"Because he is a poet, does he want to be a minister?" he said.

These words from the king's lips bespoke Racine's disgrace. Madame de Maintenon was forbidden to receive him again. Of course the historiographer, who was one of the ornaments of the court, could remain and carry on his duties; he could stay as before at Versailles, at Fontainebleau, and even at Marly. But he was banished thenceforth from the intimacy of the sovereign.

To lose the king's friendship was like being deprived of light. After this, Racine felt as much an exile at court as Arnauld was in Flanders. The most sensitive of men was cut to the heart when he knew that the sun, apparently so close, had gone away from him forever.

Another incident occurred. Always short of money, Louis XIV obliged his secretarial-councillors to turn over to him the sum of 12,000 livres. Racine had acquired one of these posts, which had been added to that of gentleman of the chamber and treasurer of France. To acquire these titles he had been forced to mortgage a large part of his property; he therefore sought to be relieved of the new tax which, he said, "has much disarranged my little affairs." Was the courtier, formerly so clever, so shaken that he had lost his sense of the fitness of things? Since he could no longer talk familiarly with the monarch, he wrote a memorandum—another one!—asking to be exempt from the tax imposed on the secretarial-councillors. The maréchal de Noailles offered to deliver the petition to Madame de Maintenon, but unfortunately satisfied himself with turning it over to his brother, the Archbishop of Paris, whom Louis XIV suspected of Jansenism. The prelate's intervention in Racine's favor was ill received by the monarch, and he dryly refused the favor solicited. The poet, ignorant of these transactions and much perturbed, asked the comtesse de Grammont to find out what had happened.

This proud Scotswoman was one of the most loyal of Port-Royal's friends, which was enough to arouse the sovereign's hostility. When he saw Madame de Grammont taking a hand in the affair, Louis XIV made his displeasure known—there were decidedly too many Jansenists rushing to the defense of "Sieur Racine's" interests.

The poet was at Marly on March 4, 1698, and wrote a letter to Madame de Maintenon, a rough draft of which is still in existence. He told her what had occurred and added: "This, Madame, is the way I have conducted myself in this affair. But I learn I have another more terrible one on my hands; I have been represented to the king as a Jansenist." Clumsily, the author of *Esther* defended himself from ever having been "a man of conspiracy." "But I know," he added, "what could have given rise to an accusation so unjust. I have an aunt who is the superior of Port-Royal, and to whom I owe an infinite debt of gratitude. It is she who taught me about God in my childhood, and he made use of her to draw me away from the aberrations and misery in which I was steeped for fifteen years." At a difficult time, Mother Agnès had asked her nephew to intervene on behalf of the Monastery of the Fields. "Could I have refused her without proving myself the basest of men?" the poet wrote.

These are the events to which he referred: In 1697, the Abbess of Port-Royal of Paris, Marie-Anne de Harlay, addressed a petition to the king asking for a portion of the revenues of the Monastery of the Fields to be allocated to the abbey on the faubourg Saint-Jacques. Immediately on learning that

Louis XIV had received this petition, Racine warned his aunt, who wrote at once in defense of her valley nuns. To give weight to the abbess' arguments, the poet went to see Father de La Chaise, Louis XIV's confessor, and pleaded the cause of the monastery.

"I dare not believe I persuaded him," the poet wrote Madame de Maintenon, "but at least he seemed pleased at my frankness and, putting his arms around me, assured me that he would be my servant and friend as long as he lived."

Since he was now accused of Jansenism, Racine thought back to this interview. Perhaps his intervention had been the final step in his own disgrace.

It is probable the poet was mistaken. It is known from Saint-Simon that Father de La Chaise was a true gentleman and incapable of betraying the confidence of a person who came to him. Moreover, Louis XIV had nothing more to learn about Racine, as he knew well the ties that bound the poet to Port-Royal. On various occasions the author of *Esther* had left the court to make retreats in the valley of the Chevreuse, without in any way concealing his intentions from the king's entourage.

That day at the château de Marly, where he was one of the few privileged to come, Racine reflected and finally understood. The sovereign's mind was set against him, and Louis XIV would never again place confidence in a defender of Port-Royal.

The poet ended his letter to Madame de Maintenon with several lines that indicated his distress. Since he was being kept at a distance both by the king and by his patroness, he would seek consolation in his duties as historiographer. "But consider," he wrote, "what bitterness is cast over this work by the thought that the great prince with whom I am constantly concerned regards me perhaps as a man more deserving of his anger than of his kindness."

Madame de Maintenon was touched by this discreet expression of suffering; she could well appreciate its extent, for she knew that she too ran the risk of falling from favor. Disobeying the king, she granted Racine an interview in the gardens of Versailles.

"Let this cloud pass," she told him. "I will bring back the good weather."

As the poet continued to look sad, Madame de Maintenon added: "Are you doubtful of my good heart or of my influence?"

To this Racine replied quickly but without concealing his discouragement: "I know what your influence is and how kind you are. But I have an aunt who loves me in a way quite different; every day this saintly woman asks God on my behalf for disgrace, humiliation, subjects for repentance. She will have more influence than you have."

Immediately an incident took place that gave meaning to his disillusioned words. The barouche of Louis XIV was heard approaching, and Madame de Maintenon exclaimed in fright:

"Be off! It is the king."

Be off! Like Adam after the fall, Racine had to hide when the ruler of this Garden of Eden appeared.

Stripped of ambition, with his dreams come to naught, the poet advanced toward his death, which took place the following year, with the serenity of a Roman condemned by Caesar. From his wife he received the calm affection of a faithful companion. His children had no inkling of the exalting and somber joys that had brought him so much happiness and so much suffering; thus sheltered, they grew up each day around him.

Since Nanon, the youngest, was unable to become a novice at Port-Royal, she took the veil at the Ursuline convent in Melun; Racine wept when he saw her surrounded by the nuns who were thenceforth to be her only family. His eldest daughter, Catherine, also wished to become a religious, but only if she could enter the Abbey of the Fields. She had to abandon the idea, for the gates of Zion were closed by the order of the king. So Catherine remained in the world, and eventually married.

La Champmeslé died on May 17, 1698. Racine had but one anxiety regarding the object of his passion of earlier days—the same he had felt at the bedside of marquise du Parc. Had Berenice been reconciled to God before she died? Her lover feared she had "mounted her high horse," but was consoled to learn that La Champmeslé, in her turn, had signed the act of renunciation and met death "in a proper enough frame of mind."

Several months later Racine was stricken "on the right side." He was attended by Louis XIV's physician, Denis Dodart, to whom he entrusted his *Abridged History of Port-Royal.* The idea that he must one day die had distressed the poet in the past; now he looked forward to his last hours. To Boileau, who had hastened to his bedside, he said, "My friend, I consider I am fortunate to die before you."

Racine expired on April 21, 1699, at the age of fifty-nine. The *Mercure Galant,* formerly so harsh in its criticisms, was now unreserved in the admiration it bestowed on his memory.

In his will Racine asked to be buried in the cemetery of Port-Royal of the Fields, at the foot of Monsieur Hamon's grave. This did not please the king, but he could not refuse his historiographer's last request. The body was transferred secretly, at night.

Mother Agnès Racine lived to see the death of the spiritual son whose passions had caused her so much anguish, and whose return to the fold she counted as a blessing. She survived him by only a year.

When it was learned at court that the author of *Athaliah* wished to be buried at Port-Royal, the comte de Roucy exclaimed: "That is an announcement he would never have made in his lifetime!" These scornful words were both unjust and cruel. The poet had given his life for the valley where he had found the wellsprings of his genius.

When Racine was gravely ill, Louis XIV sent his officers several times to inquire about the poet's condition. Seeing Boileau on the day following Racine's death, he said at once in a loud voice: "Ah, Monsieur, both of us have lost a great deal in losing Monsieur Racine."

The author of the *Lutrin,* always an amused spectator of court intrigue, added that the sovereign praised the dead man "in a way that would have made the courtiers want to die merely to have him speak like that about them afterward."

Poor Racine! Only beyond the grave was he given the words that would have saved him had he lived.

Louis XIV knew how to associate the poet's fame with that of the chief of state. He even granted Racine's widow a pension of two thousand livres "in consideration of the meritorious services rendered by Sieur Racine in the employment entrusted to him."

The comtesse de Grammont rendered a more gracious tribute. This ally of Port-Royal sincerely mourned Racine, for the poet had kept hope alive in her and her intimates at court. "He encouraged, strengthened, and enlightened us," she said.

Her words may be surprising, since in the mirage that surrounds the past Versailles is often looked upon as an ideal and delightful setting. But Racine's contemporaries leave no illusions regarding what Madame de Maintenon, when she was still Madame Scarron, called "the horrible agitations of this country."

La Bruyère describes the courtiers, preyed upon by fear and ambition: "Their features are changed, their faces coarsened; those who are proud and haughty are the most downcast." And this is the testimony of a Palatine princess, the second most important noblewoman of France, regarding these harassed people: "One weeps, another hits the table with his fists, the third blasphemes; the women have the air of persons possessed."

The duchesse d'Orléans was also bold enough to tell of the monotony of court life: one entertainment followed another, always similar; she speaks of the interminable minuets, which made her think of eternity, and of tunes heard a hundred times over. "Always the same pleasures, at the same hours, in company with the same people."

Racine himself had described the king's entourage in *Britannicus:*

> How all one says is far from what one thinks!
> How seldom heart and lips agree together!
> With what joy is faith betrayed!

Later, three lines in *Esther* tell of the humiliations a courtier must suffer:

> He who cannot swallow insults
> Nor disguise himself in false colors
> Let him depart, fly, from the gaze of kings.

When Louis XIV turned devout those whom Arnauld called "the professionally pious" succeeded the former "wild beasts" of The Fronde, who had been tamed and domesticated. "At the present moment, unless one assumes an air of piety there is no salvation at court," wrote Madame de La Fayette.

This servile religiosity became so odious that it made honest men look back with nostalgia to the time when the king's palace was, in Boudaloue's words, "the center of corruption."

The elect of this false paradise found in Racine the high-mindedness and compassion which the poet owed to Port-Royal. Because of him there was a refuge for hope in the gilded Gehenna of Versailles.

A last thought is due to La Fontaine, Racine's old friend. In 1664, the fabulist had been won over to "easy devotion," and greatly relished the indulgence of the casuists, as we see from his "Ballad":

> Quite justly does Rome's condemnation fall
> On the Bishop of Ypres, author of vain debate.
> His sectarians forbid us, all in all,
> Every earthly pleasure we could taste.
> One can reach Paradise without so much haste
> No matter what it is that Arnauld tells us.
> Sensual pleasure he has banished without reason.
> If one wants to climb the towers of heaven
> The stony road is only a daydream.
> Escobar has laid down a velvet carpet.

Later on, through Boileau, he met the solitaries and admired them. He had written a very naughty tale dealing with a monk who multiplied the five talents of the Gospel in a strange manner. In the prologue to this story the fabulist praised Antoine Arnauld and naively wanted to dedicate the work to him. Boileau let his friend understand that a tribute of this sort would be considered an insult by the Port-Royal theologian, whereupon the good fellow contritely gave up publishing the tale, though not without confessing his regret, for he considered it the best he had ever written.

Later on, to give pleasure to the Messieurs, he composed a poem on "The Captivity of Saint Malc." That day, La Fontaine forgot the Muses and invoked the Virgin, renouncing, as he said:

> . . . the criminal sweetmeats
> I begged of the nine Sisters in days gone by.

Arnauld d'Andilly had published the story of Saint Malc in his *Lives of the Desert Fathers*. This pious hermit was held in slavery by the Arabs, and shared the lot of a Christian woman who was also a captive. The infidels wanted to compel them to live as man and wife, but Saint Malc refused. La Fontaine put this story into verse: "Of a hero's solitary virtue I sing. . . ."

Careful to avoid any unseemly reference, the pious epic was lifeless and gloomy. Even so, the critics found one charming image in this fastidious poem—La Fontaine pictured faith as a treasure "Coming down to us from water that has its wellspring in the sky."

One of La Fontaine's fables, "The Arbitrating Judge, the Hospitalier, and the Solitary," was dedicated to the Messieurs. Two saints decided that, in order to be saved, one would render justice "without any recompense whatever," and the other could care for the sick. A third and wiser saint retired into solitude, where he was joined by his two companions. The moral of the fable showed the irony of Molina's former disciple: "To contemplate yourself better, remain in the desert."

Again La Fontaine forced his talent, for this was one of his poorer fables.

It was also to please the Messieurs that Boileau's friend lent his name to a *Collection of Christian Poetry,* published under the ægis of Port-Royal. La Fontaine presented this book to the prince de Conti on behalf of the solitaries:

> . . . Fearing to leave the deep peace
> They secretly enjoy, far from the world's turmoil,
> They ask me to bring this to light of day for them.

The fabulist composed for this collection a paraphrase of Psalm XVII, "I love thee, O Lord, my strength. . . ." Apparently this love was not inspiring enough, for the poem is dull and lifeless.

La Fontaine was not greatly attracted by the grave manner of the Messieurs, and knew nothing of their hidden happiness. He had been given a home by Racine's enemy, the duchesse de Bouillon, and wrote his patroness on the subject of Port-Royal:

Anacreon is silent before the Jansenists.
Their lessons still seem a bit dreary to me.

In one of his fables, "The Scythian Philosopher," the poet expressed his ideas regarding Saint-Cyran's disciples with suddenly recovered verve: "They would have us stop living before we are dead!"

Yet no one escaped the destiny of the *Grand Siècle*. At the beginning of an illness that was to be his last, La Fontaine placed himself in the hands of the Lord of the Gospels and entered on the straight and narrow path of the Christian.

5

VICTORY OF THE SUN KING

Saint-Cyran, Pascal, and Racine were gone. Those defenders of Port-Royal who still survived had been imprisoned, exiled, or dispersed. Only a few nuns remained in the valley of the Chevreuse; these religious, worn out by age and tribulations, were crushed beneath the shadow of Louis XIV.

When the abbess of the Paris monastery, Marie-Anne de Harlay, tried to obtain a part of the revenues of the house of the Fields, she was greatly in debt. Her lawyer made no attempt to hide a fact well known to all. The nuns of the faubourg Saint-Jacques, he wrote, "are foolish virgins who have no oil in their lamp and are asking it from the wise ones."

The second Duchess of Orleans, the Palatine, whose best friend had retired to Port-Royal of Paris, interceded with the king in support of Madame de Harlay's request. Louis XIV was on the point of acceding when a personage close to him, the princesse de Conti, also intervened, but this time in favor of the Abbey of the Fields. "His Majesty," wrote a chronicler of the time, "then changed his mind and did not grant the favor Madame asked."

Highly irritated at her lack of success, the abbess of the Paris monastery sought revenge, and accused the religious of the Fields of receiving novices against the sovereign's orders. Monseigneur de Noailles was compelled to betake himself to the Chevreuse Valley, but he found no grounds for Madame de Harlay's accusation. Touched by the simplicity of the valley nuns, the archbishop declared that "they are truly models for other women religious," and he "wished all those in his diocese would imitate them." Despite this reminder of humility, the abbess did not consider herself beaten, and for a second time called for the abrogation of the decree separating the property

of the two houses. Monseigneur de Noailles was irritated at her stubbornness, and, on learning that Madame de Harlay had given a ball in the convent parlor, the archbishop made a remark that was repeated as far as
Versailles:

"It is really not just for Port-Royal of Paris to give a ball, and for Port-
Royal of the Fields to have to pay the violinists."

On February 22, 1703, a decree of the Council of State dismissed Madame
de Harlay's claims, thus bringing the painful lawsuit to an end.

The convent on the faubourg Saint-Jacques may be forgotten for a moment in favor of the one in the Fields.

On February 5, 1699, two months before her nephew's death and a year
before her own, Mother Agnès Racine had been relieved of her charge after
fulfilling the functions of abbess for nine years. Mother Elisabeth de Sainte-
Anne Boulard was elected in her place.

Thirty-four religious—the last survivors—took part in the election. The
new abbess was seventy-one years of age, and assumed the responsibility of
directing the community with some anxiety. No one was ignorant of the fact
that the king was more hostile than ever to the Monastery of the Fields. Madame de Grammont was barred from a visit to Marly because she had made a
retreat at the monastery. Despite this, the countess was always to remain
faithful to the memory of the abbey where she had been brought up out of
charity when her father, Lord Hamilton, was driven from England by Cromwell and sought refuge in France.

"Marly and Port-Royal do not get on well together," declared Louis XIV
as he struck Madame de Grammont's name from his list of guests. His
remark was indeed true.

Repeating Madame de Harlay's accusations, enemies of the Abbey of the
Fields declared that the nuns had taken in six novices. Louis XIV was perturbed and asked Monseigneur de Noailles, now a cardinal, for information.
The prelate reassured the king, saying the so-called novices were young girls
who had taken no vows. They were called "white-veil sisters," and came only
to assist the nuns because the latter's voices gave out when they tried to sing
the Psalms, and because of age and infirmity they could not always be certain
of having one of their community in prayer before the Blessed Sacrament.

On another occasion Louis XIV was given the truth about Port-Royal of
the Fields. In his *Memoirs,* Saint-Simon relates that one day the king's first
surgeon, Maréchal, was asked to go to the monastery because the leg of one
of the nuns had to be amputated. The surgeon was extremely surprised
when warned that he risked disgrace if he went to the Fields. Wanting
neither to fail in his duty nor to displease the sovereign, Maréchal frankly

discussed his dilemma with the king. "At the name Port-Royal," writes Saint-Simon, "the king bridled up as he always did about things that annoyed him." After reflecting "for time enough to say two or three *Paters*," Louis XIV gave his consent, but on condition Maréchal would visit the house, converse with the religious, and "make them talk."

Rather surprised at such a commission, the surgeon went to the valley and carried out his task. When he returned he told the king "he had not been so impressed by the sanctity of any house he had ever visited."

At this the sovereign sighed, saying the nuns were, indeed, saints, and that "with regard to them things have been allowed to go much too far." That day he seems to have decided to leave the remaining religious in peace so long as they lived.

But the dangerous friends of Port-Royal were on the move as usual, and with the best of intentions two of them again put the abbey in jeopardy.

A priest in Normandy wrote the confessor of the Monastery of the Fields asking for advice on a theological matter. He wanted to keep "respectful silence" on the point of recognizing whether or not the five propositions condemned by the pope had been supported by Jansenius. Could he, in conscience, sign the famous formulary which was still being circulated in every diocese?

The monastery confessor replied to his fellow priest saying everything that could allay his scruples; quite pleased with this letter he had written, Monsieur Eustace submitted it to a faithful friend of Port-Royal, Monsieur Besson, the pastor of Magny. The two priests revised it and developed it into a "consultation" which grew into a treatise on theology. Quite proud of their work, they submitted it in succession to forty Sorbonne doctors, and obtained their approbation.

A year went by during which the consultation remained buried in the coffers of the faculty of theology. Then suddenly an unknown person—apparently hostile to the Jansenists—published the unfortunate work under the title *Case of Conscience*, together with a provocative preface seemingly written for the purpose of stirring up trouble.

This time the quarrel was resumed and the battle began anew. Molina's disciples replied from every quarter; five refutations appeared in rapid succession. *Case of Conscience* was then submitted to the censorship of Rome. The new pope, Clement XI, who earlier in life had almost joined the Jesuits, greatly favored the sons of Loyola. Without asking the advice of his theologians, he condemned the book and sent two briefs, one to the king and the other to Cardinal de Noailles, informing them of his decision.

The cardinal felt compelled to condemn *Case of Conscience,* and the

Sorbonne doctors who had supported the treatise now wanted to extricate themselves from an embarrassing situation. All retracted with the exception of one who would not withdraw his approbation. By royal order he was exiled from Paris, expelled from the faculty of the Sorbonne, and even forced to leave France and take refuge in Holland.

On March 5, 1703, the Council wisely decreed that in future absolute silence must be maintained with reference to questions raised by *Case of Conscience.*

Although the peace of the Church still prevailed, it was already very precarious. Theological passions were unleashed on all sides. Fénelon considered the moment had come to be forgiven for his support of the Quietists, which had caused his disgrace, and allied himself to the Jesuits. "The Society must realize my enemies are theirs," he wrote their general. And he published his *Instructions* condemning *Case of Conscience.*

The Swan of Cambrai, described by Saint-Simon as "ingratiating and prepossessing," was sincere. He had always looked on the Jansenists, about whom he knew very little, as savage and inhuman.

On the advice of Madame de Maintenon, who took part in the struggle after Racine's death, Louis XIV asked the pope for a decision condemning the partisans of "respectful silence" even more explicitly than he had done in his briefs. The king obtained, on July 16, 1705, the bull *Vineam Domini Sabaoth,* forcing ecclesiastics to acknowledge that the five heretical propositions were indeed contained in *Augustinus.* Port-Royal's situation became highly critical, and the two priests who had caused all the trouble by giving in to the vanity of authorship were in consternation. Monsieur Besson died soon afterward; Monsieur Eustace, after being threatened with arrest, retired to the Abbey of Orval, where under a borrowed name he lived a life of severe penance.

Meanwhile, Cardinal de Noailles was compelled to publish the bull *Vineam Domini.* To this he thought he should add a decree entitled "Against Jansenism," in order to allay the suspicions raised by his benevolence toward Port-Royal of the Fields. Monsieur Marignier, the confessor who succeeded Monsieur Eustace, was given orders to read the papal bull and the cardinal's decree before the grill of the monastery. Monsieur Marignier then was to send the archbishopric a letter testifying that the decisions had been "received by the religious with the respect due His Holiness and His Eminence."

When these documents were read to them, painful memories were revived in the minds of the nuns—Arnauld's condemnation, the removal of their superiors. This persecution was like a badly extinguished fire, flaring up again and again.

Each religious was called on to declare to the confessor that she received with respect the decisions condemning Jansenius; a repudiation was once again asked of these poor women.

If the combat had to be resumed, at least let it be brought into the open! The nuns remembered the compromises imposed earlier by theologians claiming to be their protectors. One of the religious expressed the thought of all her sisters: "Our house is like an old, tumbledown cottage threatened by destruction on every side. Isn't it better to be destroyed by one fell blow for the glory of God than to sink down little by little?"

With her own death not far away, Madame Boulard's mind went back to heroic days which would never return. "I am," she said, "like a soldier who has been in the army and wants to be in it again, despite all the trouble there was."

On their knees before the crucifix, the nuns vowed not to falter. But the theologians, always so quick to unleash a storm, now thought only of finding compromises, and devised new "reservations" similar to those that had caused Jacqueline Pascal so much anguish. Mabille, a Sorbonne doctor, was quite pleased with a stratagem which, he said, could save Port-Royal. According to this, the confessor of the Monastery of the Fields would draw up the declaration of obedience required by the archbishop and add a phrase that would deprive it of all meaning—the religious were to declare they accepted the bull and decree but "without derogating from what had taken place in regard to them at the time of the peace of the Church under Clement XI." At that time the respectful silence concerning *Augustinus* had been allowed, and this reservation should make it possible for it to be permitted again. In the eyes of one theologian, appearing to obey without submitting was the best of answers to the problem.

The nuns were highly perturbed, but how could these humble women raise objections when a theologian who was "a friend of the truth" had spoken? Sadly they submitted, and the abbey confessor drew up the declaration and added the reservation devised by Mabille.

This "counter-letter" irritated Monseigneur de Noailles, for the prelate did not want to take the king an act of obedience which was illusory. He sent Monsieur Gilbert, the superior, to the Abbey of the Fields. The priest tried with as little success as the late Péréfixe to convince the abbess and the nuns one by one of the necessity of complete submission. They were destroying themselves, he told the religious, for in the king's entourage there were "wicked personages" only waiting for an opportunity of this kind to annihilate the Port-Royal community; the cardinal could do nothing to prevent them from doing so.

Simpler than their predecessors, Madame Boulard and her sisters limited themselves to kneeling before the superior and saying: "Must we surrender our consciences?"

After talking to them for two days, the vicar-general left without having obtained any result whatever.

Now as before, the friends of the monastery encouraged the nuns in their resistance. Father Quesnel, spiritual successor to Arnauld, wrote from Flanders exhorting them to have courage; their determination not to give in was, he said, "a very particular grace from Jesus Christ which should fill them with deep and humble gratitude."

Father Quesnel had earned the right to speak in this way. In defense of his beliefs he had given up a brilliant career in the Church and had been compelled to leave his country; he had been in prison, had escaped, and was to remain in exile for the rest of his life.

The nuns decided to make no further concessions, nor to take advantage of any ambiguities; yet they knew their age and declining strength put them at a greater disadvantage than ever.

The sub-prioress, Sister de Bernières, died on April 14, 1706; she was the daughter of the magistrate who had harbored in his home one of the Little Schools of Port-Royal, and who had devoted his fortune to the help of the indigent. Several days later the abbess, Madame de Sainte-Anne Boulard, suffered a heart attack, and both she and the prioress, Mother Baudraud, died one after the other.

The dying abbess, knowing that the prioress—who actually survived her by only a day—was at death's door, asked for her resignation. Then Madame Boulard gathered her last strength to appoint as prioress one of the most courageous and intelligent nuns in the monastery—Sister Sainte-Anastasie du Mesnil.

The burial of the two nuns had just taken place when the cellaress of the abbey, Sister Le Féron, was handed a decree of the Council of State. Informed of the nuns' resistance, Louis XIV was imposing his first sanction. The prohibition against reception of novices at the Fields, previously only a verbal order from the king, was now made final by a decision of the Council couched in the harshest language. The cellaress, who was seventy-three years of age and had already experienced "the fire of two persecutions," was so overcome that she died three days after informing the community of the decree of condemnation.

The new prioress, Mother du Mesnil, now in charge of the monastery, was fifty-seven years old, and had left the world at twenty-six. She had been maid-of-honor to the princesse de Conti; after refusing a wealthy marriage she had become a religious at Port-Royal. The superior who received her vows said to her at the time: "You are fortunate; you have been chosen by God. You are destined for salvation."

In this world, however, the prioress was to meet with one trial after another. When she asked for permission to have a new abbess elected, Monseigneur de Noailles refused. He was greatly displeased with the religious who, he said, had taken bad advice, and he considered their disobedience "altogether criminal."

In his anger, Monseigneur de Noailles' words were reminiscent of de Péréfixe's imprecations.

"Nothing is worse than the half-instructed," he said.

The prelate told the confessor of Port-Royal of the Fields that for a long time he had warded off the harsh measures that threatened the nuns, but in future he would not protect them. Noailles had to admit that the harsh measures could not have been avoided even had the religious signed the formulary without any restriction: "The king's decision to destroy them was taken a long time ago," the cardinal said. Nevertheless, he considered that had they obeyed their consciences would have been at peace.

Without an abbess, the religious felt helpless and abandoned, and one by one they died. Their confessor, Monsieur Marignier, lost hope, and shortly after the day he learned from Monseigneur de Noailles that the Abbey of the Fields was condemned, he died of grief at the age of forty-nine. The funereal shadow of the valley claimed all those who came within its reaches.

"Before I appear in God's presence, I must bear witness to the faith of our sisters. Never have I doubted it," the priest said as he lay dying.

The Abbess of Port-Royal of Paris, Marie-Anne de Harlay, each day proved herself more unworthy of her charge. Although she made every possible effort to retain her post, she was forced to resign. To succeed her, Louis XIV chose the niece of a Marshal of France, Château-Renaud, intending to place the Monastery of the Fields, still without an abbess, also under her authority.

Up until that time, Madame de Château-Renaud had been a religious of the diocese of Mans, and she was very anxious to live in the capital. When she paid a visit to the archepiscopal theologian, the new abbess affected detachment toward worldly possessions and a great desire for sanctity. The theologian was not deceived, for he knew for what purpose Madame de Château-Renaud had been given her post.

"She would straddle a rainbow," he said.

However, the pope thwarted the king's plans. The bulls permitting Madame de Château-Renaud to take possession of the two abbeys were not delivered until 1709, more than two years after her appointment.

Meanwhile the community of the faubourg Saint-Jacques reopened its interminable lawsuit against the nuns of the Fields. The prioress of the Paris house introduced a new petition for the nullification of the decree of separation, demanding that all possessions of Port-Royal of the Fields be turned over to her since this abbey and the one in the faubourg Saint-Jacques should rightfully be reunited. The magistrates of the Paris Parlement were favorable to the Jansenist cause and would not receive the petition, so it was turned over directly to the Council of State where its success was a foregone conclusion. A decree of this jurisdiction, dated January 9, 1707, nullified the decision that had effected the separation and ordered six thousand livres to be deducted annually from the revenue of the Monastery of the Fields. This abbey had only eight thousand livres in all and so would be left with only two thousand. Furthermore, the nuns were ordered to discharge their old servants, most of whom were too old to work and were being given a home out of charity. To furnish these unfortunate women with some money before sending them away, and to provide for the nuns' subsistence, the prioress, Mother du Mesnil, even had to sell pieces of the sacristy silver; shortly after this, bailiffs appeared and carried off the remaining objects.

On the advice of one of the last of the solitaries, Saint-Claude, a lawyer of Parlement, the Monastery of the Fields made use of every counter process—injunctions, protests, memoranda, requests, petitions—but all were rejected in succession. Saint-Claude himself was arrested and imprisoned in the Bastille, where he remained under very harsh conditions until the death of Louis XIV.

Monsieur Vuillart, a friend of Racine, was likewise taken to the Bastille for defending the interests of "the Jansenist order." The intendant of the Monastery of the Fields, more than eighty years of age, was likewise jailed. When the two prisoners were freed after the death of Louis XIV, one was dying and the second was blind.

It was known at the Abbey of the Fields that these harsh measures were only the forerunners of others. On May 8, 1707, the members of the community gathered in the chapter hall to draw up in advance a document of protest declaring the nullity of any signatures that might be extorted from them. Those errors the nuns might thenceforth commit "could be imputed only to the exhausted state to which extreme suffering had reduced poor women who were old, ill, and deprived of any counsel."

Cardinal de Noailles would have preferred to avoid such extreme harshness, but Louis XIV was in a state of high displeasure. At Versailles he had hard words for the prelate. "If the Bishop of Chartres (Monseigneur des Marais) had the Port-Royal affair in hand, he would have finished it within two weeks, and here for six months you have accomplished nothing."

The cardinal felt he was in danger, and his ire fell on the rebels.

The more I think of their conduct, the more inexcusable I find their resistance. . . . I believe them quite unworthy of the sacraments. . . . I am a man of the Church and therefore obliged to act against those who flout its authority . . . It is with much sorrow I find myself obliged to punish them for their rebelliousness, but I believe I am bound in conscience to do so.

The officials of the archbishopric who judged ecclesiastical cases began the process which would put an end to the existence of the Abbey of the Fields. The prioress appealed to the Primacy of Lyons, which held jurisdiction over the Paris diocese, but the Primate was not given sufficient time to pronounce judgment. Because they had been called upon to abjure their errors and had refused, the nuns were excommunicated by decree of the cardinal on May 22, 1707, in the same way they had been excommunicated by de Péréfixe. This punishment afflicted them far more grievously than all the others, and when the prioress wrote to tell one of the friends of the monastery what had happened, her trembling handwriting betrayed her emotion.

The religious made another appeal to the Primate of Lyons in order to receive communion on Easter Sunday, April 8, 1709, but their plea went unanswered.

Despite his bitterness, the cardinal was saddened to see the sisters of the Fields reduced to indigence, and he invited the prioress to send him a memorandum on the subject. Mother du Mesnil refused.

"Since Monseigneur the Archbishop," she said, "has taken from us the bread of heaven, we are little concerned about earthly bread."

Nevertheless, the religious received communion in secret as they had done before. The priest who distributed it to them, Monsieur de Crès, endangered both his future and his liberty, and on being discovered and prosecuted had to hide for several years in the provinces.

Monsieur Pollet, the new confessor sent the monastery by the cardinal, was moved by the nuns' fervor.

"In these seventeen women," he said, "there is enough piety to sanctify seventeen convents."

The former solitaries who survived were either in prison or in exile. Now it was a woman, Mademoiselle de Joncoux, who alone defended the Abbey of the Fields. Her birth and wit opened all doors to her, and she had access to the court, to Parlement, to the archbishop, and even to marquis d'Argenson, the lieutenant of police.

This friend of Port-Royal attempted the impossible, even getting the papal nuncio in Paris to intercede for the nuns despite the fact she placed small hope in Rome.

"There is little likelihood at present that the pope can be brought around," she said.

At Versailles, Mademoiselle de Joncoux learned that a decision had been made to disperse the nuns. "They have absolutely determined to destroy the house before the king dies," she wrote.

The support she gave the monastery permitted the nuns to exist. She did not hide this from Monseigneur de Noailles, saying "she would sell her petticoat" rather than leave the religious in want. The cardinal warned her that she ran the risk "of bringing many things down on her head."

"For a long time," replied Mademoiselle de Joncoux, "I have been above 'things.' When one wears a coif one does not trouble oneself overmuch; I would not change it for the purple."

So saying, the courageous woman made a deep bow to the confounded prelate and withdrew, thus ending the eternal dialogue between Antigone and Creon.

The Jesuits used their weapon, "Jansenian heresy," to put Saint-Cyran's followers on the horns of a dilemma: either to accept the formulary and deny their beliefs or to reject it and deny the pope.

Like Pascal, Madame de Sévigné said earlier in regard to the Jansenists: "It is a crime for them to sign and a crime not to sign." The wise and prudent marquise could never understand the mystical passion that led the nuns to lay themselves open to persecution. But this woman, whose good sense was as lively as her wit, saw through the game of the Society of Jesus. "The Spirit breathes where it wills," she wrote. "It was Saint Augustine who said this; I find him very Jansenistic, and also Saint Paul. The Jesuits have a phantom they call Jansenius on whom they heap a thousand insults, pretending not to know where all this comes from."

It comes from Christ and the Gospels!

Thereafter, any person who displeased the Society of Jesus was accused of Jansenism. The most influential Jesuit, Father de La Chaise, let fall this remark: "Jansenism is my pitch-pot. I place it where I must."

This Jesuit was held in great esteem by Saint-Simon, who praised him highly in his *Memoirs*. The author had to admit, however, that at the approach of Easter, the king's confessor had recourse more than once "to political illnesses," and thus avoided giving absolution to the king at the time his passion for Madame de Montespan made it impossible for him to profess repentance. During one of these "illnesses," the priest Father de La Chaise asked to replace him was more courageous. "Bravely, he refused absolution," Saint-Simon wrote. Another Jesuit, the famous Bourdaloue, went further. In the chapel of the château of Saint-Germain, in the course of a sermon on impurity, he dared turn to Louis XIV and accuse him publicly of leading a dissolute life. Had such men been more numerous they might have brought down trouble on their Society, but they would have given it another face in history.

Father de La Chaise's indulgence—which went so far, it was said, as to give the king communion with unconsecrated hosts when he could not absolve him—enabled him to become all powerful. Courtiers crowded into his residence in the hope of gaining his support.

"You have made a minister of your confessor," Fénelon said to the king.

Each Friday, Louis XIV assembled his Council of Conscience; all decisions concerning the Church of France were made at these meetings, for the king wished to be "both priest and king," as Daguesseau expressed it. In this Council, Father de La Chaise had more influence than even the chaplain-general; moreover, on the days after the king was given absolution and on those he received communion, appointments were made to the great ecclesiastical posts of the kingdom, and no one could obtain a bishopric unless he had given proofs of his attachment to the Society of Jesus.

Father de La Chaise rebuffed Madame de Maintenon, even though she was almost the queen. Louis XIV warned her "that she could not be at his court if she did not like the Jesuits." The sovereign's wife hated the confessor because, like Louvois, he had opposed the public announcement of her marriage to the king, but she never "dared bare her teeth to him," wrote Saint-Simon, "because she knew the king's attitude in regard to him."

When not in the company of the monarch, the Jesuit resided in a house belonging to his Society; he had it reconstructed according to new plans, and greatly embellished the vast gardens surrounding it. This land was later to become the most important cemetery of Paris and to bring a somber immortality to Père La Chaise—the priest who directed the conscience of Louis XIV reigns forever over the dead.

When the confessor felt his strength declining, he asked the king to choose his successor from among the members of his Society. On this subject Saint-Simon reports a remark made by the Jesuit which Louis XIV made no attempt to keep secret from his entourage. Father de La Chaise told his penitent that "in case he was thinking of taking a confessor from outside the Society of Jesus, this Society was made up of all kinds of people and mentalities for whom he could not be held responsible, and that they must not be driven to desperation." And the Jesuit reminded him "that a bad blow could be struck hastily and was not without a precedent.

In this connection Saint-Simon evoked the memory of Henri IV; having narrowly escaped death from the dagger of Jean Châtel, a disciple of the Jesuits, the Bearnais deemed it wise to allow them to return to France, and went so far as to take one of them, Father Cotton, as his confessor. For similar motives, Louis XIII followed his example. "When Father de La Chaise dies," added Saint-Simon, "Louis XIV will be careful not to lay himself open to the vengeance of the Society by choosing a confessor outside its ranks. He wants to live and to live in safety."

So long as the Jesuit was still alive, the sovereign intended to keep his *chaise de commodités* at his side. Father de La Chaise tried in vain to retire in favor of one of his colleagues, but was destined to die in the breach. Saint-Simon tells of the last days of this priest, a victim of the favor he had so greatly coveted "for the greater glory of God." The picture drawn is frightening: "He had to continue to carry his burden until the end; neither infirmity nor decrepitude could deliver him. His legs tottering beneath him, his memory gone, his judgment weakened, his wits confused—nothing repelled the king. Up to the end he had this corpse brought before him and transacted with it the usual business."

In this connection it is impossible not to think of the *Provincial Letters* and beyond them to the terrible words of the Gospel: "Let the dead bury their dead!"

Saint-Simon describes the priest's last hours. His superiors rushed to his bedside, asking him for an accounting. Had he always borne in mind "the welfare and honor of the Society?" The dying man reassured them: he had lived only for it, and died as a soldier in its service.

Justice must be done to the illustrious Jesuit. Although Father de La Chaise had overlooked no means of combatting Jansenism, he had always conducted himself as a man with a heart in regard to the nuns of the Fields. So long as he lived, the community survived. "He never wished to push Port-Royal to its destruction," Saint-Simon is quite correct in saying.

The new royal confessor, Father Tellier, succeeded Father de La Chaise on May 21, 1709. Appointed on the advice of the Bishop of Chartres and Madame de Maintenon, this Jesuit who already wielded authority in France as Provincial, was of a different stripe. Wishing to establish the authority of his Society in every quarter, he considered, says Saint-Simon, "that there was nothing that was not permitted him, or that he could not undertake." It was, the duke adds, "a passion that wholly possessed him, a constant urge." The aim this priest assigned himself is described by the author of the *Memoirs:* Father Tellier intended to impose "the despotic rule of the Society, its dogmas, its maxims; and to bring about the radical destruction of everyone who did not submit to it blindly."

The portrait of the priest as drawn by Saint-Simon calls to mind the sinister grandeur of Torquemada.

His head and health were of iron, also his conduct; his nature was grim and cruel. . . . He was profoundly false and deceitful, covering up his purposes by a thousand twists and turns. . . . He would strike terror if met in a lonely corner of the forest. His countenance was dark, false, terrible; his eyes, burning and malevolent, were extremely crossed; the sight of him was dread-inspiring." He had consecrated himself "body and soul to his Society . . . he knew no other God.

From the moment this man became the spiritual guide of France's ruler, the fate of Port-Royal was sealed. The community of the Fields was lost, and even the stones of the monastery were condemned.

Louis XIV had always been hostile to Jansenism. He held it "in abomination," as told by his contemporaries. This hatred was now to be freely displayed.

For a long time the monarch had been dominated by appetites which his temperament made it impossible for him to control. Louise de La Vallière, the delicate blond who was hopelessly in love, had held the young sovereign in the bonds of an amiable passion. But the year 1667 saw the triumph of the robust charms of La Montespan, who later became, in Lauzun's words, "a fat tripe-seller." Louis XIV addressed himself to this banquet of flesh with the solid appetite of the Bourbons. Aphrodisiacs lavishly supplied by the favorite added further to the king's ardor, to the point of affecting his health; at such times he suffered passing moments of remorse.

Father Annat had earlier tried to separate Louis XIV from Louise de La Vallière, telling him that habitual sin led to hell. A satirical verse tells how the royal penitent satisfied his confessor:

> For fear of displeasing him
> I am changing La Vallière
> For La Montespan.

Louis XIV nevertheless compelled his former mistress to remain with him; she had to make others believe she was still the favorite so as to cover up a double adultery which Madame de Montespan's husband threatened to denounce to the Roman Curia. The duchesse de La Vallière lived with her rival and at times waited on her as a maid, helping her prepare for the master's bed; she did not even reply to the sarcastic remarks thrown at her.

When the king joined his armies, followed by his court, the intendants had to place three rooms at his disposal. Two of these were reserved for the mistresses, while the humble Maria Theresa remained at the Louvre awaiting the warrior's return.

Despite the fact he partook with gusto of the forbidden fruit, Louis XIV remained attached to the Church, regarding it as his insurance against hell. The God of Saint-Cyran and Pascal had never been revealed to the king, who knew only the God of Ignatius of Loyola. As a descendant of David's sacred race, he thought Christ should watch over the thrones of the sovereigns who were his vassals. "God is infinitely jealous of his glory," wrote Louis XIV. "Perhaps he has exalted us to such heights so that he may be all the more honored by our homage."

How could the king have had any doubt about his rank in the hierarchy that went from earth to heaven? "We are told," wrote Madame de Sévigné, "that the Minims have dedicated a thesis to the king in which they compare him to God, but in such a way that God can be seen as only a copy."

The Messieurs of Port-Royal refused to take part in a cult of this kind because the Gospel does not permit a man to serve two masters. Louis XIV never forgave them for the choice they made.

At this period the king had been delivered from sins of the flesh by Madame de Maintenon. On Esther's advice, Ahasuerus had driven out the haughty Vashti, and had even bestowed his good graces on the queen. Maria Theresa died shortly afterward, filled with gratitude and "in a state of perfect felicity." Thus liberated, the king discreetly married his Minerva, and finally could live in peace with his senses and with God. This is the explanation of the constant favor accorded the only woman Louis XIV could approach without danger.

Madame de Maintenon was not of a very sensual nature, and had to force herself to satisfy the king. "What grace," her confessor wrote on this subject, "to do through virtue what so many others do out of passion!"

She who was called by the Bishop of Chartres "the strong woman of Scripture," and by Fénelon "God's sentinel," regarded her conjugal duties as a means of accomplishing the will of the Almighty. "May I serve for the king's salvation," she wrote. "May I be saved with him!" On the advice of the priests around her, Madame de Maintenon, after escaping the snares of Jansenism and Quietism, influenced Louis XIV to oppose "novelties" of every kind in the name of the Church. She must "beseige" the king to this end, Fénelon told the directress of Saint-Cyr at the time he was her confidant.

Over a period of several years cleverly chosen passages from the papers of Quesnel were read, reread, and commented upon—in Madame de Maintenon's room, in the presence of the king—by the king's confessor, Father de La Chaise, in order to convince the sovereign of the danger presented by "the Jansenist sect." Louis XIV, who had combatted Port-Royal with some embarrassment during his life of sin, could now begin a fierce onslaught against the new Jerusalem with the good conscience of a Christian protecting the Church and a king defending his state.

When, in 1685, Madame de Maintenon obtained the revocation of the Edict of Nantes, she wrote: "The king is beginning to think seriously of his salvation. If God preserves him, there will be only one religion in his realm." And she added: "We are very pleased with Father de La Chaise; he inspires the king to great things. Soon all his subjects will serve God in spirit and in truth." Saint-Simon recounts the same event in a different vein. "After the revocation of the Edict of Nantes," he said, "the king never again believed he was so great in the eyes of men, nor that he had advanced so far in making reparation for his sins and the scandal of his life . . . he always pampered himself by making someone else expiate his misdeeds, and especially the Huguenots and the Jansenists.

In fact, Louis XIV considered the persecution he waged against the latter as the crown of his work. In his *Memoirs,* written for the instruction of the dauphin, Louis XIV speaks "of the long disputes on grace, knowledge of which is not necessary to anyone for salvation." These debates had provoked hostilities, the king went on, which, heightened by "zeal and stubbornness," had almost caused a schism. The sovereign told the dauphin of the danger he had combatted: "It was not only a question of certain theologians but of bishops established in their sees and capable of dragging the multitude along with them."

Events followed one another in quick succession. The peace of the Church had been granted at a time when the French armies were victorious and prosperity extended to the provinces, but evil days had come: defeat on the frontiers, famine throughout the kingdom. The king felt his strength was declining and that his death was not far off. Before he went, he wanted to destroy the living symbol of spiritual resistance—Port-Royal of the Fields—and each day Father Tellier urged him to carry out this duty.

Again Cardinal de Noailles was placed in a situation where he had to act. His nephew did not hide from him the increasing irritation of the king, who more and more suspected him of being a Jansenist. The prelate protested against these threats, saying he had never belonged to the group and had been raised "at a great distance from its doctrine."

He had expected, he wrote his nephew, to suppress the monastery within three months, but the pope had not sent him the bulls necessary for taking action. Was it his fault? If he had not yet "given the finishing touch," at least he could boast of having taken severe measures, for "he knew his business."

Hoping to redeem himself in the eyes of the king, the cardinal added:

"I have done everything that Monseigneur de Péréfixe, rightly incensed at this community, did against it. And people find this is not enough!" He said further: "I have excommunicated them and done more than any of my predecessors against this monastery. I could even suppress it entirely—which I will do as soon as my hands are free—but all this does not prevent people from saying over and over again that I show favor to these women."

Since Noailles could not suppress the monastery without the pope's authorization, the king turned to Rome. His representative, Cardinal de La Trémouille, brought pressure to bear on the pontiff, Clement IX, to obtain a bull declaring the suppression of Port-Royal of the Fields.

A French professor at the Sapienza in Rome, Maille, undertook to defend the monastery, but emissaries of Father Tellier had him arrested. He was imprisoned in the Castel Sant'Angelo and was released later only at the instance of one of his former pupils, Pope Benedict XIV.

After a vain attempt to resist, Clement XI signed the bull "at the request of the king," on March 27, 1708. The pontiff sadly declared that Louis XIV had brought such pressure to bear that "he could not refuse the solicitations of so great a prince."

The bull ordered the suppression of the Abbey of the Fields which, since it numbered only a few aged religious, "had no hope of reestablishing itself." Its possessions were to be turned over to Port-Royal of Paris. However, this suppression should not be declared until after the nuns in the valley had died; so long as they lived they should have disposition of the convent buildings, the church, and the furnishings. Each was, moreover, to receive a modest pension from the Paris monastery—two hundred livres a month.

In May 1708, the nuncio received the bull and took it to the king. Louis XIV was greatly disappointed, declaring that "if he accepted this brief he would not have the pleasure of seeing Port-Royal destroyed during his lifetime." The sovereign therefore requested a more decisive document from the pope.

Again Clement XI waited for several months—Louis XIV was seventy years of age, and if he died his successor might prove more conciliatory. Finally, under pressure from Cardinal de la Trémouille and with his states threatened by German troops against which France constituted his sole protection, the pope signed a new bull completely in keeping with the desires of Louis XIV and Father Tellier. The religious of the Fields were declared guilty "of obstinacy and stubborn efforts to foment the Jansenian heresy"; their community was suppressed and no delay was granted. The text of the pontifical decision was obviously inspired down to its last detail by the envoys of the king: "In order for this suppression to be more promptly effected and for the nest where error has flourished so perniciously to be entirely destroyed," ran the bull addressed to the Archbishop of Paris, the nuns "should be transported together or separately, in the time, manner, and form you consider proper, to other religious houses of your choosing."

Louis XIV and his confessor were satisfied at last. Monseigneur de Noailles now had "a free hand." Armed by Chancellor Pontchartrain with letters patent, the bull was registered in parlement to be acted upon at the requisition of Procurator-General Daguesseau.

Although Port-Royal's cause was lost, its defenders again tried to intervene; some among them were even in the immediate entourage of Monseigneur de Noailles. The promoter appointed by the cardinal to examine the bull was not afraid to write: "The Pope, the King, and His Eminence will have to render account before God's judgment of their reasons for destroying this house."

The abbey's lawyers unsuccessfully multiplied petitions and memoranda against the bull because the pope had pronounced judgment without hearing their case. Again on this occasion Port-Royal's friends acted with extraordinary clumsiness, deeming it opportune to send the archbishop anonymous letters recalling Monseigneur de Péréfixe's last hours, the terrifying death of Monseigneur de Harlay, and, finally, the death of the cardinal's own brother, Maréchal de Noailles, who died without being able to receive the sacraments. These letters told the prelate "he would be cast into the burning pool of fire and sulphur which is the second death."

The author of these naive letters appears to have been Mabille, the doctor of theology who had persuaded the nuns to insert into their declaration of obedience the fatal reservation: "Without derogating from what had taken place . . ." Such a defender was more dangerous than many enemies. His threats angered Monseigneur de Noailles and convinced him that "the sect" was dangerous.

The cardinal ordered an inquiry *de commodo vel incommodo,* regarding the suppression of the house of the Fields. The commissioner charged with the inquiry questioned the peasants whose lands adjoined the monastery; they declared they knew nothing of *commodo* and *incommodo,* but testified that the charity of the nuns had been extended to every poor person in the region.

Finally, on July 11, 1709, Monseigneur de Noailles published the decree putting an end to the existence of the Monastery of Port-Royal of the Fields:

> . . . Taking everything into consideration and invoking the Holy Name of God, We, Archbishop of Paris, with our authority both as ordinary and that of the Holy and Apostolic Sovereign Pontiff, suppress

and extinguish by the present act and in perpetuity the title of the Abbey of Port-Royal of the Fields. In consequence, We join all the possessions, furnishings, and property of this abbey to the monastery of Port-Royal of Paris.

Thus did the ancient monastery vanish forever from the eyes of the Church.

Going to the faubourg Saint-Jacques, Cardinal de Noailles read his decree to the Paris nuns; however, he told them that he hoped their future conduct would be as commendable as that of their sisters of the Fields.

Still without an abbess, the condemned monastery had a prioress capable of facing misfortune. In the midst of all this turmoil, Mother du Mesnil kept her serenity. "I pity the prelate," she wrote Mademoiselle de Joncoux, and added this great truth: "How blessed we are to be of little consquence in the eyes of the world; it makes it impossible for us to oppress anyone."

Gathered around the prioress, the nuns, old and sick, could not hide their anxiety concerning the future. "Love of the roof-tree," Mother du Mesnil wrote with melancholy, "is very strong in the spirit of certain of them." For some, the Monastery of the Fields had never meant more than a house built of stone, yet the prioress gave this assurance in the name of all her sisters: "We will do our duty until our last breath."

Thinking of her enemies, today victorious, she made a remark worthy of Saint-Cyran: "Those who make us suffer are more to be pitied than we are."

With much the same thought as Angélique de Saint-Jean in earlier years, the prioress expressed surprise that so great a monarch as Louis XIV, who could hold all Europe at bay, would be so obstinately bent on the destruction of a monastery. With discreet malice like that of the dead abbess, Mother du Mesnil wrote: "The great affairs of the king do not keep him busy enough to make him forget us. We do not forget him either, and pray personally for one who has such need of it."

But what did the world matter? "For myself, I leave everything to God," the prioress ended.

Thus, beyond the contrivances of lawyers, the subtlety of theologians, and the ruses of the Jesuits, the voices of the daughters of Port-Royal as they echo the Gospels are heard.

The Abbess of Port-Royal of Paris, Madame de Château-Renaud, was given full powers over the house of the Fields, which henceforth would be under her jurisdiction. She arrived in the valley on October 1, 1709, accompanied by two notaries, and presented herself in the parlor. Mother du Mesnil received her there and raised her veil; for a moment the two nuns looked at one another, both much moved. However, Madame de Château-Renaud steadied her voice to read a letter from the archbishop which ordered the daughters of Port-Royal of the Fields to receive her as their abbess. To this the prioress replied that an appeal had been made to the Primate of Lyons, whereupon Madame de Château-Renaud invoked a decree of Parlement. Mother du Mesnil observed that this decision had been rendered in default and that her community had brought an injunction against it.

Mother du Mesnil further said that her community had never obeyed anyone other than a superior it had itself elected, and she would not have made her profession at Port-Royal had things been otherwise. Here the prioress put her hand on a sore spot: this community which freely chose its abbess constituted in the heart of the kingdom a sort of republic where equality was held in as high respect as among the solitaries—this had been the desire of the Arnaulds. It was precisely this spirit of independence that Louis XIV wanted to eradicate. Without success the sovereign had asked the pope many years earlier for authorization to appoint the Abbess of Port-Royal of the Fields. It was the only means, he wrote the Holy Father, "to cut off the head of a hydra which had grown too large over a period of thirty years."

To return to Madame de Château-Renaud: the notaries accompanying her reminded the prioress that the Paris abbess had the power to "break down the doors" and enter the monastery by force. But these were no longer the times of the turbulent Angélique d'Estrées—it was the century of Racine. Madame de Château-Renaud spoke calmly, saying she did not want to go to extremes and preferred to have recourse "to other ways, just as certain."

The abbess went to the monastery church where she placed her hand, as was the custom, on the abbatial chair to signify that she took possession, and she had the bell rung. The people in her suite believed they, too, should ring it loudly, and continued to do so until the convent servants cut the rope.

Madame de Château-Renaud then went up to Les Granges, now abandoned by the solitaries, to have her mid-day meal. At the beginning of the afternoon the notaries brought Mother du Mesnil a copy of the minutes they had taken. It contained mention of the opposition the prioress had registered that morning and to which her sisters had subscribed during the day—regular procedure, so dear to the *Grand Siècle*, was followed even at the most tragic moments.

Madame de Château-Renaud went to spend the night at the house of Saint-Cyr, close by, and was received by Madame de Maintenon, who questioned her closely. Had the abbess felt in the church of the Fields "that holy chrism it is said to possess?" The nun answered she had this feeling only at Saint-Cyr, when she saw "the modesty, the silence, and recollection of so many young persons assembled in one place." Madame de Château-

Renaud expressed her admiration at the order reigning at Saint-Cyr, and said she was still convinced that "she who had begun a work so successful was one of those geniuses who rarely appear in a century."

Maréchal de Château-Renaud's niece had breathed the air of Versailles and knew that in addressing the new Esther it was possible to get quite far with flattery.

As the fate of Port-Royal of the Fields was being accomplished, its prioress mastered her fears. "Although I love repose, I do not want it to be false," she wrote. "I therefore follow the advice I have been given, hoping God will bear me up."

On her return to Paris, Madame de Château-Renaud sent a petition to the king: since Mother du Mesnil refused to recognize her authority as abbess, she requested Louis XIV to give an order for the two houses to be joined into one.

On October 8, 1709, a decree of the Council of State ordered the religious of the Fields to receive Madame de Château-Renaud as their abbess; the doors of the monastery must be opened to her, the keys handed over, and her orders obeyed.

This time the prioress and the nuns made no opposition; they intended to obey without listening further to the lawyers who still wanted to involve them in useless suits. Madame de Château-Renaud would be their superior, and the poor women asked only to be allowed to subsist in the valley until the end if they could be allowed not to deny their faith.

Father Tellier was not at all satisfied with such an arrangement; he said "piously" to the king that Madame de Château-Renaud did not dare go to Port-Royal of the Fields because she was "persuaded that those stubborn, disobedient, rebellious women would only sneer at the decree of the royal Council." The Jesuit asked his all-powerful penitent for "precise orders" to disperse the nuns; without such orders, he said, "one could never have done with them."

His words were an appeal to Louis XIV's pride. After the Messieurs, it was the nuns who wanted to go against him. He must put an end to it. A second decree of the Council, signed by the king on October 26th, ordered the lieutenant general of police, the marquis d'Argenson, to remove all the religious and disperse them in various convents.

On October 29th, when the nuns returned from the church, where they had gone during the night to sing matins, they found the lights of the dormitory had gone out—something that had never happened since the foundation of the monastery. Many of them saw this darkness as a portent.

That same day, after prime, a peasant rushed in to warn the prioress that carriages had just entered the valley and were headed toward the monastery. Shortly thereafter, the police lieutenant appeared; surrounded by men-at-arms, he had come to carry out the decree.

The king's men had arrived in the Chevreuse Valley the previous day, October 28th. But a violent storm had delayed them and their carriages had been hidden, under various pretexts, behind the walls of neighboring villages. The archers had passed the night in the shelter of trees in the woodland surrounding the abbey, where they had lighted great bonfires.

At dawn the carriage of Police Lieutenant d'Argenson, accompanied by a commissary and two mounted policemen, entered the monastery courtyard. In the parlor the prioress received the magistrate, who ordered all doors opened, took the keys, and handed them over to his police. Under Mother du Mesnil's eyes cupboards and coffers were opened, and all papers and documents of value seized.

Despite all this, their religious offices had to go on according to the Rule, and the prioress went to rejoin her sisters and lead them to the church. At that moment, despite the law of silence, she felt she must answer the mute questions in the eyes of her religious.

"It is just another visit," she told them with her customary affability. "I do not know what its consequences will be. We must always put ourselves into the arms of God who knows our needs better than we do. Let us go in to tierce."

Again a silence fell, to be broken in the church by the chanting of the Psalm: *"Ad te, Domine, levavi."* Never before had their hearts been lifted so high as on this day when by one instinct their voices rose to add the *Veni Creator* to the office of tierce.

When the singing stopped the prioress went to find D'Argenson, who ordered her to assemble the community in the chapter hall. The bells were rung and the religious came in to take their places. The prioress, who knew she had been dispossessed, gave her customary seat to the police lieutenant, flanked by the commissary and his police.

"Are all the religious here?" asked D'Argenson.

"There is still one other," replied Mother du Mesnil. "But she is very old and sick, and is paralyzed."

"If she can't come, let her be brought in," said the police lieutenant. "It is necessary for her to be present."

The nuns then went to get Sister Robert, the sister of a counselor of the High Chamber of Parlement, and brought in the eighty-six-year-old woman on a stretcher.

"Where are the lay sisters?" asked D'Argenson.

"It is not customary," the prioress said, "for them to attend chapter."

"They must be here, for they, too, have a part in this affair."

The seven lay sisters arrived, and joined the fifteen choir religious.

D'Argenson had the door of the chapter hall closed and placed two police before it.

Then he declared, "Mesdames, I have come to tell you of the sacrifice you must make today. Although I am grieved to be the bearer of the king's orders, they nevertheless must be carried out. You are to leave this assembly and never to see one another again. I am announcing your general dispersion, commanded by His Majesty. You have only three hours to get yourselves ready."

This was a far cry from the day when Archbishop de Péréfixe came in person to designate the exiled religious and Arnauld d'Andilly ceremoniously led them to their carriages. Today the weight of years had fallen on the condemned community, and it was a man of the police who was to conduct the aging women into exile. No longer was persecution hailed with heroic words—instead there fell a dreary silence.

It was broken by Mother du Mesnil: "Monseigneur, we are ready to obey."

The three-hour delay granted the nuns was more than enough.

"What you have to do, do quickly," Jesus had said to Judas.

"A half-hour is more than enough for us to say our last farewells," the prioress told the police lieutenant.

D'Argenson was touched by this unexpected submissiveness. Saint-Simon says of him "he was always inclined toward the milder course of action, and humanity easily found favor in his eyes." The magistrate was thinking of the future, with which none of the exiled women were concerned at that time.

"Mesdames, my orders designate different houses. I can fill the places as I deem proper. See between yourselves what you consider most suitable. Madame Prioress, where do you want to go?"

"Sir," she replied, "it is indifferent to me. I hope to find God in any place I may be."

For Mother du Mesnil, the world was powerless; but she must think of her sisters who were old and sick and who would be sorely tried by removal to another place.

"It seems to me," she added, "it would be better for those who are sick to go to houses closest to us so they will be less inconvenienced by the journey."

Following her advice, D'Argenson drew up and read to them the *lettres de cachet* dispersing the nuns to many divers convents: at Rouen, Autun, Chartres, Compiegne, Meaux, Nevers, Nantes.

As it was already past noon, the police lieutenant gave the nuns permission to have a collation served them in the chapter hall while he was drawing up his report. Displeased at not having been able to prepare the meal as usual, one of the lay sisters exclaimed: "How can you expect us, Monsieur, to prepare dinner for our Mothers when you keep us here."

The prioress looked at the impertinent nun with sadness, and, completely shamed, the lay sister bowed her head and went to kneel before D'Argenson to ask pardon. The chief of police was surprised and embarrassed; he turned to his papers and began the execution of the king's orders. Then, according to an account of the affair, the religious, who were like "a little flock without a shepherd," said to one another: "Farewell until Eternity," and asked pardon for anything they had done to hurt the other in times past. Marquis d'Argenson could not hide his emotion as he looked on this final scene of what had been a great dream.

Nevertheless three hundred archers, armed as for the seige of a fortress, filed into the abbey courtyard. This deployment of force allows one to imagine under what colors the Monastery of the Fields had been painted to Louis XIV by Father Tellier.

The arm of one of the nuns was bleeding, and she asked Mother du Mesnil's permission to go to the infirmary.

"Sister," the prioress replied, "the community is disbanded; I no longer have authority. You must address yourself to Monsieur d'Argenson who has his authority from the king."

The police lieutenant granted the requested permission, but asked the nun to return as soon as her arm had been bandaged. The religious were given permission to go two by two to take some food and to find their belongings. Some did so, but most of them remained prostrate in the chapter hall.

Soon afterward, the whole community reassembled and went in procession to the door of the cloister. Before getting into the twelve carriages which were to carry them to various convents, the religious went into their church to pray before the Blessed Sacrament, and then gathered around Mother du Mesnil to have her blessing. As she gave it, the prioress asked her sisters to remain faithful to their rule, to their consciences, and to rise above misfortunes. She tried to remain firm and calm, knowing that if she betrayed her true feelings she would weaken her companions at a time they needed all their strength. What no one could prevent were the demonstrations of the peasants and poor people who wept as they saw their protectresses depart. The nuns separated after vowing to remain together in thought and "to find Port-Royal everywhere."

Their departure was so precipitate that one of the nuns was forgotten—

Sister Robert, paralyzed and lying motionless on her stretcher. When one of the servants went up to her to commiserate, the religious replied: "Today is the day of man. The day of God will come in its turn."

These were the last words spoken by a nun at Port-Royal of the Fields. The following day, at six in the morning, Sister Robert was put on a litter and carried to Nantes.

Placed in solitary confinement, and deprived of the sacraments, almost all the exiles later agreed, one by one, to sign the formulary; but certain of them were overcome by remorse and later retracted. Sister Boiscervoise, an octogenarian, had just enough time to sign, for she was exhausted by her journey and died of pneumonia five days after she reached the convent of the Franciscan Sisters in Amiens.

The lay sisters, who because of their status had not been required to sign earlier, were thenceforth subjected to this demand. Coming out of their kitchens, they had to condemn the five propositions and declare they were contained in Jansenius' Latin text! Blessed are the humble—one of the lay sisters could sign only with a cross, for she did not know how to write.

The prioress herself never submitted, despite the exhortations and threats heaped upon her during her six years of captivity in the Ursuline convent at Blois. In vain did Monseigneur de Noailles announce to her that her sisters had successively signed. "This news," said the nun, "can cause me grief, but it does not shake me because such examples do not destroy the principles that make me act."

Alone with the prioress, one other nun resisted to the end. Her name was Madeleine du Valois. Drawn toward the religious life by Angélique de Saint-Jean, she remained always faithful to the latter's memory.

The conveyances carrying the nuns into exile under the archers' guard rolled through the streets of Versailles. The spectacle impressed many people, even at the court, where the wealth and noise of the château was contrasted to the poverty and silence of the monastery.

Fénelon, an avowed enemy of Jansenism, expressed the general feeling when he wrote the duc de Chevreuse: "Such a blow from authority as the one just given by Versailles cannot fail to excite public compassion for these women and indignation against their persecutors."

The day after the nuns were taken away, a priest, Abbot Madot, was sent by Father Tellier to the valley to examine the books, manuscripts, and pictures. Even a few pious maxims the nuns had copied and placed in their missals were scrutinized in case they contained heresy. The envoy of the royal confessor tore up pictures of Saint-Cyran and Antoine Arnauld so that the memory of those men might be erased forever.

However, Abbot Madot could find nothing that could provide Father

Tellier with a weapon against the Messieurs. "They are cleverer than we," the priest muttered spitefully.

After his departure D'Argenson, who had remained in the monastery with the garrison, took it upon himself to gather up the manuscripts and turn them over to Mademoiselle Joncoux, since he was aware of her devotion to Port-Royal. Most of the manuscripts which survive today were saved in this manner. According to the royal orders these archives should have been turned over to Monseigneur de Noailles, but the police lieutenant gave the cardinal only printed matter and leaflets of no interest. The objects that filled the monastery were collected in a hall, and many were stolen by the archers and by vagabonds.

The garrison occupied not only the abbey but the hills above, and all means of access were guarded by soldiers. D'Argenson had been ordered to take every measure to prevent the peasants from assembling around the abandoned convent.

The Abbess of Port-Royal of Paris, Madame de Château-Renaud, returned to the Fields on November 27, 1709, this time as its sovereign ruler. Everything that had been seized—outside books and papers—became her property. Derisory booty! The paltry, worthless objects were highly encumbering; a hundred and fifty wagons were needed to haul away the accumulation of five centuries.

Madame de Château-Renaud did not long enjoy the revenues of the Monastery of the Fields, which were joined to those of her own abbey. Less than a year after her victory, on August 25, 1710, she died suddenly.

After the departure of the garrison, the buildings of the Abbey of the Fields remained empty and deserted. Yet for the Jansenists its walls were the image of Zion—like the ruins of Jerusalem, the monastery was God's abode.

Monseigneur de Noailles had thought of transferring the Paris religious to the Fields, but they refused to go to "that desert." After several days spent in packing the furniture, Madame de Château-Renaud had returned to Paris with a swelling of the legs which she attributed to the valley's unhealthy climate—nothing could induce her to leave the faubourg Saint-Jacques.

Shortly after this it was rumored that the Jesuits wanted to buy the buildings of Port-Royal of Paris for the purpose of starting a seminary; it could have been they who asked Monseigneur de Noailles to send the Paris religious to the Fields so he might dispose of the monastery of faubourg Saint-Jacques.

The Jansenists were perturbed, for they wanted the Abbey of the Fields to remain empty, in the hope that when times were better the dispersed community could return. Certain of them believed it opportune to disclose

the Jesuit project to the priests of Saint Sulpice. The latter were opposed
to the foundation by the Society of Jesus of a seminary similar to their own
and its installation in the buildings of Port-Royal of Paris. The Sulpicians
were very powerful at that time, for Madame de Maintenon had placed her
spiritual guidance in the hands of the pastor of their parish. Was it at their
request, transmitted through his wife, that Louis XIV decided to keep the
Paris nuns at the faubourg Saint-Jacques, and to destroy the Monastery of
the Fields, which had become useless? Happily, this conjecture can be dispelled, for it would be sad to think that the abbey's demolition was due to
a supreme stroke of clumsiness on the part of its defenders. Moreover, no
intervention was needed to persuade Louis XIV to wipe out the memory of
this great spiritual enterprise. The king intended to destroy everything that
could serve as a rallying point "for the sect of the Jansenists." After the
dispersal of the religious, engravings of the cloister, of the church, the chapter
house, the infirmary, and the refectory were seized by the police at the
king's orders, and the plates used in making them were destroyed.

A decree of the Council of State, under date of January 22, 1710, ordered
the demolition of the Abbey of the Fields with the exception of the church.
According to the reasons given for the decree, the upkeep of the abandoned
buildings had become an unnecessary expense.

On February 8, 1710, D'Argenson signed an order putting up for auction
the materials remaining after the demolition. The houses of the duchesse de
Longueville and of Mademoiselle de Vertus and the guest-house were torn
down in succession, and finally the monastery itself.

Since it was no longer used for worship the church became a shelter for
vagabonds, and it also was ordered to be torn down. However, many dead
persons lay buried beneath its stones; even more in the nuns' cemetery in the
enclosure surrounded by the cloister, and also outside the walls where most
of the solitaries had been interred. In five centuries more than three thousand
bodies had been buried there—all were to be driven from their last resting
place.

Monsieur de Pomponne, the son of the minister, was the first to be
alarmed when he learned that the bodies of the members of his family, the
Arnaulds, were to be exhumed and their ashes cast into a common grave.
As early as August, 1710, the marquis asked Louis XIV for permission to
remove his dead. Posterity should not be reminded, he wrote the king, "that
these bodies were buried in a place which had the misfortune to come under
His Majesty's displeasure."

What would the great Arnauld have said about such repudiation? But
at least the ashes of those dear to him could be transported to the church
of Palaiseau at this price.

The relatives of other dead persons in their turn sent petitions to the king, asking to obtain bodies and sometimes relics. At a time when medieval simplicity still prevailed, certain of those who loved Port-Royal had requested that after they died their hearts be allowed to remain in the monastery. Antoine Arnauld's heart had been returned in this way to his native land, and, thanks to the marquis de Pomponne, his heart and that of Angélique Arnauld were saved. Racine's remains rejoined those of Pascal in the Church of Saint-Etienne-du-Mont in Paris; the hearts of Madame de Longueville and of her son were transported to Saint-Jacques-du-Haut-Pas. The Abbess of Malnoue obtained the remains of her sister, Mademoiselle de Vertus.

Indeed, the time had come for the living to shelter their dead, for in 1711 the king ordered the exhumation of the corpses that remained in the valley. Drunken grave-diggers mutilated them as, roaring with laughter, they piled them on the pavement of the church; at night dogs came and fed on them. Beneath the trees of the cemetery where Racine had been given a sepulchre, Athaliah's dream became a reality:

> I found only a horrible heap of bones
> And mangled flesh, and tatters steeped in blood
> Dragged through the mire, and limbs unspeakable
> For which voracious dogs were wrangling there.

Among the profaned bodies were those of Jacqueline Pascal, of Monsieur Hamon, and of Monsieur de Sévigné. Heaped into tumbrils, they were taken for burial to a ditch dug in the middle of the cemetery of a nearby village—Saint-Lambert. Tavernkeepers in the neighborhood used the tombstones beneath which the nuns and solitaries had slept as tables for drinkers.

Thus arrived the "day of man." Less than a century later the future caught up with His Christian Majesty, and his remains and those of his family were taken by revolutionaries from the Basilica of Saint-Denis and thrown into a common grave with the same macabre cynicism. All that was accomplished reveals the greatness of Holy Writ.

These lines, inspired by hatred of Port-Royal, were written by Joseph de Maistre, the admirer of absolute power: "Louis XIV, by having wheat planted on land which had produced nothing but bad books, was acting as a wise husbandman."

Just as the great king was bringing his work to an end a famous witness, the duc de Saint-Simon, decided to include in his *Memoirs* a brief outline of the history of Port-Royal up to the day of its destruction. Even Racine in his *Abridged History* did not attain to the forcefulness of these pages.

Saint-Simon told of Saint Augustine's proclamation of the sovereign power of grace, of its defense by Saint Thomas, of its recognition by the Councils of the Church. He showed the Jesuits casting a veil over this dogma which impeded their conquest of minds, and seeking refuge in the ancient heresy of the Pelagian monks.

In a few words the duke described the nature of the power wielded by the Society of Jesus: the fathers were "masters, through the confessional, of almost all kings," and "of almost all the public through the education of youth, and through their talents and artfulness." Moreover, they made themselves "agreeable through permissive devices which had never before been used in the tribunal of penance."

Saint-Simon rendered justice to these religious men who, devoured by ambition for their Society, personally led hard lives, devoted to study and combat. But this self-abnegation made their policies all the more formidable. These policies were "the most refined and went the deepest, rising high above every consideration other than their determination to dominate." Saint-Simon expressed admiration for "the authority, the procedure, the elasticity, the secrecy, the uniformity of opinion, and the multiplicity of means employed" by the Society.

Nevertheless, he went on to say, when the Jesuits wished to deviate from the Gospel, the Church of France had risen up against "those agreeable novelties which had made so many conquests." The successors of Molina had then invented a heresy—Jansenism—to combat the Christians who defended their faith.

Saint-Simon told of the manner in which the king's confessor, Father Tellier, had caused the nuns of the Fields to be torn from their convent "like trollops from a house of sin." His lines expressed the unanimous feeling of all honest men.

The last act in the tragedy of Port-Royal had come to an end. The drama that had begun on the Day of the Grating, September 25, 1609, ended on October 29, 1709, when the last nuns were removed from the valley. A hundred years had gone by between these two dates—the century of Port-Royal. Louis XIV believed he had triumphed, and the Society of Jesus which had inspired his victory was about to win another. The bull *Unigenitus,* signed on September 8, 1713, condemned as tainted with heresy a hundred propositions extracted from *Moral Reflections on the New Testament.* This book by Father Quesnel, Antoine Arnauld's successor, defended the dogma of grace. The Oratorian was described in the bull as "a ravening wolf, a false prophet, a master of lies, a cheat, a hypocrite, a poisoner of souls."

Cardinal de Noailles had given high approval to Quesnel's book, and could not obey the pope without reversing himself. Since he refused to do this, he had the sorrow of seeing himself condemned by Rome.

"Monseigneur," Mademoiselle de Joncoux said to him, "the stones of Port-Royal are falling on your head."

Louis XIV was highly irritated when he learned Monseigneur de Noailles had not submitted; he forbade him access to Versailles and demanded that Parlement register the bull *Unigenitus*. The magistrates, who supported the morality of Port-Royal and were inimical to the Jesuits, were at heart on the side of the Jansenists, and, moreover, wanted to defend the liberty of the Gallican Church against the authority of a pope upheld by the Society of Jesus.

The procurator-general, Daguesseau, received the king's order to register the bull. The jurist was indignant at the pontifical decision which, he said, "rejected the necessity of grace, erased the Gospels, and overthrew religion."

Daguesseau was one of the "king's men" who had a seat in the well of the court at the foot of the dais reserved for the judges; as he represented the interests of the sovereign, he did not have the independence of the presidents and counselors of Parlement. Moreover, the procurator-general had a large family which could be ruined were he to resist. He therefore hesitated to oppose the king.

"Go, Monsieur," his wife said to him. "Act as though you had neither wife nor family. I would prefer to see you led to the Bastille with honor than to witness your dishonor here."

In that century, as in many others, women surpassed their men in courage when the moment came to act. Daguesseau made his decision, and presented himself before Louis XIV in the company of the first president. The two magistrates announced to the king that they opposed the registration of the pontifical decision and of the royal declaration enjoining the bishops to submit.

The sovereign broke into a rage. These "gentlemen of the robe" had seized the sword of justice which had been surrendered through the weakness of their ancestors. Louis XIV confronted them with the rudeness of his own forebears.

"Be careful," he said. "I have my foot raised, and if you make a move I will walk on your stomachs. It's not far from my office to the Bastille."

The magistrates did not flinch at the sovereign's threat. Formerly, at the height of his fame, the monarch would have dealt with them severely, but he could do so no longer. Weakened and close to death, Louis had lost much of his authority; the most glorious of reigns had reached its twilight hour. France was opposed by all Europe, where there was much agitation since the sovereign had secured the Spanish throne for his grandson. Although the great king had triumphed over a few nuns, he had met with less success on the field of battle. Already, in 1706, the maréchal de Villeroi had suffered a harsh defeat at Ramillies. Louis XIV had received the beaten old soldier with melancholy. "Monsieur le Maréchal," he said, "one is no longer lucky at our age."

In 1708, the French armies were beaten at Oudenarde and, far more cruelly, the following year at Malplaquet. The ruler of France was placed in a shameful position and had to sue for peace. When his enemies demanded that he remove his grandson from the Spanish throne, Louis XIV sadly replied: "Since we must continue the war, it is better to do so against our enemies than against our children."

The situation of the French armies was so grave that the sovereign envisioned a time when he would die at the head of his soldiers under the Empire's fire. The kingdom was saved by Vendôme, and especially by the maréchal de Villars. The country, however, was exhausted, and in the provinces the misery had become so great that there were rumblings of revolt. During the terrible winter of 1709, soldiers had to disperse a parade of marketwomen from Les Halles who marched on Versailles demanding bread.

At such a time the arrest of the first president and of the procurator-general could have brought about a violent upheaval in Parlement, and might lead to a new Fronde. Louis XIV no longer had sufficient power to run this risk.

"These people are going to kill me," he muttered after his interview with the magistrates.

Even so, Father Tellier exhorted his penitent to continue the struggle to the end. He was so insistent that on two occasions indignant servants forbade him access to the bedchamber where the king lay ill with the malady that would cause his death.

Louis XIV thought that he had destroyed Jansenism forever by removing the nuns from the valley and selling the stones of their monastery. On the contrary, he had created what he had always feared—a party which was to constitute a mortal threat to royalty.

The solitaries and the nuns had struggled to defend their faith in the spiritual domain, but they had been loyal subjects. Arnauld considered the King of France the Lord's anointed. But now that Port-Royal no longer existed, Parlement entered the fight at the side of the Archbishop of Paris. The magistrates did not limit themselves to defending evangelical morality. As the enemies of absolute power, they used Jansenism as a banner which was rendered the more formidable because it could rally around it the multitude of honest people.

In 1715, Louis XIV was afflicted with gangrene and lost all hope of being cured. Cardinal de Noailles wrote him expressing his sorrow at being kept apart from his sovereign at such a time. He accused the king's confessor and other Jesuits of having "in their house an open shop for simony." Louis XIV replied that "his greatest desire would be to die in his arms," but that he could not do so because the prelate obstinately refused to accept the bull *Unigenitus*. So the sovereign prepared to enter eternity attended by Father Tellier, whom he obeyed by preventing the Archbishop of Paris from coming to his bedside.

Earlier, when within a matter of several days Louis XIV had lost his grandson, the latter's wife, and one of their children, he had said: "God is punishing me."

Now he felt his power waning, and was heard to murmur: "When I was king . . ."

Before he appeared in the presence of his Judge, the monarch took a measure of precaution. He had all the churchmen who had guided him come into his bedchamber and there he threw upon their shoulders the responsibility for his actions in religious matters during the last years of his reign. Had he not acted according to their advice? Therefore, he said, if he had acted wrongly, it was on their consciences and they would have to answer for it before God. Strangled with fear of the Beyond, the dying Caesar uttered words worthy of Pilate.

When Massillon delivered the monarch's funeral oration, he pointed to the escutcheons carrying the letters L L G—*Louis le Grand*. Then turning to the congregation the preacher exclaimed: "God alone is great!"

6

THE HIGH WALLS FALL

The century of Port-Royal had come to a close, but the fates hovered over the powers that had destroyed the new Jerusalem: the Archbishop of Paris, royalty, and the Society of Jesus.

"The King is dead! Long live the King! Liberated France is trembling with joy," wrote Saint-Simon. The Paris Parlement now held sovereign power, and declared the will of Louis XIV to be null and void. He had stipulated that the duc de Maine, born of his affair with Madame de Montespan, would wield considerable power in the Council of the Regency, but the successors of those magistrates who had earlier handed the scepter to Marie de' Medici after the death of Henri IV, and to Anne of Austria on the death of Louis XIII, placed control in the hands of the Duke of Orleans. This prince became the ruler of the kingdom and the legitimatized bastard was cast into the shadows.

On becoming regent, the Duke of Orleans had the Jansenists released from prison; more than two thousand had been incarcerated by Louis XIV at the request of Father Tellier. Thanks to the atheist called by His Most Christian Majesty "a criminal swashbuckler," the followers of Saint Augustine were delivered of their chains.

From every direction the frontiers were crossed by exiles returning to France. Father Quesnel, Arnauld's spiritual heir, thought of the words of the chorus in Esther. "It seems to me," he wrote, "that they are singing with the late Monsieur Racine: "The roads of Zion are open at last, / Assemble from the ends of the universe."

The nuns themselves were forgotten for nearly a year; Mademoiselle de

Joncoux, who had defended them so ardently, died before she could obtain their release.

Finally on March 19, 1716, an order from the regent arrived at Blois: Mother du Mesnil was to be transferred to the Abbey of Etrée, in the Eure, where she was awaited by a community of admirers. The favor was received too late—the day previous, March 18th, the last prioress of Port-Royal of the Fields had died at the age of sixty-six.

The Ursulines at Blois had grown to love her, having discovered with surprise that a Jansenist could be rich in heart. Their surprise was no less when they saw the prioress die "with great tranquility of spirit," after the last sacraments had been denied her. Mother du Mesnil was buried in consecrated ground, but apart from the graves of the other religious and without chanting or tolling of bells. The nuns recited the Vespers of the Dead for her, and a priest said the *Libera* before her bier.

Sister Madeleine de Valois, who was the only nun besides the prioress who refused to sign the formulary, was freed in 1716 through the intercession of the princesse de Condé, daughter-in-law of the victor of Rocroi. This nun was taken to Paris, then to the Abbey of Etrée, and Cardinal de Noailles gave her permission to receive the sacraments. Sister Valois carried some precious relics to the monastery that gave her hospitality, among them the death-mask of Mother Angélique Arnauld. At the Abbey of Etrée she brought about a revival of religious fervor that was the last reflecting ray of the Chevreuse Valley.

The other exiles were also authorized to leave the houses to which they had been sent. Some of them had made friends with their jailers, and remained of their own free will. Others found shelter in monasteries where the spirit of Port-Royal was still alive, as at Malnoue.

"They were great religious," said a nun who had known them. "They often spoke of Mother Angélique and tried to imitate her."

Over the following years these survivors successively passed away. The last, a lay sister, Sister Agnès de Sainte-Blaindine Forget, died at Amiens in 1738.

Seven days before the death of Louis XIV, Father Tellier made him sign a codicil to his will designating the priest confessor of the future Louis XV. The Jesuit was preparing to take over the direction of the royal child when he learned of his downfall; the Duke of Orleans was exiling him to La Flèche for the rest of his life.

As Louis XIV grew weaker, Monseigneur de Noailles took courage again, and now he felt quite daring. Appointed to preside over the young king's

Council of Conscience, the prelate forbade the Jesuits access to the churches of his diocese.

"He is no longer afraid of being strangled by Father Tellier," said the regent, who was highly amused.

On September 24, 1718, the cardinal had been excommunicated for his failure to accept the bull *Unigenitus*. He had appealed to a forthcoming council which was to say whether the pontifical decision was orthodox. But this council never assembled, and with the passage of time his resistance subsided. Ten years later Louis de Noailles decided to give up the fight, and on October 11, 1728, he declared that he received the bull "with very sincere respect and submission." Six months later the cardinal retracted this at the point of death.

This prince of the Church, never guilty of anything save weakness, suffered until the end the trial formerly inflicted on the nuns of Port-Royal. A Parisian wrote this epitaph for him:

> Here lies Louis Cahin-Caha,
> He twisted and turned
> When urged for a yea or nay,
> Then said this, then said that,
> Lost his head and went away.

Most of Port-Royal's friends and enemies had now died. The parlementarians continued the struggle, which was soon reduced to political rivalry between the sovereign and the magistrates.

Worse was to come. Certain Jansenists became so fanatical that the solitaries would never have recognized them as their adherents. A loyal and humble successor of Saint-Cyran, Deacon Pâris, had been buried in the cemetery of the Church of Saint Médard; in 1713 a group of convulsionaries assembled around his tomb. A witness writes: "They could be heard moaning, yelling, whistling, prophesying, caterwauling. But above all, they danced, danced until they were out of breath."

This *danse macabre* is the closing note of a great adventure that had become frightful and ridiculous.

Although triumphant under Louis XIV, the Society of Jesus had to humble itself before the Regent. Its members knew they could have no hold on the mind of the Duke of Orleans, who was completely indifferent to heaven, to hell, and to his own salvation. In addition, all the populace was against the Society. "The good city of Paris is Jansenist from head to toe," a contemporary wrote in his diary.

After the stones of Port-Royal fell on Cardinal de Noailles, they were also to fall upon the Jesuits. Like Louis XIV, they had struggled against phantoms, for the solitaries and nuns were quite incapable of harming the Society. But it had now come face to face with an enemy dangerous in another way: the Parlement of Paris. The magistrates who composed it considered a congregation blindly submitted to the pope as a grave threat to France's independence. The parlementarians, who were Gallican and Jansenistic, set out to crush this occult power, and were able to achieve their purpose because of an imprudent action that was to prove fatal to the Society of Jesus.

The fathers had not contented themselves with gaining mastery over minds, but in various parts of the world had taken earthly goods into their possession. In Paraguay and Uruguay, after freeing the Indians from oppression by the Spanish and Portuguese colonists, then grouping them into "reductions," they had set up happy and prosperous republics. The Jesuits ruled them with a mildness that won over the natives, and taught them to exploit the riches of the soil and subsoil—forests and gold mines.

In other countries the Fathers had set up commercial companies, always managed by lay associates. Unfortunately the day came when one Jesuit, Father Lavalette, superior of the missions, decided to direct an enterprise for selling products from Martinique to Europe under his own name. This ancestor of certain adventurers of the present century had ideas which were too ambitious for his day; in debt to the amount of several millions, he was summoned before the judges of the Court of Marseilles. They ordered him to reimburse his creditors, and declared that the Society of Jesus as a whole was responsible for his debts.

Appeal was made to the Parlement of Paris, where the Society's lawyers argued that a religious congregation whose work was the salvation of souls could not involve itself in the bankruptcy of one of its members. In order to show that Father Lavalette had no right to engage in commercial transactions, the French Provincial made a mistake that was to destroy his entire Society. He submitted to Parlement the Constitutions of the order drawn up by Ignatius Loyola.

Quite wisely, the saint had forbidden the text to be placed in secular hands. His sons were to learn the cost of disobeying their founder. The magistrates lost no time in finding out not only whether or not the Companions of Jesus could engage in commerce, but they also closely scrutinized the articles of the constitution which ordered every religious to obey the pope "like a corpse which of itself can take no action."

On May 8, 1761, Parlement issued a first decree which confirmed the decision of the Marseilles judges. The Society of Jesus must pay Father

Lavalette's debts, and all its possessions in France were to constitute security for his creditors. Only shortly after this, Parlement declared that the Constitutions of the Society, which obliged the Jesuits of France to recognize no other authority than that of the pope, were contrary to the fundamental laws of the realm and a threat to its sovereigny.

The magistrates ordered burnt in the court of the Palace of Justice the works of the Company's casuists—Suarez, Bellarmine—as "seditious destroyers of every principle of Christian morality." Though separated by a hundred years, the flames of this fire corresponded to those that had consumed the *Provincial Letters*.

The following year, on April 1, 1762, Parlement closed all establishments of the Jesuits. Louis XV saw that if he did not intervene the Society itself would be dissolved. He attempted to save it: the French province was to be made subject to a superior appointed by the king and independent of the pope. The Jesuit general nobly refused to accept this compromise, correctly considering that if he freed his Society from the obedience due the sovereign pontiff he would betray his mission. Pope Clement XIII was in full accord with him and expressed the superior's thinking in these words: "Let the Constitutions remain what they are or what they are not."

The die was cast. The Society of Jesus was too much hated in France for Louis XV to defend it further. On August 6, 1762, Parlement issued a decree suppressing the Society. The "so-called Jesuits" must leave their houses, never wear their habits, no longer obey their general, nor live in community. The decree described them "as a political body and not a religious order" which was destroying faith and morals; it blamed the fathers for fomenting sedition and for being always ready to make attempts against the king's safety. The magistrates judged the Jesuits more harshly than had Pascal, who said: "They keep corruption in the hearts of men."

The provincial parlements imitated that of Paris. In November, 1764, Louis XV had to sign an edict abolishing the Society of Jesus throughout the kingdom. Its possessions were to be confiscated, its members banished, and any who attempted resistance were to be imprisoned. Thus, as the result of a bankruptcy, the all-powerful Society of Jesus was dissolved in France.

In Portugal, the expulsion of the Jesuits had been ordered even before the decree of the Paris Parlement. The sovereign of that kingdom, Joseph I, had taken action against them; an attempt on his life followed, and the conspirators declared they had acted at the instigation of the Jesuits. Several theologians of the Society had long since proclaimed that it was lawful to kill a king when he betrays the God to whom he owes his crown, persecutes his Church, and becomes a tyrant.

Since Joseph I and his minister, the marquis de Pombal, were not convinced of the legitimacy of "tyrannicide," they had six Jesuits condemned to death as accomplices of the attackers; these Jesuits were drawn and quartered alive while two hundred more were cast into prison. All the rest had to leave Portugal.

The example given by this nation and by France determined other Catholic monarchs to throw off the yoke imposed on them by the Society of Jesus. These princes rose up in revolt against confessors who were not content with threatening them with hell but gave them to understand that in this world they ran the risk of being "piously assassinated," as Pascal expressed it, if they did not obey the Society. King Charles III of Spain banished the Jesuits; thousands were thrown into the holds of ships and sent to the pope. The sovereign pontiff was highly embàrrassed when he learned that his formidable militia was thenceforth to be installed in his Papal States. At his orders, the cannons of Cività-Vecchia opened fire when the first of the vessels bearing these religious appeared, and they were compelled to seek haven elsewhere. The holy cargo was disembarked on the coasts of Corsica belonging to the republic of Genoa, but only shortly thereafter that nation ceded the island to Louis XV, since it little desired to hold on to a territory peopled by Jesuits. The King of the Two Sicilies also drove them out of Naples, after having their houses occupied by soldiers. Ferdinand of Parma, the Spanish infante, expelled them from his duchy; the grand master of the Order of Malta banished them from that island.

But this was not enough. Fearing the vengeance of the proscribed men, the sovereigns did not feel themselves safe until they saw Rome abolish the order which they had wiped out in their own kingdoms. The rulers of France, Spain, Portugal, and the Two Sicilies threatened the pope with schism if he himself did not suppress the Society of Jesus.

For four years Clement XIV, a former pupil of the Jesuits, tried to defend them, but on July 21, 1773, he had to sign the brief *Dominus ac Redemptor*, which put an end to the existence of the Society. Desiring to justify his decision before history, the pope enumerated the complaints aroused by the Jesuits who were "accused of seeking the goods of this earth with too much avidity and eagerness." Many people, in fact, accused the Society of adding inheritances which were wrested from the dying to the gold from its American colonies and the profits from its commercial enterprises. The papal brief also alluded to certain pagan ceremonies tolerated by the Jesuits while those of the Church itself were neglected.

Actually, in order to be "all things to all men," Jesuit missionaries in the Far East had not been content to bear Chinese names and wear the silken robes of mandarins: they had authorized their converts to continue the celebration of the cult of Confucius, sometimes going so far as to conceal from their neophytes those things which might have shocked them about the crucifixion of Jesus. In India, Father Beschi had become "Grand Virama-muni," and wore ornaments of precious stones, sat on tiger-skins, and was carried on a palanquin and fanned by slaves. Several missionaries affected to ignore the lower classes so as not to compromise themselves with pariahs in the eyes of an élite they desired to win over. Did not the end justify the means?

Such attitudes as these, said the pope, "had led to the loss of souls and to the great scandal of peoples." The time had come when the Holy Father must himself pronounce judgment on his soldiers; he did so with regret but without leaving anything unclear. His brief reminded the Society of the exceptional powers granted to it—absolute power of the General and exemption from episcopal jurisdiction. These privileges had provoked the hostility of the secular clergy of other religious orders, of universities, and finally of kings. "The peace of Christianity had long been disturbed." Unknown struggles were doubtless going on among the Jesuits themselves, for he said, "the bosom of the Society is rent asunder by internal dissensions." The pope intended to put an end to all this tumult.

"We suppress and We abolish the Society of Jesus. We declare null and void forever the authority of the General, the Provincials, the Visitors, and the Superiors. Let all Christendom join with Us."

During the months following the publication of the brief, Father Lorenzo Ricci, superior general of the Jesuits, was imprisoned with his assistants in Castel Sant'Angelo; Father Ricci was to remain in captivity until his death.

The Society was subjected to the harshest persecution. The fathers had to seek asylum in Russia, where they were received by Catherine the Great; and in the kingdom of Prussia, where Frederick II opened the frontiers to them. It came about that the last refuge found by the sons of Loyola was granted them by schismatics and heretics. Thus was fulfilled Isaiah's prophecy, quoted by Pascal in his sixth "Provincial Letter": "Your ruin will be like that of a high wall which falls."

A year after the publication of the brief, on September 22, 1774, Clement XIV died under peculiar circumstances. It was said he had been poisoned by "tufana water," and the Society of Jesus was openly accused. In his book *Grandeur et misère des Jésuites*, François Ribadeau-Dumas quotes a letter from Cardinal Bernis to the young King Louis XV. The prince of the Church said that the pope's death had caused "horror and compassion," and he added: "The vicar of Christ prayed, as did the Redeemer, for his most implacable enemies, and carried delicacy of conscience to the point of scarcely permitting himself to mention the cruel suspicions by which he was devoured."

After this, neither Louis XVI nor any other Catholic monarchs wanted to allow the Society of Jesus to re-enter their territories. Napoleon also excluded from France what he termed "a religious militia." The emperor's abdication and the Restoration finally permitted Pius VII to reestablish the Society on August 7, 1814.

The destruction of the Society of Jesus in the eighteenth century, a revolution brought about by kings, had important consequences. The Jesuits were not only Rome's supporters: through their influence over minds they contributed within each nation to the maintenance of the absolute power of kings who ruled by divine right. The downfall of the Society was to break the authority of the very sovereigns who believed they had freed themselves.

The end of Louis XV's reign was spent in a long struggle against the Jansenist Parlement. The king was temporarily victorious; but his successor, Louis XVI, restored the parlementarians' powers. The latter ungratefully resumed the combat, and in 1788 refused to allow the imposition of necessary taxes, thereby forcing the king into bankruptcy and compelling him to convoke the Estates-General. Having thus paved the way for revolution, the magistrates of the old regime saw the downfall of the monarchy, and they themselves were destroyed along with it.

After the storm, when Napoleon was overthrown in turn, royalty was restored and, at the same time, the Society of Jesus again found its place in Catholic Europe. But these new manifestations of the great figures of centuries past were mere shadows of the two ramparts which had been destroyed.

After collecting the spoils from its sister Abbey of the Fields, Port-Royal of Paris grew so extravagant that in 1723 Cardinal de Noailles had to appoint an administrator to receive and disburse the monastery revenues.

In 1790, the nuns of the faubourg Saint-Jacques were driven out of their convent by the Revolution. To erase the memory of these "tyrants," the buildings the religious had occupied were given the name *Port-Libre*. In conformity with a time-honored custom, the revolutionaries turned Port-Libre into a jail where a thousand political prisoners were held successively; several of them were to die on the scaffold. Afterwards, the ancient abbey was made into a home for foundlings, and then it became what it is today—the Maternity Hospital on the Boulevard de Port-Royal. Children like those who might have been seen in the countryside of Galilee are now born in a dwelling where, in former times, virgins spent their time in contemplation before their invisible Spouse.

Today pilgrims to the Chevreuse Valley find only a few vestiges of the Jerusalem that was destroyed. Although the ancient church was razed in 1652 because it became inundated during rainstorms, the shafts of its columns were buried so deeply in the ground that the wreckers could not remove them. They have now been excavated, and give an idea of the original sanctuary. A small chapel built over the original site of the choir contains relics—a copy of *Augustinus,* the death masks of Mother Angélique and of Pascal, copies of portraits of the nuns and the solitaries, engravings, archives.

Here and there among the foliage can be seen the few edifices that escaped destruction—the fat, round pigeontower and the caretaker's house. A whole century lies asleep in the peace of the fields.

The spiritual heirs of Saint-Cyran, Arnauld, and Nicole watch over these reminders of a great past. The Society of Friends of Port-Royal keeps its memory alive. A building—badly restored—built by the solitaries in 1651 near the farm of Les Granges to house the Little Schools, was purchased by the state in 1952, together with its surrounding park. Today it is a museum of objects connected with the history of Jansenism.

In Utrecht, Holland, a Jansenist church grew up around the exiled Arnauld and Quesnel. It still exists, but as it is excluded from the Catholic community by Rome, each year it grows farther apart from those who have rejected it.

Of the high hopes of yesteryear, there apparently remain nothing but ruins.

A SPIRITUAL DESTINY

We have been created only for love; in the evening of this life, we will be judged by our love." Thus the grain of seed sown within each of us will take root; this seed will then be destroyed so that it may bear fruit and become a tree that grows forever.

If grace is granted us, we will be reborn and we will live in the Kingdom. But if it is refused, if the seed does not die, it will decay; a glowing fire will consume our appetites and our hates like dried stalks thrown into a fire. Thus heaven and hell are found in the depths of our own souls.

This revelation in the Gospel was accepted as a guiding light by the religious and solitaries of Port-Royal. They proclaimed it, and all honest men responded to their call. A combat between light and darkness took place in those times. Life was a tremendous adventure; each one wanted to know himself completely in order to rise to his superhuman destiny. In Saint-Cyran's words, "a soul is a world." Thinkers and poets explored this universe, not as spectators or bystanders but as heroes who played out their own tragedy. In this way Pascal and Racine discovered the secrets of the mind and heart. It was a great century.

Then began once more the combat that princes, priests, and pharisees once waged against Christ. "If the world hate you, know ye that it hated me before you," Jesus said to his disciples. All powers united to oppose this law of love; the cleverness of the Society of Jesus and the hostility of a great king forced Rome to condemn the disciples of Christ. All hope of resurrection was destroyed, and in the struggle between Jacob and the angel, Jacob won, to his own detriment.

Joyously, and like an underground stream gushing to the surface, the Regency rakes, the authors of the *Encyclopedia,* and the philosophers proclaimed "the Enlightenment," and mocked at "superstitions."

A victory both easy and futile. By the end of the reign of Louis XIV, royal confessors, ecclesiastical courtiers, and casuists had already destroyed the love that once had animated the apostles and martyrs, that had mapped out the roads of the Crusades, that had built cathedrals, that had inspired the *Pensées.*

The Jansenists, who carried the Gospel message, were accused by their enemies of inhumanity, a calumny that continues to besmirch their memory today.

In bygone times when crucifixes were chiseled from ivory tusks, the image-makers did not have space wide enough to show Christ stretching out his arms to sinners. The Jesuits falsely claimed that Saint-Cyran's successors had created the "Christs with narrow arms." Even today the Jansenists are said to have been responsible for these crucifixes, many of them carved before their time. Nevertheless, are we not voluntary accomplices of such injustice when we sternly cast the memory of Port-Royal into the past as though throwing a shroud over the dead?

Still, we must admit the convenience of a brand of religion that leads neither to the tragedy of Calvary nor to Pascal's night of fire, but to the calm meditations of the enlightened humanist, to learned evolutionary ideas, and to the scientific paradise proclaimed by Teilhard de Chardin. We are offered two types of Christianity: one heroic, intended for saints; the other intellectual and comfortable, reserved to right-thinking men.

In truth, unless it is not veiled and betrayed, the Gospel seems inaccessible. With all the violence of love, Christ set out to strip us of our possessions and our desires so he might fill his Kingdom with himself alone. There is something within us that refuses the destruction of all that is mortal. We refuse grace so long as grace is not granted. With all his strength Pascal fought against a surrender that he feared and desired at the same time. Nevertheless, we resist in vain, because we are destined to make the gift of our whole being; to refuse means death. If we want to escape from our prison and from the void, we must enter the order of the heart. We can build, invent, and go very far in the domain of the mind, but thought, admirable as it is, remains one of the mechanisms of the universe. Only love, the fruit of the soul, can raise what is immortal within us beyond nature and earthly life. This mysterious treasure is not acquired by work as is science: it is given to the elect. To obtain it, we must set out as Pascal did in search of the unknown—blindly, and with empty hands.

In this domain "which reason does not know," man, the prey of selfishness and ambition, remains very inferior to woman. With no effort she who is entrusted with carrying within her the greatest of miracles—the gift of life— fulfills each day the words of Saint Bernard: "The measure of life is to love without measure."

So, throughout the history of Port-Royal, Eve appears higher than Adam. Saint-Cyran brought the Christ of the Gospels to the nuns; Pascal led his young sister to the threshold of the infinite. The men planted the seed, but the ground in which the miracle was accomplished was the hearts of celibate women who brought forth a God.

Many of them surpassed their guides. While the doctors of Port-Royal engaged in sterile debates, the nuns were mute behind their cloister grill and welcomed persecution as a gift from heaven. Pascal made his greatest discovery when he realized the sovereignty of the heart, but it was his sister who led him to the summit he yearned for, but could not reach. Mother Agnès Racine brought the gift of grace as well as genius to the solitary's young pupil; later she drew the prodigal son back to the new Jerusalem and buried his body there. She was the heroine of the poet's finest tragedy—a drama never written.

"These are our queens," the solitaries said in speaking of the nuns. They were indeed queens in the highest of all realms.

Today from the valley where "the daughters of silence dwelled," there rises a hope. On our journey along the straight road toward the beyond shines a light, distant and yet near. A song of love mounts toward heaven, and if we unite ourselves to it, if only for a moment, we will triumph over the fixed and empty gaze of death.

This was the destiny of Port-Royal—to open to us the only future that is worthy of mankind.

DOCUMENTS

TEXT OF THE FIVE CONDEMNED PROPOSITIONS

First proposition

Some of God's commandments are impossible for just men [to observe], even when they wish and strive [to keep them], if the grace which makes them possible is lacking.

Second proposition

In the state of fallen nature, no one [can] ever resist interior grace.

Third proposition

To merit or demerit in the state of fallen nature, it is not required that man be free from the necessity of willing and acting; it is sufficient for him to be free from constraint.

Fourth proposition

The Semi-pelagians admitted the necessity of interior prevenient [antecedent] grace for all good works, even for the beginning of faith; but they were heretical in claiming that this grace is such that the human will may either resist or obey it.

Fifth proposition

To say that Jesus Christ died and shed his blood for all men, without a single exception, is to speak as a Semi-pelagian.

TEXT OF THE FORMULARY
(As drawn up in 1661)

"I submit sincerely to the constitution of Pope Innocent X of May 31, 1653, according to its true meaning, which was determined by the constitution of our Holy Father, Pope Alexander VII, of October 16, 1656.

"I recognize that I am obliged in conscience to obey these constitutions, and I condemn in heart and speech the doctrine of the five propositions of Cornelius Jansenius, contained in his book entitled *Augustinus,* which these two popes and the bishops have condemned; said doctrine not being that of Saint Augustine which Jansenius has ill-interpreted, contrary to the true meaning of this Doctor."

TEXT OF PASCAL'S
MEMORIAL

The Year of Grace 1654

Monday, November 23, Feast of Saint Clement, Pope and Martyr
and of others in the Martyrology
Eve of Saint Chrysogonus and other Martyrs
From about half past ten at night until about
half past twelve

fire

God of Abraham, God of Isaac, God of Jacob
not of the philosophers and scientists
Certitude   Certitude   Feeling   Joy   Peace
God of Jesus Christ
My God and your God
Thy God shall be my God
Forgetfulness of the world and all things, except only God
He is to be found only by the ways taught in the Gospel
Greatness of the human soul
Righteous Father, the world has not known thee, but I have known thee
Joy, joy, joy, tears of joy
I have fallen away from him
They have forsaken me, the fountain of living water
My God, wilt thou forsake me?
May I not be separated from him for all eternity
This is life eternal, that I know only thee, God,
and Jesus Christ whom thou hast sent
Jesus Christ
Jesus Christ
I have fallen away from him, I have fled him, denied him, crucified him
May I never be separated from him
We hold him only by the ways taught in the Gospel
Renunciation total and sweet

RACINE'S WILL

In the name of the Father, and of the Son, and of the Holy Spirit

I desire that after my death my body be taken to Port-Royal of the Fields and buried there in the cemetery, at the foot of the grave of Monsieur Hamon.

I humbly beseech the Mother abbess and the religious to grant me this honor, although I realize I am quite unworthy of it both by the scandals of my past life and by the little use I made of the excellent education I earlier received in this house and of the great examples of piety and penance I saw there and of which I have been only a sterile admirer.

But the greater my offenses against God, the greater need I have of the prayers of this holy community to bring down mercy on my head. I also beg the Mother abbess and the religious to accept the sum of eight hundred livres which I have ordered to be given them after my death.

Made in Paris, in my office, on October tenth, sixteen hundred and ninety-eight.

Racine.

THE ARNAULD FAMILY

Antoine ARNAULD (1560-1619)
husband of Catherine MARION
had twenty children,
of whom ten survived

Robert ARNAULD
d'ANDILLY
1588-1674

Mother Angélique
1591-1661
Religious
at
Port-Royal

Anne
1594-1653
Religious
at
Port-Royal

Catherine
1590-1651
Religious
at
Port-Royal

Mother Agnes
1593-1671
Religious
at
Port-Royal

Robert ARNAULD D'ANDILLY
had, among other children

Catherine
1615-1643
Religious
at
Port-Royal

Charles-Henri
de LUZANCY
1623-1684
Solitary
of
Port-Royal

Marie-Charlotte
1624-1678
Religious
at
Port-Royal

Simon
Marquis
de
Pomponne
1616-1699
Minister
of State

Angélique
de
Saint-Jean
1624-1684
Religious
at
Port-Royal

Marie-
Angélique
1630-1700
Religious
at
Port-Royal

Henri	Simon	Antoine
1597-1692	1603-1639	1612-1694
Bishop	killed	called
of	in war	"the Great Arnauld"
Angers		

Marie	Madeleine
1600-1642	1607-1649
Religious	Religious
at	at
Port-Royal	Port-Royal

Anne-Marie
1631-1660
died
a novice at
Port-Royal

Catherine ARNAULD, who,
before becoming a religious, was
the wife of Isaac LE MAITRE,
had, among other children

Simon LE MAITRE
de SERICOURT
1611-1650
Solitary
of
Port-Royal

Antoine	Isaac LE MAITRE
LE MAITRE	de SACI
1608-1658	1613-1684
Solitary	Priest
of	at
Port-Royal	Port-Royal

CHRONOLOGY

History of Port-Royal	Literary History	Political History
1602 (September 29). Jacqueline Arnauld (Mother Angélique) made abbess of the monastery of Port-Royal at the age of eleven years.		
1609 (September 25). Day of the Grating.		1610 (May 14). Assassination of Henri IV.
	1623 (June 19). Birth of Blaise Pascal.	
		1630 (November 10). Richelieu is victorious over Marie de'Medici (Day of the Dupes).
		1635. Richelieu declares war on Spain.
	1636. Corneille: *The Cid*.	
1637. Antoine Le Maître becomes the first of the solitaries.	1637. Descartes: *Discourse on Method*.	
1638 (May 14). Arrest of Saint-Cyran.		1638 (September 5). Birth of Louis XIV.
	1639 (December 22). Racine's baptism.	
1640. Publication of *Augustinus*.		
1642 (March 6). Urban VIII condemns *Augustinus*.		1642 (December 4). Death of Richelieu.
1643 (August). Antoine Arnauld: *Of Frequent Communion*.	1643. Corneille: *Polyeucte*.	1643 (May 14). Death of Louis XIII.
1643 (October 11). Death of Saint-Cyran.		1643 (May 19). Victory of Rocroi.
		1648 (October 24). Treaties of Westphalia.
		1648 (August 26). Day of the Barricades.
1653 (May 31). The five propositions denounced by Nicholas Cornet and condemned by Innocent X.		1648–1652: the Fronde.
	1654 (November 23). Pascal's Night of Fire and *Memorial*.	

History of Port-Royal	Literary History	Political History
1655 (July 10). Arnauld: "Letter to a Duke and Peer."		
1656 (January 14). Arnauld is condemned on the question of *fact* by the Faculty of Theology.		
1656 (January 23). First "Provincial Letter."		
1656 (March 24). Miracle of the Holy Thorn.		
1657 (March 24). Eighteenth and last "Letter" of Pascal.		
		1659 (November 7). Peace of the Pyrenees.
		1660 (June 9). Louis XIV marries Maria Theresa, Infanta of Spain.
1661 (August 6). Death of Mother Angélique Arnauld. 1661 (October 4). Death of Jacqueline Pascal.		1661 (March 9). Death of Mazarin.
	1662 (August 19). Death of Blaise Pascal. 1664 (June 20). *The Thebaid.*	
1664 (August 26). The nuns of Port-Royal of Paris are imprisoned in various convents by the order of Monseigneur de Péréfixe.		
1665 (July). The religious are reunited at Port-Royal of the Fields.	1665 (December 11). *Alexander.*	
	1666. Racine: "Letter" against Port-Royal.	
	1667 (January 1). *Phaedra.*	1668. Peace of Aix-la-Chapelle.
1668 (October 8). A brief of Clement IX proclaims "The Peace of the Church."	1667 (November 17). *Andromache.*	
	1669. *Tartuffe.*	
1671 (February 19). Death of Mother Agnès Arnauld.	1670 (January). Publication of *Pensées* (Port-Royal edition).	
		1678. Treaties of Nijmegen.

History of Port-Royal	Literary History	Political History
1679. Second persecution (Monseigneur de Harlay).		
1684 (January). Death of Monsieur de Saci, then of Mother Angélique de Saint-Jean.		
		1685 (October 18). Revocation of Edict of Nantes.
	1689 (January 26). *Esther.*	
	1691 (January 10). *Athaliah.*	
1694 (August 8). Death of Antoine Arnauld.		
	1695 (April 13). Death of La Fontaine.	
	1699 (April 21). Death of Racine.	
		1701–1714. War of the Spanish Succession.
1709 (October 29). Dispersal of the nuns of Port-Royal of the Fields.		
1710. Destruction of the monastery.		
1711. Exhumation of the bodies at Port-Royal of the Fields.	1711 (March 13). Death of Boileau.	
1712. Demolition of the church.		
1713 (September 8). Clement XI signs the bull *Unigenitus.*		
		1715 (September 1). Death of Louis XIV.

Bibliography

Sources

These are numerous and highly informative. The defenders of Port-Royal collected everything that might perpetuate its memory. Most of these documents were published outside France, sometimes in Germany but generally in Holland, the haven of the Jansenist refugees. The most vivid and animated accounts are contained in the memoirs of the solitaries and their friends.

Mémoires touchant la vie de M. de Saint-Cyran par M. Lancelot pour servir d'éclaircissement à l'histoire de Port-Royal. Cologne, 1738.

Mémoires de Pierre Thomas, sieur du Fossé. First edition, Cologne, 1739; another edition, greatly expanded, appeared at Rouen, 1876–1879.

Mémoires pour servir à l'histoire de Port-Royal by N. Fontaine. Utrecht, 1736.

Mémoires de Messire Robert Arnauld d'Andilly. Hamburg, 1734.

Mémoires du P. Rapin, of the Society of Jesus. Extremely hostile to the Messieurs. 3 vols. Ed. L. Aubineau. Paris-Lyon, 1865.

Mémoires of Godefroi Hermant—who also wrote *Histoire du jansénisme*—are, on the other hand, very favorable to Port-Royal. Ed. A. Gazier, 1905–1908.

Recueil de plusieurs pièces pour servir à l'Histoire de Port-Royal. Utrecht, 1740. Known as the *Recueil d'Utrecht,* this work was intended to complete the *Mémoires* of Lancelot, Du Fossé, and Fontaine. It gives particularly valuable details concerning the life of Pascal.

Nécrologes. These obituaries furnish a great deal of information on Port-

Royal. The best known is by the Benedictine scholar Dom Rivet de la Grange (*Nécrologe de l'Abbaye de Notre-Dame de Port-Royal des Champs*. Amsterdam, 1723. A *Supplément* to this *Nécrologe* was published in 1735, the work of Le Febvre de Saint-Marc. Others appeared in 1760, 1764, 1767, and 1778; the one of 1760, entitled *Nécrologe des plus célèbres défenseurs et confesseurs de la vérité* is devoted to the solitaries and their spiritual directors.

Lettres chrétiennes et spirituelles of Saint-Cyran were published in 1679 and in 1744.

Histoire de la vie et des ouvrages de Messire Antoine Arnauld was written by Père Quesnel. Liège, 1697; Paris, 1783. The same Oratorian priest also wrote *Justification de M. Arnauld.* Liège, 1702. The writings of Antoine Arnauld (*Oeuvres*, 43 vols. in quarto) appeared between 1775 and 1783. The last volume includes his biography by Larrière.

Fantôme du jansénisme by Antoine Arnauld. Addressed to Louis XIV. Cologne, 1686.

Essais de morale by Pierre Nicole. Complete edition, 1715.

Lettres of Arnauld d'Andilly. Printed in Paris, 1680; *Lettres* of M. de Saci were also issued in Paris in 1690.

M. Hamon left a collection of his writings, *Recueil de lettres et opuscules.* Amsterdam, 1734. Also *Relation de plusieurs circonstances de sa vie faite par lui-même.* 1734.

With regard to the Bishop of Alet, the protector of Port-Royal, Lancelot wrote the *Relation* of the journey he made to see this prelate and also *Mémoires pour servir à l'Histoire de Messire Nicolas Pavillon.* A biography of the same bishop was published by Abbé Goujet in 1697 and another by Le Febvre de Saint-Marc in 1738.

Lettres of Père Quesnel appeared in 1721, 1722 and 1728.

Histoire des cinq propositions de Jansénius. Trevoux, 1702. Very hostile to Port-Royal; attributed, although apparently erroneously, to Père Tellier.

Journal de M. de Saint-Amour (1662), on the other hand, was written by a Jansenist defender.

Histoire de la Paix de l'Eglise (1698) is the work of Dom Gerberon. This Benedictine is also the author of *Histoire générale du jansénisme.* Amsterdam, 1700.

Histoire du cas de conscience. Nancy, 1705–1711.

Best known of the works concerning the monastery written by its contemporaries are:

Histoire de l'abbaye de Port-Royal by Jérôme Besoigne. Cologne, 1752.

Histoire générale de Port-Royal by Dom Clémencet. Amsterdam, 1755–1757.

Mémoires historiques et chronologiques sur l'abbaye des Champs by Abbé Guilbert. Utrecht, 1758–1759.

Histoire abrégée de l'abbaye de Port-Royal by Jacques Fouillou. 1710.

Mémoires sur la destruction de Port-Royal des Champs. 1711.

The opinions of the Society of Jesus were expressed by Père Rapin in his *Histoire du Jansénisme* (text revised and published by Abbé Domenech in 4 vols., 1861–1865).

The most important work on the subject was written by Racine. The first part of his *Abrégée de l'Histoire de Port-Royal* appeared at Cologne in 1742; the integral text was published at Paris in 1767. An excellent edition of the work was prepared by Augustin Gazier with a foreword and notes, 1908.

We also cite:

Abrégé chronologique de l'histoire de Port-Royal des Champs (1760), and *Nouvelle Histoire abrégée de l'abbaye de Port-Royal* (1786).

With reference to the nuns, one of the principal sources is *Les Vies . . . intéressantes et édifiantes des religieuses de Port-Royal* (1790).

Antoine Arnauld, Nicole and Sainte-Marthe wrote an *Apologie* for the nuns.

Desmarets de Saint-Sorlin immediately published *Réponse à l'insolente Apologie des religieuses de Port-Royal*. Paris, 1666.

Divers actes, lettres et relations des religieuses de Port-Royal (1725), and especially *Histoire des persécutions* (1753), are of much interest in all that concerns the life of the community and the signing of the formulary.

Constitutions of the Port-Royal monastery. Mons, 1665.

Mémoires pour servir à l'histoire de Port-Royal et la vie de la Révérende Mère Marie-Angélique de Sainte-Madeleine Arnauld. Utrecht, 1742. Contains a number of tributes to her.

Entretiens of Mère Angélique Arnauld. Records of conversations to which have been joined the *Pensées* of Jacqueline Pascal on the mystery of the death of Christ.

Lettres of Mère Angélique. Utrecht, 1742–1744.

Lettres of Mère Agnès Arnauld. Published with an introduction by Prosper Faugère, 1858.

Lettres of Jacqueline Pascal, of her older sister Gilberte and of her niece Marguerite Périer were also published by Prosper Faugère in 1845.

Two drafts of Bossuet's letter to the religious of Port-Royal on the subject of the formulary are contained in his collected works (*Les Grands Ecrivains de la France,* vol. I, p. 84).

Mémoires of Saint-Simon and *Lettres* of Madame de Sévigné—published in their entirety in the *Collection des Grands Ecrivains de la France*—express the opinion of "honest people" on the subject of Port-Royal.

Finally, numerous manuscripts which have never been published or have been published only in part are to be found in the public libraries of France (Bibliothèque Nationale, Bibliothèque Sainte-Geneviève, Bibliothèque Mazarine, Bibliothèque de l'Arsenal) and in private collections.

Fragments of the various works just cited have been published in recent years under the following titles:

Chroniques de Port-Royal, with a preface by François Mauriac. Paris, 1946.
Relation écrite par la Mère Angélique Arnauld sur Port-Royal. Preface and notes by Louis Cognet, 1949.
Relation de captivité d'Angélique de Saint-Jean. Introduction by Louis Cognet, 1954.
Les Ecrivains de Port-Royal. Presented by Maurice Catel, 1962.
Saint-Cyran's writings consist of his *Théologie familière,* his *Lettres chrétiennes et spirituelles,* and *Instructions,* which were excerpted from the two books by Robert Arnauld d'Andilly. In 1944 Henri Perruchot published a selection of the *Pensées morales* of Saint-Cyran with an introduction. The *Ecrits de piété inédits* of Saint-Cyran were published by Jean Orcibal in 1962.

However, it is impossible really to know the spiritual director of Port-Royal unless one reads the works of his teacher, Pierre de Bérulle. The essential book of the latter is *Discours de l'état et des grandeurs de Jésus,* published in 1623; his complete works were published by the Maison d'Institution de l'Oratoire in 1960. Several sections have been published separately: *Opuscles de piété* (1956), *Le Mystère de Marie,* and *Vie de Jésus* (1962).

Bérulle's *Correspondance* was published by Jean Dagens. Louvain, 1939.

The life and works of the founder of the Oratory have been treated by Houssaye in *Le cardinal de Bérulle et le cardinal de Richelieu,* 1872–1875. Also by Henri Brémond in *Histoire littéraire du sentiment religieux en France,* vol. IV, *La conquête mystique,* Part 1, "L'Ecole française," 1921. More recent works are: Molien, *Le cardinal de Bérulle* (1947); Jean Dagens, *Bérulle et les origines de la restauration catholique* (1952); Bellemare, *Le sens de la créature dans la doctrine de Bérulle* (1959); Paul Cochoix, *Bérulle et l'école française* (1963).

Works on Port-Royal and Jansenism

These studies are so numerous that it is possible to cite here only those of particular interest.

The major work is still Sainte-Beuve's *Port-Royal* (5 vols., 1840–1860; vol. 6, 1867). A seventh volume contains an alphabetical and analytical table by A. de Montaiglon (1871). This work was published in the Bibliothèque de la Pléiade in 3 vols. presented and annotated by Maxime Leroy, 1953–1962.

Sainte-Beuve's work has been considerably augmented in our time by researches on Saint-Cyran, on Angélique Arnauld, on Pascal, on the origins of Jansenism and on the influence of Bérulle. But the wide scope of Sainte-Beuve's study, his sure judgment, and the purity of his style make it one of the monuments to the past. Certain omissions—which were inevitable—have been pointed out by Griselle in his article "Les lacunes du Port-Royal de Sainte-Beuve," in *Etudes*, May 20, 1907.

A more serious reproach can be made against Sainte-Beuve as the historian of the nuns and the solitaries. He was proud of belonging to the nineteenth century and wanted to remain aloof from those whose lives he had recounted; addressing them, he said in his conclusion: "I have been your biographer. . . . I am not one of you." This "servitor of science" considered that the Jansenists had a "sick side." Upon finishing his work, he congratulated himself on having retained "a mind as free, as serene in its coldness, and as impartial as before."

Nevertheless, on reading the last lines of his text, Sainte-Beuve admitted his uneasiness: ". . . overpowered by final weakness and inevitable disgust, he perceived in his turn that he was only one of the most fugitive of illusions in the heart of the infinite Illusion."

Wasn't this weakness the finest tribute ever rendered to Port-Royal and to Pascal by a writer who had become an unbeliever?

Abbé Brémond devotes a part of his *Histoire littéraire du sentiment religieux en France* to Jansenism (vol. IV, *La conquête mystique,* part 2, "L'Ecole de Port-Royal," 1920).

This priest had close ties to the Jesuits and displayed a veritable hatred toward the Jansenists. In Saint-Cyran, Henri Brémond saw "pietistic charlatanism, mental disequilibrium, foolish vanity, repulsive egotism." Saint-Cyran's exalted concept of his priestly mission brought forth the accusation of "megalomania." His *Lettres spirituelles,* which contributed to Pascal's conversion, were, according to Abbé Brémond, only "a tissue of theological cock and bull." When he thought of the imprisonment that cost Saint-Cyran's life, the friend of the Jesuits could not repress a cry of triumph: "Vincennes finished him off!"

A strange inconsistency is that in the same work we find admirable pages on Bérulle who had earlier expressed the same line of thought as the director of Port-Royal.

Abbé Brémond was preceded by a much more violent adversary of the Jansenists—Joseph de Maistre. In his book *De l'Eglise gallicane* (1821), the latter denounced the "bitter and hateful passions of the solitaries," their "incurable rage," their rigorism, "that masquerade of pride," the severity of their writings, which had "the polish, hardness and coldness of ice," and finally "the mock-heroic revolt of these men religious." The most ultramontane of writers outdid himself when he recalled the persecution inflicted on the Jansenists: "Certain incarcerations of short duration, certain *lettres de cachet* were *very probably pleasing to men who* . . . based their entire existence on the attention paid them by the government."

But let us forsake this votary of violence—who, unfortunately, gave rise to a frightening posterity—to return to the historians.*

Augustin Gazier was one of the most ardent defenders of the spirit of Saint-Cyran, Arnauld, and Pascal. In 1905 he published a historical study of the monastery under the title *Port-Royal des Champs*. His *Histoire générale du mouvement janséniste depuis ses origines jusqu'à nos jours* (1922) gives a substantial view of the whole subject. *Histoire du Monastère de Port-Royal* (1921), the work of his niece, Mlle. Cécile Gazier, retraces the succession of events that led to the destruction of the abbey.

Mlle. Gazier also devoted a book to the *Messieurs de Port-Royal* (1932), and another to the best known of the penitents, under the title *Les Belles Amies de Port-Royal* (1930).

Angélique Arnauld has inspired panegyrics (Guillaume Dall, *La Mère Angélique,* 1893), but also certain hostile accounts (Monlaur, *Angélique Arnauld,* 1901).

Louis Cognet has published studies on *La Réforme de Port-Royal* (1950), and *La Mère Angélique et saint François de Sales* (1951).

Augustin Gazier has published a work on *Jeanne de Chantal et Angélique Arnauld,* followed by their letters (1915).

Saint-Cyran is the subject of a rather unfavorable but scholarly study by J. Laferrière, *Etude sur Jean Duvergier de Hauranne, abbé de Saint-Cyran.*

---

* Except where otherwise indicated, all the following books were published in Paris.

We are obligated to Jean Orcibal for the following important books relative to the origins of Jansenism: *Correspondence de Jansénius* (1947); *Le Premier Port-Royal* (1956); *Jean Duvergier de Hauranne, abbé de Saint-Cyran, et son temps* (1947–1948); *Lettres inédites* of Saint-Cyran (1961); *La spiritualité de l'abbé de Saint-Cyran* (1961); *Saint-Cyran et le jansénisme* (1961).

A. Delplanque has written on *Les Femmes de Port-Royal;* C. Cochin on *Henri Arnauld;* and E. Dejean on *Nicolas Pavillon.*

The Little Schools, whose origin and development was treated by Sainte-Beuve (*Port-Royal*, book IV) are the subject of several works: Carré, *L'Education à Port-Royal* (1887); Cadet, *Les Pédagogues de Port-Royal* (1887). L. Prunel has written a biography of the bishop of Langres, *Sebastien Zamet* (1912).

Recollections of the monastery in the Chevreuse Valley are contained in *Le Pèlerinage de Port-Royal* by André Hallays (1909).

Bernard Dorival, curator of the Musée des Granges, has published a very complete guide to the vestiges of Port-Royal still standing and on the documents collected there: *Le Musée National des Granges de Port-Royal* (1963).

On the level of ideology, the doctrine of Port-Royal has been remarkably well explained by Jean Laporte in (1) *Saint-Cyran;* (2) *Les Vérités de la Grâce* (1923); and (3) *La Morale d'après Arnauld* (1951–1952).

A more summary work is *Essai sur la morale de Port-Royal* by J. F. Thomas (1942).

We further cite:

Fuzet, *Les Jansénistes du XVIIe siècle* (1876).

Bournet, *La Querelle janséniste* (1924).

J. Paquier, *Qu'est-ce que le jansénisme?* (1909).

A. de Meyer, *Les Premières Controverses jansénistes en France.* Louvain, 1917.

J. Chaix-Ruy, *Le Jansénisme, Pascal et Port-Royal* (1930).

J. Willaert, *Les Origines du jansénisme dans les Pays-Bas catholiques* (1948).

L. Ceyssens, *Sources relatives aux débuts du jansénisme et de l'anti-jansénisme.* Louvain, 1957.

L. Cognet, *Les Origines de la spiritualité française au XVIIIe siècle* (1944); *Le jansénisme* (1961).

Y. de la Brière, *Le Jansénisme, étude critique sur les cinq propositions* (1916).

Particular attention is drawn to the above books by Augustin Gazier, Louis

Cognet and Jean Orcibal; to them we owe the broader knowledge of the life and spirit of Port-Royal which we have today.

The doctrine of the Catholic Church regarding Predestination and Grace is explained, under those words, in the *Dictionnaire de théologie catholique* by Vacant and Mangenot (1935). These questions were treated more extensively by Père Gayraud in *Thomisme et Molinisme* (1889); by Gaillard in *Etude sur l'histoire du dogme de la grâce* (1897); by L. Labauche in *Leçons de théologie dogmatique* (1921) and, more recently, by Père Henri de Lubac in *Surnaturel* (1956).

The ideology of the Jansenists and the events to which they gave rise were treated by Fernand Mourret in *Histoire générale de l'Eglise,* vol. V, *L'Ancien Régime* (1931). But the most extensive, up-to-date and lively study of Jansenism and the surrounding spiritual atmosphere was written by Daniel-Rops in *L'Eglise des temps classiques* (vol. V of *Histoire de l'Eglise du Christ,* Part I, "Le Grand Siècle des Ames" [1958]).

The persecution suffered by the nuns of Port-Royal inspired a modern play that has already become a classic in France: *Port-Royal* by Henri de Montherlant. It was performed for the first time by the Théâtre Français on December 8, 1954, and published that same year (Paris: Gallimard). In it are found echos of the *Relations* and also of certain of the writings of Saint-Cyran. Péréfixe is represented as a comic character, a caricature that might seem severe but which is very close to reality. The nuns themselves appear as theological "bluestockings," women who oscillate between heresy and atheism. Poor Mère Agnès, so gentle and humble, is shown as stern and haughty. Angélique de Saint-Jean actually did know the anxieties that afflict many believers but she was very far from the doubt-ridden and at times inhuman nun depicted by Montherlant.

Books in English on Port-Royal and the Jansenists

Very few of the numerous French works listed in the author's Bibliography are available to the English reader. Even the major works of Racine and Sainte-Beuve on Port-Royal have not been translated. On the other hand, there are various translations of Racine's plays which are analyzed by M. Escholier, and of the Memoirs of Saint-Simon and the *Letters* of Madame de Sévigné dealing in part with the Jansenist controversy. Varying viewpoints are expressed by the authors of the following books in English or translations from the French:

Abercrombie, N. J. *The Origins of Jansenism.* Oxford: Clarendon Press, 1936.

Brémond, Henri. *A Literary History of Religious Thought in France.* Trans. by K. L. Montgomery. 4 vols. London: The Macmillan Company, 1928– .

Cadet, Felix: *Port Royal Education.* Trans. by A. D. Jones. New York: Charles Scribner, 1898.

Chevalier, Jacques. *Pascal.* London: Sheed & Ward, 1930.

Clark, Ruth. *Strangers and Sojourners at Port-Royal.* Cambridge: The University Press, 1932.

Clark, William Robinson. *Pascal and the Port Royalists.* New York: Charles Scribner's Sons, 1902.

Cognet, L. J. Articles on the "Arnauld Family," on "Jansenius" and on "Jansenism" in *Catholic Encyclopedia,* vols. 2 and 7. New York: McGraw-Hill, 1966.

Cousin, Victor, and Faugère, Prosper and others. *Jacqueline Pascal; Or a Glimpse of Convent Life at Port-Royal.* Trans. by H. N. with an Introduction by W. R. Williams. New York: Carter & Brothers, 1860.

Daniel-Rops, Henri. *The Church in the Seventeenth Century* (part 1, vol. V of *Histoire de l'Eglise du Christ*). Trans. by J. J. Buckingham. London: J. M. Dent; New York: E. P. Dutton [1963].

Gleason, Robert W., S.J. (ed.). *The Essential Pascal.* Selected and edited with Introduction and Commentary. Portions of Pascal's writings newly translated by G. F. Pullen. New York and Toronto: Mentor-Omega Book, The New American Library, 1966.

Hay, Malcolm Vivian. *The Prejudices of Pascal, Concerning in Particular the Jesuit Order and the Jewish People.* London: N. Spearman, 1962.

Knox, Ronald. *Enthusiasm: A Chapter in the History of Religion, with Special Reference to the Seventeenth and Eighteenth Centuries.* New York: Oxford University Press, 1961.

Mesnard, Jean. *Pascal, His Life and Works.* Trans. by G. S. Fraser. Preface by Ronald Knox. London: Harvill Press, 1952.

Pascal, Blaise. *Pensées.* Trans. by W. F. Trotter. London: J. M. Dent; New York: E. P. Dutton, 1940.

———. *The Provincial Letters.* Trans. with an historical introduction and notes by Rev. Thomas M'Crie. New York: Hurd and Houghton, 1866.

Pastor, Ludwig von. *The History of the Popes.* 34 vols. St. Louis, Mo.: Herder, 1923– . Vols. 3–34 (1644–1721) deal with the pontificates during which the Jansenists were active.

Racine, Jean Baptiste. *Confessions; Unpublished Sonnets.* Trans. by Walter Roberts. London: Mowbray, 1936.

Rea, Lillian. *The Enthusiasts of Port-Royal.* London: Methuen, 1912.

Romanes, Ethel. *The Story of Port-Royal.* London: J. Murray, 1907.

Sanders, Ella K. *Angélique of Port-Royal, 1591–1661.* London: S.P.C.K., 1928.

Schimmelpennick, M. A. *Narrative of the Demolition of Port-Royal des Champs.* London: J. and A. Arch, 1816.

—— (ed.). *Select Memoirs of Port-Royal.* 2 vols. Hamilton, Adams & Co., 1835.

Steinmann, Jean. *Pascal.* Trans. by Martin Turnell. New York: Harcourt, Brace and World, 1966.

Trouncer, Margaret. *The Reluctant Abbess: Angélique Arnauld of Port-Royal (1591–1661).* New York: Sheed & Ward, 1957.

Woodgate, M. V. *Jacqueline Pascal and Her Brother.* Dublin: Browne & Nolan, 1944.

Index